INSTRUCTOR'S MANUAL
with Program Disk

VISUAL BASIC® 6 HOW TO PROGRAM

DEITEL & DEITEL
T. R. NIETO

Prentice Hall, Upper Saddle River, NJ 07458

Editor in Chief: Marcia Horton
Supplement Editor: Dolores Mars
Special Projects Manager: Barbara A. Murray
Production Editor: Jonathan Boylan
Supplement Cover Manager: Paul Gourhan
Supplement Cover Designer: PM Workshop Inc.
Manufacturing Buyer: Pat Brown

Printed in the United States of America

10 9 8 7 6 5 4 3 2

ISBN 0-13-020522-2

Prentice-Hall International (UK) Limited, London
Prentice-Hall of Australia Pty. Limited, Sydney
Prentice-Hall Canada, Inc., Toronto
Prentice-Hall Hispanoamericana, S.A., Mexico
Prentice-Hall of India Private Limited, New Delhi
Prentice-Hall (Singapore) Pte. Ltd.
Prentice-Hall of Japan, Inc., Tokyo
Editora Prentice-Hall do Brazil, Ltda., Rio de Janeiro

Contents

Preface

Thank you for considering and/or adopting our text *Visual Basic 6 How to Program*. If you have not read the preface to *Visual Basic 6 How to Program*, please take a moment to do so. The preface contains a careful walkthrough of the book's key features. We worked hard to produce a textbook and ancillary materials that we hope you and your students will find valuable.

The following ancillary resources for *Visual Basic 6 How to Program* are available:

- *Visual Basic 6 How to Program's 178 program examples* are included on a CD-ROM in the back of the book. The examples help instructors prepare lectures faster and aid students in their study of Visual Basic. These examples are also available as a ZIP archive file for download at

  http://www.deitel.com/products_and_services/publications/index.htm

  When extracting the source code from the ZIP archive, you must use a ZIP archive reader that understands directories such as WinZip (**http://www.winzip.com**) or PKZIP (**http://www.pkware.com**). The file should be extracted into a separate directory (e.g., **vb_solutions**).

- The *Visual Basic 6 How to Program Instructor's Manual* (ISBN# 0-13-020522-2) contains answers to most of the exercises in *Visual Basic 6 How to Program*. The *Instructor's Manual* also contains a PC-formatted disk containing solutions to 233 programming exercises in a ZIP archive, **vb_solutions.zip**. The programs are separated into directories by chapter and by problem number.

- The *Visual Basic 6 Multimedia Cyber Classroom* is an interactive multimedia version of the book. Its features include audio "walkthroughs" of programs, section review questions (these are only available on the *Visual Basic 6 Multimedia Cyber Classroom*), a full-text-search engine, the ability to execute example programs, and more. The *Cyber Classroom* helps students get more out of their courses. The *Cyber Classroom* also helps students who miss a class catch up quickly. The *Cyber Classroom* is available as a stand-alone product (ISBN# 0-13-083116-6) or bundled with the textbook in a product called *The Complete Visual Basic 6 Training Course* (ISBN# 0-13-082928-5).

- *Microsoft's Visual Basic 6 Working Model Edition Software* is wrapped with *Visual Basic 6 How to Program* and *The Complete Visual Basic 6 Training Course*. This version of Visual Basic allows students to continue their study of Visual Basic at home.

- *The Visual Basic 6 How to Program Companion Website* provides a variety of resources to both instructors and students. For instructors, the *Companion Website* includes a *Syllabus Manager* to help instructors plan their courses interactively (the syllabus can then be accessed by students on-line), *Adobe Acrobat PDF slides* containing all the programs and illustrations in the text (great for creating transparencies or displaying with a projector in class) and *reference materials* from the appendices of the book (such as the operator precedence chart, the ANSI character set and web resources). The site also contains several features for each chapter in the book such as the *chapter objectives*, a set of *true/false exercises* and *matching exercises* (great for instructors to gauge their students' comprehension of chapter concepts), *chapter highlights*, the *reference materials* mentioned previously and a *message board* where students and instructors worldwide can share information with others. The companion web site is located on the Prentice Hall web site at

  http://www.prenhall.com/pubguide/index.html

  Click the *Computer Science* link on this page, locate the link for *Visual Basic 6 How to Program* and click it. This will bring you to the companion web site.

- *Adobe Acrobat PDF Slide Show* which contains a PDF slide for each source-code listing, figure and table in the textbook. The slide show is available at no charge from the companion web site for *Visual Basic 6 How to Program* (described above) and from our FTP site

      ftp://208.230.131.215/downloads/pdf_files/vb6_pdf.zip

  The slide show can be viewed or printed using the Adobe Acrobat reader which is available at no charge from **http://www.adobe.com**.

We would sincerely appreciate your comments, criticisms and corrections. Please send them to:

      deitel@deitel.com

We will respond immediately. Please watch our Deitel & Associates, Inc. web site and our Prentice Hall web site for book and product updates:

      http://www.deitel.com
      http://www.prenhall.com/deitel

We would like to thank the extraordinary team of publishing professionals at Prentice Hall who made *Visual Basic 6 How to Program* and its ancillary materials possible. Our Computer Science editor, Laura Steele, worked closely with us to ensure the timely availability and professional quality of these ancillary materials. We would also like to thank Mr. Chris Poirier of Deitel & Associates, Inc. for his extensive contributions to the ancillary materials.

Harvey M. Deitel
Paul J. Deitel
Tem R. Nieto

Chapter 1 Solutions
Computing Concepts

1.6   [CD] Categorize each of the following items as either hardware or software.
a) CPU
ANS: hardware.
b) Visual Basic IDE
ANS: software.
c) ALU
ANS: hardware.
d) mouse
ANS: hardware.
e) input unit
ANS: hardware.
f) Windows operating system
ANS: software.
g) Monitor
ANS: hardware.
h) CD-ROM/DVD player
ANS: hardware.

1.7   [CD] Fill in the blanks in each of the following statements.
a) Which logical unit of the computer receives information from outside the computer for use by the computer? _____.
ANS: the input unit.
b) The process of instructing the computer to solve specific problems is called _____.
ANS: computer programming.
c) What type of computer language uses English-like abbreviations for machine language instructions? _____.
ANS: a high-level language.
d) Which logical unit of the computer sends information that has already been processed by the computer to various devices so that the information may be used outside the computer? _____.
ANS: the output unit.

1.8   Fill in the blanks in each of the following statements.
a) Which logical unit of the computer retains information? _____.
ANS: memory unit and secondary storage unit.
b) Which logical unit of the computer performs calculations? _____.
ANS: arithmetic and logical unit.
c) Which logical unit of the computer makes logical decisions? _____.
ANS: arithmetic and logical unit.
d) The level of computer language most convenient to the programmer for writing programs quickly and easily is _____.
ANS: high-level.
e) The only language that a computer can directly understand is called that computer's _____.
ANS: machine language.
f) Which logical unit of the computer coordinates the activities of all the other logical units? _____.
ANS: central processing unit.

1.9   Fill in the blanks in each of the following statements.
a) The most powerful desktop machines are called _____.
ANS: workstations.

b) Information is easily shared across computer networks, where some computers called file servers offer a common store of programs and data that may be used by client computers distributed throughout the network, hence the term _____.

ANS: client/server.

c) Any computer can directly understand only its own _____ language.

ANS: machine.

d) Translator programs called _____ convert assembly language programs to machine language at computer speeds.

ANS: assemblers.

e) The translator programs that convert high-level language programs into machine language are called _____.

ANS: compilers.

f) _____ is the preferred programming language for scientific and engineering applications that require complex mathematical computations.

ANS: FORTRAN.

g) _____ is the popular system implementation language that was first used to develop the UNIX operating system.

ANS: C.

h) _____, an extension of C, provides a number of features that "spruce up" the C language and add capabilities for doing object-oriented programming (OOP).

ANS: C++.

i) The _____ programming language was developed by Sun Microsystems, is based on C and C++ and incorporates features from other object-oriented languages.

ANS: Java.

1.10 State whether each of the following is *true* or *false*. If *false*, explain why.

a) Sequential files are preferred in transaction-processing systems like point-of-sale systems.

ANS: False. Random-access files are preferred.

b) You can build ActiveX components with any of Microsoft's key programming languages, like Visual Basic, Visual C++ and Visual J++. No matter which of these languages is used to build an ActiveX component, the component can be used by any of them.

ANS: True.

c) The trend in the computer field is to get away from how things are represented in the computer, and instead, focus on the way information is used in real-world applications.

ANS: True.

d) The programmer's and user's time is more precious than the computer's time.

ANS: True.

Chapter 2 Solutions

Integrated Development Environment

2.4 [CD] Fill in the blanks in each of the following statements:

a) The _____ contains a variety of colors, from which the programmer selects one.
ANS: palette.

b) The three values of the **Alignment** property are _____, _____ and _____.
ANS: Left Justify, **Right Justify**, and **Center**.

c) The _____ property changes a control's foreground color.
ANS: ForeColor.

d) IDE is an abbreviation for _____.
ANS: Integrated Development Environment.

e) Clicking the _____ on the toolbar executes the program.
ANS: Start button.

f) The _____ property identifies a form and is often prefixed with **frm**.
ANS: Name.

g) GUI is an abbreviation for _____.
ANS: Graphical User Interface.

h) A _____ is a group of related files.
ANS: project.

2.5 State which of the following are *true* and which are *false*. If *false*, explain why.

a) At run-time, a form's grid is visible.
ANS: False.

b) A tool tip identifies an IDE feature.
ANS: True.

c) A **Label**'s **Text** property determines what text is displayed to the user.
ANS: False. The **Caption** property determines what text is displayed.

d) At design-time, almost every IDE feature is available.
ANS: True.

e) When placed over an enabled sizing handle, the mouse pointer changes.
ANS: True.

f) A **Label** displays uneditable text to the user.
ANS: True.

g) A form and **Label** have an identical set of properties.
ANS: False. They are two different objects—each of which is used differently. The properties cannot be identical for these two objects.

2.6 Build the following GUIs (you need not provide any functionality). Execute each program and determine what happens when a control is clicked with the mouse.

a) [CD] This GUI consists of three **Label**s colored yellow, red and black.

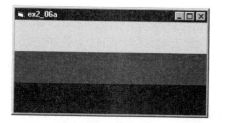

b) This GUI consist of one **Label** and eighteen **CommandButtons**. Note: You must modify the **Label**'s **BorderStyle** property. Also note that the dotted line around the six (**6**) button (it can be any of your buttons) appears during run mode.

c) **[CD]** The following GUI consists of one **Label**, one **CommandButton** and four **OptionButtons**. Note: The black dot in **Dog** automatically appears at run-time but may appear in a different one of your buttons.

d) The following GUI consists of three **VScrollBar**s and two **Label**s. Note: One **Label** requires its **BorderStyle** property changed. Also note that one **VScrollBar**'s *scroll box* automatically flashes at run-time.

Flashing
scroll box

2.7   Briefly describe each of the following IDE features:
a) tool bar
ANS: The tool bar provides many short cuts to menu items.
b) menu bar
ANS: The menu bar contains menus which list the commands a developer can use to create Windows programs.

c) toolbox

ANS: The toolbox contains predefined building blocks called controls.

d) control

ANS: A predefined building block that can be used in a program.

e) form

ANS: The Window that represents a program's graphical user interface.

f) project

ANS: A collection of files that comprise a program.

g) title bar

ANS: The top portion of a window that displays the window's name.

2.8 [CD] Briefly describe the differences between design mode and run mode.

ANS: During design mode most of the IDE features are available. The programmer uses these features to create Windows programs. During run mode, many IDE features are not available. The program is executing.

2.9 Compare a form's properties to a **Label**'s properties. Make a list of all the properties that are common to both. Now, summarize only the properties on the list we have discussed in this chapter.

2.10 Why do you think that the toolbox, the form and the **Properties** window are crucial to the concept of visual programming?

ANS: These allow programs to be rapidly created. The developer does not have to be a windows expert to create fully functional programs. These features allow the Visual Basic developer to write only a fraction of the code they would normally have to write if these features were not available.

Chapter 3 Solutions
Introduction to Visual Basic Programming

3.9 Identify and correct the error(s) in each of the following statements:

a) Assume that **Option Explicit** has been set.

```
' Event code for procedure
Private Sub cmdDisplay_Click()
    value1 = 5 : value2 = 10

    If value1 > value2 Then
        Print value1
    End If
End Sub
```

ANS: **value1** and **value2** must explictly be declared.

b) Assume that **Option Explicit** has not been set.

```
' Event code for procedure
Private Sub lblGreeting_Click()
    Low1Val = 8

    ' Display the value in lblGreeting's Caption property
    lblGreeting = LowlVal
End Sub
```

ANS: The name **Low1Val** is different than **LowlVal**. One name uses a one, "**1**", and the other uses the letter "**l**". One name should be changed to match the other.

c) `animalName = "Giant " Cat "Parrot"   ' Concatenate strings`
ANS: The string concatenation operator is **&** not **Cat**.

d) `thisIsAnIncrediblyLongVariableNameOf45Letters As Integer`
ANS: Missing keyword **Dim**. The correct declaration should read
```
Dim thisIsAnIncrediblyLongVariableNameOf45Letters As Integer
```

e) Assume that the **Integer** variables **c** and **j** are declared and initialized to **47** and **55**, respectively.

```
Dim x As Integer

If c =< j Then
    x = 79
    frmMyForm.Print x
End If
```

ANS: The **If** condition uses an incorrect operator, **=>**. The correct operator is **<=**.

f) Assume that the variables **q**, **pcm** and **qp** are declared as **Integer**s.

```
' Executable statement
q = 76 ; qp =    ' Hard return after =
78 ; pcm = 61
```

ANS: Semicolons, **;**, should be colons, **:**. A line-continuation characte needs to be added and the comment removed. The corrected code should read

```
q = 76: qp = _
78: pcm = 61
```

3.10   **[CD]** Write a single statement or line that accomplishes each of the following:

a) Print the message `"Visual Basic 6!!!!"` on the form.

ANS: `Print "Visual Basic 6!!!!"`

b) Assign the product of variables `width22` and `height88` to variable `area51`.

ANS: `area51 = width22 * height88`

c) State that a program performs a sample payroll calculation (i.e., use text that helps to document a program).

ANS: `' Program performs a sample payroll calculation`

d) Calculate the area of a circle and assign it to the `Integer` variable `circleArea`. Use the formula *area* = (πr^2), the variable `radius` and the value 3.14159 for π.

ANS: `circleArea = 3.14159 * radius ^ 2`

e) Concatenate the following two strings using the string concatenation operator and assign the result to **Label lblHoliday**'s Caption: `"Merry Christmas"` and `" and a Happy New Year"`.

ANS: `lblHoliday.Caption = "Merry Christmas" & " and a Happy New Year"`

3.11   **[CD]** Fill in the blanks in each of the following:

a) _____ are used to document a program and improve its readability.

ANS: Comments.

b) A statement that makes a decision is _____.

ANS: `If/Then`.

c) Calculations are normally performed by _____ statements.

ANS: Assignment.

d) The _____ statement terminates program execution.

ANS: `End`.

e) The _____ method is used to display information to the form.

ANS: `Print`.

f) A _____ is a message to the user indicating that some action is required.

ANS: Prompt.

3.12   State which of the following are *true* and which are *false*. If *false*, explain why.

a) `Integer` division has the same precedence as floating-point division.

ANS: False. Floating-point division has a higher precedence.

b) The following are all valid variable names: `_under_bar_`, `m928134`, `majestic12`, `her_sales`, `hisAccountTotal`, `cmdWrite`, `b`, `creditCardBalance1999`, `YEAR_TO_DATE`, `__VoLs__LiSt__`.

ANS: False. Names `_under_bar_` and `__VoLs__LiSt__` are invalid names.

c) The statement `squareArea = side ^ 2` is a typical example of an assignment statement.

ANS: True.

d) A valid arithmetic expression with no parentheses is evaluated from left to right regardless of the operators used in that expression.

ANS: False. The expression is evaluated according to operator precedence. An operator with a higher precedence can be to the right of an operator with lower precedence.

e) The following are all invalid variable names: `2quarts`, `1988`, `&67h2`, `vols88`, `*true_or_FALSE`, `99_DEGREES`, `_this`, `Then`.

ANS: False. The name `vols88` is a valid identifier.

f) Visual Basic automatically generates the beginning and end code of event procedures.

ANS: True.

3.13   Given the following declarations, list the type for each variable declared.

a) `Dim traveler88 As Integer`

ANS: `Integer`

b) `number% = 76`

ANS: `Integer`

c) `Dim cars As Integer, trucks`

ANS: `Integer`, `Variant`

d) `Dim touchDowns, fieldGoals As Integer`

ANS: `Variant`, `Integer`

e) `portNumber = 80     ' Implicit declaration`

ANS: `Variant`

3.14   Given the equation $y = ax^3 + 7$, which of the following, if any, are correct statements for this equation?

a) `y = a * ( x ^ 3 + 7 )`

b) `y = ( a * x ) ^ 3 ) + 7`

c) `y = ( a * x * x * x + 7 )`

d) `y = ( a * ( x * ( x * x ) ) + 7 )`

```
e) y = ( a * ( x * x ) ^ 2 ) + 7
f) y = (a) * (x) * (x) * (x) + (7)
```
ANS: c, d, e, and f.

3.15   State the order of evaluation of the operators in each of the following statements, and show the value of **x** after each statement is performed. Assume **x** to be an **Integer** variable.

```
a) x = ( 3 * 9 * ( 3 + ( 9 * 3 / ( 3 ) ) ) )
```
ANS: **x** = 324.

```
x = ( 3 * 9 * ( 3 + ( 9 * 3 / ( 3 ) ) ) )
x = ( 3 * 9 * ( 3 + ( 27 / ( 3 ) ) ) )
x = ( 3 * 9 * ( 3 + ( 9 ) ) )
x = ( 3 * 9 * ( 12 ) )
x = ( 27 * ( 12 ) )
x = 324
```
```
b) x = 1 + 2 * 3 - 4 / 4 - 12 \ 6 * 6
```
ANS: **x** = 6

```
x = 1 + 2 * 3 - 4 / 4 - 12 \ 6 * 6
x = 1 + 6 - 4 / 4 - 12 \ 6 * 6
x = 1 + 6 - 1 - 12 \ 6 * 6
x = 1 + 6 - 1 - 12 \ 36
x = 1 + 6 - 1 - 0
x = 7 - 1 - 0
x = 6 - 0
x = 6
```
```
c) x = ( ( 10 - 4 * 2 ) \ 2 + ( 13 - 2 * 5 ) ) ^ 2
```
ANS: **x** = 16.

```
x = ( ( 10 - 4 * 2 ) \ 2 + ( 13 - 2 * 5 ) ) ^ 2
x = ( ( 10 - 8 ) \ 2 + ( 13 - 2 * 5 ) ) ^ 2
x = ( ( 2 ) \ 2 + ( 13 - 2 * 5 ) ) ^ 2
x = ( ( 2 ) \ 2 + ( 13 - 10 ) ) ^ 2
x = ( ( 2 ) \ 2 + ( 3 ) ) ^ 2
x = ( 1 + ( 3 ) ) ^ 2
x = ( 4 ) ^ 2
x = 16
```
```
d) x = 8.2 Mod 3 + 2 / 2 - -3
```
ANS: **x** = 6.

```
x = 8.2 Mod 3 + 2 / 2 - -3
x = 8.2 Mod 3 + 1 - -3
x = 2 + 1 - -3
x = 3 - -3
x = 6
```
```
e) x = -2 + 7.4 \ 5 - 6 / 4 Mod 2
```
ANS: **x** = -1.

```
x = -2 + 7.4 \ 5 - 6 / 4 Mod 2
x = -2 + 7.4 \ 5 - 1.5 Mod 2
x = -2 + 1 - 1.5 Mod 2
x = -2 + 1 - 0
x = -1 - 0
x = -1
```

3.16   [CD] Which, if any, of the following statements contain variables involved in destructive read-in?

```
a) myVariable = txtTextBox.Text
b) V = O + L + S + 8 * 8
c) Print "Destructive read-in"
d) Print "a = 8"
e) Print x = 22
f) Print userName
```
ANS: a and b.

3.17   What, if anything, prints when each of the following statements is performed? If nothing prints, then answer "nothing." Assume that **x** = 2 and **y** = 3.

```
a) Print x
```
ANS: **2**

b) `Print -y ^ 2`
ANS: -9
c) `Print x + x`
ANS: 4
d) `Print "x ="`
ANS: x =
e) `txtTextBox.Text = "x + y"`
ANS: Nothing.
f) `z = x + y`
ANS: Nothing.
g) `Print x + y * 4 ^ 2 / 4 & " is the magic number!"`
ANS: 14

3.18 Write a program that inputs three different **Integer**s using function **InputBox** and prints the sum, the average, the product, the smallest and the largest of these numbers on the form using **Print**. Use only the single-selection version of the **If/Then** statement you learned in this chapter. Provide an **Exit** button to terminate program execution. (Hint: Each **Print** statement is similar to `Print "Sum is "; sum`. The semicolon (`;`) instructs Visual Basic to print the variable's value immediately after the last character printed.)
ANS:

```
1   ' Exercise 3.18 Solution
2   Option Explicit
3
4   Private Sub cmdPrint_Click()
5       Dim a As Integer, b As Integer
6       Dim total As Integer, smallest As Integer
7       Dim largest As Integer
8
9       a = InputBox("Enter first number:")
10      b = InputBox("Enter second number:")
11      largest = InputBox("Enter third number:")
12
13      smallest = largest
14      total = a + b + largest
15
16      Print "Sum is "; total
17      Print "Average is "; (total / 3)
18      Print "Product is "; (a * b * largest)
19
20      If a > b Then
21
22          If a > largest Then
23              largest = a
24          End If
25
26      End If
27
28      If b > a Then
29
30          If b > largest Then
31              largest = b
32          End If
33
34      End If
35
36      Print "Largest is "; largest
37
38      If a < b Then
39
40          If a < smallest Then
41              smallest = a
42          End If
43
44      End If
45
```

```
46      If b < a Then
47
48         If b < smallest Then
49            smallest = b
50         End If
51
52      End If
53
54      Print "Smallest is "; smallest
55   End Sub
56
57   Private Sub cmdExit_Click()
58      End
59   End Sub
```

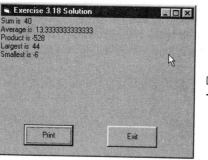

Data values input were **44**, **-6** and **2**.

3.19 [CD] Write a program that reads in the radius of a circle as an **Integer** and prints the circle's diameter, circumference and area to the form using the **Print** method. Do each of these calculations inside a **Print** statement. Use the following formulas (r is the radius): *diameter = 2r, circumference = 2πr, area = πr²*. Use the value 3.14159 for π. (Note: In this chapter, we have discussed only **Integer** variables. In Chapter 4 we will discuss floating-point numbers (i.e., values that can have decimal points and data type **Single**).

ANS:

```
1   ' Exercise 3.19 Solution
2   Option Explicit
3
4   Private Sub cmdPrint_Click()
5      Dim radius As Integer
6
7      radius = txtInput.Text
8
9      Print "Diameter: " & radius * 2
10     Print "Area: " & 3.14159 * radius ^ 2
11     Print "Circumference : " & 2 * 3.14159 * radius
12  End Sub
```

3.20 Enhance Exercise 3.19 by displaying the diameter, circumference and area in **Label**s.
ANS:

```
1   ' Exercise 3.20 Solution
2   Option Explicit
3
```

```
4   Private Sub cmdPrint_Click()
5      Dim radius As Integer
6
7      radius = txtInput.Text
8
9      lblDiameter.Caption = "Diameter: " & radius * 2
10     lblArea.Caption = "Area: " & 3.14159 * radius ^ 2
11     lblCircumference.Caption = "Circumference : " & 2 * 3.14159 * radius
12  End Sub
```

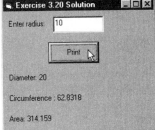

3.21 Write a temperature conversion program that converts a Fahrenheit temperature to a Celsius temperature. Provide a **Text-Box** for user input and a **Label** for displaying the converted temperature. Provide a **Input** button to read the value from the **Text-Box**. Also provide the user with an **Exit** button to end program execution. Use the following formula: *Celsius = 5 / 9 ∞ (Fahrenheit – 32)*.

ANS:

```
1   ' Exercise 3.21 Solution
2   Option Explicit
3
4   Private Sub cmdInput_Click()
5      Dim fahrenheitTemp As Integer
6
7      fahrenheitTemp = txtInput.Text
8
9      lblCelsius.Caption = "Celcius equivalent is " & 5 / 9 * (fahrenheitTemp - 32)
10  End Sub
```

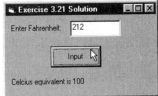

3.22 Enhance Exercise 3.21 to provide a conversion from Fahrenheit to Kelvin. Display the converted Kelvin temperature in a second **Label**. Use the formula: *Kelvin = Celsius + 273*.

ANS:

```
1   ' Exercise 3.22 Solution
2   Option Explicit
3
4   Private Sub cmdInput_Click()
5      Dim fahrenheitTemp As Integer
6      Dim celsiusTemp As Integer
7
8      fahrenheitTemp = txtInput.Text
9      celsiusTemp = 5 / 9 * (fahrenheitTemp - 32)
10
11     lblCelsius.Caption = "Celcius equivalent is " & _
12                          celsiusTemp
13
14     lblKelvin.Caption = "Kelvin equivalent is " & _
15                         celsiusTemp + 273
16  End Sub
```

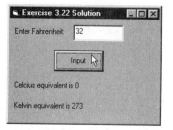

3.23   Modify Exercise 3.21 to use function **InputBox** for input.
          ANS:

```
1   ' Exercise 3.23 Solution
2   Option Explicit
3
4   Private Sub cmdInput_Click()
5       Dim fahrenheitTemp As Integer
6       Dim celsiusTemp As Integer
7
8       fahrenheitTemp = InputBox("Enter Fahrenheit temperature:", _
9                                 "Exercise 3.22")
10
11      celsiusTemp = 5 / 9 * (fahrenheitTemp - 32)
12
13      lblCelsius.Caption = "Celcius equivalent is " & _
14                           celsiusTemp
15
16      lblKelvin.Caption = "Kelvin equivalent is " & _
17                          celsiusTemp + 273
18  End Sub
```

Chapter 4 Solutions
Control Structures: Part I

4.6   Identify and correct the error(s) in each of the following:

a) Assume that the variable **age** is declared and has a valid value.

```
If age >= 65
    lblAge = "Age is greater than or equal to 65"
Else
    lblAge.Caption = Age is less than 65
```

ANS: Then is missing. **End If** is missing. Double quotes are missing. Corrected code should read:

```
If age >= 65 Then
    lblAge = "Age is greater than or equal to 65"
Else
    lblAge.Caption = "Age is less than 65"
End If
```

b) Assume that the variable **x** is declared and initialized to 1. The loop should iterate from 1 to 10.

```
Dim total As Integer

Do Until x <= 10
    total = total + x
    x = x + 1
```

ANS: Loop is missing. Corrected code should read:

```
Dim total As Integer

Do Until x <= 10
    total = total + x
    x = x + 1
Loop
```

c) Assume that the variable **y** is declared and initialized to 1. The loop should sum the numbers from 1 to 100.

```
While y <= 100
    total = total + y
Wend

y = y + 1
```

ANS: Statement that modifies control variable **y** should be inside the loop. Corrected code should read:

```
While y <= 100
    total = total + y
    y = y + 1
Wend
```

d) Assume that the variable **z** is declared and initialized to 1000. The loop should iterate from 1000 to 1.

```
While (z > 0)
    Print z
    z = z + 1
Wend
```

ANS: Variable **z** should be decremented. Corrected code should read:

```
While (z > 0)
   Print z
   z = z - 1
Wend
```

e) Assume that the variable **k** is declared as an **Integer**. The loop should iterate until –1 is input.

```
Do While k <> -1
    InputBox("Enter a number -1 to quit:", VB6)
Loop
```

ANS: Variable **k** should be assigned the value returned from **InputBox**. **VB6** should be enclosed in a set of double quotes. Corrected code should read:

```
Do While k <> -1
   k = InputBox( "Enter a number -1 to quit:", "VB6")
Loop
```

f) Assume that **u** and **t** are declared as **Integer**s.

```
Let u = 8
Let t = 22

' If u is not equal to t then print t; otherwise print
' the value of u.
If u <> t Then Print t : Print u
```

ANS: Wrong character is used for comments. **If/Then** statement always prints both values and therefore should be converted to an **If/Then/Else** (function **IIf** or function **Switch** can be used as well). Corrected code should read:

```
Let u = 8
Let t = 22

' If u is not equal to t then print t; otherwise print
' the value of u.
If u <> t Then
   Print t
Else
   Print u
End If
```

4.7   What does the following event procedure do?

```
Private Sub CommandButton1_Click()
    Dim y As Integer, x As Integer, mysteryValue As Integer

    x = 1
    mysteryValue = 0

    While x <= 10
        y = x ^ 2
        Print y
        mysteryValue = mysteryValue + y
        x = x + 1
    Wend

    Caption = "Value is " & mysteryValue
End Sub
```

ANS: The squares of the numbers 1 to 10 are printed to the form and the form's caption displays **Value is 385**.

4.8   **[CD]** Fill in the blanks in each of the following:

a) The solution to any problem involves performing a series of actions in a specific _____.

ANS: order.

b) A variable that accumulates the sum of several numbers is called a _____.

ANS: total.

c) A special value used to indicate "end of data entry" is called a _____, a _____, a _____ or a _____ value.

ANS: sentinel, flag, dummy, signal.

d) A _____ is a graphical representation of an algorithm.

ANS: flowchart.

e) The item written inside a decision symbol is called a _____.

ANS: condition.

f) In a flowchart, the order in which the steps should be performed is indicated by _____ symbols.

ANS: flowline.

g) The termination symbol indicates the _____ and _____ of every algorithm.

ANS: start or beginning, end.

h) Rectangle symbols correspond to calculations that are normally performed by _____ statements.

ANS: assignment.

4.9   State which of the following are *true* and which are *false*. If *false*, explain why.

a) Experience has shown that the most difficult part of solving a problem on a computer is producing a working program from an algorithm.

ANS: False. The most difficult part of solving a problem is developing an algorithm.

b) A sentinel value must be a value that cannot be confused with a legitimate data value.

ANS: True.

c) Flowlines indicate the actions to be performed.

ANS: False. Flowlines indicate the flow of control.

d) In top-down stepwise refinement, each refinement is a complete representation of the algorithm.

ANS: True.

e) Conditions written inside decision symbols always contain arithmetic operators (i.e., **+**, **-**, **/**, ****, **^**, etc.).

ANS: False. Comparison operators are frequently used in conditions.

f) The **!** is the type declaration character for type **Single**.

ANS: True.

g) Function **Format$** returns a formatted **Single**.

ANS: False. A formatted **String** is returned.

4.10   **[CD]** Write a single pseudocode statement to accomplish each of the following:

a) Display the message **"Enter two numbers"** on the form.

ANS: *Display "Enter two numbers"*

b) Assign the sum of the variables **x**, **y**, **z** to variable **p**.

ANS: *p gets the sum of x, y and z*

c) The following condition is to be tested in an **If/Then/Else** selection structure: The current value of variable **m** is greater than twice the current value of variable **v**. If the condition is **True**, print the value of **m** to the form. Otherwise print twice the value of **v** to the form.

ANS: *If m is greater than twice v then*
           Display m
       Else
           Display v multiplied by 2

d) Obtain values for variables **r**, **y** and **u** from the user.

ANS: *Input r*
       Input y
       Input u

4.11   Formulate a pseudocode algorithm for each of the following:

a) Obtain two numbers from the user, compute the sum of the numbers and display the result.

ANS: *Input first number*
       Input second number

       Calculate the sum of the two numbers input
       Display the sum

b) Obtain two numbers from the user, and determine and display which (if either) is the larger of the two numbers.

ANS: *Input first number*
       Input second number

       If the first number is greater than the second number then
           Display the first number
       ElseIf the second number is greater than the first number then
           Display the second number

c) Obtain a series of positive numbers from the user, and determine and display the sum of the numbers. Assume that the user types the sentinel value **-1** to indicate "end of data entry."

ANS: *Prompt for the first value*
       Input the first value (possibly the sentinel)

       While the user has not as yet entered the sentinel
           If the value input is positive then
               Add the value to the sum
           Input the next value (possibly the sentinel)
       Display the sum

4.12   Convert each of the following **While** loops to **Do While** loops.

a)
```
While x > 500
    Print x;
    x = x - 5
Wend
```
ANS:
```
Do While x > 500
    Print x;
    x = x - 5
Loop
```

b)
```
While pcm = q
   qFactor = qFactor + pcm
   pcm = txtInput.Text
Wend
```
ANS:
```
Do While pcm = q
   qFactor = qFactor + pcm
   pcm = txtInput.Text
Loop
```

c)
```
While J <> hugeJ
    largeJ = largeJ + J
    J = J Mod bigJ
Wend
```
ANS:
```
Do While J <> hugeJ
    largeJ = largeJ + J
    J = J Mod bigJ
Loop
```

d)
```
While n <= display
    Print "Visual Basic 6 How To Program!"
    n = n * 7
Wend
```
ANS:
```
Do While n <= display
    Print "Visual Basic 6 How To Program!"
    n = n * 7
Loop
```

4.13   Convert each **While** loop in Exercise 4.12 to a **Do Until** loop.

a)
```
While x > 500
    Print x;
    x = x - 5
Wend
```

ANS:
```
      Do Until x = 500
         Print x;
         x = x - 5
      Loop
```

b) While pcm = q
```
         qFactor = qFactor + pcm
         pcm = txtInput.Text
   Wend
```
ANS:
```
      Do Until pcm <> q
         qFactor = qFactor + pcm
         pcm = txtInput.Text
      Loop
```

c) While J <> hugeJ
```
         largeJ = largeJ + J
         J = J Mod bigJ
   Wend
```
ANS:
```
      Do Until J = hugeJ
         largeJ = largeJ + J
         J = J Mod bigJ
      Loop
```

d) While n <= display
```
         Print "Visual Basic 6 How To Program!"
         n = n * 7
   Wend
```
ANS:
```
      Do Until n > display
         Print "Visual Basic 6 How To Program!"
         n = n * 7
      Loop
```

4.14   Convert the pseudocode statements you wrote in Exercise 4.10 to Visual Basic code.

a) Display the message **"Enter two numbers"** on the form.

ANS: **Print "Enter two numbers"**

b) Assign the sum of the variables **x**, **y**, **z** to variable **p**.

ANS: **p = x + y + z**

c) The following condition is to be tested in an **If/Then/Else** selection structure: The current value of variable **m** is greater than twice the current value of variable **v**. If the condition is **True**, print the value of **m** to the form. Otherwise print twice the value of **v** to the form.

ANS: **If m > 2 * v Then**
```
         Print m
      Else
         Print v * 2
      End If
```

d) Obtain values for variables **r**, **y**, and **u** from the user.

ANS: **r = InputBox("Enter r", "Input #1")**
```
      y = InputBox("Enter y", "Input #2")
      u = InputBox("Enter u", "Input #3")
```

4.15   Convert the pseudocode algorithms you wrote in Exercise 4.11 to Visual Basic code.

a) Obtain two numbers from the user, compute the sum of the numbers, and display the result.

ANS: **num1 = InputBox("Enter first number", "Input")**
```
      num2 = InputBox("Enter second number", "Input")

      sum = num1 + num2
      Print sum
```

b) Obtain two numbers from the user, and determine and display which (if either) is the larger of the two numbers.

```
ANS: num1 = InputBox("Enter first number", "Input")
     num2 = InputBox("Enter second number", "Input")

     If num1 > num2 Then
         Print num1
     ElseIf num1 < num2 Then
         Print num2
     End If
```

c) Obtain a series of positive numbers from the user, and determine and display the sum of the numbers. Assume that the user types the sentinel value **-1** to indicate "end of data entry."

```
ANS: num1 = InputBox("Enter a number -1 to Quit:")

     While num1 != -1

         If num1 >= 0 Then
             sum = sum + num
         End If

         num1 = InputBox("Enter a number -1 to Quit:")
     Wend

     Display the sum
```

For Exercises 4.16 to 4.19, perform each of these steps:

1. Read the problem statement.

2. Formulate the algorithm using pseudocode and top-down stepwise refinement.

3. Write a Visual Basic program.

4. Test, debug and execute the program.

4.16 [CD] Drivers are concerned with the mileage obtained by their automobiles. One driver has kept track of several tankfuls of gasoline by recording miles driven and gallons used for each tankful. Develop a program that will input the miles driven and gallons used for each tankful. The program should calculate and display the miles per gallon obtained for each tankful. After processing all input information, the program should calculate and print the combined miles per gallon obtained for all tankfuls.

ANS:

```
1   ' Exercise 4.16 Solution
2   ' Pseudocode
3   '
4   ' Top:
5   '       Determine the average miles/gallon for each tank of gas, and
6   '       the overall miles/gallon for an arbitrary number of tanks of gas.
7   '
8   ' First refinement:
9   '       Input the gallons used and the miles driven, and calculate and
10  '       print the miles/gallon for each tank of gas.
11  '           Keep track of the total miles and total gallons.
12  '       Calculate and print the overall average miles/gallon.
13  '
14  ' Second refinement:
15  '       Input the gallons used.
16  '       While the sentinel value (-1) has not been entered for the gallons
17  '           Input the miles driven.
18  '           Add gallons to the total gallons.
19  '           Add miles to the total miles.
20  '           Display the miles/gallon.
21  '           Input the gallons used.
22  '       Display the overall miles/gallon.
23  Option Explicit
24
```

```
25   Private Sub cmdCalculate_Click()
26      Dim miles As Single, gallons As Single
27      Dim totalMiles As Single, totalGallons As Single
28
29      lblMpg.Caption = "MPG: 0"
30      lblTotalMpg.Caption = "Total MPG: 0"
31
32      gallons = InputBox("Enter Gallons (-1 to end):")
33
34      While gallons <> -1
35         miles = InputBox("Enter Miles: ")
36         totalGallons = totalGallons + gallons
37         totalMiles = totalMiles + miles
38         lblMpg.Caption = "MPG: " & miles / gallons
39         gallons = InputBox("Enter Gallons (-1 to end):")
40      Wend
41
42      lblTotalMpg.Caption = "Total MPG: " & (totalMiles / totalGallons)
43   End Sub
```

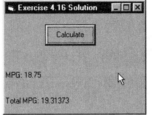

The following data was input: 12, 220, 14, 290, 13, 250, 12, 225.

4.17   Develop a program that will determine if a department store customer has exceeded the credit limit on a charge account. For each customer, the following facts are available:

1. Account number.

2. Balance at the beginning of the month.

3. Total of all items charged by this customer this month.

4. Total of all credits applied to this customer's account this month.

5. Credit limit.

The program should input each of these facts, calculate the new balance (= *beginning balance + charges – credits*) and determine if the new balance exceeds the customer's credit limit. For those customers whose credit limit is exceeded, the program should beep and display the message **"Credit Limit Exceeded."**

    ANS:

```
1    ' Exercise 4.17 Solution
2    '
3    ' Top: Determine if a customer has exceeded the credit limit
4    '     on a charge account.
5    '
6    ' First refinement:
7    '     Input the account number, beginning balance, total charges,
8    '         total credits, and credit limit
9    '     Calculate and display the new balance
10   '     Determine if the new balance exceeds the credit limit
11   '
12   ' Second refinement:
13   '     Enter the customer's account number
14   '     Enter the customer's beginning balance
15   '     Enter the customer's total charges
16   '     Enter the customer's total credits
17   '     Enter the customer's credit limit
18   '     Calculate the customer's new balance
19   '     Display the new balance
20   '     If the balance exceeds the credit limit
21   '         Print "Credit Limit Exceeded"
22   Option Explicit
23
```

```
24  Private Sub cmdEnter_Click()
25     Dim account As Integer, balance As Single, limit As Single
26     Dim charges As Single, credits As Single
27
28     lblDisplay.Caption = ""
29     account = txtAccount.Text
30     balance = txtBegBalance.Text
31     charges = txtTotalCharges.Text
32     credits = txtTotalCredits.Text
33     limit = txtCreditLimit.Text
34
35     If ((balance + charges - credits) > limit) Then
36        Beep
37        lblDisplay.Caption = "Credit Limit Exceeded!"
38     End If
39
40  End Sub
```

4.18 One large chemical company pays its salespeople on a commission basis. The salespeople receive $200 per week plus 9 percent of their gross sales for that week. For example, a salesperson who sells $5000 worth of chemicals in a week receives $200 plus 9 percent of $5000, or a total of $650. Develop a program that will input each salesperson's gross sales for last week and will calculate and display the salesperson's earnings. Process one salesperson's figures at a time.

ANS:

```
1  ' Exercise 4.18 Solution
2  '
3  ' Top: Determine a salesperson's earnings for a week.
4  '
5  ' First refinement:
6  '    Initialize variables and input items sold
7  '    Calculate and display salesperson's earnings
```

```
8   '
9   ' Second refinement:
10  '    Initialize gross to zero
11  '    Enter item
12  '    Determine the item's value and add it to the gross
13  '    Calculate salesperson's earnings
14  '    Display salesperson's earnings
15  Option Explicit
16
17  Private Sub cmdEnter_Click()
18     Dim gross As Single, salary As Single
19
20     gross = txtInput.Text
21
22     salary = 200 + 0.09 * gross
23     lblDisplay.Caption = "Salary is $" & salary
24  End Sub
```

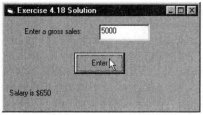

4.19   The simple interest on a loan is calculated by the formula

$$interest = principal \infty rate \infty days \div 365$$

The preceding formula assumes that rate is the annual interest *rate*, and therefore includes the division by 365 (days). Develop a program that will input principal, rate and days for several loans, and will calculate and display the simple interest for each loan, using the preceding formula. Use **TextBox**es for input and **Label**s for display.

ANS:

```
1   ' Exercise 4.19 Solution
2   '
3   ' Top: Determine and print the simple interest givin the
4   '      principal, annual interest rate and days.
5   '
6   ' First refinement:
7   '    Input principal, rate and days
8   '    Calculate and display simple interest
9   '
10  ' Second refinement:
11  '    Enter principal, rate and days
12  '    Calculate simple interest
13  '    Display simple interest
14  Option Explicit
15
16  Private Sub cmdCalculate_Click()
17     Dim principal As Single, rate As Single
18     Dim days As Single
19
20     principal = txtPrincipal.Text
21     rate = txtRate.Text / 100
22     days = txtDays.Text
23
24     lblDisplay.Caption = "Simple interest is $" & _
25                          principal * rate * days / 365
26  End Sub
```

4.20   [CD] Develop a program that will determine the gross pay for each of several employees. The company pays "straight-time" for the first 40 hours worked by each employee and pays "time-and-a-half" for all hours worked in excess of 40 hours. You are given a list of employees of the company, the number of hours each employee worked last week and the hourly rate of each employee. Your program should input this information for each employee, and should determine and display the employee's gross pay. Use **TextBox**es for input and **Label**s for display.

ANS:

```
1   ' Exercise 4.20 Solution
2   Option Explicit
3
4   Private Sub cmdCalculate_Click()
5       Dim hours As Single, wages As Single
6
7       hours = txtHours.Text
8       wages = txtWage.Text
9
10      If hours > 40 Then
11          lblDisplay.Caption = "$" & (40 * wages) + (hours - 40) * _
12                               (wages * 1.5)
13      Else
14          lblDisplay.Caption = "$" & (40 * wages)
15      End If
16
17  End Sub
```

4.21   The process of finding the largest number (i.e., the maximum of a group of numbers) is used frequently in computer applications. For example, a program that determines the winner of a sales contest would input the number of units sold by each salesperson. The salesperson who sells the most units wins the contest. Write a program that inputs a series of 10 numbers, and determines and prints the largest of the numbers. Hint: Your program should use three variables as follows:

1. **counter:**   A counter to count 10 (i.e., to keep track of how many numbers have been input, and to determine when all 10 numbers have been processed).

2. **number:**   The current number input to the program.

3. **largest:**   The largest number found so far.

ANS:

```
1   ' Exercise 4.21 Solution
2   Option Explicit
3
4   Dim largest As Integer
5   Dim counter As Integer
6
7   Private Sub cmdEnter_Click()
8      Dim number As Integer
9
10     If counter = 10 Then
11        cmdEnter.Enabled = False
12     End If
13
14     number = txtInput.Text
15     txtInput.Text = ""
16
17     If (number > largest) Then
18        largest = number
19     End If
20
21     counter = counter + 1
22     lblDisplay.Caption = "Largest is " & largest
23  End Sub
```

The following values were input: 67, 85, 14, 9, 77, 84 and 8.

4.22   [CD] What does the following event procedure do?

```
Private Sub cmdDisplay_Click()
   Dim count As Integer

   count = 1

   While count <= 10
      Print IIf(count Mod 2, "$$$$", "????????")
      count = count + 1
   Wend

End Sub
```

ANS:

```
$$$$
????????
$$$$
????????
$$$$
????????
$$$$
????????
$$$$
????????
```

4.23   What does the following event procedure do?

```
Private Sub cmdDisplay_Click()
   Dim row As Integer, column As Integer

   row = 10

   Do While row >= 1
      column = 1

      Do While column <= 10
         If row Mod 2 Then
            Print "j";
         Else
            Print "c";
         End If

         column = column + 1
      Loop

      row = row - 1
      Print
   Loop
End Sub
```

ANS:

```
cccccccccc
jjjjjjjjjj
cccccccccc
jjjjjjjjjj
cccccccccc
jjjjjjjjjj
cccccccccc
jjjjjjjjjj
cccccccccc
jjjjjjjjjj
```

4.24   [CD] Write a program that prints a hollow square on the form. The square length should be input in a **TextBox**.
ANS:

```
1   ' Exercise 4.24 Solution
2   Option Explicit
3
4   Private Sub cmdPrint_Click()
5      Dim number As Integer
6      Dim row As Integer, column As Integer
7
8      Cls
9      number = txtInput.Text
10
11     If number > 0 Then
12
13        If number <= 20 Then
14           row = number
15
16           While row >= 1
17              column = 1
18
19              While column <= number
20
21                 If row = number Then
22                    Print "*";
23                 ElseIf row = 1 Then
24                    Print "*";
25                 ElseIf column = 1 Then
```

```
26                         Print "*";
27                      ElseIf column = number Then
28                         Print "*";
29                      Else
30                         Print " ";
31                      End If
32
33                      column = column + 1
34                   Wend
35
36                   Print
37                   row = row - 1
38                Wend
39
40          End If
41
42       End If
43
44    End Sub
```

4.25 [CD] Write a program that keeps printing to the form powers of 2, namely 2, 4, 8, 16, 32, 64, etc. Your loop should not terminate (i.e., you should create an infinite loop). What happens when you run this program?

ANS:

```
1   ' Exercise 4.25 Solution
2   ' This solution will create an Overflow error
3   ' because the range of type Integer is exceeded.
4   Option Explicit
5
6   Private Sub cmdPrint_Click()
7      Dim x As Integer, y As Integer
8
9      x = 1
10     y = 2
11
12     While True
13
14        If x Mod 10 = 0 Then
15           Print              ' Print on next line
16        End If
17
18        Print y & "   ";
19        x = x + 1
20        y = y * 2             ' Will cause Overflow error
21     Wend
22
23  End Sub
```

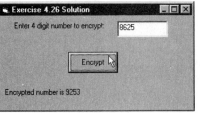

4.26　A company wants to transmit data over the telephone, but they are concerned that their phones may be tapped. All of their data is transmitted as four-digit **Integer**s. They have asked you to write a program that will encrypt their data so that it may be transmitted more securely. Your program should read a four-digit **Integer** and encrypt it as follows: Replace each digit by (the sum of that digit plus 7) modulus 10. Then, swap the first digit with the third, and swap the second digit with the fourth. Then print the encrypted **Integer**.

　　ANS:

```
1   ' Exercise 4.26 Solution
2   Option Explicit
3
4   Private Sub cmdEncrypt_Click()
5       Dim first As Integer, second As Integer, third As Integer
6       Dim fourth As Integer, digit As Integer, temp As Integer
7       Dim encryptedNumber As Integer
8
9       digit = txtInput.Text
10
11      first = (digit \ 1000 + 7) Mod 10
12      second = ((digit Mod 1000) \ 100 + 7) Mod 10
13      third = ((digit Mod 1000 Mod 100) \ 10 + 7) Mod 10
14      fourth = (digit Mod 1000 Mod 100 Mod 10 + 7) Mod 10
15
16      temp = first
17      first = third * 1000
18      third = temp * 10
19
20      temp = second
21      second = fourth * 100
22      fourth = temp
23
24      encryptedNumber = first + second + third + fourth
25      lblDisplay.Caption = "Encrypted number is " & encryptedNumber
26  End Sub
```

4.27　Write a program that takes an encrypted **Integer** from Exercise 4.26 and decrypts it.

　　ANS:

```
1   ' Exercise 4.27 Solution
2   Option Explicit
3
4   Private Sub cmdDecrypt_Click()
5       Dim first As Integer, second As Integer, third As Integer
6       Dim fourth As Integer, digit As Integer, temp As Integer
7       Dim decrypted As Integer, num As Integer
8
```

```
9       num = txtInput.Text
10
11      first = num \ 1000
12      second = (num Mod 1000) \ 100
13      third = (num Mod 1000 Mod 100) \ 10
14      fourth = num Mod 1000 Mod 100 Mod 10
15
16      temp = (first + 3) Mod 10
17      first = (third + 3) Mod 10
18      third = temp
19
20      temp = (second + 3) Mod 10
21      second = (fourth + 3) Mod 10
22      fourth = temp
23
24      decrypted = first * 1000 + second * 100 + third * 10 + fourth
25      lblDisplay.Caption = "Decrypted number is " & decrypted
26   End Sub
```

4.28   Write a program that reads in one five-digit **Integer** and determines and prints how many digits in the **Integer** are 7s. Use a loop to solve the problem. Note: The range for an **Integer** is –32,768 to 32,767.

ANS:

```
1   ' Exercise 4.28 Solution
2   Option Explicit
3
4   Private Sub cmdEnter_Click()
5       Dim first As Integer, second As Integer, third As Integer
6       Dim divisor As Integer, num As Integer, count As Integer
7       num = txtInput.Text
8       divisor = 10000
9
10      While divisor >= 1
11
12         If (num \ divisor = 7) Then
13            count = count + 1
14         End If
15
16         num = num Mod divisor
17         divisor = divisor / 10
18      Wend
19
20      lblDisplay.Caption = "Number of 7s: " & count
21   End Sub
```

4.29   Modify Exercise 4.28 so that it determines and prints the number of 7s for any number of digits up to five digits. Use a **TextBox** for input and a **Label** for display.

ANS:

```
1   ' Exercise 4.29 Solution
2   ' This is somewhat of a trick question--assuming the solution is
3   ' similar to Exercise 4.28 NO modification is necessary.
4   Option Explicit
5
6   Private Sub cmdEnter_Click()
7      Dim first As Integer, second As Integer, third As Integer
8      Dim divisor As Integer, num As Integer, count As Integer
9
10     num = txtInput.Text
11     divisor = 10000
12
13     While divisor >= 1
14
15        If (num \ divisor = 7) Then
16           count = count + 1
17        End If
18
19        num = num Mod divisor
20        divisor = divisor / 10
21     Wend
22
23     lblDisplay.Caption = "Number of 7s: " & count
24   End Sub
```

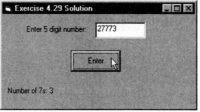

4.30   How can you determine how fast your machine operates? Write a program with the **Do While** loop that counts from 1 to 50,000,000 by 1s. Every time the count reaches a multiple of 10,000,000, print that number to the form. Use your watch to time how long each 10 million repetitions of the loop takes. Use the **Single** variable **counter** to do the counting. Today's personal computers execute so quickly that you might need to count each 20 million, 50 million or even 100 million items to be able to time the intervals manually.

       ANS:

```
1   ' Exercise 4.30 Solution
2   Option Explicit
3
4   Private Sub cmdGo_Click()
5      Dim count As Single
6
7      count = 1
8
9      Do While count <= 50000000
10
11        If count Mod 10000000 = 0 Then
12           Print count
13        End If
14
15        count = count + 1
16     Loop
17
18   End Sub
```

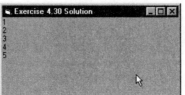

4.31   **[CD]** Write a program that prints 100 asterisks to the form one at a time. After every tenth asterisk, your program should print a blank line. (Hint: Count from 1 to 100. Use the modulus operator to recognize each time the counter reaches a multiple of 10.) Note: You should change the **Font** property of the form to **Courier**.

ANS:

```
1   ' Exercise 4.31 Solution
2   Option Explicit
3
4   Private Sub cmdPrint_Click()
5      Dim x As Integer
6
7      Cls
8      x = 1
9
10     While x <= 100
11        Print "*";
12
13        If ((x Mod 10) = 0) Then
14           Print
15        End If
16
17        x = x + 1
18     Wend
19  End Sub
```

4.32   Modify the program of Fig. 4.8 to perform validation on the user input. Invalid input should be rejected. Note: this may require you to rewrite portions of the example code.

ANS:

```
1   ' Exercise 4.32 Solution
2   Option Explicit                  ' General Declaration
3
4   Private Sub cmdPrint_Click()
5      Dim counter As Integer        ' Declaration
6
7      counter = txtInput.Text       ' Get number of characters
8
9      If counter = 0 Then
10        Caption = "The number input is out of range!"
11     Else
12        lblDisplay.Caption = ""        ' Clear Label
13        Caption = ""                   ' Clear Caption
14
15        ' Repeat the statements between Do While and Loop
16        ' until counter has a value of 0.
17        Do While counter > 0
18           lblDisplay.Caption = lblDisplay.Caption & "#"
19           counter = counter - 1       ' Decrement number
20        Loop
21
22     End If
23  End Sub
```

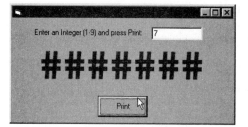

Chapter 5 Solutions
Control Structures: Part II

5.6 Identify and correct the error(s) in each of the following:

a) Assume that the variable **x** is declared as **Integer**.

```
For x = 100 To 1
    Print x
```

ANS: **Step** and **Next** are missing.

```
For x = 100 to 1 Step -1
    Print x
Next x
```

b) The following code should print whether **Integer value** is odd or even:

```
Select (value Mod 2)
    Case 0
        Print "Even integer"
    Case 1
        Print "Odd integer"
Select End
```

ANS: **Select End** should be **End Select**.

```
Select (value Mod 2)
    Case 0
        Print "Even integer"
    Case 1
        Print "Odd integer"
End Select
```

c) The following code should output the odd **Integer**s from 19 to 1:

```
For (x = 19 To 1 Step 2)
    Print x
Next
```

ANS: **Step** value should be negative.

```
For (x = 19 To 1 Step -2)
    Print x
Next x
```

d) The following code should output the even **Integer**s from 2 to 100:

```
counter = 2

Do Loop
    counter = counter + 2
    Print counter
While counter < 100
```

ANS: The statements in the loop body should be reversed and **<** should be **<=**.

```
Do Loop
    Print counter
    counter = counter + 2
While counter <= 100
```

e) `lstMyListBox.AddItem = "adding a string!"`
ANS: `Call lstMyListBox.AddItem("adding a string!")`
f) Assume that variables **a**, **b** and **j** are declared as **Integer**.

```
For j = 1 To 200

    For j = 11 To 777 Step 11
        Print a * b
    Next j

Next j
```

ANS: The same control variable cannot be used for nested loops. Another variable must be declared and used.
```
For j = 1 To 200

    For k = 11 To 777 Step 11
        Print a * b
    Next k

Next j
```
g) Assume that the variables **x**, **y** and **z** are declared as **Integer**s.

```
For x = 800 To 900

    For y = -50 To 150
        Print z + 8 * y + x - 3
    Next x

Next z
```

ANS: The wrong variable names are specified in the **Next** statements.
```
For x = 800 To 900

    For y = -50 To 150
        Print z + 8 * y + x - 3
    Next y

Next x
```

5.7   **[CD]** State whether the following are *true* or *false*. If the answer is *false*, explain why.
a) The **$** is the type declaration character for the **Currency** type.
ANS: False. The **@** character is the type declaration character for **Currency**.
b) A **Do/Loop Until** structure may be used to replace a **For/Next** structure.
ANS: True.
c) A **Do/Loop While** structure may be used to replace a **For/Next** structure.
ANS: True.
d) Keyword **Is** may be used in a **Select Case** structure.
ANS: True.
e) A module-level variable is accessible to multiple event procedures in the same module.
ANS: True.
f) **Case** statements are tested sequentially until either a match occurs or the **End Select** is executed.
ANS: True.

5.8   Write a statement or a set of statements to accomplish each of the following:
a) Declare the variable **nationalDebtInterest** as a **Long**.
ANS: `Dim nationalDebtInterest As Long`
b) Declare constant variable **general76** as an **Integer** and assign it the value **76**.
ANS: `Const general76 As Integer = 76`
c) Print the value of **mDie1** using the **Print** method. Variable **mDie1** contains a number in the range 1 to 6.
ANS: `Print mDie1`
d) Write a **Select Case** structure that tests variable **s** against the odd numbers between 1 and 10. If **s** is indeed an odd number in the range 1 to 10, print value of **s** as "**One**," "**Three**," etc. Otherwise, print "**Out of range**."

```
ANS: Select Case s
        Case 1
            Print "One"
        Case 3
            Print "Three"
        Case 5
            Print "Five"
        Case 7
            Print "Seven"
        Case 9
            Print "Nine"
        Case Else
            Print "Out of range"
     End Select
```
e) Add **"Sorted Values are: "** to **ListBox lstSortedNames**.
ANS: **Call lstSortedName.AddItem("Sorted Values are: ")**

5.9   Answer each of the following questions.
a) Of the three logical operators introduced in this chapter, _____ has the highest precedence.
ANS: **Not**
b) The_____ statement causes an immediate exit from a **Do While/Loop, Do/Loop While, Do Until/Loop** and **Do/ Loop Until**.
ANS: **Exit Do**
c) Operator _____ reverses the result of a condition.
ANS: **Not**
d) Visual Basic constant _____ represents a tab character.
ANS: **vbTab**

5.10   What does the following event procedure do?

```
Private Sub cmdButton_Click()
    Dim x As Integer, y As Integer
    Dim i As Integer, j As Integer

    x = InputBox("Enter a number in the range 1-20:")
    y = InputBox("Enter a number in the range 1-20:")

    For i = 1 To y
       For j = 1 To x
           Print "&";
       Next j

       Print
    Next i

End Sub
```

ANS: The program draws a rectangle of **&**s. Variable **y** specifies the row and variable **x** specifies the column.

5.11   [CD] What does the following do?

```
For i = 1 To 2
   For j = 1 To 3
      For k = 1 To 4
          Print "*";
      Next k

      Print
   Next j
Next i
```

ANS:

```
****
****
****
****
****
****
```

5.12   What does the following print?

```
1   Dim p As Integer, c As Integer, m As Integer
2
3   For p = 0 To 4
4
5      While c < p
6
7         Select Case (p + c - 1)
8            Case -1 Or 0
9               m = m + 1
10           Case 1, 2, 3
11              m = m + 2
12           Case Else
13              m = m + 3
14        End Select
15
16        Print m, ;
17        c = c + 1
18     Wend
19
20   Next p
21
22   Print
23   Print m
```
   ANS: 3, 5, 8, and 11 separated by tabs on one line. 11 on next line.

5.13   What does the following print?

```
1   Dim e As Integer, b As Integer
2   Dim t As Integer, w As Integer
3
4   For e = 4 To 0 Step -1
5
6      For b = 0 To e - 1
7         t = e + b + 1
8
9         If Not t Mod 2 Then
10            w = w + t
11         ElseIf Not t Mod 3 Then
12            w = w + t - 2
13         End If
14
15         lstListBox.AddItem w
16      Next b
17
18   Next e
19
20   lstListBox.AddItem w & "*"
```
   ANS: 5, 11, 18, 26, 30, 35, 41, 44, 48, 50 and 50* are displayed in **ListBox lstListBox**.

5.14   Assume that **a = 1, b = 2, c = 3** and **d = 2**. What does each of the following statements print? Are the parentheses necessary in each case?

a) **Print (a = 1)**
ANS: True. No.

b) **Print (b = 3)**
ANS: False. No.

c) **Print (a >= 1 And b < 4)**
ANS: True. No.

d) **Print (d <= 99 And c < d)**
ANS: False. No.

e) **Print (b >= a Or c = d)**
ANS: True. No.

f) **Print (c + d < b Or 3 - b >= c)**
ANS: False. No.

g) **Print (True)**
ANS: True. No.

h) **Print ((False) + False)**
ANS: 0. No.

i) **Print (Not(c > d))**
ANS: False. No.

5.15   (*De Morgan's Laws*) In this chapter, we discussed the logical operators **And**, **Or** and **Not**. De Morgan's Laws can sometimes make it more convenient for us to express a logical expression. These laws state that the expression **Not**(condition1 **And** condition2) is logically equivalent to the expression (**Not** condition1 **Or Not** condition2). Also, the expression **Not** (condition1 **Or** condition2) is logically equivalent to the expression (**Not** condition1 **And Not** condition2). Use De Morgan's Laws to write equivalent expressions for each of the following. (Note: In some cases there may be more than one correct answer.)

a) **Not (x < 5) And Not (y >= 7)**
ANS: Not ((x < 5) Or (y >= 7))

b) **Not (a = b) Or Not (g <> 5)**
ANS: Not ((a = b) And (g <> 5))

c) **Not ((x <= 8) And (y > 4))**
ANS: Not ((x <= 8) Or (y > 4))

d) **Not ((i > 4) Or (j <= 6))**
ANS: Not ((i > 4) And (j <= 6))

5.16   Write a program that prints the following patterns separately on the form each time a button is pressed. Provide four buttons **A**, **B**, **C** and **D**. When button **A** is pressed, the triangle shown in part (A) is printed, etc. Use **For/Next** loops to generate the patterns. Each triangle's asterisks (*) should be printed by a single statement of the form **Print "*";** (this causes the asterisks to print side by side). Hint: The last two patterns require that each line begin with an appropriate number of blanks. Set the form's **Font** to **Courier Bold**.

```
(A)            (B)            (C)            (D)
*              **********     **********            *
**             *********      *********            **
***            ********       ********            ***
****           *******        *******            ****
*****          ******         ******            *****
******         *****          *****            ******
*******        ****           ****            *******
********       ***            ***            ********
*********      **             **            *********
**********     *              *            **********
```

ANS:

```
1   ' Exercise 5.16 Solution
2   Option Explicit
3
4   Private Sub cmdA_Click()
5       Dim r As Integer, c As Integer
6
7       Cls
8
```

```
 9        For r = 1 To 10
10
11           For c = 1 To r
12              Print "*";
13           Next c
14
15           Print
16        Next r
17
18     End Sub
19
20     Private Sub cmdB_Click()
21        Dim r As Integer, c As Integer
22
23        Cls
24
25        For r = 10 To 1 Step -1
26
27           For c = 1 To r
28              Print "*";
29           Next c
30
31           Print
32        Next r
33
34     End Sub
35
36     Private Sub cmdC_Click()
37        Dim r As Integer, c As Integer, a As Integer
38
39        Cls
40
41        For r = 1 To 10
42
43           For c = 2 To r
44              Print " ";
45           Next c
46
47           For a = 10 To r Step -1
48              Print "*";
49           Next a
50
51           Print
52        Next r
53
54     End Sub
55
56     Private Sub cmdD_Click()
57        Dim r As Integer, c As Integer, a As Integer
58
59        Cls
60
61        For r = 1 To 10
62
63           For c = 10 To r Step -1
64              Print " ";
65           Next c
66
67           For a = 1 To r
68              Print "*";
69           Next a
70
71           Print
72        Next r
73
74     End Sub
```

5.17   Combine your code from the four separate problems of Exercise 5.16 into a single program that prints all four patterns side by side on the form by making clever use of nested **For/Next** loops.

   ANS:

```
1   ' Exercise 5.17 Solution
2   Option Explicit
3
4   Private Sub cmdPrint_Click()
5      Dim r As Integer, c As Integer
6
7      Cls
8
9      For r = 1 To 10
10
11        For c = 1 To r
12           Print "*";
13        Next c
14
```

```
15          For c = 10 To (r + 1) Step -1
16             Print " ";
17          Next c
18
19          Print Space$(4);
20          ' B
21          For c = 10 To r Step -1
22             Print "*";
23          Next c
24
25          For c = 1 To (r - 1)
26             Print " ";
27          Next c
28
29          Print Space$(4);
30
31          ' C
32          For c = 2 To r
33             Print " ";
34          Next c
35
36          For c = 10 To r Step -1
37             Print "*";
38          Next c
39
40          Print Space$(4);
41          'D
42          For c = 10 To (r + 1) Step -1
43             Print " ";
44          Next c
45
46          For c = 1 To r
47             Print "*";
48          Next c
49
50          Print
51       Next r
52
53    End Sub
```

5.18 [CD] A criticism of the **Exit Do** statement and the **Exit For** statement is that each is unstructured. Actually, **Exit Do** statements and **Exit For** statements can always be replaced by structured statements, although doing so can be awkward. Describe in general how you would remove any **Exit Do** statement from a loop in a program and replace that statement with some structured equivalent. (Hint: The **Exit Do** statement leaves a loop from within the body of the loop. The other way to leave is by failing the loop-continuation test. Consider using in the loop-continuation test a second test that indicates "early exit because of an "exit" condition.") Use the technique you developed here to remove the **Exit Do** statement from the program of Fig. 5.16 and the **Exit For** statement from the program of Fig. 5.17.

   ANS:

```
1    ' Exercise 5.18 Solution
2    Option Explicit
3
4    Private Sub cmdPrint_Click()
5       Dim x As Integer, flag As Boolean
6       x = 1
```

```
7
8      Do
9
10         If x = 5 Then
11             flag = True
12         End If
13
14         Print x & Space$(2);
15         x = x + 1
16     Loop While x <= 10 And flag = False
17
18     Print "Exited loop at x = " & x
19 End Sub
```

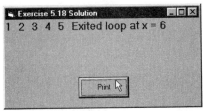

```
1  ' Exercise 5.18 Solution
2  Option Explicit
3
4  Private Sub cmdPrint_Click()
5     Dim x As Integer
6
7     For x = 1 To 10
8
9        If x = 5 Then
10           x = 10          ' Set value to fail condition
11        End If
12
13        Print x & Space$(2);
14     Next x
15
16     Print
17     Print "Exited loop at x = " & x
18  End Sub
```

5.19   Using the series

$$\sin(x) = x - x^3 / 3! + x^5 / 5! - x^7 / 7! + \ldots$$

calculate the sine x to n terms. The GUI should consist of two **TextBox**es, three **Label**s and a button. One **TextBox** should allow the user to input the value of x in radians (2π radians in a circle). The second **TextBox** should allow the user to input the number of terms n. The larger the term, the more accurate the value. Display the results in a **Label**. The other two **Label**s should be used as prompts. The calculation should be performed and displayed when the button is pressed.

   ANS:

```
1  ' Exercise 5.19 Solution
2  Option Explicit
3
4  Private Sub cmdCalculate_Click()
5     Dim x As Double, n As Long, i As Long
6     Dim sine As Double, exp As Long
7     Dim f As Long, factorial As Double
8
```

```
9    x = txtX.Text
10   n = txtTerms.Text
11   exp = 1
12   factorial = 1
13
14   For i = 1 To n
15
16      For f = exp To 1 Step -1
17         factorial = factorial * f
18      Next f
19
20      If i Mod 2 = 0 Then
21         sine = sine - (x ^ exp / factorial)
22      Else
23         sine = sine + (x ^ exp / factorial)
24      End If
25
26      factorial = 1
27      exp = exp + 2
28   Next i
29
30   lblDisplay.Caption = "sin(" & x & ") = " & sine
31 End Sub
```

Exercise 5.19 Solution

Enter the value of x in radians: 1.570795

Enter the number of terms: 10

Calculate

sin(1.570795) = 0.999999999999119

5.20   [CD] (*Pythagorean Triples*) A right triangle can have sides that are all **Integer**s. The set of three **Integer** values for the sides of a right triangle is called a Pythagorean triple. These three sides must satisfy the relationship that the sum of the squares of two of the sides is equal to the square of the hypotenuse. Write a program to find all Pythagorean triples for **side1**, **side2** and the **hypotenuse**, all no larger than 500. Use a triple-nested **For/Next** loop that tries all possibilities. This is an example of "brute force" computing. You will learn in more advanced computer science courses that there are large numbers of interesting problems for which there is no known algorithmic approach other than using sheer brute force.

ANS:

```
1  ' Exercise 5.20 Solution
2  Option Explicit
3
4  Private Sub cmdCalculate_Click()
5     Dim h As Integer, s1 As Integer, s2 As Integer
6
7     lstTriples.AddItem "Calculating...button will disable when finished"
8
9     For h = 1 To 500
10
11       For s1 = 1 To 500
12
13         For s2 = 1 To 500
14
15           If (h ^ 2 = s1 ^ 2 + s2 ^ 2) Then
16              lstTriples.AddItem h & vbTab & s1 & vbTab & s2
17           End If
18
19           DoEvents      ' Allow other events to happen
20         Next s2
21
22       Next s1
23
24    Next h
25
```

```
26       cmdCalculate.Enabled = False
27   End Sub
```

5.21   Write a program that prints the following diamond shape. You may use an output statement that prints a single asterisk (*). Maximize your use of repetition (with nested **For/Next** structures) and minimize the number of output statements. Print the diamond on the form. Set the form's **Font** to **Courier Bold**.

```
        *
       ***
      *****
     *******
    *********
     *******
      *****
       ***
        *
```

ANS:

```
 1   ' Exercise 5.21 Solution
 2   Option Explicit
 3
 4   Private Sub cmdPrint_Click()
 5      Dim r As Integer, c As Integer, s As Integer
 6
 7      ' Top
 8      For r = 1 To 5
 9
10         For s = 1 To 5 - r
11            Print " ";
12         Next s
13
14         For c = 1 To 2 * r - 1
15            Print "*";
16         Next c
17
18         Print
19      Next r
20
21      ' Bottom
22      For r = 4 To 1 Step -1
23
24         For s = 1 To 5 - r
25            Print " ";
26         Next s
27
28         For c = 1 To 2 * r - 1
29            Print "*";
30         Next c
31
32         Print
33      Next r
34
35   End Sub
```

5.22   Modify the program you wrote in Exercise 5.21 to allow the user to input an odd number in the range 1 to 25. The odd number input specifies the number of rows in the diamond. Your program should provide a button which when clicked displays the diamond on the form.

ANS:

```
1    ' Exercise 5.22 Solution
2    Option Explicit
3
4    Private Sub cmdPrint_Click()
5        Dim r As Integer, c As Integer, s As Integer
6        Dim n As Integer
7
8        Cls
9        n = txtNumber.Text
10
11       If (n Mod 2 <> 0) And (n >= 1) And (n <= 25) Then
12
13           ' Top
14           For r = 1 To (n - 2) Step 2
15
16               For s = ((n - r) / 2) To 1 Step -1
17                   Print " ";
18               Next s
19
20               For c = 1 To r
21                   Print "*";
22               Next c
23
24               Print
25           Next r
26
27           ' Bottom
28           For r = n To 0 Step -2
29
30               For s = ((n - r) / 2) To 1 Step -1
31                   Print " ";
32               Next s
33
34               For c = 1 To r
35                   Print "*";
36               Next c
37
38               Print
39           Next r
40
41       Else
42           Print "Invalid input!"
43       End If
44
45   End Sub
```

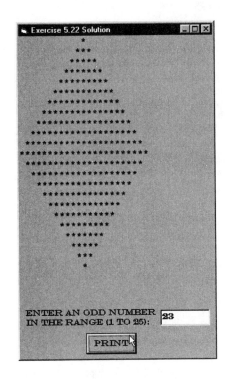

Chapter 6 Solutions

Sub Procedures and *Function* Procedures

6.6 [CD] State whether each of the following is *true* or *false*. If *false*, explain why.
 a) All procedure calls pass arguments call-by-value by default.
 ANS: False. Call-by-reference is the default.
 b) **Rnd** returns a number in the range $0 < x < 1$.
 ANS: False. **Rnd** returns a number in the range $0 \le$ **Rnd** < 1.
 c) Keyword **Static** may be applied to procedures.
 ANS: True.
 d) Keyword **ByVal** applies to all variables in the parameter list that follow it.
 ANS: False. It only applies to one parameter.
 e) **Static** variables are always declared in a procedure.
 ANS: True.
 f) In a **Function** procedure call, the argument(s) passed are enclosed in parentheses.
 ANS: True.
 g) A variable's storage class is determined by its scope.
 ANS: False.
 h) A control may be passed to a procedure as an argument.
 ANS: True.
 i) **Static** may not be applied to a procedure that has **Static** variables declared in the body.
 ANS: False.
 j) To pass arguments call-by-value to a procedure, keyword **ByVal** is used in the call.
 ANS: False. **ByVal** is used in the definition. Parentheses may be used in the call.

6.7 Answer the following questions about enumeration **Z**:
```
Enum Z
    value1
    value2
    value3 = -6
    value4
    value5 = value2
    value6
End Enum
```
 a) What is the value of **value1**?
 ANS: 0
 b) What is the value of **value2**?
 ANS: 1
 c) What is the value of **value4**?
 ANS: -5
 d) What is the value of **value5**?
 ANS: 1
 e) What is the value of **value6**?
 ANS: 2
 f) What happens if another enumeration constant, **value4**, is added to the existing enumeration, which already contains an enumeration constant **value4**?
 ANS: A syntax error occurs.

6.8   Determine if the following program segments contain error(s). For each error, explain how it can be corrected. Note: For a particular program segment, it is possible that no errors are present in the segment.

a) `Call ByRef MyProcedure(1, 2, 3)`

ANS: The `ByRef` keyword needs to be removed.

```
Call MyProcedure(1, 2, 3)
```

b) `Call RXZ 9, 8, 7`

ANS: The arguments passed to RXZ must be enclosed in parentheses.

```
Call RXZ(9, 8, 7)
```

c) `Call ANLT(varOne=:100)`

ANS: The colon and equal characters should be reversed.

```
Call ANLT(varOne:=100)
```

d)
```
Public Sub C(number As Single)
    lstValue.AddItem number & "*"
    Exit Sub
End Sub
```

ANS: No errors.

e) Assume that the following declaration resides in a code module's general declaration.

```
Static Public gMyNumber As Double
```

ANS: Keyword `Static` should be removed.

```
Public gMyNumber As Double
```

f)
```
Private Sub R(number As Integer ByVal, s As String)
    Print s & number
End Sub
```

ANS: Keyword `ByVal` is in the wrong place.

```
Private Sub R(ByVal number As Integer, s As String)
    Print s & number
End Sub
```

g)
```
Public Function RedLineIX(x%, y%, z%)%
    Print x: Print y: Print z
    RedLineIX = x * y * z
End Function
```

ANS: Type-declaration for the return type is in the wrong place.

```
Public Function RedLineIX%(x%, y%, z%)
    Print x: Print y: Print z
    RedLineIX = x * y * z
End Function
```

h)
```
Private Function PrintResults(x&, y As Long) As Long
    Print "The sum is " & x + y
    PrintResults = x + y
End Function
```

ANS: No error.

i)
```
Private Static Function Square(number As Long) As Long
    Dim number As Long, temp As Long
    temp = number ^ 2
    Function Square = temp
End Function
```

ANS: Keyword `Function` needs to be removed from the return value line.

```
Private Static Function Square(number As Long) As Long
    Dim number As Long, temp As Long
    temp = number ^ 2
    Square = temp
End Function
```

j)
```
Private Static Bft(x%, y%)
    Static z as Integer
    Print x; y
    If z = 0 Then
        z = 100
    End If
    z = z + 1
End Sub
```

ANS: Keyword **Sub** is missing from the header.

```
Private Static Sub Bft(x%, y%)
   Static z as Integer
   Print x; y

   If z = 0 Then
      z = 100
   End If


   z = z + 1
End Sub
```
k) **Call Static Procedure003(x, y)**
ANS: Keyword **Static** needs to be removed.

6.9 Answer each of the following questions.
a) What does it mean to choose numbers "at random"?
ANS: Every number has an equal chance of being chosen at any time.
b) Why is **Rnd** useful for simulating games of chance?
ANS: Because it produces a sequence of pseudo-random numbers that when scaled appear to be random.
c) Why would you randomize a program by using **Randomize**? Under what circumstances is it desirable not to randomize?
ANS: The sequence of numbers produced by the random number generator differ each time function **srand** is called. Not randomizing is useful for debugging purposes—the programmer knows the sequence of numbers.
d) Why is it often necessary to scale and/or shift the values produced by **Rnd**?
ANS: To produce random values in a specific range.
e) How does using the **Int** instead of the **Fix** affect the random numbers generated by **Rnd**?
ANS: The random numbers are not affected.
f) Why is computerized simulation of real-world situations a useful technique?
ANS: It enables more accurate predictions of random events such as cars arriving at a toll booth, people arriving in lines, birds arriving at a tree, etc. The results of a simulation can help determine how many toll booths to have open or how many cashiers to have open at specified times.

6.10 [CD] Write statements that assign random **Integer**s to the variable **n** in the following ranges:
a) $1 \le n \le 2$
ANS: **n = 1 + Int(Rnd() * 2)**
b) $1 \le n \le 100$
ANS: **n = 1 + Int(Rnd() * 100)**
c) $0 \le n \le 9$
ANS: **n = Int(Rnd() * 10)**
d) $1000 \le n \le 1112$
ANS: **n = 1000 + Int(Rnd() * 113)**
e) $-1 \le n \le 1$
ANS: **n = -1 + Int(Rnd() * 3)**
f) $-3 \le n \le 11$
ANS: **n = -3 + Int(Rnd() * 15)**

6.11 For each of the following sets of **Integer**s, write a single **Print** statement that prints a number at random from the set.
a) 2, 4, 6, 8, 10.
ANS: **Print 2 * (1 + Int(Rnd() * 5))**
b) 3, 6, 7, 9, 11.
ANS: **Print 1 + 2 * (1 + Int(Rnd() * 5))**
c) 6, 10, 14, 18, 22.
ANS: **Print 6 + 4 * (Int(Rnd() * 5))**

6.12 [CD] Find the error(s) in the following recursive **Function** procedure and explain how to correct it/them:
```
Private Function Sum(n As Integer) As Integer
   If (n = 0) Then
      Exit Function
   Else
      Sum = n + Sum(n)
   End If
End Function
```

```
ANS: Private Function Sum(n As Integer) As Integer
         If (n = 0) Then
             Sum = 0
         Else
             Sum = n + Sum(n - 1)
         End If
     End Function
```

6.13   What does the following **Function** procedure do?
```
' Parameter b must be a positive Integer
' to prevent infinite recursion
Public Function Mystery(a As Integer, b As Integer) As Integer
   If b = 1 Then
       Mystery = a
       Exit Function
   Else
       Mystery = a + Mystery(a, b - 1)
   End If
End Function
```
ANS: The procedure simulates exponentiation.

6.14   After you determine what the procedure of Exercise 6.13 does, modify it to operate properly after removing the restriction of the second argument being non-negative.

ANS:

```
1    ' Exercise 6.14 Solution
2    Option Explicit
3
4    Private Sub Form_Load()
5       Print Mystery(2, 3)
6    End Sub
7
8    Public Function Mystery(a As Integer, b As Integer) As Integer
9
10      If ((a < 0 And b < 0) Or b < 0) Then
11         a = a * -1
12         b = a * -1
13      End If
14
15      If b = 1 Then
16         Mystery = a
17         Exit Function
18      Else
19         Mystery = a + Mystery(a, b - 1)
20      End If
21
22   End Function
```

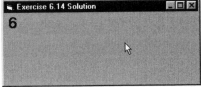

6.15   Write a program that simulates coin tossing. For each toss of the coin the program should print **Heads** or **Tails**. Let the program toss the coin 100 times, and count the number of times each side of the coin appears. Print the results. The program should call a separate **Function** procedure **Flip** that takes no arguments and returns **0** for tails and **1** for heads. Note: If the program realistically simulates the coin tossing, then each side of the coin should appear approximately half the time.

ANS:

```
1    ' Exercise 6.15 Solution
2    Option Explicit
3
```

```
 4   Private Sub Form_Load()
 5      Dim c As Integer, heads As Integer, tails As Integer
 6
 7      Call Randomize
 8
 9      For c = 1 To 100
10         If Flip() Then
11            heads = heads + 1
12         Else
13            tails = tails + 1
14         End If
15      Next c
16
17      Print "Heads: " & heads & vbTab & "Tails: " & tails
18   End Sub
19
20   Private Function Flip() As Integer
21      Flip = Int(Rnd() * 2)
22   End Function
```

Exercise 6.15 Solution
Heads: 51   Tails: 49

6.16   [CD] Write a program that obtains a character and an **Integer** from the user and displays a square out of whatever character is contained in character parameter **fillCharacter**. Thus if side is 6 and **fillCharacter** is "#", then this procedure should print

```
#####
#####
#####
#####
#####
```

Note: The form's **Font** property should be changed to **Courier**.

ANS:

```
 1   ' Exercise 6.16 Solution
 2   Option Explicit
 3
 4   Private Sub cmdDraw_Click()
 5      Dim fillCharacter As String, side As Integer
 6
 7      side = txtSide.Text
 8      fillCharacter = txtChar.Text
 9      Call Cls
10      Call DrawSquare(fillCharacter, side)
11   End Sub
12
13   Private Sub DrawSquare(fillChar As String, s As Integer)
14      Dim row As Integer, column As Integer
15      row = s
16
17      While row > 0
18         column = 1
19
20         While column <= s
21            Print fillChar;
22            column = column + 1
23         Wend
24
25         Print
26         row = row - 1
27      Wend
28
29   End Sub
```

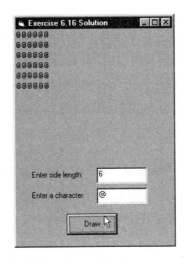

6.17   A mail order house sells five different products whose retail prices are product 1— $2.98, product 2—$4.60, product 3—$9.98, product 4—$4.49 and product 5—$6.87. Write a program that reads a series of pairs of numbers as follows:

1. Product number
2. Quantity sold for one day

Your program should use a **Select Case** statement in a programmer-defined procedure to help determine the retail price for each product. Your program should calculate and display the total retail value of all products sold last week.

ANS:

```
1   ' Exercise 6.17 Solution
2   Option Explicit
3
4   Private Sub cmdEnter_Click()
5       Dim productNumber As Integer, quantity As Integer
6
7       productNumber = txtProductNumber.Text
8       quantity = txtQuantity.Text
9
10      If productNumber < 1 Or productNumber > 5 Then
11         Exit Sub
12      End If
13
14      Call Evaluate(productNumber, quantity)
15  End Sub
16
17  Private Sub Evaluate(p As Integer, q As Integer)
18      Static product1Total As Currency, product2Total As Currency
19      Static product3Total As Currency, product4Total As Currency
20      Static product5Total As Currency
21
22      Call lstDisplay.Clear
23
24      Select Case p
25         Case 1
26            product1Total = product1Total + q * 2.98
27         Case 2
28            product2Total = product2Total + q * 4.6
29         Case 3
30            product3Total = product3Total + q * 9.98
31         Case 4
32            product4Total = product4Total + q * 4.49
33         Case 5
34            product5Total = product5Total + q * 6.87
35      End Select
36
37      Call lstDisplay.AddItem("Product" & vbTab & "Total")
38      Call lstDisplay.AddItem("1" & vbTab & Format$(product1Total, "Currency"))
39      Call lstDisplay.AddItem("2" & vbTab & Format$(product2Total, "Currency"))
```

```
40    Call lstDisplay.AddItem("3" & vbTab & Format$(product3Total, "Currency"))
41    Call lstDisplay.AddItem("4" & vbTab & Format$(product4Total, "Currency"))
42    Call lstDisplay.AddItem("5" & vbTab & Format$(product5Total, "Currency"))
43 End Sub
```

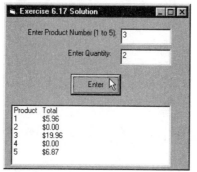

6.18   A parking garage charges a $6.00 minimum fee to park for up to three hours. The garage charges an additional $1.50 per hour for each hour or part thereof in excess of three hours. The maximum charge for any given 24-hour period is $25.00. Assume that no car parks for longer than 24 hours at a time. Write a program that will calculate and print the parking charges for each customer who parked his or her car in this garage yesterday. You should enter the hours parked for each customer. Your program should print the results in a neat tabular format and should calculate and print the total of yesterday's receipts. The program should use the procedure **CalculateCharges** to determine the charge for each customer.

ANS:

```
1  ' Exercise 6.18 Solution
2  Option Explicit
3
4  Private Sub cmdEnter_Click()
5      Dim hours As Single
6      hours = txtHours.Text
7      Call CalculateCharges(hours)
8  End Sub
9
10 Private Sub CalculateCharges(hrs As Single)
11     Static carNumber As Integer, totalReceipts As Currency
12     Dim charge As Currency
13
14     carNumber = carNumber + 1
15
16     If hrs < 3 Then
17        charge = 6
18     ElseIf hrs < 19 Then
19        charge = 6 + 1.5 * Round(hrs - 3)
20     Else
21        charge = 25
22     End If
23
24     totalReceipts = totalReceipts + charge
25     Call lstDisplay.AddItem("Car number: " & carNumber & vbTab & _
26                           Format$(charge, "Currency"))
27     lblTotal.Caption = "Total charges: " & Format$(totalReceipts, "currency")
28 End Sub
```

Exercise 6.18 Solution

Enter Hours Parked: 7

Enter

Car number: 1	$9.00
Car number: 2	$6.00
Car number: 3	$12.00

Total charges: $27.00

6.19   Computers are playing an increasing role in education. Write a program that will help an elementary school student learn multiplication. Use **Rnd** to produce two positive one-digit **Integer**s. It should then type a question such as

How much is 6 times 7?

The student then types the answer. Your program checks the student's answer. If it is correct, print **"Very good!"** and then ask another multiplication question. If the answer is wrong, print **"No. Please try again."** and then let the student try the same question again repeatedly until the student finally gets it right.

ANS:

```
1   ' Exercise 6.19 Solution
2   Option Explicit
3
4   Dim mX As Integer
5   Dim mY As Integer
6
7   Private Sub Form_Load()
8       Call SetUp
9   End Sub
10
11  Private Sub cmdAnswer_Click()
12      Dim guess As Integer
13
14      guess = txtInput.Text
15
16      If guess = mX * mY Then
17          Caption = "Very good!"
18          Call SetUp
19      Else
20          Caption = "No. Please try again."
21      End If
22
23  End Sub
24
25  Private Sub SetUp()
26      Call Randomize
27      mX = 1 + Int(Rnd() * 9)
28      mY = 1 + Int(Rnd() * 9)
29      lblLabel.Caption = "How much is " & mX & _
30                         " times " & mY & "?"
31      txtInput.Text = ""
32  End Sub
```

6.20   The use of computers in education is referred to as computer-assisted instruction (CAI). One problem that develops in CAI environments is student fatigue. This can be eliminated by varying the computer's dialogue to hold the student's attention. Modify the program of Exercise 6.19 so that the various comments are printed for each correct answer and each incorrect answer as follows:

Responses to a correct answer

Very good!
Excellent!
Nice work!
Keep up the good work!

Responses to an incorrect answer

```
No. Please try again.
Wrong. Try once more.
Don't give up!
No. Keep trying.
```

Use the random number generator to choose a number from 1 to 4 to select an appropriate response to each answer. Use a **Select Case** structure to issue the responses. Your solution should use programmer-defined procedures.

ANS:

```
1   ' Exercise 6.20 Solution
2   Option Explicit
3
4   Dim mX As Integer
5   Dim mY As Integer
6
7   Private Sub Form_Load()
8      Call SetUp
9   End Sub
10
11  Private Sub cmdAnswer_Click()
12     Dim guess As Integer
13
14     guess = txtInput.Text
15
16     If guess = mX * mY Then
17        Select Case (1 + Int(Rnd() * 4))
18           Case 1
19              Caption = "Very good!"
20           Case 2
21              Caption = "Excellent"
22           Case 3
23              Caption = "Nice work!"
24           Case 4
25              Caption = "Keep up the good work!"
26        End Select
27
28        Call SetUp
29     Else
30
31        Select Case (1 + Int(Rnd() * 4))
32           Case 1
33              Caption = "No. Please try again."
34           Case 2
35              Caption = "Wrong. Try once more."
36           Case 3
37              Caption = "Don't give up!"
38           Case 4
39              Caption = "No. Keep trying."
40        End Select
41
42     End If
43
44  End Sub
45
46  Private Sub SetUp()
47     Call Randomize
48     mX = 1 + Int(Rnd() * 9)
49     mY = 1 + Int(Rnd() * 9)
50     lblLabel.Caption = "How much is " & mX & _
51                        " times " & mY & "?"
52     txtInput.Text = ""
53  End Sub
```

6.21   More sophisticated computer-aided instruction systems monitor the student's performance over a period of time. The decision to begin a new topic is often based on the student's success with previous topics. Modify the program of Exercise 6.20 to count the number of correct and incorrect responses typed by the student. After the student types 10 answers, your program should calculate the percentage of correct responses. If the percentage is lower than 70 percent, your program should print "**Please ask your instructor for extra help**."

ANS:

```
1   ' Exercise 6.21 Solution
2   Option Explicit
3
4   Dim mX As Integer
5   Dim mY As Integer
6   Dim mProblemNumber As Integer
7   Dim mCorrect As Integer
8
9   Private Sub Form_Load()
10      Call SetUp
11  End Sub
12
13  Private Sub cmdAnswer_Click()
14      Dim guess As Integer
15
16      guess = txtInput.Text
17
18      If guess = mX * mY Then
19
20          Select Case (1 + Int(Rnd() * 4))
21             Case 1
22                Caption = "Very good!"
23             Case 2
24                Caption = "Excellent"
25             Case 3
26                Caption = "Nice work!"
27             Case 4
28                Caption = "Keep up the good work!"
29          End Select
30
31          mCorrect = mCorrect + 1
32      Else
33
34          Select Case (1 + Int(Rnd() * 4))
35             Case 1
36                Caption = "No. Please try again."
37             Case 2
38                Caption = "Wrong. Try once more."
39             Case 3
40                Caption = "Don't give up!"
41             Case 4
42                Caption = "No. Keep trying."
43          End Select
44
45          Caption = Caption & "    " & mX & " * " & mY & " is " & mX * mY
46      End If
```

```
47
48        lblPercent.Caption = "Percent correct: " & _
49                          Format$(mCorrect / mProblemNumber, _
50                          "Percent")
51
52        If mProblemNumber = 10 Then
53
54           If mCorrect / mProblemNumber < 0.7 Then
55              Caption = "Please ask your instructor for extra help"
56              cmdAnswer.Enabled = False
57           End If
58
59        End If
60
61        Call SetUp
62     End Sub
63
64     Private Sub SetUp()
65        Call Randomize
66        mX = 1 + Int(Rnd() * 9)
67        mY = 1 + Int(Rnd() * 9)
68        lblLabel.Caption = "How much is " & mX & _
69                          " times " & mY & "?"
70        txtInput.Text = ""
71        mProblemNumber = mProblemNumber + 1
72     End Sub
```

| Please ask your instructor for extra help |
| How much is 1 times 8? [   ] |
| Answer   Percent correct: 50.00% |

6.22   Write a program that plays the game of "guess the number" as follows: Your program chooses the number to be guessed by selecting an **Integer** at random in the range 1 to 1000. The program then types:

```
I have a number between 1 and 1000.
Can you guess my number?
Please enter your first guess.
```

The player then types a first guess. The program responds with one of the following:

```
Excellent! You guessed the number!
Would you like to play again (y or n)?

Too low. Try again.

Too high. Try again.
```

If the player's guess is incorrect, your program should loop until the player finally gets the number right. Your program should keep telling the player "**Too high**" or "**Too low**" to help the player "zero in" on the correct answer.

   ANS:

```
1    ' Exercise 6.22 Solution
2    Option Explicit
3
4    Dim mAnswer As Integer
5    Dim mGuess As Integer
6    Dim mGameOver As Boolean
7
8    Private Sub Form_Load()
9       Call GameSetUp
10   End Sub
11
12   Private Sub cmdEnter_Click()
13
14      If mGameOver = False Then
15         mGuess = txtGuess.Text
```

```
16          Call CheckGuess
17      Else
18          Dim s As String
19
20          s = txtGuess.Text
21
22          If s = "Y" Or s = "y" Then
23              txtGuess.Text = ""
24              mGameOver = False
25              Call GameSetUp
26          Else
27              End
28          End If
29
30      End If
31
32  End Sub
33
34  Private Sub GameSetUp()
35      lblPrompt.Caption = "I have a number between 1 and 1000. " & _
36                          "Can you guess my number? Enter your guess."
37      mAnswer = GetNumber()
38  End Sub
39
40  Private Function GetNumber() As Integer
41      Call Randomize
42      GetNumber = 1 + Int(Rnd() * 1000)
43  End Function
44
45  Private Sub CheckGuess()
46
47      If mGuess = mAnswer Then
48          lblPrompt.Caption = "Excellent. You guessed the number! " & _
49                              "Would you like to play again (y or n)?"
50          mGameOver = True
51      ElseIf mGuess > mAnswer Then
52          lblPrompt.Caption = "Too High. Try again."
53      Else  ' mGuess < mAnswer
54          lblPrompt.Caption = "Too Low. Try again."
55      End If
56
57  End Sub
```

6.23   Modify the program of Exercise 6.22 to count the number of guesses the player makes. If the number is 10 or fewer, print "**Either you know the secret or you got lucky!**" If the player guesses the number in 10 tries, then print "**Ahah! You know the secret!**" If the player makes more than 10 guesses, then print "**You can do better!**" Why should it take no more than 10 guesses? Well, with each "good guess" the player should be able to eliminate half of the numbers. Now show why any number 1 to 1000 can be guessed in 10 or fewer tries.

ANS:

```vb
1    ' Exercise 6.23 Solution
2    Option Explicit
3
4    Dim mAnswer As Integer
5    Dim mGuess As Integer
6    Dim mGameOver As Boolean
7    Dim mGuesses As Integer
8
9    Private Sub Form_Load()
10       Call GameSetUp
11   End Sub
12
13   Private Sub cmdEnter_Click()
14
15       If mGameOver = False Then
16          mGuess = txtGuess.Text
17          mGuesses = mGuesses + 1
18          Call CheckGuess
19       Else
20          Dim s As String
21
22          s = txtGuess.Text
23
24          If s = "Y" Or s = "y" Then
25             txtGuess.Text = ""
26             mGameOver = False
27             Call GameSetUp
28          Else
29             End
30          End If
31
32       End If
33
34   End Sub
35
36   Private Sub GameSetUp()
37       lblPrompt.Caption = "I have a number between 1 and 1000. " & _
38                           "Can you guess my number? Enter your guess."
39       mAnswer = GetNumber()
40       Caption = ""
41       mGuesses = 0
42   End Sub
43
44   Private Function GetNumber() As Integer
45       Call Randomize
46       GetNumber = 1 + Int(Rnd() * 1000)
47   End Function
48
49   Private Sub CheckGuess()
50
51       If mGuess = mAnswer Then
52          lblPrompt.Caption = "Excellent. You guessed the number! " & _
53                              "Would you like to play again (y or n)?"
54          mGameOver = True
55
56          If mGuesses < 10 Then
57             Caption = "Either you know the secret or you got lucky!"
58          ElseIf mGuesses = 10 Then
59             Caption = "Ahah! You know the secret!"
60          Else
61             Caption = "You can do better!"
62          End If
63
```

```
64        ElseIf mGuess > mAnswer Then
65           lblPrompt.Caption = "Too High. Try again."
66        Else  ' mGuess < mAnswer
67           lblPrompt.Caption = "Too Low. Try again."
68        End If
69
70   End Sub
```

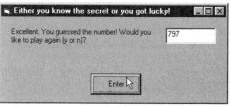

6.24   Modify the craps program of Fig. 6.22 to allow wagering. Package as multiple procedures the portion of the program that runs the game of craps. Initialize variable **bankBalance** to 1000 dollars. Prompt the player to enter a **wager**. Use a procedure to check that **wager** is less than or equal to **bankBalance** and if not, prompt the user to reenter **wager** until a valid **wager** is entered. Also check for **wager**s less than or equal to zero. After a correct **wager** is entered, allow the player to play a game of craps.

If the player wins, increase **bankBalance** by **wager** and display the new **bankBalance**. If the player loses, decrease **bankBalance** by **wager**, display the new **bankBalance**, check if **bankBalance** has become zero, and if so, print the message "**Sorry. You busted!**" The game should continue until either the player runs out of money or the player quits.

Write a procedure called **Chatter** that displays various messages as the game progresses to create some "chatter" such as "**Oh, you're going for broke, huh?**", or "**Aw c'mon, take a chance!**", or "**You're up big. Now's the time to cash in your chips!**" Procedure **Chatter** should use random number generation and a **Select Case** structure to display the chatter. Note: The chatter does not have to be relevant to what is occurring in the game.

ANS:

```
1    ' Exercise 6.24 Solution
2    Option Explicit       ' General declaration
3
4    ' Declare module variables
5    Dim mMyPoint As Integer
6    Dim mDie1 As Integer
7    Dim mDie2 As Integer
8    Dim mBankBalance As Currency
9    Dim mWager As Currency
10   Const mWIN As Integer = 1
11   Const mLOSE As Integer = 2
12
13   Enum Names
14      snakeEyes = 2    ' Explicitly assign 2
15      trey             ' Implicitly assign 3
16      [yo leven] = 11  ' Explicitly assign 11
17      boxCars          ' Implicitly assign 12
18   End Enum
19
20   Private Sub Form_Load()
21      Icon = LoadPicture("\vb_solutions\ch06\ex06_24\die.ico")
22      cmdPlay.Enabled = False
23      mBankBalance = 1000
24      txtBankBalance.Text = Format$(mBankBalance, "Currency")
25   End Sub
26
27   Private Sub cmdPlay_Click()
28      Call Craps
29   End Sub
30
31   Private Sub cmdEnter_Click()
32      mWager = txtWager.Text
33      Caption = ""
34
35      If ValidateWager = True Then
```

```
36          cmdEnter.Enabled = False
37          cmdPlay.Enabled = True
38       Else
39          Caption = "You must enter a valid wager."
40       End If
41
42    End Sub
43
44    Private Sub Craps()
45       Dim sum As Integer
46
47       ' initialization
48       mMyPoint = 0
49       fraPoint.Caption = "Point"
50       lblStatus.Caption = ""
51       imgPointDie1.Picture = LoadPicture("")
52       imgPointDie2.Picture = LoadPicture("")
53       Call Randomize
54
55       sum = RollDice()       ' Invoke rollDice
56
57       ' Determine outcome of first roll
58       Select Case sum
59          Case 7, [yo leven]
60             cmdRoll.Enabled = False    ' Disable Roll button
61             cmdPlay.Enabled = False
62             cmdEnter.Enabled = True
63             lblStatus.Caption = "You Win!!!"
64             Call UpdateBank(mWIN)
65          Case snakeEyes, trey, boxCars
66             cmdRoll.Enabled = False
67             lblStatus.Caption = "Sorry. You lose."
68             Call UpdateBank(mLOSE)
69          Case Else
70             Call Chatter
71             mMyPoint = sum
72             fraPoint.Caption = "Point is " & sum
73             lblStatus.Caption = "Roll Again."
74             Call DisplayDie(imgPointDie1, mDie1)
75             Call DisplayDie(imgPointDie2, mDie2)
76             cmdPlay.Enabled = False    ' Disable Play button
77             cmdRoll.Enabled = True     ' Enable Roll button
78       End Select
79    End Sub
80
81    Private Sub cmdRoll_Click()
82       Dim sum As Integer
83
84       sum = RollDice()              ' Invoke rollDice
85       ' Check for a win or loss
86       If sum = mMyPoint Then           ' Win
87          lblStatus.Caption = "You Win!!!"
88          cmdRoll.Enabled = False
89          cmdPlay.Enabled = False
90          cmdEnter.Enabled = True
91          Call UpdateBank(mWIN)
92       ElseIf sum = 7 Then              ' Loss
93          lblStatus.Caption = "Sorry. You lose."
94          cmdRoll.Enabled = False
95          cmdPlay.Enabled = False
96          cmdEnter.Enabled = True
97          Call UpdateBank(mLOSE)
98       End If
99
100   End Sub
101
102   Private Sub DisplayDie(imgDie As Image, face As Integer)
```

```
103       imgDie.Picture = LoadPicture("\vb_solutions\ch06\ex06_24\die" & _
104                                 face & ".gif")
105   End Sub
106
107   Private Sub UpdateBank(result As Integer)
108
109       If result = mWIN Then
110           mBankBalance = mBankBalance + mWager
111       Else   ' mLOSE
112           mBankBalance = mBankBalance - mWager
113
114           If mBankBalance = 0 Then
115               cmdRoll.Enabled = False
116               cmdPlay.Enabled = False
117               cmdEnter.Enabled = False
118               Caption = "SORRY. YOU BUSTED!"
119           End If
120
121       End If
122
123       txtBankBalance.Text = Format$(mBankBalance, "Currency")
124   End Sub
125
126   Private Function RollDice() As Integer
127       Dim die1 As Integer, die2 As Integer, dieSum As Integer
128       Dim a As Integer, b As Integer
129
130       die1 = 1 + Int(6 * Rnd())       ' Roll die1
131       die2 = 1 + Int(6 * Rnd())       ' Roll die2
132
133       Call DisplayDie(imgDie1, die1) ' Draw die image
134       Call DisplayDie(imgDie2, die2) ' Draw die image
135       Call Chatter
136
137       mDie1 = die1                    ' Store die1 value
138       mDie2 = die2                    ' Store die2 value
139       dieSum = die1 + die2            ' Sum dice
140       RollDice = dieSum               ' Return dieSum to caller
141   End Function
142
143   Private Function ValidateWager() As Boolean
144
145       If mWager <= 0 Or mWager > mBankBalance Then
146           ValidateWager = False
147           Exit Function
148       End If
149
150       ValidateWager = True
151   End Function
152
153   Private Sub Chatter()
154       Select Case Int(Rnd() * 10)
155           Case 0
156               Caption = "Oh, you're going for broke, huh?"
157           Case 1
158               Caption = "Aw cmon, take a chance!"
159           Case 2
160               Caption = "You're up big. Now's the time to cash in your chips!"
161           Case 3
162               Caption = "Way to lucky! Must be a cheat!!"
163           Case 4
164               Caption = "Shooter is hot!"
165           Case 5
166               Caption = "Hey! Keep your hands away from my chips!"
167           Case 6
168               Caption = "Bet it all! Bet it all!"
169           Case 7
```

```
170              Caption = "Pass me those lucky dice."
171          Case 8
172              Caption = "Can I borrow a few chips?"
173          Case 9
174              Caption = "I gonna make some money tonight!"
175      End Select
176
177  End Sub
```

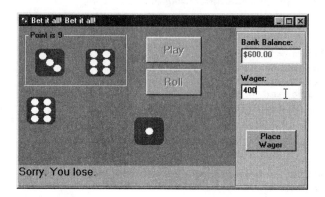

6.25   Modify Exercise 6.24 to support up to four different players. Allow each player to enter his or her name. Each player's name and bank balance should be displayed at all times.

ANS:

```
1   ' Exercise 6.25 Solution
2   ' NOTE: THIS SOLUTION CONTAINS THE USE OF THE GOTO STATEMENT
3   ' WHICH IS NOT DISCUSSED IN THE BOOK. IN THE NEXT EDITION OF
4   ' THIS BOOK--THIS EXERCISE WILL BE MOVED TO A CHAPTER PAST THE
5   ' ARRAYS CHAPTER SUCH THAT ARRAYS AND CONTROL ARRAYS CAN BE
6   ' USED IN THE SOLUTION.
7   Option Explicit
8
9   ' Declare module variables
10  Dim mMyPoint As Integer
11  Dim mDie1 As Integer
12  Dim mDie2 As Integer
13  Dim mBankBalance1 As Currency
14  Dim mBankbalance2 As Currency
15  Dim mBankbalance3 As Currency
16  Dim mBankbalance4 As Currency
17  Dim mWager1 As Currency
18  Dim mWager2 As Currency
19  Dim mWager3 As Currency
20  Dim mWager4 As Currency
21  Dim mHasPlayer As Boolean
22  Dim mCurrentPlayer As Integer
23  Const mWIN As Integer = 1
24  Const mLOSE As Integer = 2
25
26  Enum Names
27      snakeEyes = 2    ' Explicitly assign 2
28      trey             ' Implicitly assign 3
29      [yo leven] = 11  ' Explicitly assign 11
30      boxCars          ' Implicitly assign 12
31  End Enum
32
33  Private Sub Form_Load()
34      Dim players As Integer, i As Integer
35
36      Icon = LoadPicture("\vb_solutions\ch06\ex06_25\die.ico")
37      cmdPlay.Enabled = False
38
39      Do
```

```
40          players = InputBox("Enter number of players (1 to 4):")
41      Loop While players < 1 Or players > 4
42
43      If players = 4 Then
44          fraPlayer4.Caption = InputBox("Enter Player 4's Name:")
45          fraPlayer4.Enabled = True
46          mBankbalance4 = 1000
47          txtBankBalance4.Text = Format$(mBankbalance4, "Currency")
48          players = 3
49      End If
50
51      If players = 3 Then
52          fraPlayer3.Caption = InputBox("Enter Player 3's Name:")
53          fraPlayer3.Enabled = True
54          mBankbalance3 = 1000
55          txtBankBalance3.Text = Format$(mBankbalance3, "Currency")
56          players = 2
57      End If
58
59      If players = 2 Then
60          fraPlayer2.Caption = InputBox("Enter Player 2's Name:")
61          fraPlayer2.Enabled = True
62          mBankbalance2 = 1000
63          txtBankBalance2.Text = Format$(mBankbalance2, "Currency")
64      End If
65
66      fraPlayer1.Caption = InputBox("Enter Player 1's Name:")
67      fraPlayer1.Enabled = True
68      mBankBalance1 = 1000
69      txtBankBalance1.Text = Format$(mBankBalance1, "Currency")
70      mCurrentPlayer = 1
71      Caption = fraPlayer1.Caption & " is the shooter."
72      mHasPlayer = True
73      cmdEnter.Enabled = True
74  End Sub
75
76  Private Sub cmdPlay_Click()
77      Call Craps
78  End Sub
79
80  Private Sub cmdEnter_Click()
81      Dim w As Currency, b As Currency
82
83      lblStatus.Caption = ""
84
85      If mCurrentPlayer = 1 Then
86          mWager1 = txtWager1.Text
87          w = mWager1
88          b = mBankBalance1
89          Caption = fraPlayer1.Caption & " roll the dice."
90      ElseIf mCurrentPlayer = 2 Then
91          mWager2 = txtWager2.Text
92          w = mWager2
93          b = mBankbalance2
94          Caption = fraPlayer2.Caption & " roll the dice."
95      ElseIf mCurrentPlayer = 3 Then
96          mWager3 = txtWager3.Text
97          w = mWager3
98          b = mBankbalance3
99          Caption = fraPlayer3.Caption & " roll the dice."
100     Else  ' 4
101         mWager4 = txtWager4.Text
102         w = mWager4
103         b = mBankbalance4
104         Caption = fraPlayer4.Caption & " roll the dice."
105     End If
106
```

```vb
107         If ValidateWager(w, b) = True Then
108             cmdEnter.Enabled = False
109             cmdPlay.Enabled = True
110         Else
111             Caption = "You must enter a valid wager."
112         End If
113     End Sub
114
115     Private Sub Craps()
116         Dim sum As Integer
117
118         ' initialization
119         mMyPoint = 0
120         fraPoint.Caption = "Point"
121         lblStatus.Caption = ""
122         imgPointDie1.Picture = LoadPicture("")
123         imgPointDie2.Picture = LoadPicture("")
124         Call Randomize
125         Call lstMsg.Clear
126         sum = RollDice()        ' Invoke rollDice
127
128         ' Determine outcome of first roll
129         Select Case sum
130             Case 7, [yo leven]
131                 cmdRoll.Enabled = False    ' Disable Roll button
132                 cmdPlay.Enabled = False
133                 cmdEnter.Enabled = True
134                 lblStatus.Caption = "You Win!!!"
135                 Call UpdateBank(mWIN)
136             Case snakeEyes, trey, boxCars
137                 cmdRoll.Enabled = False
138                 lblStatus.Caption = "Sorry. You lose."
139                 Call UpdateBank(mLOSE)
140             Case Else
141                 Call Chatter
142                 mMyPoint = sum
143                 fraPoint.Caption = "Point is " & sum
144                 lblStatus.Caption = "Roll Again."
145                 Call DisplayDie(imgPointDie1, mDie1)
146                 Call DisplayDie(imgPointDie2, mDie2)
147                 cmdPlay.Enabled = False    ' Disable Play button
148                 cmdRoll.Enabled = True     ' Enable Roll button
149         End Select
150     End Sub
151
152     Private Sub cmdRoll_Click()
153         Dim sum As Integer
154
155         Call lstMsg.Clear
156         sum = RollDice()            ' Invoke rollDice
157         ' Check for a win or loss
158
159         If sum = mMyPoint Then          ' Win
160             lblStatus.Caption = "You Win!!!"
161             cmdRoll.Enabled = False
162             cmdPlay.Enabled = False
163             cmdEnter.Enabled = True
164             Call UpdateBank(mWIN)
165         ElseIf sum = 7 Then             ' Loss
166             lblStatus.Caption = "Sorry. You lose."
167             cmdRoll.Enabled = False
168             cmdPlay.Enabled = False
169             cmdEnter.Enabled = True
170             Call UpdateBank(mLOSE)
171         End If
172     End Sub
173
```

```
174  Private Sub DisplayDie(imgDie As Image, face As Integer)
175      imgDie.Picture = LoadPicture("\vb_solutions\ch06\ex06_25\die" & _
176                                   face & ".gif")
177  End Sub
178
179  Private Sub UpdateBank(result As Integer)
180
181      If result = mWIN Then
182
183          Select Case mCurrentPlayer
184              Case 1
185                  mBankBalance1 = mBankBalance1 + mWager1
186                  txtBankBalance1.Text = Format$(mBankBalance1, "Currency")
187              Case 2
188                  mBankbalance2 = mBankbalance2 + mWager2
189                  txtBankBalance2.Text = Format$(mBankbalance2, "Currency")
190              Case 3
191                  mBankbalance3 = mBankbalance3 + mWager3
192                  txtBankBalance3.Text = Format$(mBankbalance3, "Currency")
193              Case 4
194                  mBankbalance4 = mBankbalance4 + mWager4
195                  txtBankBalance4.Text = Format$(mBankbalance4, "Currency")
196          End Select
197
198      Else   ' mLOSE
199
200          Select Case mCurrentPlayer
201              Case 1
202                  mBankBalance1 = mBankBalance1 - mWager1
203                  txtBankBalance1.Text = Format$(mBankBalance1, "Currency")
204
205                  If mBankBalance1 = 0 Then
206                      Call lstMsg.AddItem(fraPlayer1.Caption & " BUSTED!")
207                      fraPlayer1.Enabled = False
208                  End If
209
210              Case 2
211                  mBankbalance2 = mBankbalance2 - mWager2
212                  txtBankBalance2.Text = Format$(mBankbalance2, "Currency")
213
214                  If mBankbalance2 = 0 Then
215                      Call lstMsg.AddItem(fraPlayer2.Caption & " BUSTED!")
216                      fraPlayer2.Enabled = False
217                  End If
218
219              Case 3
220                  mBankbalance3 = mBankbalance3 - mWager3
221                  txtBankBalance3.Text = Format$(mBankbalance3, "Currency")
222
223                  If mBankbalance3 = 0 Then
224                      Call lstMsg.AddItem(fraPlayer3.Caption & " BUSTED!")
225                      fraPlayer3.Enabled = False
226                  End If
227
228              Case 4
229                  mBankbalance4 = mBankbalance4 - mWager4
230                  txtBankBalance4.Text = Format$(mBankbalance4, "Currency")
231
232                  If mBankbalance4 = 0 Then
233                      Call lstMsg.AddItem(fraPlayer4.Caption & " BUSTED!")
234                      fraPlayer4.Enabled = False
235                  End If
236
237          End Select
238
239      End If
240
```

```
241        ' Variable c is used to determine if all players are out
242        Dim c As Integer
243
244        c = 1
245   y:
246        mCurrentPlayer = (mCurrentPlayer Mod 4) + 1
247        mHasPlayer = False
248
249        If mCurrentPlayer = 1 And fraPlayer1.Enabled Then
250           Caption = fraPlayer1.Caption & " is the shooter"
251           mHasPlayer = True
252           GoTo x
253        End If
254
255        If mCurrentPlayer = 2 And fraPlayer2.Enabled Then
256           Caption = fraPlayer2.Caption & " is the shooter"
257           mHasPlayer = True
258           GoTo x
259        End If
260
261        If mCurrentPlayer = 3 And fraPlayer3.Enabled Then
262           Caption = fraPlayer3.Caption & " is the shooter"
263           mHasPlayer = True
264           GoTo x
265        End If
266
267        If mCurrentPlayer = 4 And fraPlayer4.Enabled Then
268           Caption = fraPlayer4.Caption & " is the shooter"
269           mHasPlayer = True
270           GoTo x
271        End If
272
273        ' If we have looped more than 10 times get out of goto cycle
274        If c >= 10 Then
275           GoTo x
276        End If
277
278        c = c + 1
279
280        ' If this point is reached the current player has not
281        ' yet been determined. Go back and find current player.
282        GoTo y
283
284        ' If this point is reached the current player is either known or
285        ' all players are out of the game.
286   x:
287        cmdEnter.Enabled = True
288
289        If mHasPlayer = False Then
290           Caption = "Game Over. All players are out."
291           cmdRoll.Enabled = False
292           cmdPlay.Enabled = False
293           cmdEnter.Enabled = False
294        End If
295   End Sub
296
297   Private Function RollDice() As Integer
298      Dim die1 As Integer, die2 As Integer, dieSum As Integer
299      Dim a As Integer, b As Integer
300
301      die1 = 1 + Int(6 * Rnd())      ' Roll die1
302      die2 = 1 + Int(6 * Rnd())      ' Roll die2
303      Call DisplayDie(imgDie1, die1) ' Draw die image
304      Call DisplayDie(imgDie2, die2) ' Draw die image
305      Call Chatter
306      mDie1 = die1                   ' Store die1 value
307      mDie2 = die2                   ' Store die2 value
```

```
308        dieSum = die1 + die2              ' Sum dice
309        RollDice = dieSum                ' Return dieSum to caller
310   End Function
311
312   Private Function ValidateWager(wager As Currency, _
313                                 bankBalance As Currency) As Boolean
314
315       If wager <= 0 Or wager > bankBalance Then
316           ValidateWager = False
317           Exit Function
318       End If
319
320       ValidateWager = True
321   End Function
322
323   Private Sub Chatter()
324       Select Case Int(Rnd() * 13)
325           Case 0
326               Call lstMsg.AddItem("Oh, you're going for broke, huh?")
327           Case 1
328               Call lstMsg.AddItem("Aw cmon, take a chance!")
329           Case 2
330               Call lstMsg.AddItem("You're up big. Now's the time " & _
331                                   "to cash in your chips!")
332           Case 3
333               Call lstMsg.AddItem("Way to lucky! Must be a cheat!!")
334           Case 4
335               Call lstMsg.AddItem("Shooter is hot!")
336           Case 5
337               Call lstMsg.AddItem("Hey! Keep your hands away from my chips!")
338           Case 6
339               Call lstMsg.AddItem("Bet it all! Bet it all!")
340           Case 7
341               Call lstMsg.AddItem("Pass me those lucky dice.")
342           Case 8
343               Call lstMsg.AddItem("Can I borrow a few chips?")
344           Case 9
345               Call lstMsg.AddItem("I gonna make some money tonight!")
346           Case 10
347               Call lstMsg.AddItem("Its all in the wrist.")
348           Case 11
349               Call lstMsg.AddItem("Shooter looks cold. Bet carefully.")
350           Case 12
351               Call lstMsg.AddItem("Hey " & fraPlayer1.Caption & ", do you " & _
352                                   "know how to play craps??? Get with the " & _
353                                   "program!")
354       End Select
355   End Sub
```

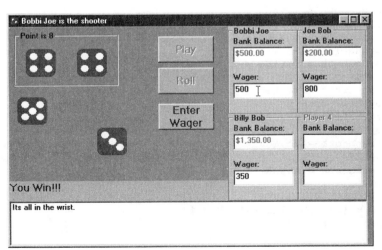

6.26   [CD] Procedures are capable of returning enumeration constants. Write a **Function** procedure that returns an enumerated constant representing the month of the year. Create an enumeration, **MonthsOfYear**, which defines enumerated constants **Jan**, **Feb**, etc. Both the procedure and enumeration should reside in a code module. Write a program which verifies that the procedure is properly written.

ANS:

```
1    ' Exercise 6.26 Solution
2    Option Explicit
3
4    Dim mMonthValue As Integer
5
6    Public Enum MonthsOfYear
7       moyJAN
8       moyFEB
9       moyMAR
10      moyAPR
11      moyMAY
12      moyJUN
13      moyJUL
14      moyAUG
15      moySEP
16      moyOCT
17      moyNOV
18      moyDEC
19   End Enum
20
21   Public Function GetNextMonth() As MonthsOfYear
22      Dim currentMonth As MonthsOfYear
23
24      Select Case mMonthValue
25         Case moyJAN
26            currentMonth = moyJAN + 1
27         Case moyFEB
28            currentMonth = moyFEB + 1
29         Case moyMAR
30            currentMonth = moyMAR + 1
31         Case moyAPR
32            currentMonth = moyAPR + 1
33         Case moyMAY
34            currentMonth = moyMAY + 1
35         Case moyJUN
36            currentMonth = moyJUN + 1
37         Case moyJUL
38            currentMonth = moyJUL + 1
39         Case moyAUG
40            currentMonth = moyAUG + 1
41         Case moySEP
42            currentMonth = moySEP + 1
43         Case moyOCT
44            currentMonth = moyOCT + 1
45         Case moyNOV
46            currentMonth = moyNOV + 1
47         Case moyDEC
48            currentMonth = moyDEC + 1
49      End Select
50
51      mMonthValue = (mMonthValue + 1) Mod 12
52      GetNextMonth = currentMonth
53   End Function
```

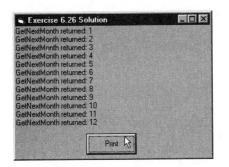

6.27   [CD] Write a procedure **Maximum3** that returns the largest of three **Single** numbers. Use Visual Basic function **IIf** to implement **Maximum3**. Write a program which verifies that the procedure is properly written.

ANS:

```
1   ' Exercise 6.27 Solution
2   Option Explicit
3
4   Private Sub cmdLargest_Click()
5      Dim value1 As Long, value2 As Long, value3 As Long
6      value1 = txtOne.Text
7      value2 = txtTwo.Text
8      value3 = txtThree.Text
9
10     lblDisplay.Caption = "Largest value is " & Maximum(value1, value2, value3)
11  End Sub
12
13  Private Function Maximum(max As Long, y As Long, z As Long) As Long
14     max = IIf(y > max, y, max)
15     max = IIf(z > max, z, max)
16     Maximum = max
17  End Function
```

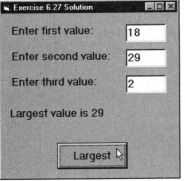

6.28   Write a procedure that takes an **Integer** value and returns the number with its digits reversed. For example, given the number 8456, the procedure should return 6548. Write a program which verifies that the procedure is properly written.

ANS:

```
1   ' Exercise 6.28 Solution
2   Option Explicit
3
4   Private Sub cmdPrint_Click()
5      Dim n As Integer
6
7      Call Cls
8      n = txtInput.Text
9
10     Print ReverseDigits(n)
11  End Sub
12
```

```
13    Private Function ReverseDigits(ByVal number As Integer) As String
14       Dim reverse As Integer, divisor As Integer
15       Dim multiplier As Integer
16
17       divisor = 1000
18       multiplier = 1
19
20       While number > 10
21
22          If number >= divisor Then
23             reverse = reverse + (number \ divisor) * multiplier
24             number = number Mod divisor
25             multiplier = multiplier * 10
26          End If
27
28          divisor = divisor \ 10
29       Wend
30
31       reverse = reverse + number * multiplier
32       ReverseDigits = reverse
33    End Function
```

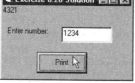

6.29   Write a program that uses a programmer-defined procedure called **CircleArea** to calculate and print the area of a circle. The user should input the radius in a **TextBox**.

   ANS:

```
1    ' Exercise 6.29 Solution
2    Option Explicit
3
4    Private Sub cmdPrint_Click()
5       Dim r As Integer
6
7       Call Cls
8       r = txtInput.Text
9       Print "Area: " & CircleArea(r)
10   End Sub
11
12   Private Function CircleArea(ByVal radius As Double) As Double
13      CircleArea = 3.14159 * radius ^ 2
14   End Function
```

6.30   The *greatest common divisor (GCD)* of two **Integer**s is the largest **Integer** that evenly divides each of the two numbers. Write a procedure **Gcd** that returns the greatest common divisor of two **Integer**s. Incorporate the procedure into a program that reads two values from the user.

   ANS:

```
1    ' Exercise 6.30 Solution
2    Option Explicit
3
4    Private Sub cmdEnter_Click()
5       Dim a As Integer, b As Integer
6
```

```
7      a = txtInput1.Text
8      b = txtInput2.Text
9      lblDisplay.Caption = "GCD: " & Gcd(a, b)
10   End Sub
11
12   Private Function Gcd(x As Integer, y As Integer) As Integer
13      Dim k As Integer, divisor As Integer, c As Integer
14
15      k = 2
16      divisor = 1
17      c = IIf(x < y, x, y)
18
19      Do While k <= c
20
21         If (x Mod k = 0) And (y Mod k = 0) Then
22            divisor = k
23         End If
24
25         k = k + 1
26      Loop
27
28      Gcd = divisor
29   End Function
```

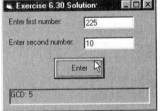

6.31   [CD] Write a recursive version of the **Gcd** procedure you developed in Exercise 6.30. The **Gcd** of **x** and **y** is defined recursively as follows: If **y** is equal to **0**, then **Gcd(x, y)** is **x**; otherwise, **Gcd(x, y)** is **Gcd(y, x Mod y)**, where **Mod** is the modulus
operator.

ANS:

```
1    ' Exercise 6.31 Solution
2    Option Explicit
3
4    Private Sub cmdEnter_Click()
5       Dim a As Integer, b As Integer
6
7       a = txtInput1.Text
8       b = txtInput2.Text
9
10      lblDisplay.Caption = "GCD: " & Gcd(a, b)
11   End Sub
12
13   Private Function Gcd(x As Integer, y As Integer) As Integer
14      If y = 0 Then
15         Gcd = x
16      Else
17         Gcd = Gcd(y, x Mod y)
18      End If
19   End Function
```

6.32 *(Towers of Hanoi)* Every budding computer scientist must grapple with certain classic problems, and the Towers of Hanoi (see Fig. 6.35) is one of the most famous of these. Legend has it that in a temple in the Far East, priests are attempting to move a stack of disks from one peg to another. The initial stack had 64 disks threaded onto one peg and arranged from bottom to top by decreasing size. The priests are attempting to move the stack from this peg to a second peg under the constraints that exactly one disk is moved at a time, and at no time may a larger disk be placed above a smaller disk. A third peg is available for temporarily holding disks. Supposedly the world will end when the priests complete their task, so there is little incentive for us to facilitate their efforts.

Let us assume that the priests are attempting to move the disks from peg 1 to peg 3. We wish to develop an algorithm that will print the precise sequence of peg-to-peg disk transfers.

If we were to approach this problem with conventional methods, we would rapidly find ourselves hopelessly knotted up in managing the disks. Instead, if we attack the problem with recursion in mind, it immediately becomes tractable. Moving n disks can be viewed in terms of moving only
$n - 1$ disks (and hence the recursion) as follows:

    a) Move $n - 1$ disks from peg 1 to peg 2, using peg 3 as a temporary holding area.
    b) Move the last disk (the largest) from peg 1 to peg 3.
    c) Move the $n - 1$ disks from peg 2 to peg 3, using peg 1 as a temporary holding area.

The process ends when the last task involves moving $n = 1$ disk (i.e., the base case). This is accomplished by trivially moving the disk without the need for a temporary holding area.

Write a program to solve the Towers of Hanoi problem. Allow the user to enter the number of disks in a **TextBox**. Use a recursive **Tower** procedure with four parameters:

    a) The number of disks to be moved
    b) The peg on which these disks are initially threaded
    c) The peg to which this stack of disks is to be moved
    d) The peg to be used as a temporary holding area

Your program should display in a **ListBox** the precise instructions it will take to move the disks from the starting peg to the destination peg. For example, to move a stack of three disks from peg 1 to peg 3, your program should print the following series of moves:

        $1 \rightarrow 3$ (This means move one disk from peg 1 to peg 3.)
        $1 \rightarrow 2$
        $3 \rightarrow 2$
        $1 \rightarrow 3$
        $2 \rightarrow 1$
        $2 \rightarrow 3$
        $1 \rightarrow 3$

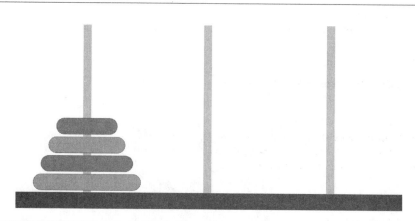

Fig. 6.35   The Towers of Hanoi for the case with four disks.

ANS:

```
1    ' Exercise 6.32 Solution
2    Option Explicit
3
4    Private Sub cmdEnter_Click()
5       Dim ndisks As Integer
6
7       Call lstDisplay.Clear
8       ndisks = txtInput.Text
9
10      If ndisks > 64 Or ndisks < 1 Then
11         Call lstDisplay.AddItem("Enter 1 to 64 disks")
12         Exit Sub
13      End If
14
15      Call Towers(ndisks, 1, 3, 2)
16   End Sub
17
18   Private Sub Towers(disks As Integer, start As Integer, _
19                      last As Integer, temp As Integer)
20
21      If (disks = 1) Then
22         Call lstDisplay.AddItem(start & " --> " & last)
23         Exit Sub
24      End If
25
26      ' Move disks - 1 disks from start to temp
27      Call Towers(disks - 1, start, temp, last)
28
29      ' Move last disk from start to last
30      Call lstDisplay.AddItem(start & " --> " & last)
31
32      ' Move disks - 1 disks from temp to last
33      Call Towers(disks - 1, temp, last, start)
34   End Sub
```

6.33   Any program that can be implemented recursively can be implemented iteratively, although sometimes with more difficulty and less clarity. Try writing an iterative version of the Towers of Hanoi. If you succeed, compare your iterative version with the recursive version you developed in Exercise 6.32. Investigate issues of performance, clarity and your ability to demonstrate the correctness of the programs.

6.34   [CD] Write a procedure **IntegerPower(base, exponent)** that returns the value of

$$base^{exponent}$$

For example, **IntegerPower(3, 4) = 3 * 3 * 3 * 3**. Assume that **exponent** is a positive, non-zero **Integer**, and **base** is an **Integer**. Procedure **IntegerPower** should use a loop to control the calculation. Do not use any Visual Basic math functions. Incorporate this procedure into a program that reads **Integer** values from **TextBox**es for **base** and **exponent** from the user and performs the calculation with procedure **IntegerPower**.

ANS:

```
1    ' Exercise 6.34 Solution
2    Option Explicit
3
```

```
4    Private Sub cmdCalculate_Click()
5       Dim b As Integer, exp As Integer
6
7       b = txtBase.Text
8       exp = txtExp.Text
9
10      lblDisplay.Caption = "Result: " & IntegerPower(b, exp)
11   End Sub
12
13   Private Function IntegerPower(base As Integer, exponent As Integer) _
14                                 As Integer
15
16      Dim x As Integer, result As Integer
17
18      result = 1
19
20      For x = 1 To exponent
21         result = result * base
22      Next x
23
24      IntegerPower = result
25   End Function
```

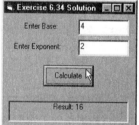

6.35   Write a recursive version of procedure **IntegerPower** that you developed in Exercise 6.34. The recursion step would use the relationship

$$base^{exponent} = base \cdot base^{exponent-1}$$

and the terminating condition occurs when **exponent** is equal to **1** because

$$base^1 = base$$

Incorporate this procedure into a program that enables the user to enter the **base** and **exponent**.

ANS:

```
1    ' Exercise 6.35 Solution
2    Option Explicit
3
4    Private Sub cmdCalculate_Click()
5       Dim b As Integer, exp As Integer
6
7       b = txtBase.Text
8       exp = txtExp.Text
9
10      lblDisplay.Caption = "Result: " & IntegerPower(b, exp)
11   End Sub
12
13   Private Function IntegerPower(base As Integer, _
14                                 exponent As Integer) _
15                                 As Integer
16
17      If exponent = 1 Then
18         IntegerPower = base
19         Exit Function
20      End If
21
22      IntegerPower = base * IntegerPower(base, exponent - 1)
23   End Function
```

6.36 An **Integer** number is said to be a *perfect number* if its factors, including 1 (but not the number itself), sum to the number. For example, 6 is a perfect number because 6 = 1 + 2 + 3. Write a procedure **Perfect** that determines if parameter **number** is a perfect number. Use this procedure in a program that determines and prints all the perfect numbers between 1 and 1000. Print the factors of each perfect number to confirm that the number is indeed perfect. Challenge the computing power of your computer by testing numbers much larger than 1000.

ANS:

```
1    ' Exercise 6.36 Solution
2    Option Explicit
3
4    Private Sub Form_Load()
5       Dim k As Integer
6
7       For k = 2 To 1000
8
9          If IsPerfect(k) Then
10            Call lstList.AddItem(k)
11         End If
12
13      Next k
14
15   End Sub
16
17   Private Function IsPerfect(ByVal n As Integer) As Boolean
18      Dim factorSum As Integer, j As Integer
19
20      factorSum = 1
21
22      For j = 2 To n \ 2
23
24         If n Mod j = 0 Then
25            factorSum = factorSum + j
26         End If
27
28      Next j
29
30      IsPerfect = IIf(factorSum = n, True, False)
31   End Function
```

Exercise 6.36 Solution

```
6
28
496
```

6.37 An **Integer** is said to be *prime* if it is divisible only by 1 and itself. For example, 2, 3, 5 and 7 are prime, but 4, 6, 8 and 9 are not.
  a) Write a procedure that determines if a number is prime.
  b) Use this procedure in a program that determines and prints all the prime numbers between 1 and 10000. How many of these 10000 numbers do you really have to test before being sure that you have found all the primes?
  c) Initially you might think that *n*/2 is the upper limit for which you must test to see if a number is prime, but you need only go as high as the square root of *n*. Why? Rewrite the program, and run it both ways. Estimate the performance improvement.

ANS:

```
1   ' Exercise 6.37 Part B Solution
2   Option Explicit
3
4   Private Sub Form_Load()
5      Dim count As Integer, i As Integer
6
7      Call lstList.AddItem("Primes from 1 to 10000 are:")
8
9      For i = 2 To 10000
10
11        If (Prime(i)) Then
12           count = count + 1
13           Call lstList.AddItem(i)
14        End If
15
16     Next i
17
18  End Sub
19
20  Private Function Prime(n As Integer) As Boolean
21     Dim i As Integer
22
23     i = 2
24
25     While i <= n / 2
26
27        If n Mod i = 0 Then
28           Prime = False
29           Exit Function
30        End If
31
32        i = i + 1
33     Wend
34
35     Prime = True
36  End Function
```

```
1   ' Exercise 6.37 Part C Solution
2   Option Explicit
3
4   Private Sub Form_Load()
5      Dim count As Integer, i As Integer
6
7      Call lstList.AddItem("Primes from 1 to 10000 are:")
8
9      For i = 2 To 10000
10
11        If (Prime(i)) Then
12           count = count + 1
13           Call lstList.AddItem(i)
14        End If
15
16     Next i
```

```
17
18  End Sub
19
20  Private Function Prime(n As Integer) As Boolean
21     Dim i As Integer
22
23     i = 2
24
25     While i <= Sqr(n)
26
27        If n Mod i = 0 Then
28           Prime = False
29           Exit Function
30        End If
31
32        i = i + 1
33     Wend
34
35     Prime = True
36  End Function
```

6.38   Write program segments that accomplish each of the following:
   a) Calculate the **Integer** part of the quotient when **Integer a** is divided by **Integer b**.
   b) Calculate the **Integer** remainder when **Integer a** is divided by **Integer b**.
   c) Use the program pieces developed in a) and b) to write a procedure **DisplayDigits** that receives an **Integer** between **1** and **99999** and prints it as a series of digits, each pair of which is separated by two spaces. For example, the **Integer 4562** should be printed as

        4 5 6 2.

   d) Incorporate the procedure developed in part (c) into a program that inputs an **Integer** from the user and invokes **DisplayDigits** from a button's **Click** event procedure by passing the procedure the **Integer** entered.

   ANS:

```
1   ' Exercise 6.38 Solution
2   Option Explicit
3
4   Private Sub cmdCalculate_Click()
5      Dim j As Long
6
7      j = txtInput1.Text
8
9      Call DisplayDigits(j)
10  End Sub
11
12  ' Part A: determine quotient using integer division
13  Private Function Quotient(a As Long, b As Long) As Integer
14     Quotient = a \ b
15  End Function
16
17  ' Part B: determine remainder using the modulus operator
18  Private Function Remainder(a As Long, b As Long) As Integer
19     Remainder = a Mod b
20  End Function
21
```

```
22  ' Part C
23  Private Sub DisplayDigits(number As Long)
24     Dim divisor As Long, s As String, k As Integer
25
26     If number < 1 Or number > 99999 Then
27        Exit Sub
28     End If
29
30     divisor = 10000
31     lblDisplay.Caption = ""
32
33     Do While divisor >= 1
34        k = Quotient(number, divisor)
35
36        If k <> 0 Then
37           s = s & "  " & k
38        End If
39
40        number = Remainder(number, divisor)
41        divisor = Quotient(divisor, 10)
42     Loop
43
44     lblDisplay.Caption = s
45  End Sub
```

Exercise 6.38 Solution

Enter an Integer: 58393

Calculate

5   8   3   9   3

6.39   Implement the following **Integer** procedures:

a) Procedure **Celsius** returns the Celsius equivalent of a Fahrenheit temperature using the calculation

```
C = 5 / 9 * (F - 32)
```

b) Procedure **Fahrenheit** returns the Fahrenheit equivalent of a Celsius temperature.

```
F = 9 / 5 * C + 32
```

c) Use these procedures to write a program that enables the user to enter either a Fahrenheit temperature and display the Celsius equivalent or enter a Celsius temperature and display the Fahrenheit equivalent.

ANS:

```
1   ' Exercise 6.39 Solution
2   Option Explicit
3
4   Private Sub cmdFahrenheit_Click()
5      Dim fahrenheitTemp As Integer
6
7      fahrenheitTemp = InputBox("Enter Fahrenheit Temperature:")
8
9      lblCelsius.Caption = "Celsius equivalent is " & _
10                          Celsius(fahrenheitTemp)
11  End Sub
12
13  Private Sub cmdCelsius_Click()
14     Dim celsiusTemp As Integer
15
16     celsiusTemp = InputBox("Enter Celsius Temperature:")
17
18     lblCelsius.Caption = "Fahrenheit equivalent is " & _
19                          Fahrenheit(celsiusTemp)
20  End Sub
21
```

```
22    Private Function Celsius(ByVal t As Integer) As Integer
23       Celsius = 5 / 9 * (t - 32)
24    End Function
25
26    Private Function Fahrenheit(ByVal t As Integer) As Integer
27       Fahrenheit = 9 / 5 * t + 32
28    End Function
```

6.40   [CD] Write a procedure **Multiple** that determines for a pair of **Integer**s whether the second **Integer** is a multiple of the first. The procedure should take two **Integer** arguments and return **True** if the second is a multiple of the first, and **False** otherwise. Incorporate this procedure into a program that inputs a series of **Integer** pairs (one pair at a time using **TextBox**es).

   ANS:

```
1     ' Exercise 6.40 Solution
2     Option Explicit
3
4     Private Sub cmdMultiple_Click()
5        Dim a As Integer, b As Integer
6
7        a = txtFirst.Text
8        b = txtSecond.Text
9
10       If Not Multiple(a, b) Then
11          lblDisplay.Caption = b & " is not a multiple of " & a
12       Else
13          lblDisplay.Caption = b & " is a multiple of " & a
14       End If
15    End Sub
16
17    Private Function Multiple(number1 As Integer, number2 As Integer) As Boolean
18
19       If number2 Mod number1 = 0 Then
20          Multiple = True
21       Else
22          Multiple = False
23       End If
24
25    End Function
```

6.41   Write a program that inputs **Integer**s (one at a time) and passes them one at a time to procedure **IsEven**, which uses the modulus operator to determine if an **Integer** is even. The procedure should take an **Integer** argument and return **True** if the **Integer** is even and **False** otherwise.

ANS:

```
1   ' Exercise 6.41 Solution
2   Option Explicit
3
4   Private Sub cmdEnter_Click()
5
6      If IsEven(txtInput.Text) Then
7         lblDisplay.Caption = "Even"
8      Else
9         lblDisplay.Caption = "Odd"
10     End If
11
12  End Sub
13
14  Private Function IsEven(ByVal v As Integer) As Boolean
15     IsEven = (v Mod 2 = 0)
16  End Function
```

6.42   [CD] Write a **Function** procedure that takes two **String** arguments representing a first name and a last name, concatenates the two **String**s to form a new **String** representing the full name and returns the concatenated **String**.

ANS:

```
1   ' Exercise 6.42 Solution
2   Option Explicit
3
4   Private Sub cmdDisplay_Click()
5      lblDisplay.Caption = ConcatName(txtFirst.Text, txtLast.Text)
6   End Sub
7
8   Private Function ConcatName(fName As String, lName As String) As String
9      ConcatName = fName & " " & lName
10  End Function
```

6.43   Write a procedure that keeps count of how many times it is called. Write this procedure two different ways. First, use a module value to keep count. Then write a version that uses a **Static** local variable to keep count. In what situations might the programmer prefer to write the procedure one way versus the other?

   ANS:

```
1   ' Exercise 6.43 Solution
2   Option Explicit
3
4   Dim mCounter As Integer
5
6   Private Sub cmdCall_Click()
7      lblDisplay.Caption = ""
8      Call UseModule
9      Call UseStaticLocal
10  End Sub
11
12  Private Sub UseModule()
13     mCounter = mCounter + 1
14     lblDisplay.Caption = "mCounter = " & mCounter
15  End Sub
16
17  Private Sub UseStaticLocal()
18     Static localStatic As Integer
19
20     localStatic = localStatic + 1
21     lblDisplay.Caption = lblDisplay.Caption & _
22                      "          localStatic " & localStatic
23  End Sub
```

6.44   Write a **Function** procedure **ToMorseCode** that takes one **String** argument (containing either a single letter or digit) and returns a **String** containing the Morse code equivalent. Figure 6.36 lists the Morse code for letters and digits.

Character	Code	Character	Code
A	.-	T	-
B	-...	U	..-
C	-.-.	V	...-
D	-..	W	.--
E	.	X	-..-
F	..-.	Y	-.--
G	--.	Z	--..
H	....		
I	..	Digits	
J	.---	1	.----
K	-.-	2	..---
L	.-..	3	...--
M	--	4	....-
N	-.	5	.....
O	---	6	-....

Fig. 6.36   The letters of the alphabet as expressed in international Morse code.

Character	Code	Character	Code
P	.--.	7	--...
Q	--.-	8	---..
R	.-.	9	----.
S	...	0	-----

Fig. 6.36   The letters of the alphabet as expressed in international Morse code.

ANS:

```
1    ' Exercise 6.44 Solution
2    Option Explicit
3
4    Private Sub cmdEnter_Click()
5       lblDisplay.Caption = "Morse code equivalent: " & ToMorseCode(txtInput.Text)
6    End Sub
7
8    Private Function ToMorseCode(s As String) As String
9
10      Select Case s
11         Case "A", "a"
12            ToMorseCode = ".-"
13         Case "B", "b"
14            ToMorseCode = "-..."
15         Case "C", "c"
16            ToMorseCode = "-.-."
17         Case "D", "d"
18            ToMorseCode = "-.."
19         Case "E", "e"
20            ToMorseCode = "."
21         Case "F", "f"
22            ToMorseCode = "..-."
23         Case "G", "g"
24            ToMorseCode = "--."
25         Case "H", "h"
26            ToMorseCode = "...."
27         Case "I", "i"
28            ToMorseCode = ".."
29         Case "J", "j"
30            ToMorseCode = ".---"
31         Case "K", "k"
32            ToMorseCode = "-.-."
33         Case "L", "l"
34            ToMorseCode = ".-.."
35         Case "M", "m"
36            ToMorseCode = "--"
37         Case "N", "n"
38            ToMorseCode = "-."
39         Case "O", "o"
40            ToMorseCode = "---"
41         Case "P", "p"
42            ToMorseCode = ".--."
43         Case "Q", "q"
44            ToMorseCode = "--.-"
45         Case "R", "r"
46            ToMorseCode = ".-."
47         Case "S", "s"
48            ToMorseCode = "..."
49         Case "T", "t"
50            ToMorseCode = "-"
51         Case "U", "u"
52            ToMorseCode = "..-"
```

```
53          Case "V", "v"
54             ToMorseCode = "...-"
55          Case "W", "w"
56             ToMorseCode = ".--"
57          Case "X", "x"
58             ToMorseCode = "-..-"
59          Case "Y", "y"
60             ToMorseCode = "-.--"
61          Case "Z", "z"
62             ToMorseCode = "--.."
63          Case "0"
64             ToMorseCode = "-----"
65          Case "1"
66             ToMorseCode = ".----"
67          Case "2"
68             ToMorseCode = "..---"
69          Case "3"
70             ToMorseCode = "...--"
71          Case "4"
72             ToMorseCode = "....-"
73          Case "5"
74             ToMorseCode = "....."
75          Case "6"
76             ToMorseCode = "-...."
77          Case "7"
78             ToMorseCode = "--..."
79          Case "8"
80             ToMorseCode = "---.."
81          Case "9"
82             ToMorseCode = "----."
83          Case Else
84             ToMorseCode = "none"
85       End Select
86
87    End Function
```

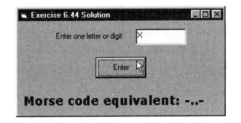

Chapter 7 Solutions
Arrays

7.6 [CD] Fill in the blanks in each of the following:
a) The elements of an array are related by the fact that they _____.
ANS: have the same name and type.
b) When referring to an array element, the position number contained within parentheses is called a _____.
ANS: index.
c) Naming an array, stating its type, and specifying the number of elements in the array is called _____ the array.
ANS: declaring.
d) The process of placing the elements of an array into either ascending or descending order is called _____.
ANS: sorting.
e) In a two-dimensional array, the first index (by convention) identifies the _____ of an element, and the second index (by convention) identifies the _____ of an element.
ANS: row, column.
f) An *m*-by-*n* array contains _____ rows, _____ columns and _____ elements.
ANS: *m*, *n*, *m*-by-*n*.

7.7 State which of the following are *true* and which are *false*. If *false*, explain why.
a) To refer to a particular location or element within an array, we specify the name of the array and the value of the particular element.
ANS: False. The name and index of the element is specified.
b) An array declaration reserves space for the array.
ANS: True.
c) To indicate that 100 locations should be reserved for **Integer** array **p**, the programmer could write the declaration (**Option Base** is **1**)
```
Static p[100] As Integer
```
ANS: False. The proper declaration should be
```
Static p(100) As Integer
```
d) A program that initializes the elements of a 15-element array to 0 must contain at least one **For** statement.
ANS: False. Arrays are initialized to 0 when declared. The **Erase** statement could be used as well to initialize the array to all 0s. Other loops besides a **For** may be used as well.
e) A program that totals the elements of a two-dimensional array must contain nested **For** statements.
ANS: False. Loops are not required to access array elements.

7.8 Write statement(s) that perform the following one-dimensional array operations:
a) Initialize the 10 elements of **Integer** array **counts** to zeros.
ANS: Dim counts(10) as Integer   ' Option Base is 1
b) Add 1 to each of the 15 elements of **Integer** array **bonus**.
```
ANS: For q = LBound(bonus) To UBound(bonus)
         bonus(q) = bonus(q) + 1
      Next q
```
c) Print the 12 values of **Single** array **monthlyTemperatures**.
```
ANS: For t = LBound(monthlyTemperatures) To UBound(monthlyTemperatures)
         Print monthlyTemperatures(t)
      Next t
```

7.9   Find the error(s) in each of the following statements and if possible, correct the error(s).
   a) `Print Count(x)      ' Print total elements in control array x`
   ANS: `Print x.Count`
   b) `Print b.Caption.Item(1) ' b is a control array of TextBoxes`
   ANS: `Print b.Item(1).Text`
   c) `Print UBound(c), LBound(c); "**" ' c is a control array`
   ANS: `Print c.UBound, c.LBound; "**"`

7.10   Label the elements of 3-by-5 two-dimensional array **sales** to indicate the order in which they are set to 0 by the following program segment (**Option Base** is **0**):

```
For row = 0 To 3
   For column = 0 To 5
      sales(row, column) = 0
   Next column
Next row
```

   ANS: `sales(0, 0), sales(0, 1), sales(0, 2), sales(0, 3), sales(0, 4),`
        `sales(0, 5), sales(1, 0), sales(1, 1), sales(1, 2), sales(1, 3),`
        `sales(1, 4), sales(1, 5), sales(2, 1), sales(2, 2), sales(2, 3),`
        `sales(2, 4), sales(2, 5), sales(3, 1), sales(3, 2), sales(3, 3),`
        `sales(3, 4), sales(3, 5), sales(4, 1), sales(4, 2), sales(4, 3),`
        `sales(4, 4), sales(4, 5), sales(5, 1), sales(5, 2), sales(5, 3),`
        `sales(5, 4), sales(5, 5)`

7.11   Write statement(s) to accomplish each of the following (assume that indexes begin at 1):
   a) Display the value of the seventh element of **String** array **f**.
   ANS: `Print f(7)`
   b) Place the value 762 into element 7 of one-dimensional **Single** array **b**.
   ANS: `b(7) = 762`
   c) Initialize each of the five elements of one-dimensional **Integer** array **g** to 8.
   ANS: `For t = LBound(g) to UBound(g)`
           `g(t) = 8`
        `Next t`
   d) Total and print the 100 elements of **Currency** array **c**.
   ANS: `For d = LBound(c) to UBound(c)`
           `total = total + c(d)`
           `Print c(d)`
        `Next d`
   e) Copy array **a** into the first portion of array **b**. Assume that **a(11)** and **b(37)** are declared as fixed-size **Double**
       arrays.
   ANS: `For e = LBound(a) to UBound(a)`
           `b(e) = a(e)`
        `Next e`
   f) Print the smallest and largest values contained in 99-element **Long** array **w**.
   ANS: `' Assume all variables are declared`
        `For j = LBound(w) to UBound(w)`
           `If (w(j) < smallest) Then`
              `smallest = w(j)`
           `ElseIf (w(j) > largest) Then`
              `largest = w(j)`
           `End If`
        `Next j`

7.12   Consider a 2-by-3 **Integer** array **t** (assume that **Option Base** is **1**):
   a) Write a local declaration for **t**.
   ANS: `Dim t(2, 3) As Integer`
   b) How many rows does **t** have?
   ANS: 2.
   c) How many columns does **t** have?
   ANS: 3.
   d) How many elements does **t** have?
   ANS: 6.
   e) Write the names of all the elements in the second row of **t**.
   ANS: `t(2, 1), t(2, 2), t(2, 3)`.

f) Write the names of all the elements in the third column of **t**.

ANS: `t(1, 3), t(2, 3)`.

g) Write a single statement that sets the element of **t** in row 1 and column 2 to 0.

ANS: `t(1, 2) = 0`

h) Write a statement that initializes each element of **t** to 0. Do not use a repetition structure.

ANS: `Erase t`.

i) Write a nested **For** statement that initializes each element of **t** to 0.

ANS:
```
For r = LBound(t) To UBound(t)
      For c = LBound(t, 2) to UBound(t, 2)
          t(r, c) = 0
      Next c
   Next r
```

7.13   [CD] Use a one-dimensional array to solve the following problem. A company pays its salespeople on a commission basis. The salespeople receive $200 per week plus 9 percent of their gross sales for that week. For example, a salesperson who grosses $5000 in sales in a week receives $200 plus 9 percent of $5000, or a total of $650. Write a program (using an array of counters) that determines how many of the salespeople earned salaries in each of the following ranges (assume that each salesperson's salary is truncated to an **Integer** amount):

1. $200-$299

2. $300-$399

3. $400-$499

4. $500-$599

5. $600-$699

6. $700-$799

7. $800-$899

8. $900-$999

9. $1000 and over

ANS:

```
1   ' Exercise 7.13 Solution
2   Option Explicit
3
4   Private Sub cmdeCalculate_Click()
5      Dim sales As Integer, i As Integer
6      Dim salary As Double
7
8      sales = txtInput.Text
9
10     If sales < 0 Then
11        Exit Sub
12     End If
13
14     salary = 0.09 * sales + 200
15
16     i = salary \ 100
17
18     If i > 10 Then
19        i = 10
20     End If
21
22     Call UpdateDisplay(i)
23  End Sub
24
25  Private Sub UpdateDisplay(ByVal x As Integer)
26     Dim t As Integer
27
28     t = lblNumber(x) + 1
29     lblNumber(x) = t
30  End Sub
```

7.14 Use a one-dimensional array to solve the following problem. Read in 20 numbers, each of which is between 10 and 100, inclusive. As each number is input, print it only if it is not a duplicate of a number already input. Provide for the "worst case" in which all 20 numbers are different.

     ANS:

```
1    ' Exercise 7.14 Solution
2    Option Explicit
3    Option Base 1
4
5    Dim mArray(20) As Integer
6    Dim mSubscript As Integer
7
8    Private Sub Form_Load()
9       mSubscript = 1
10      lblPrompt.Caption = "Input integer (10-100): "
11   End Sub
12
13   Private Sub cmdEnter_Click()
14      Dim duplicate As Boolean, value As Integer
15      Dim j As Integer, message As String
16
17      message = "Enter #"
18      value = txtInput.Text
19      lblPrompt.Caption = message & (mSubscript + 1)
20
21      mSubscript = mSubscript + 1
22
23      If value < 10 Or value > 100 Then
24         Exit Sub
25      End If
26
27      For j = LBound(mArray) To mSubscript
28
29         If (value = mArray(j)) Then
30            duplicate = True
31            Exit For
32         End If
33
34      Next j
35
36      If (Not duplicate) Then
37         mArray(mSubscript) = value
38         lblDisplay.Caption = lblDisplay.Caption & " " & value
39      End If
40
41      If mSubscript = 20 Then
42         cmdEnter.Enabled = False
```

```
43      End If
44
45  End Sub
```

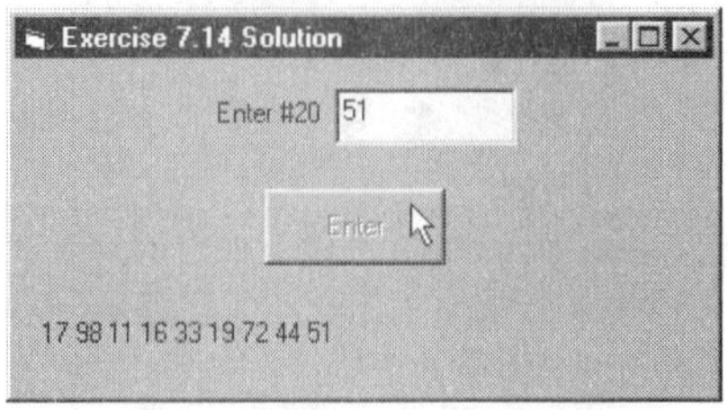

7.15 Write a program that simulates the rolling of two dice. The program should use function **Rnd** to roll the first die, and should use **Rnd** again to roll the second die. The sum of the two values should then be calculated. Note: Since each die can show an **Integer** value from 1 to 6, the sum of the two values will vary from 2 to 12, with 7 being the most frequent sum and 2 and 12 being the least frequent sums. Figure 7.20 shows the 36 possible combinations of the two dice. Your program should roll the two dice 36,000 times. Use a one-dimensional array to tally the number of times each possible sum appears. Print the results in a tabular format. Also, determine if the totals are reasonable (i.e., there are six ways to roll a 7), so approximately one sixth of all the rolls should be 7.

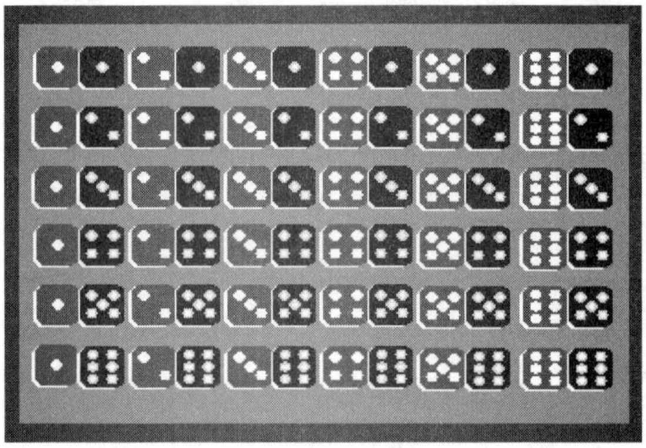

Fig. 7.20   The 36 possible outcomes of rolling two dice.

ANS:

```
1   ' Exercise 7.15 Solution
2   Option Explicit
3
4   Private Sub Form_Load()
5       ' Array expected contains counts for the expected
6       ' number of times each sum occurs in 36 rolls of the dice
7       Dim expected() As Variant, i As Long
8       Dim x As Integer, y As Integer, totals(2 To 12) As Long
9
10      expected = Array(0, 0, 1, 2, 3, 4, 5, 6, 5, 4, 3, 2, 1)
11      Call Randomize
12
13      For i = 1 To 36000
14          x = 1 + Int(Rnd() * 6)
15          y = 1 + Int(Rnd() * 6)
16          totals(x + y) = totals(x + y) + 1
17      Next i
18
19      Print Format$("Sum", String$(10, "@")) & _
20          Format$("Total", String$(10, "@")) & _
21          Format$("Expected", String$(10, "@")) & _
22          Format$("Actual", String$(8, "@"))
23
24      For i = 2 To 12
25          Print Format$(i, String$(10, "@")) & _
```

```
26                    Format$(totals(i), String$(10, "@")) & _
27                    Format$(Format$(FormatNumber(expected(i) / 36, 3), _
28                        "Percent"), String$(9, "@")) & _
29                    Format$(Format$(FormatNumber(totals(i) / 36000, 3), _
30                        "Percent"), String$(9, "@"))
31       Next i
32   End Sub
```

7.16   Write a program that runs 1000 games of craps and uses arrays to answer the following questions:
   a) How many games are won on the first roll, second roll, ..., twentieth roll, and after the twentieth roll?
   b) How many games are lost on the first roll, second roll, ..., twentieth roll, and after the twentieth roll?
   c) What are the chances of winning at craps? (Note: You should discover that craps is one of the fairest casino games. What do you suppose this means?)
   d) What is the average length of a game of craps?
   e) Do the chances of winning improve with the length of the game?
   ANS:

```
1    ' Exercise 7.16 Solution
2    Option Explicit
3    Option Base 1
4
5    Public Enum Outcome
6        outCONTINUE
7        outWIN
8        outLOSE
9    End Enum
10
11   Private Sub cmdRoll_Click()
12       Const SIZE As Integer = 21, ROLLS = 1000
13       Dim gameStatus As Outcome, sum As Integer, myPoint As Integer
14       Dim roll As Integer, length As Integer, wins(SIZE) As Integer
15       Dim losses(SIZE) As Integer, winSum As Integer, loseSum As Integer
16       Dim i As Integer
17
18       Call Randomize
19       Call Cls
20
21       For i = 1 To ROLLS
22           sum = RollDice()
23           roll = 1
24
25           Select Case sum
26               Case 7, 11
27                   gameStatus = outWIN
28               Case 2, 3, 12
29                   gameStatus = outLOSE
30               Case Else
31                   gameStatus = outCONTINUE
32                   myPoint = sum
33           End Select
```

```
34
35          While gameStatus = outCONTINUE
36              sum = RollDice()
37              roll = roll + 1
38
39              If sum = myPoint Then
40                  gameStatus = outWIN
41              ElseIf sum = 7 Then
42                  gameStatus = outLOSE
43              End If
44
45          Wend
46
47          If roll > 21 Then
48              roll = 21
49          End If
50
51          If gameStatus = outWIN Then
52              wins(roll) = wins(roll) + 1
53              winSum = winSum + 1
54          Else
55              losses(roll) = losses(roll) + 1
56              loseSum = loseSum + 1
57          End If
58
59      Next i
60
61      Print "Games won or lost after the 20th roll"
62      Print "are displayed as the 21st roll."
63      Print
64
65      For i = 1 To 21
66          Print Format$(wins(i), "@@@@") & _
67                  " game(s) won and" & _
68                  Format$(losses(i), "@@@@") & _
69                  " game(s) lost on roll " & i
70      Next i
71
72      Print
73
74      ' Calculate chances of winning
75      Print "The chances of winning are " & winSum & " / " & _
76              (winSum + loseSum) & " = " & _
77              Format$((100 * (winSum / (winSum + loseSum))), "Fixed") _
78              & "%"
79
80      ' Calculate average length of game
81      For i = 1 To 21
82          length = length + wins(i) * i + losses(i) * i
83      Next i
84
85      Print "The average game length is " & _
86              Format$(length / 1000, "Fixed") & " rolls."
87  End Sub
88
89  Private Function RollDice() As Integer
90      Dim die1 As Integer, die2 As Integer, workSum As Integer
91
92      die1 = 1 + Int(Rnd() * 6)
93      die2 = 1 + Int(Rnd() * 6)
94      workSum = die1 + die2
95      RollDice = workSum
96  End Function
```

7.17   (*Airline Reservations System*) A small airline has just purchased a computer for its new automated reservations system. You have been asked to program the new system. You are to write a program to assign seats on each flight of the airline's only plane (capacity: 10 seats).

Your program should display the following menu of alternatives:

```
Please type 1 for "smoking"
Please type 2 for "nonsmoking"
```

If the person types 1, then your program should assign a seat in the smoking section (seats 1-5). If the person types 2, then your program should assign a seat in the nonsmoking section (seats 6-10). Your program should then print a boarding pass indicating the person's seat number and whether it is in the smoking or nonsmoking section of the plane.

Use a one-dimensional array to represent the seating chart of the plane. Initialize all the elements of the array to 0 to indicate that all seats are empty. As each seat is assigned, set the corresponding elements of the array to 1 to indicate that the seat is no longer available.

Your program should, of course, never assign a seat that has already been assigned. When the smoking section is full, your program should ask the person if it is acceptable to be placed in the nonsmoking section (and vice versa). If yes, then make the appropriate seat assignment. If no, then print the message "Next flight leaves in 3 hours."

7.18   Use a two-dimensional array to solve the following problem. A company has four salespeople (with salesperson numbers 1 to 4) who sell five different products (with product numbers 1 to 5). Once a day, each salesperson passes in a slip for each different type of product sold. Each slip contains:

1. The salesperson number

2. The product number

3. The total dollar value of that product sold that day

Thus, each salesperson passes in 0 to 5 sales slips per day. Assume that the information from all of the slips for last month is available. Write a program that will read all this information for last month's sales and summarize the total sales by salesperson by product. All totals should be stored in the two-dimensional array **sales**. After processing all the information for last month, print the results in tabular format with each of the columns representing a particular salesperson and each of the rows representing a particular product. Cross total each row to get the total sales of each product for last month; cross total each column to get the total sales by salesperson for last month. Your neat tabular printout should include these cross totals to the right of the totaled rows and to the bottom of the totaled columns.

ANS:

```
1    ' Exercise 7.18 Solution
2    Option Explicit
3
4    Dim mSales(1 To 4, 1 To 5) As Currency
5    Dim mGrandTotal As Currency
6    Const mFORMAT As Integer = 10
7
8    Private Sub Form_Load()
9        Call CalculateAndPrint
10   End Sub
11
12   Private Sub cmdEnter_Click()
13       Dim i As Integer, j As Integer
14
15       i = txtSalesPerson.Text
16       j = txtProductNumber.Text
17       mSales(i, j) = mSales(i, j) + txtTotal.Text
18       mGrandTotal = mGrandTotal + mSales(i, j)
19       Call CalculateAndPrint
20   End Sub
21
22   Private Sub CalculateAndPrint()
23       Dim i As Integer, j As Integer, productSales(1 To 5) As Currency
24       Dim totalSales As Currency
25
26       Call Cls
27       Print "The total sales for each salesperson are displayed"
28       Print "at the end of each row, and the total sales for"
29       Print "each product are displayed at the bottom of each column. "
30       Print
31       Print Format$(1, String$(mFORMAT + 3, "@"));
32
33       For i = 2 To 5
34           Print Format$(i, String$(mFORMAT, "@"));
35       Next i
36
37       Print Format$("Total", String$(mFORMAT, "@"));
38
39       For i = 1 To 4
40           totalSales = 0
41           Print
42           Print i;
43
44           For j = 1 To 5
45               totalSales = totalSales + mSales(i, j)
46               Print Format$(Format$(mSales(i, j), "Currency"), _
47                           String$(mFORMAT, "@"));
48               productSales(j) = productSales(j) + mSales(i, j)
49           Next j
50
51           Print Format$(Format$(totalSales, "Currency"), _
52                       String$(mFORMAT, "@"));
53       Next i
54
55       Print
56       Print "Total";
57       Print Format$(Format$(productSales(1), "Currency"), _
58                   String$(mFORMAT - 2, "@"));
59
60       For j = 2 To 5
61           Print Format$(Format$(productSales(j), "Currency"), _
62                       String$(mFORMAT, "@"));
63       Next j
64
65       Print Format$(Format$(mGrandTotal, "Currency"), _
```

```
66                String$(mFORMAT, "@"))
67    End Sub
```

Exercise 7.18 Solution

The total sales for each salesperson are displayed at the end of each row, and the total sales for each product are displayed at the bottom of each colum.

	1	2	3	4	5	Total
1	$0.00	$3.46	$0.00	$0.00	$0.00	$3.46
2	$0.00	$0.00	$0.00	$96.54	$0.00	$96.54
3	$0.00	$0.00	$0.00	$0.00	$0.00	$0.00
4	$0.00	$0.00	$0.00	$0.00	$0.00	$0.00
Total	$0.00	$3.46	$0.00	$96.54	$0.00	$90.00

Salesperson #: 1   Product #: 2   Total: 3.46

Enter

7.19 (*Knight's Tour*) One of the more interesting puzzlers for chess buffs is the Knight's Tour problem, originally proposed by the mathematician Euler. The question is this: Can the chess piece called the knight move around an empty chessboard and touch each of the 64 squares once and only once? We study this intriguing problem in depth here.

The knight makes L-shaped moves (over two in one direction and then over one in a perpendicular direction). Thus, from a square in the middle of an empty chessboard, the knight can make eight different moves (numbered 0 through 7), as shown in Fig. 7.21.

a) Draw an 8-by-8 chessboard on a sheet of paper and attempt a Knight's Tour by hand. Put a 1 in the first square you move to, a 2 in the second square, a 3 in the third, etc. Before starting the tour, estimate how far you think you will get, remembering that a full tour consists of 64 moves. How far did you get? Was this close to your estimate?

b) Now let us develop a program that will move the knight around a chessboard. The board is represented by an 8-by-8 two-dimensional array board. Each of the squares is initialized to zero. We describe each of the eight possible moves in terms of both their horizontal and vertical components. For example, a move of type 0 as shown in Fig. 7.21 consists of moving two squares horizontally to the right and one square vertically upward. Move 2 consists of moving one square horizontally to the left and two squares vertically upward. Horizontal moves to the left and vertical moves upward are indicated with negative numbers. The eight moves may be described by two one-dimensional arrays, horizontal and vertical, as shown in Fig. 7.22.

Let the variables **currentRow** and **currentColumn** indicate the row and column of the knight's current position. To make a move of type **moveNumber**, where **moveNumber** is between 0 and 7, your program uses the statements

```
currentRow = currentRow + vertical(moveNumber)
currentColumn = currentColumn + horizontal(moveNumber)
```

Keep a counter that varies from 1 to 64. Record the latest count in each square the knight moves to. Remember to test each potential move to see if the knight has already visited that square. And, of course, test every potential move to make sure that the knight does not land off the chessboard. Now write a program to move the knight around the chessboard. Run the program. How many moves did the knight make?

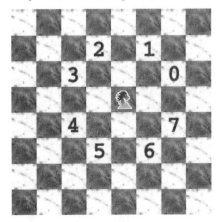

Fig. 7.21   The eight possible moves of the knight.

Horizontal component	Vertical component
`horizontal(0) = 2`	`vertical(0) = -1`
`horizontal(1) = 1`	`vertical(1) = -2`
`horizontal(2) = -1`	`vertical(2) = -2`
`horizontal(3) = -2`	`vertical(3) = -1`
`horizontal(4) = -2`	`vertical(4) = 1`
`horizontal(5) = -1`	`vertical(5) = 2`
`horizontal(6) = 1`	`vertical(6) = 2`
`horizontal(7) = 2`	`vertical(7) = 1`

Fig. 7.22   Arrays that describe the knight's moves.

c) After attempting to write and run a Knight's Tour program, you have probably developed some valuable insights. We will use these to develop a heuristic (or strategy) for moving the knight. Heuristics do not guarantee success, but a carefully developed heuristic greatly improves the chance of success. You may have observed that the outer squares are more troublesome than the squares nearer the center of the board. In fact, the most troublesome, or inaccessible, squares are the four corners.

Intuition may suggest that you should attempt to move the knight to the most troublesome squares first and leave open those that are easiest to get to so that when the board gets congested near the end of the tour there will be a greater chance of success.

We may develop an "accessibility heuristic" by classifying each of the squares according to how accessible they are, and then always moving the knight to the square (within the knight's L-shaped moves, of course) that is most inaccessible. We label a two-dimensional array accessibility with numbers indicating from how many squares each particular square is accessible. On a blank chessboard, each center square is rated as 8, each corner square is rated as 2, and the other squares have accessibility numbers of 3, 4 or 6, as shown in Fig. 7.23.

Write a version of the Knight's Tour program using the accessibility heuristic. At any time, the knight should move to the square with the lowest accessibility number. Therefore, the tour may begin in any of the four corners. In case of a tie, the knight may move to any of the tied squares. (Note: As the knight moves around the chessboard, your program should reduce the accessibility numbers as more and more squares become occupied. At any given time during the tour, each available square's accessibility number reflects the precise number of squares from which that square may be reached.) Run this version of your program. Did you get a full tour? Now modify the program to run 64 tours, one starting from each square of the chessboard. How many full tours did you get?

d) Write a version of the Knight's Tour program which, when encountering a tie between two or more squares, decides what square to choose by looking ahead to those squares reachable from the "tied" squares. Your program should move to the square for which the next move would arrive at a square with the lowest accessibility number.

Fig. 7.23   Accessibility numbers for Knight's Tour heuristic.

ANS:

```vb
1   ' Exercise 7.19 Solution
2   Option Explicit
3
4   Private Sub cmdTour_Click()
5       Call KnightTourAccess
6       Call PrintBoard(Me)        ' Me is this form
7   End Sub
```

```vb
8   ' modKnightAccess
9   Option Explicit
10
11  Dim mMoveNumber As Integer
12  Dim mBoard(7, 7) As Integer
13  Dim mAccess(7) As Variant
14  Dim mHorizontal As Variant
15  Dim mVertical As Variant
16
17  Public Sub KnightTourAccess()
18      mHorizontal = Array(2, 1, -1, -2, -2, -1, 1, 2)
19      mVertical = Array(-1, -2, -2, -1, 1, 2, 2, 1)
20
21      Call Randomize
22      Call CreateAccess
23      Call ClearBoard
24      Call RunTour
25  End Sub
26
27  Private Sub CreateAccess()
28      ' mAccess is an array of Variants. Each element of the array
29      ' is an array. To access an individual element of mAccess the
30      ' syntax:
31      '      mAccess(r)(c)
32      ' is used.
33      mAccess(0) = Array(2, 3, 4, 4, 4, 4, 3, 2)
34      mAccess(1) = Array(3, 4, 6, 6, 6, 6, 4, 3)
35      mAccess(2) = Array(4, 6, 8, 8, 8, 8, 6, 4)
36      mAccess(3) = Array(4, 6, 8, 8, 8, 8, 6, 4)
37      mAccess(4) = Array(4, 6, 8, 8, 8, 8, 6, 4)
38      mAccess(5) = Array(4, 6, 8, 8, 8, 8, 6, 4)
39      mAccess(6) = Array(3, 4, 6, 6, 6, 6, 4, 3)
40      mAccess(7) = Array(2, 3, 4, 4, 4, 4, 3, 2)
41  End Sub
42
43  Private Sub ClearBoard()
44      Dim a As Integer, b As Integer
45
46      mMoveNumber = 0
47
48      For a = 0 To 7
49
50         For b = 0 To 7
51            mBoard(a, b) = 0
52         Next b
53
54      Next a
55
56  End Sub
57
58  Private Sub RunTour()
59      Dim testRow As Integer, testColumn As Integer
60      Dim minRow As Integer, minColumn As Integer, minAccess As Integer
61      Dim accessNumber As Integer, done As Boolean, moveType As Integer
62      Dim currentRow As Integer, currentColumn As Integer
```

```
63
64        minAccess = 9      ' Set initial value to an out of range value
65        done = False
66
67        ' Randomly place knight on the board
68        currentRow = Int(Rnd() * 8)
69        currentColumn = Int(Rnd() * 8)
70        mMoveNumber = mMoveNumber + 1
71        mBoard(currentRow, currentColumn) = mMoveNumber
72
73        ' Perform the tour based upon the first move
74        While (Not done)
75           accessNumber = minAccess
76
77           ' Test all possible moves based on the current position
78           ' Moves include those that are off the board
79           For moveType = 0 To 7
80              testRow = currentRow + mVertical(moveType)
81              testColumn = currentColumn + mHorizontal(moveType)
82
83              ' Test for a valid move
84              If (ValidMove(testRow, testColumn)) Then
85
86                 ' If the access is lower than the current accessNumber
87                 ' then remember it
88                 If (mAccess(testRow)(testColumn) < accessNumber) Then
89                    accessNumber = mAccess(testRow)(testColumn)
90                    minRow = testRow
91                    minColumn = testColumn
92                 End If
93
94                 ' Reduce the accessibility for locations we can move to
95                 mAccess(testRow)(testColumn) = mAccess(testRow)(testColumn) - 1
96              End If
97
98           Next moveType
99
100          ' If we never found a valid move then fail loop. If we did find a
101          ' move then move there and update the current position
102          If (accessNumber = minAccess) Then
103             done = True
104          Else
105             currentRow = minRow
106             currentColumn = minColumn
107             mMoveNumber = mMoveNumber + 1
108             mBoard(currentRow, currentColumn) = mMoveNumber
109          End If
110
111       Wend
112
113   End Sub
114
115   Private Function ValidMove(row As Integer, col As Integer) As Boolean
116
117       If ((row >= 0 And row < 8) And (col >= 0 And col < 8)) Then
118
119           ' Visual Basic logical operators do not short circuit
120           ' therefore this is written as a separate condition
121           If (mBoard(row, col) = 0) Then
122               ValidMove = True
123               Exit Function
124           End If
125
126       End If
127
128       ValidMove = False
129   End Function
```

```
130
131  Public Sub PrintBoard(f As Form)
132     Dim r As Integer, c As Integer
133
134     Call f.Cls
135     f.Print Format("0", "@@@@@") & " ";
136     ' Header for columns
137
138     For c = 1 To 7
139        f.Print Format(c, "@@") & " ";
140     Next c
141
142     f.Print
143
144     For r = 0 To 7
145        f.Print Format$(r, "@@") & " ";
146
147        For c = 0 To 7
148           f.Print Format$(mBoard(r, c), "@@") & " ";
149        Next c
150
151        f.Print
152     Next r
153
154     f.Print
155     f.Print "The tour ended with " & mMoveNumber & " moves."
156
157     If (mMoveNumber = 64) Then
158        f.Print "This was a full tour!"
159     Else
160        f.Print "This was not a full tour."
161     End If
162
163  End Sub
```

```
▄ Exercise 7.19 Solution              _ □ ✕
         0   1   2   3   4   5   6   7
    0    7  52   9  54   5  58  19  56
    1   10  43   6  59  20  55   4  47
    2   51   8  53  44  63  48  57  18
    3   42  11  64  49  60  21  46   3
    4   39  50  41  34  45  62  17  22
    5   12  33  38  61  30  25   2  27
    6   37  40  31  14  35  28  23  16
    7   32  13  36  29  24  15  26   1

    The tour ended with 64 moves.
    This was a full tour!

                    [ One Tour ]
```

7.20   (*Knight's Tour: Brute Force Approaches*) In Exercise 7.19 we developed a solution to the Knight's Tour problem. The approach used, called the "accessibility heuristic," generates many solutions and executes efficiently.

As computers continue increasing in power, we will be able to solve more problems with sheer computer power and relatively unsophisticated algorithms. Let us call this approach "brute force" problem solving.

    a) Use random number generation to enable the knight to walk around the chessboard (in its legitimate L-shaped moves, of course) at random. Your program should run one tour and print the final chessboard. How far did the knight get?

    b) Most likely, the preceding program produced a relatively short tour. Now modify your program to attempt 1000 tours. Use a one-dimensional array to keep track of the number of tours of each length. When your program finishes attempting the 1000 tours, it should print this information in neat tabular format. What was the best result?

    c) Most likely, the preceding program gave you some "respectable" tours but no full tours. Now "pull all the stops out" and simply let your program run until it produces a full tour. (Caution: This version of the program could run for hours on a powerful computer.) Once again, keep a table of the number of tours of each length, and print this table when the first full tour is found. How many tours did your program attempt before producing a full tour? How much time did it take?

d) Compare the brute force version of the Knight's Tour with the accessibility heuristic version. Which required a more careful study of the problem? Which algorithm was more difficult to develop? Which required more computer power? Could we be certain (in advance) of obtaining a full tour with the accessibility heuristic approach? Could we be certain (in advance) of obtaining a full tour with the brute force approach? Argue the pros and cons of brute force problem solving in general.

ANS:

```
1    ' Exercise 7.20 Part A Solution
2    Option Explicit
3
4    Private Sub cmdTour_Click()
5        Call KnightTourBrute
6        Call PrintBoard(Me)      ' This form
7    End Sub
```

```
8    ' modKnightBrute
9    Option Explicit
10
11   Dim mMoveNumber As Integer
12   Dim mBoard(7, 7) As Integer
13
14   Public Sub KnightTourBrute()
15       Dim horizontal As Variant, vertical As Variant, done As Boolean
16       Dim currentRow As Integer, currentColumn As Integer
17       Dim moveType As Integer, testRow As Integer
18       Dim testColumn As Integer, goodMove As Boolean
19
20       horizontal = Array(2, 1, -1, -2, -2, -1, 1, 2)
21       vertical = Array(-1, -2, -2, -1, 1, 2, 2, 1)
22
23       Call Randomize
24       Call ClearBoard
25
26       ' Randomly place knight on the board
27       currentRow = Int(Rnd() * 8)
28       currentColumn = Int(Rnd() * 8)
29
30       mMoveNumber = mMoveNumber + 1
31       mBoard(currentRow, currentColumn) = mMoveNumber
32
33       While (Not done)
34           moveType = Int(Rnd() * 8)
35           testRow = currentRow + vertical(moveType)
36           testColumn = currentColumn + horizontal(moveType)
37           goodMove = ValidMove(testRow, testColumn)
38
39           If (goodMove) Then
40               currentRow = testRow
41               currentColumn = testColumn
42               mMoveNumber = mMoveNumber + 1
43               mBoard(currentRow, currentColumn) = mMoveNumber
44           Else
45               Dim c As Integer
46
47               c = 0
48
49               While (c < 8 And Not goodMove)
50                   moveType = moveType + 1
51                   moveType = moveType Mod 8
52                   testRow = currentRow + vertical(moveType)
53                   testColumn = currentColumn + horizontal(moveType)
54                   goodMove = ValidMove(testRow, testColumn)
55
```

```
56                    If (goodMove) Then
57                        currentRow = testRow
58                        currentColumn = testColumn
59                        mMoveNumber = mMoveNumber + 1
60                        mBoard(currentRow, currentColumn) = mMoveNumber
61                    End If
62
63                    c = c + 1
64                Wend
65
66                If (Not goodMove) Then
67                    done = True
68                End If
69
70            End If
71
72            If (mMoveNumber = 64) Then
73                done = True
74            End If
75
76        Wend
77
78    End Sub
79
80    Private Sub ClearBoard()
81        Dim a As Integer, b As Integer
82
83        mMoveNumber = 0
84
85        For a = 0 To 7
86
87            For b = 0 To 7
88                mBoard(a, b) = 0
89            Next b
90
91        Next a
92
93    End Sub
94
95    Private Function ValidMove(row As Integer, col As Integer) As Boolean
96
97        If ((row >= 0 And row < 8) And (col >= 0 And col < 8)) Then
98
99            ' Visual Basic logical operators do not short circuit
100           ' therefore this is written as a separate condition
101           If (mBoard(row, col) = 0) Then
102               ValidMove = True
103               Exit Function
104           End If
105
106       End If
107
108       ValidMove = False
109   End Function
110
111   Public Sub PrintBoard(f As Form)
112       Dim r As Integer, c As Integer
113
114       Call f.Cls
115       f.Print Format("0", "@@@@@") & " ";
116
117       ' Header for columns
118       For c = 1 To 7
119           f.Print Format(c, "@@") & " ";
120       Next c
121
122       f.Print
```

```
123
124     For r = 0 To 7
125         f.Print Format$(r, "@@") & " ";
126
127         For c = 0 To 7
128             f.Print Format$(mBoard(r, c), "@@") & " ";
129         Next c
130
131         f.Print
132     Next r
133
134     f.Print
135     f.Print "The tour ended with " & mMoveNumber & " moves."
136
137     If (mMoveNumber = 64) Then
138         f.Print "This was a full tour!"
139     Else
140         f.Print "This was not a full tour."
141     End If
142
143 End Sub
```

Exercise 7.20 Part A Solution

```
    0  1  2  3  4  5  6  7
0   0 39  0 35 32  5  8  0
1   0 36 33  6  0  2 11  4
2  40  0 38 31 34  7  0  9
3  37 30  0 14  1 10  3 12
4   0 41 16 25  0 13 50 23
5  29 18 27 44 15 24 47  0
6  42  0 20 17 26 45 22 49
7  19 28 43  0 21 48  0 46

The tour ended with 50 moves.
This was not a full tour.
```

Exercise 7.20 Part A Solution

```
    0  1  2  3  4  5  6  7
0   0  0  0  0  0  0  3 10
1   0  0  0  1  0  5  0  0
2   0  0  0  0  0  2  9  4
3   0  0  0  0  0  0  6  0
4   0  0  0  0  0  0  0  8
5   0  0  0  0  0  7  0  0
6   0  0  0  0  0  0  0  0
7   0  0  0  0  0  0  0  0

The tour ended with 10 moves.
This was not a full tour.
```

```
 1   ' Exercise 7.20 Part B Solution
 2   Option Explicit
 3
 4   Private Sub cmdTour_Click()
 5       Dim frequency(1 To 64) As Integer, c As Integer
 6
 7       For c = 1 To 1000
 8           Call KnightTourBrute
 9           frequency(mMoveNumber) = frequency(mMoveNumber) + 1
10       Next c
11
```

```
12          For c = 1 To 64
13
14              If (c Mod 2) = 0 Then
15                  Print Format$(frequency(c), "@@") & " tours with " & _
16                        Format$(c, "@@") & " moves."
17              Else
18                  Print Format$(frequency(c), "@@") & " tours with " & _
19                        Format$(c, "@@") & " moves." & Space$(4);
20              End If
21
22          Next c
23
24      End Sub
```

```
25      ' modKnightBruteB
26      Option Explicit
27      Public mMoveNumber As Integer
28      Dim mBoard(7, 7) As Integer
29
30      Public Sub KnightTourBrute()
31          Dim horizontal As Variant, vertical As Variant, done As Boolean
32          Dim currentRow As Integer, currentColumn As Integer
33          Dim moveType As Integer, testRow As Integer
34          Dim testColumn As Integer, goodMove As Boolean
35
36          horizontal = Array(2, 1, -1, -2, -2, -1, 1, 2)
37          vertical = Array(-1, -2, -2, -1, 1, 2, 2, 1)
38
39          Call Randomize
40          Call ClearBoard
41
42          ' Randomly place knight on the board
43          currentRow = Int(Rnd() * 8)
44          currentColumn = Int(Rnd() * 8)
45          mMoveNumber = mMoveNumber + 1
46          mBoard(currentRow, currentColumn) = mMoveNumber
47
48          While (Not done)
49              moveType = Int(Rnd() * 8)
50              testRow = currentRow + vertical(moveType)
51              testColumn = currentColumn + horizontal(moveType)
52              goodMove = ValidMove(testRow, testColumn)
53
54              If (goodMove) Then
55                  currentRow = testRow
56                  currentColumn = testColumn
57                  mMoveNumber = mMoveNumber + 1
58                  mBoard(currentRow, currentColumn) = mMoveNumber
59              Else
60                  Dim c As Integer
61
62                  c = 0
63
64                  While (c < 8 And Not goodMove)
65                      moveType = moveType + 1
66                      moveType = moveType Mod 8
67                      testRow = currentRow + vertical(moveType)
68                      testColumn = currentColumn + horizontal(moveType)
69                      goodMove = ValidMove(testRow, testColumn)
70
71                      If (goodMove) Then
72                          currentRow = testRow
73                          currentColumn = testColumn
74                          mMoveNumber = mMoveNumber + 1
75                          mBoard(currentRow, currentColumn) = mMoveNumber
76                      End If
```

```
77
78                       c = c + 1
79               Wend
80
81               If (Not goodMove) Then
82                   done = True
83               End If
84
85           End If
86
87           If (mMoveNumber = 64) Then
88               done = True
89           End If
90
91       Wend
92   End Sub
93
94   Private Sub ClearBoard()
95       Dim a As Integer, b As Integer
96
97       mMoveNumber = 0
98
99       For a = 0 To 7
100
101          For b = 0 To 7
102              mBoard(a, b) = 0
103          Next b
104
105      Next a
106  End Sub
107
108  Private Function ValidMove(row As Integer, col As Integer) As Boolean
109      If ((row >= 0 And row < 8) And (col >= 0 And col < 8)) Then
110
111          ' Visual Basic logical operators do not short circuit
112          ' therefore this is written as a separate condition
113          If (mBoard(row, col) = 0) Then
114              ValidMove = True
115              Exit Function
116          End If
117      End If
118
119      ValidMove = False
120  End Function
121
122  Public Sub PrintBoard(f As Form)
123      Dim r As Integer, c As Integer
124
125      Call f.Cls
126      f.Print Format("0", "@@@@@") & " ";
127
128      ' Header for columns
129      For c = 1 To 7
130          f.Print Format(c, "@@") & " ";
131      Next c
132
133      f.Print
134
135      For r = 0 To 7
136          f.Print Format$(r, "@@") & " ";
137
138          For c = 0 To 7
139              f.Print Format$(mBoard(r, c), "@@") & " ";
140          Next c
141
142          f.Print
143      Next r
```

```
144
145     f.Print
146     f.Print "The tour ended with " & mMoveNumber & " moves."
147
148     If (mMoveNumber = 64) Then
149        f.Print "This was a full tour!"
150     Else
151        f.Print "This was not a full tour."
152     End If
153
154  End Sub
```

```
1   ' Exercise 7.20 Part C Solution
2   Option Explicit
3
4   Private Sub cmdTour_Click()
5      Dim frequency(1 To 64) As Long, c As Integer
6
7      While mMoveNumber <> 64
8         Call KnightTourBrute
9         frequency(mMoveNumber) = frequency(mMoveNumber) + 1
10
11        ' DoEvents is discussed later in the book
12        ' This will allow the program to be exited
13        ' when you click the close box
14        DoEvents
15        Call PrintBoard(Me)
16     Wend
17
18     For c = 1 To 64
19
20        If (c Mod 2) = 0 Then
21           Print Format$(frequency(c), "@@@@") & " tours with " & _
22                 Format$(c, "@@@@") & " moves."
23        Else
24           Print Format$(frequency(c), "@@@@") & " tours with " & _
25                 Format$(c, "@@@@") & " moves." & Space$(4);
26        End If
27
28     Next c
29  End Sub
```

```
30   ' modKnightBruteC
31   Option Explicit
32   Public mMoveNumber As Integer
33   Dim mBoard(7, 7) As Integer
34
35   Public Sub KnightTourBrute()
36      Dim horizontal As Variant, vertical As Variant, done As Boolean
37      Dim currentRow As Integer, currentColumn As Integer
38      Dim moveType As Integer, testRow As Integer
39      Dim testColumn As Integer, goodMove As Boolean
40
41      horizontal = Array(2, 1, -1, -2, -2, -1, 1, 2)
42      vertical = Array(-1, -2, -2, -1, 1, 2, 2, 1)
43
44      Call Randomize
45      Call ClearBoard
46
47      ' Randomly place knight on the board
48      currentRow = Int(Rnd() * 8)
49      currentColumn = Int(Rnd() * 8)
50      mMoveNumber = mMoveNumber + 1
51      mBoard(currentRow, currentColumn) = mMoveNumber
52
53      While (Not done)
54         moveType = Int(Rnd() * 8)
55         testRow = currentRow + vertical(moveType)
56         testColumn = currentColumn + horizontal(moveType)
57         goodMove = ValidMove(testRow, testColumn)
58
59         If (goodMove) Then
60            currentRow = testRow
61            currentColumn = testColumn
62            mMoveNumber = mMoveNumber + 1
63            mBoard(currentRow, currentColumn) = mMoveNumber
64         Else
65            Dim c As Integer
66
67            c = 0
68
69            While (c < 8 And Not goodMove)
70               moveType = moveType + 1
71               moveType = moveType Mod 8
72               testRow = currentRow + vertical(moveType)
73               testColumn = currentColumn + horizontal(moveType)
74               goodMove = ValidMove(testRow, testColumn)
75
76               If (goodMove) Then
77                  currentRow = testRow
78                  currentColumn = testColumn
79                  mMoveNumber = mMoveNumber + 1
80                  mBoard(currentRow, currentColumn) = mMoveNumber
81               End If
82
83               c = c + 1
84            Wend
85
86            If (Not goodMove) Then
87               done = True
88            End If
89         End If
90
91         If (mMoveNumber = 64) Then
92            done = True
93         End If
94      Wend
95   End Sub
96
```

```
97   Private Sub ClearBoard()
98      Dim a As Integer, b As Integer
99
100     mMoveNumber = 0
101
102     For a = 0 To 7
103
104        For b = 0 To 7
105           mBoard(a, b) = 0
106        Next b
107
108     Next a
109
110  End Sub
111
112  Private Function ValidMove(row As Integer, col As Integer) As Boolean
113
114     If ((row >= 0 And row < 8) And (col >= 0 And col < 8)) Then
115
116        ' Visual Basic logical operators do not short circuit
117        ' therefore this is written as a separate condition
118        If (mBoard(row, col) = 0) Then
119           ValidMove = True
120           Exit Function
121        End If
122
123     End If
124
125     ValidMove = False
126  End Function
127
128  Public Sub PrintBoard(p As Form)
129     Dim r As Integer, c As Integer
130
131     Call p.Cls
132     p.Print Format("0", "@@@@@") & " ";
133
134     ' Header for columns
135     For c = 1 To 7
136        p.Print Format(c, "@@") & " ";
137     Next c
138
139     p.Print
140
141     For r = 0 To 7
142        p.Print Format$(r, "@@") & " ";
143
144        For c = 0 To 7
145           p.Print Format$(mBoard(r, c), "@@") & " ";
146        Next c
147
148        p.Print
149     Next r
150
151     p.Print
152     p.Print "The tour ended with " & mMoveNumber & " moves."
153
154     If (mMoveNumber = 64) Then
155        p.Print "This was a full tour!"
156     Else
157        p.Print "This was not a full tour."
158     End If
159
160  End Sub
```

7.21 (*Knight's Tour: Closed Tour Test*) In the Knight's Tour, a full tour occurs when the knight makes 64 moves touching each square of the chessboard once and only once. A closed tour occurs when the 64th move is one move away from the location in which the knight started the tour. Modify the Knight's Tour program you wrote in Exercise 7.19 (or Exercise 7.20) to test for a closed tour if a full tour has occurred.

ANS:

```
1   ' Exercise 7.21 Solution
2   Option Explicit
3
4   Private Sub cmdTour_Click()
5      Call KnightTourAccess
6      Call PrintBoard(Me)      ' Me is this form
7   End Sub
```

```
8   ' modKnightAccess
9   Option Explicit
10
11  Dim mMoveNumber As Integer
12  Dim mBoard(7, 7) As Integer
13  Dim mAccess(7) As Variant
14  Dim mHorizontal As Variant
15  Dim mVertical As Variant
16  Dim mClosedTour As Boolean
17
18  Public Sub KnightTourAccess()
19     mHorizontal = Array(2, 1, -1, -2, -2, -1, 1, 2)
20     mVertical = Array(-1, -2, -2, -1, 1, 2, 2, 1)
21
22     Call Randomize
23     Call CreateAccess
24     Call ClearBoard
25     Call RunTour
26  End Sub
27
```

```
28    Private Sub CreateAccess()
29        ' mAccess is an array of Variants. Each element of the array
30        ' is an array. To access an individual element of mAccess the
31        ' syntax:
32        '      mAccess(r)(c)
33        ' is used.
34        mAccess(0) = Array(2, 3, 4, 4, 4, 4, 3, 2)
35        mAccess(1) = Array(3, 4, 6, 6, 6, 6, 4, 3)
36        mAccess(2) = Array(4, 6, 8, 8, 8, 8, 6, 4)
37        mAccess(3) = Array(4, 6, 8, 8, 8, 8, 6, 4)
38        mAccess(4) = Array(4, 6, 8, 8, 8, 8, 6, 4)
39        mAccess(5) = Array(4, 6, 8, 8, 8, 8, 6, 4)
40        mAccess(6) = Array(3, 4, 6, 6, 6, 6, 4, 3)
41        mAccess(7) = Array(2, 3, 4, 4, 4, 4, 3, 2)
42    End Sub
43
44    Private Sub ClearBoard()
45        Dim a As Integer, b As Integer
46
47        mMoveNumber = 0
48        mClosedTour = False
49
50        For a = 0 To 7
51
52            For b = 0 To 7
53                mBoard(a, b) = 0
54            Next b
55
56        Next a
57
58    End Sub
59
60    Private Sub RunTour()
61        Dim testRow As Integer, testColumn As Integer
62        Dim minRow As Integer, minColumn As Integer, minAccess As Integer
63        Dim accessNumber As Integer, done As Boolean, moveType As Integer
64        Dim currentRow As Integer, currentColumn As Integer
65        Dim firstMoveRow As Integer, firstMoveCol As Integer
66
67        minAccess = 9      ' Set initial value to an out of range value
68        done = False
69
70        ' Randomly place knight on the board
71        currentRow = Int(Rnd() * 8)
72        currentColumn = Int(Rnd() * 8)
73
74        mMoveNumber = mMoveNumber + 1
75        mBoard(currentRow, currentColumn) = mMoveNumber
76        firstMoveRow = currentRow
77        firstMoveCol = currentColumn
78
79        ' Perform the tour based upon the first move
80        While (Not done)
81            accessNumber = minAccess
82
83            ' Test all possible moves based on the current position
84            ' Moves include those that are off the board
85            For moveType = 0 To 7
86                testRow = currentRow + mVertical(moveType)
87                testColumn = currentColumn + mHorizontal(moveType)
88
89                ' Test for a valid move
90                If (ValidMove(testRow, testColumn)) Then
91
92                    ' If the access is lower than the current accessNumber
93                    ' then remember it
```

```
 94            If (mAccess(testRow)(testColumn) < accessNumber) Then
 95                accessNumber = mAccess(testRow)(testColumn)
 96                minRow = testRow
 97                minColumn = testColumn
 98            End If
 99
100            ' Reduce the accessibility for locations we can move to
101            mAccess(testRow)(testColumn) = mAccess(testRow)(testColumn) - 1
102        End If
103
104    Next moveType
105
106    ' If we never found a valid move then fail loop. If we did find a
107    ' move then move there and update the current position
108    If (accessNumber = minAccess) Then
109        done = True
110    Else
111        currentRow = minRow
112        currentColumn = minColumn
113        mMoveNumber = mMoveNumber + 1
114        mBoard(currentRow, currentColumn) = mMoveNumber
115
116        ' Check for closed tour
117        If (mMoveNumber = 64) Then
118            Dim c As Integer
119
120            For c = 0 To 7
121                testRow = currentRow + mVertical(c)
122                testColumn = currentColumn + mHorizontal(c)
123
124                If (testRow = firstMoveRow And testColumn = firstMoveCol) Then
125                    mClosedTour = True
126                End If
127
128            Next c
129
130        End If
131
132    End If
133
134    Wend
135
136 End Sub
137
138 Private Function ValidMove(row As Integer, col As Integer) As Boolean
139
140    If ((row >= 0 And row < 8) And (col >= 0 And col < 8)) Then
141
142        ' Visual Basic logical operators do not short circuit
143        ' therefore this is written as a separate condition
144        If (mBoard(row, col) = 0) Then
145            ValidMove = True
146            Exit Function
147        End If
148
149    End If
150
151    ValidMove = False
152 End Function
153
154 Public Sub PrintBoard(f As Form)
155    Dim r As Integer, c As Integer
156
157    Call f.Cls
158    f.Print Format("0", "@@@@@") & " ";
159
160    ' Header for columns
```

```
161     For c = 1 To 7
162         f.Print Format(c, "@@") & " ";
163     Next c
164
165     f.Print
166
167     For r = 0 To 7
168         f.Print Format$(r, "@@") & " ";
169
170         For c = 0 To 7
171             f.Print Format$(mBoard(r, c), "@@") & " ";
172         Next c
173
174         f.Print
175     Next r
176
177     f.Print
178     f.Print "The tour ended with " & mMoveNumber & " moves."
179
180     If (mMoveNumber = 64 And mClosedTour = True) Then
181         f.Print "This was a CLOSED tour!"
182     ElseIf (mMoveNumber = 64) Then
183         f.Print "This was a full tour!"
184     Else
185         f.Print "This was not a full tour."
186     End If
187
188 End Sub
```

7.22 (*Eight Queens*) Another puzzler for chess buffs is the Eight Queens problem. Simply stated: Is it possible to place eight queens on an empty chessboard so that no queen is "attacking" any other (i.e., no two queens are in the same row, the same column, or along the same diagonal)? Use the thinking developed in Exercise 7.19 to formulate a heuristic for solving the Eight Queens problem. Run your program. (Hint: It is possible to assign a value to each square of the chessboard indicating how many squares of an empty chessboard are "eliminated" if a queen is placed in that square. Each of the corners would be assigned the value 22, as in Fig. 7.24.) Once these "elimination numbers" are placed in all 64 squares, an appropriate heuristic might be: Place the next queen in the square with the smallest elimination number. Why is this strategy intuitively appealing?

ANS:

```
1  ' Exercise 7.22 Solution
2  Option Explicit
3
4  Private Sub cmdQueens_Click()
5     Call Setup
6
7     ' Keyword Me indicates the this form
8     Call PrintBoard(Me)
9  End Sub
```

```
10   ' modQueensBrute
11   Option Explicit
12   Dim mQueens As Integer
13   Dim mBoard(7, 7) As Integer
14   Dim mDone As Boolean
15   Dim mAccess(7)
16
17   Public Sub Setup()
18       Call Randomize
19       Call CreateAccess
20       Call ClearBoard
21       Call FirstMove
22       Call PlaceQueens
23   End Sub
24
25   Private Sub CreateAccess()
26       ' mAccess is an array of Variants. Each element of the array
27       ' is an array. To access an individual element of mAccess the
28       ' syntax:
29       '        mAccess(r)(c)
30       ' is used.
31       mAccess(0) = Array(22, 22, 22, 22, 22, 22, 22, 22)
32       mAccess(1) = Array(22, 24, 24, 24, 24, 24, 24, 22)
33       mAccess(2) = Array(22, 24, 26, 26, 26, 26, 24, 22)
34       mAccess(3) = Array(22, 24, 26, 28, 28, 26, 24, 22)
35       mAccess(4) = Array(22, 24, 26, 28, 28, 26, 24, 22)
36       mAccess(5) = Array(22, 24, 26, 26, 26, 26, 24, 22)
37       mAccess(6) = Array(22, 24, 24, 24, 24, 24, 24, 22)
38       mAccess(7) = Array(22, 22, 22, 22, 22, 22, 22, 22)
39   End Sub
40
41   Private Sub ClearBoard()
42       Dim a As Integer, b As Integer
43
44       mQueens = 0
45
46       For a = 0 To 7
47
48           For b = 0 To 7
49               mBoard(a, b) = 32     ' ASCII value for a space
50           Next b
51
52       Next a
53
54   End Sub
55
56   Private Sub FirstMove()
57       Dim rowMove As Integer, colMove As Integer
58
59       mQueens = 0
60       mDone = False
61       rowMove = Int(Rnd() * 8)
62       colMove = Int(Rnd() * 8)
63       mBoard(rowMove, colMove) = 81   ' ASCII value for Q
64       Call XconflictSquares(rowMove, colMove)
65       mQueens = mQueens + 1
66       Call NewAccess
67   End Sub
68
69   Private Sub PlaceQueens()
70
71       While (Not mDone)
72           Call NextMove
73       Wend
74
75   End Sub
76
```

```
77  Private Sub NextMove()
78     Dim lowestAccess As Integer, currentRow As Integer
79     Dim currentCol As Integer, rowMove As Integer, colMove As Integer
80
81     lowestAccess = 100   ' Assign a value greater than the highest access
82     mDone = True
83
84     For currentRow = 0 To 7
85
86        For currentCol = 0 To 7
87
88            If mBoard(currentRow, currentCol) = 32 Then
89               mDone = False
90
91               If mAccess(currentRow)(currentCol) < lowestAccess Then
92                  lowestAccess = mAccess(currentRow)(currentCol)
93                  rowMove = currentRow
94                  colMove = currentCol
95               End If
96
97            End If
98
99         Next currentCol
100
101    Next currentRow
102
103    If mDone Then
104       Exit Sub
105    End If
106
107    mBoard(rowMove, colMove) = 81   ' ASCII value for Q
108    Call XconflictSquares(rowMove, colMove)
109    mQueens = mQueens + 1
110    Call NewAccess
111 End Sub
112
113 Private Sub NewAccess()
114    Dim r As Integer, c As Integer
115
116    For r = 0 To 7
117
118       For c = 0 To 7
119
120          If (mBoard(r, c) = 32) Then
121             Call UpdateAccess(r, c)
122          End If
123       Next c
124    Next r
125 End Sub
126
127 Private Sub UpdateAccessDiagonals(r As Integer, c As Integer, _
128                                   rowAdjust As Integer, _
129                                   colAdjust As Integer, _
130                                   row As Integer, col As Integer)
131    Dim a As Integer
132
133    While (a < 8 And ValidMove(r, c))
134
135       If mAccess(r)(c) = 0 Then
136          mAccess(row)(col) = mAccess(row)(col) - 1
137       End If
138
139       r = r + rowAdjust
140       c = c + colAdjust
141       a = a + 1
142    Wend
143 End Sub
```

```
144
145   Private Sub UpdateAccess(row As Integer, col As Integer)
146       Call UpdateAccessDiagonals(row - 1, col - 1, -1, -1, row, col)
147       Call UpdateAccessDiagonals(row - 1, col + 1, -1, 1, row, col)
148       Call UpdateAccessDiagonals(row + 1, col + 1, 1, -1, row, col)
149       Call UpdateAccessDiagonals(row + 1, col + 1, 1, 1, row, col)
150       Call UpdateAccessRowsAndCols(row, col)
151   End Sub
152
153   Private Sub UpdateAccessRowsAndCols(row As Integer, col As Integer)
154       Dim a As Integer
155
156       For a = 0 To 7
157
158           If (mAccess(row)(a) = 0) Then
159               mAccess(row)(col) = mAccess(row)(col) - 1
160           End If
161
162           If (mAccess(a)(col) = 0) Then
163               mAccess(row)(col) = mAccess(row)(col) - 1
164           End If
165
166       Next a
167
168   End Sub
169
170   Private Function ValidMove(row As Integer, col As Integer) As Boolean
171       ValidMove = (row >= 0 And row < 8 And col >= 0 And col < 8)
172   End Function
173
174   Private Function AvailableSquare() As Boolean
175       Dim r As Integer, c As Integer
176
177       For r = 0 To 7
178
179           For c = 0 To 7
180
181               If mBoard(r, c) = 32 Then
182                   AvailableSquare = False   ' At least one open square is available
183                   Exit Function
184               End If
185
186           Next c
187
188       Next r
189
190       AvailableSquare = True
191   End Function
192
193   Private Sub XconflictSquares(row As Integer, col As Integer)
194       Dim a As Integer
195
196       For a = 0 To 7
197
198           ' Place a 35 in the row occupied by the queen
199           If (mBoard(row, a) = 32) Then
200               mBoard(row, a) = 35     ' ASCII value for #
201               mAccess(row)(a) = 0
202           End If
203
204           ' Place a 35 in the col occupied by the queen
205           If (mBoard(a, col) = 32) Then
206               mBoard(a, col) = 35
207               mAccess(a)(col) = 0
208           End If
209
210       Next a
```

```
211
212       ' Place a 35 in the diagonals occupied by the queen
213       Call Xdiagonals(row, col)
214   End Sub
215
216   Private Sub Xdiagonals(row As Integer, col As Integer)
217       Call XdiagonalHelper(row - 1, col - 1, -1, -1)
218       Call XdiagonalHelper(row - 1, col + 1, -1, 1)
219       Call XdiagonalHelper(row + 1, col - 1, 1, -1)
220       Call XdiagonalHelper(row + 1, col + 1, 1, 1)
221   End Sub
222
223   Private Sub XdiagonalHelper(r As Integer, c As Integer, rAdjust As Integer, _
224                               cAdjust As Integer)
225       Dim a As Integer
226
227       While (a < 8 And ValidMove(r, c))
228          mBoard(r, c) = 35
229          mAccess(r)(c) = 0
230          r = r + rAdjust
231          c = c + cAdjust
232          a = a + 1
233       Wend
234   End Sub
235
236   Public Sub PrintBoard(f As Form)
237       Dim queens As Integer, r As Integer, c As Integer
238
239       Call f.Cls
240
241       ' Header for columns
242       f.Print "   0 1 2 3 4 5 6 7"
243
244       For r = 0 To 7
245          f.Print Format$(r, "@@") & " ";
246
247          For c = 0 To 7
248
249             ' Function Chr$ prints the ASCII character
250             ' representation of an Integer.
251             f.Print Chr$(mBoard(r, c)) & " ";
252
253             If (mBoard(r, c) = 81) Then
254                queens = queens + 1
255             End If
256
257          Next c
258
259          f.Print
260       Next r
261
262       f.Print
263       f.Print queens & " Queens were placed on the board."
264   End Sub
```

7.23   (*Eight Queens: Brute Force Approaches*) In this exercise you will develop several brute force approaches to solving the Eight Queens problem introduced in Exercise 7.22.

    a) Solve the Eight Queens exercise using the random brute force technique developed in Exercise 7.20.

    b) Use an exhaustive technique (i.e., try all possible combinations of eight queens on the chessboard).

    c) Why do you suppose the exhaustive brute force approach may not be appropriate for solving the Knight's Tour problem?

    d) Compare and contrast the random brute force and exhaustive brute force approaches in general.

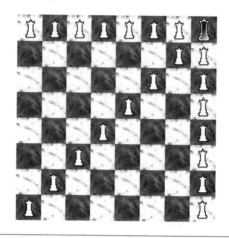

Fig. 7.24   The 22 squares eliminated by placing a queen in the upper-right corner.

       ANS:

```
1    ' Exercise 7.23 Solution
2    Option Explicit
3
4    Private Sub cmdQueens_Click()
5       Call Setup
6
7       ' Keyword Me indicates the this form
8       Call PrintBoard(Me)
9    End Sub
```

```
10   ' modQueensBrute
11   Option Explicit
12   Dim mBoard(7, 7) As Integer
13
14   Public Sub Setup()
15      Call Randomize
16      Call ClearBoard
17      Call PlaceQueens
18   End Sub
19
20   Private Sub ClearBoard()
21      Dim a As Integer, b As Integer
22
23      For a = 0 To 7
24
25         For b = 0 To 7
26            mBoard(a, b) = 32    ' ASCII value for a space
27         Next b
28
29      Next a
30
31   End Sub
32
33   Private Sub PlaceQueens()
34      Dim rowMove As Integer, colMove As Integer, queens As Integer
```

```
35        Dim done As Boolean
36
37        While (queens < 8 And Not done)
38           rowMove = Int(Rnd() * 8)
39           colMove = Int(Rnd() * 8)
40
41           If (QueenCheck(rowMove, colMove)) Then
42              mBoard(rowMove, colMove) = 81   ' ASCII value for Q
43              Call XconflictSquares(rowMove, colMove)
44              queens = queens + 1
45           End If
46
47           done = AvailableSquare()
48        Wend
49
50   End Sub
51
52   Private Function ValidMove(row As Integer, col As Integer) As Boolean
53        ValidMove = (row >= 0 And row < 8 And col >= 0 And col < 8)
54   End Function
55
56   Private Function AvailableSquare() As Boolean
57        Dim r As Integer, c As Integer
58
59        For r = 0 To 7
60
61           For c = 0 To 7
62
63              If mBoard(r, c) = 32 Then
64                 AvailableSquare = False   ' At least one open square is available
65                 Exit Function
66              End If
67
68           Next c
69
70        Next r
71
72        AvailableSquare = True
73   End Function
74
75   Private Sub XconflictSquares(row As Integer, col As Integer)
76        Dim a As Integer
77
78        For a = 0 To 7
79
80           ' Place a 35 in the row occupied by the queen
81           If (mBoard(row, a) = 32) Then
82              mBoard(row, a) = 35      ' ASCII value for #
83           End If
84
85           ' Place a 35 in the col occupied by the queen
86           If (mBoard(a, col) = 32) Then
87              mBoard(a, col) = 35
88           End If
89
90        Next a
91
92        ' Place a 35 in the diagonals occupied by the queen
93        Call Xdiagonals(row, col)
94   End Sub
95
96   Private Function QueenCheck(row As Integer, col As Integer) As Boolean
97        Dim r As Integer, c As Integer, a As Integer
98
99        ' Check row and column for a queen
100       For a = 0 To 7
101
```

```
102        If (mBoard(row, a) = 81 Or mBoard(a, col) = 81) Then
103            QueenCheck = False
104            Exit Function
105        End If
106    Next a
107
108    r = row - 1
109    c = col - 1
110    a = 0
111
112    ' Check upper left diagonal for a queen
113    While (a < 8 And ValidMove(r, c))
114        If (mBoard(r, c) = 81) Then
115            QueenCheck = False
116            Exit Function
117        End If
118
119        r = r - 1
120        c = c - 1
121        a = a + 1
122    Wend
123
124    r = row - 1
125    c = col + 1
126    a = 0
127
128    ' Check upper right diagonal for a queen
129    While (a < 8 And ValidMove(r, c))
130        If (mBoard(r, c) = 81) Then
131            QueenCheck = False
132            Exit Function
133        End If
134
135        r = r - 1
136        c = c + 1
137    Wend
138
139    r = row + 1
140    c = col - 1
141    a = 0
142
143    ' Check lower left diagonal for a queen
144    While (a < 8 And ValidMove(r, c))
145
146        If (mBoard(r, c) = 81) Then
147            QueenCheck = False
148            Exit Function
149        End If
150
151        r = r + 1
152        c = c - 1
153        a = a + 1
154    Wend
155
156    r = row + 1
157    c = col + 1
158    a = 0
159
160    ' Check lower right diagonal for a queen
161    While (a < 8 And ValidMove(r, c))
162
163        If (mBoard(r, c) = 81) Then
164            QueenCheck = False
165            Exit Function
166        End If
167
168        r = r + 1
```

```
169         c = c + 1
170         a = a + 1
171     Wend
172
173     QueenCheck = True   ' No queen in conflict
174 End Function
175
176 Private Sub Xdiagonals(row As Integer, col As Integer)
177     Call XdiagonalsHelper(row - 1, col - 1, -1, -1)
178     Call XdiagonalsHelper(row - 1, col + 1, -1, 1)
179     Call XdiagonalsHelper(row + 1, col - 1, 1, -1)
180     Call XdiagonalsHelper(row + 1, col + 1, 1, 1)
181 End Sub
182
183 Private Sub XdiagonalsHelper(r As Integer, c As Integer, _
184                             rAdjust As Integer, cAdjust As Integer)
185     Dim a As Integer
186
187     While (a < 8 And ValidMove(r, c))
188         mBoard(r, c) = 35
189         r = r + rAdjust
190         c = c + cAdjust
191         a = a + 1
192     Wend
193 End Sub
194
195 Public Sub PrintBoard(f As Form)
196     Dim queens As Integer, r As Integer, c As Integer
197
198     Call f.Cls
199
200     ' Header for columns
201     f.Print "   0 1 2 3 4 5 6 7"
202
203     For r = 0 To 7
204         f.Print Format$(r, "@@") & " ";
205
206         For c = 0 To 7
207
208             ' Function Chr$ prints the ASCII character
209             ' representation of an Integer.
210             f.Print Chr$(mBoard(r, c)) & " ";
211
212             If (mBoard(r, c) = 81) Then
213                 queens = queens + 1
214             End If
215         Next c
216
217         f.Print
218     Next r
219
220     f.Print
221     f.Print queens & " Queens were placed on the board."
222 End Sub
```

7.24   **[CD]** Modify the die-rolling program of Fig. 7.5 to use a control array for the **Image**s.

ANS:

```
1   ' Exercise 7.24 Solution
2   Option Explicit                           ' General declaration
3
4   ' Declare module variables
5   Dim mTotalRolls As Integer                ' General declaration
6   Dim mFrequency(1 To 6) As Integer         ' General declaration
7
8   Private Sub cmdRoll_Click()
9      Dim k As Integer
10
11      Call Randomize      ' Seed function Rnd
12      mTotalRolls = mTotalRolls + 12
13
14      For k = 0 To 11
15         Call displayDie(imgDie(k))
16      Next k
17
18      Call lstStatistics.Clear
19      Call DisplayStats
20   End Sub
21
22   Private Sub displayDie(imgDie As Image)
23      Dim face As Integer
24
25      face = 1 + Int(Rnd() * 6)
26      mFrequency(face) = mFrequency(face) + 1
27      imgDie.Picture = LoadPicture("\vb_solutions\ch07\ex07_24\die" _
28                                 & face & ".gif")
29   End Sub
30
31   Private Sub DisplayStats()
32      Dim j As Integer, n As Integer
33
34      Call lstStatistics.AddItem("Face" & vbTab & "Frequency" & _
35                                 vbTab & "Percent")
36      For j = 1 To 6
37         n = mFrequency(j)
38         Call lstStatistics.AddItem(j & vbTab & n & vbTab & _
39                                 vbTab & Format$(n / mTotalRolls, _
40                                 "Percent"))
41      Next j
42
43   End Sub
```

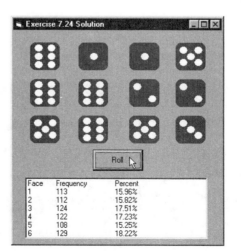

7.25 The bubble sort presented in Fig. 7.7 is inefficient for large arrays. Make the following simple modifications to improve the performance of the bubble sort.

a) After the first pass, the largest number is guaranteed to be in the highest-numbered element of the array; after the second pass, the two highest numbers are "in place," and so on. Instead of making nine comparisons on every pass, modify the bubble sort to make eight comparisons on the second pass, seven on the third pass, and so on.

b) The data in the array may already be in the proper order or near-proper order, so why make nine passes if fewer will suffice? Modify the sort to check at the end of each pass if any swaps have been made. If none has been made, then the data must already be in the proper order, so the program should terminate. If swaps have been made, then at least one more pass is needed.

ANS:

```
1   ' Exercise 7.25 Part A Solution
2   Option Explicit
3   Option Base 1
4   Dim mArray(10) As Integer
5
6   Private Sub cmdGenerate_Click()
7      Dim x As Integer
8
9      Call Randomize            ' Randomize Rnd
10     Call lstOriginal.Clear   ' Clear data
11     Erase mArray             ' Clear array
12
13     ' Generate numbers
14     For x = LBound(mArray) To UBound(mArray)
15        mArray(x) = 1 + Int(100 * Rnd())
16        Call lstOriginal.AddItem(mArray(x))
17     Next x
18
19     Call lstSorted.Clear     ' Clear ListBox
20     cmdSort.Enabled = True   ' Enable Sort button
21  End Sub
22
23  Private Sub cmdSort_Click()
24     Dim x As Integer
25
26     Call lstSorted.Clear     ' Clear ListBox
27     Call BubbleSort(mArray)  ' Sort the array
28
29     For x = LBound(mArray) To UBound(mArray)
30        Call lstSorted.AddItem(mArray(x))
31     Next x
32
33     cmdSort.Enabled = False
34  End Sub
35
36  Private Sub cmdExit_Click()
37     End
38  End Sub
```

```
39  ' modBubble
40  Option Explicit
41
42  Public Sub BubbleSort(theArray() As Integer)
43     Dim pass As Integer, compare As Integer
44     Dim hold As Integer, arraySize As Integer
45
46     If LBound(theArray) = 0 Then
47        arraySize = UBound(theArray) - LBound(theArray)
48     Else
49        arraySize = UBound(theArray) - LBound(theArray) + 1
50     End If
51
52     For pass = 1 To arraySize - 1
53
```

```
54          For compare = LBound(theArray) To arraySize - pass
55
56              If theArray(compare) > theArray(compare + 1) Then
57                  hold = theArray(compare)
58                  theArray(compare) = theArray(compare + 1)
59                  theArray(compare + 1) = hold
60              End If
61
62          Next compare
63
64      Next pass
65
66  End Sub
```

```
1   ' Exercise 7.25 Part B Solution
2   Option Explicit
3   Option Base 1
4   Dim mArray(10) As Integer
5
6   Private Sub cmdGenerate_Click()
7       Dim x As Integer
8
9       Call lstOriginal.Clear  ' Clear data
10      mArray(LBound(mArray)) = 3
11      Call lstOriginal.AddItem(mArray(LBound(mArray)))
12      mArray(LBound(mArray) + 1) = 2
13      Call lstOriginal.AddItem(mArray(LBound(mArray) + 1))
14      mArray(LBound(mArray) + 2) = 1
15      Call lstOriginal.AddItem(mArray(LBound(mArray) + 2))
16
17      ' Generate numbers
18      For x = (LBound(mArray) + 3) To UBound(mArray)
19          mArray(x) = x
20          Call lstOriginal.AddItem(mArray(x))
21      Next x
22
23      Call lstSorted.Clear     ' Clear ListBox
24      cmdSort.Enabled = True   ' Enable Sort button
25  End Sub
26
27  Private Sub cmdSort_Click()
28      Dim x As Integer
29
30      Call lstSorted.Clear     ' Clear ListBox
31      Call BubbleSort(mArray)  ' Sort the array
32
33      For x = LBound(mArray) To UBound(mArray)
34          Call lstSorted.AddItem(mArray(x))
35      Next x
36
37      cmdSort.Enabled = False
38  End Sub
```

```
39
40   Private Sub cmdExit_Click()
41       End
42   End Sub
```

```
44   ' modBubble
45   ' This code contains the enhancement from 7.25 Part A's modBubble
46   Option Explicit
47
48   Public Sub BubbleSort(theArray() As Integer)
49       Dim pass As Integer, compare As Integer
50       Dim hold As Integer, arraySize As Integer
51       Dim swapped As Boolean
52
53       pass = 1
54       swapped = True
55
56       If LBound(theArray) = 0 Then
57           arraySize = UBound(theArray) - LBound(theArray)
58       Else
59           arraySize = UBound(theArray) - LBound(theArray) + 1
60       End If
61
62       While ((pass <= arraySize - 1) And swapped = True)
63           swapped = False    ' Assume no swaps are made
64
65           For compare = LBound(theArray) To (arraySize - pass)
66
67               If theArray(compare) > theArray(compare + 1) Then
68                   hold = theArray(compare)
69                   theArray(compare) = theArray(compare + 1)
70                   theArray(compare + 1) = hold
71                   swapped = True    ' At least one swap has been made
72               End If
73
74           Next compare
75
76           pass = pass + 1
77       Wend
78
79   End Sub
```

Exercise 7.25 Part B Solution

Original values:

```
3
2
1
4
5
6
7
8
```

Sorted values:

```
1
2
3
4
5
6
7
8
```

Create Data   Sort   Exit

7.26   [CD] (*Selection Sort*) A selection sort searches an array looking for the smallest element in the array. Then, the smallest element is swapped with the first element of the array. The process is repeated for the subarray beginning with the second element of the array. Each pass of the array results in at least one more element being placed into its proper location. This sort performs comparably to the bubble sort—for an array of n elements, $n - 1$ passes must be made, and for each subarray, $n - 1$ comparisons must be made to find the smallest value. When the subarray being processed contains one element, the array is sorted. Write a program to perform this algorithm.

ANS:

```
1   ' Exercise 7.26 Solution
2   Option Explicit
3
4   Private Sub Form_Load()
5       Call Randomize
6       Print "Click the form to start..."
7   End Sub
8
9   Private Sub Form_Click()
10      Const MAXRANGE As Integer = 1000
11      Dim sortThisArray(10) As Integer, i As Integer
12
13      Call Cls
14
15      For i = LBound(sortThisArray) To UBound(sortThisArray)
16          sortThisArray(i) = 1 + Int(Rnd() * MAXRANGE)
17      Next i
18
19      Print "Unsorted array is:"
20      For i = LBound(sortThisArray) To UBound(sortThisArray)
21          Print " " & sortThisArray(i);
22      Next i
23
24      Call SelectionSort(sortThisArray, LBound(sortThisArray))
25      Print
26      Print
27
28      Print "Sorted array is:"
29      For i = LBound(sortThisArray) To UBound(sortThisArray)
30          Print " " & sortThisArray(i);
31      Next i
32
33  End Sub
```

7.27 (*Bucket Sort*) A bucket sort begins with a one-dimensional array of positive **Integer**s to be sorted and a two-dimensional array of **Integer**s with rows indexed from 0 to 9 and columns indexed from 0 to $n - 1$, where n is the number of values in the array to be sorted. Each row of the two-dimensional array is referred to as a "bucket." Write a function **BucketSort** that takes an integer array and the array size as arguments and performs as follows:

1. Place each value of the one-dimensional array into a row of the bucket array based on the value's ones digit. For example, 97 is placed in row 7, 3 is placed in row 3 and 100 is placed in row 0. This is called a "distribution pass."

2. Loop through the bucket array row-by-row and copy the values back to the original array. This is called a "gathering pass." The new order of the preceding values in the one-dimensional array is 100, 3 and 97.

3. Repeat this process for each subsequent digit position (tens, hundreds, thousands, etc.).

4. On the second pass, 100 is placed in row 0, 3 is placed in row 0 (because 3 has no tens digit) and 97 is placed in row 9. After the gathering pass, the order of the values in the one-dimensional array is 100, 3 and 97. On the third pass, 100 is placed in row 1, 3 is placed in row zero and 97 is placed in row zero (after the 3). After the last gathering pass, the original array is now in sorted order.

Note that the two-dimensional array of buckets is ten times the size of the **Integer** array being sorted. This sorting technique provides better performance than a bubble sort, but requires much more memory. The bubble sort requires space for only one additional element of data. This is an example of the space-time trade-off: The bucket sort uses more memory than the bubble sort, but performs better. This version of the bucket sort requires copying all the data back to the original array on each pass. Another possibility is to create a second two-dimensional bucket array and repeatedly swap the data between the two bucket arrays.

ANS:

```
 1   ' Exercise 7.27 Solution
 2   Option Explicit
 3   Dim mArray(50) As Integer
 4
 5   Private Sub Form_Load()
 6      Dim r As Integer
 7
 8      Call Randomize
 9
10      For r = LBound(mArray) To UBound(mArray)
11         mArray(r) = Int(Rnd() * 1000)
12         Call lstData.AddItem(mArray(r))
13      Next r
14   End Sub
15
16   Private Sub cmdSort_Click()
17      Dim r As Integer
18
19      Call BucketSort(mArray, UBound(mArray) - LBound(mArray))
20
21      For r = LBound(mArray) To UBound(mArray)
22         Call lstSortedData.AddItem(mArray(r))
23      Next r
24
25      cmdSort.Enabled = False
26   End Sub
```

```
28   ' modBucketSort
29   Option Explicit
30
31   ' Perform the bucket sort algorithm
32   Public Sub BucketSort(a() As Integer, arraySize As Integer)
33      Dim i As Integer, totalDigits As Integer
34      Dim bucket() As Integer        ' Dynamic array
35
36      ReDim bucket(9, arraySize)
37
38      totalDigits = NumberOfDigits(a, arraySize)
39
40      For i = 1 To totalDigits
41         Call DistributeElements(a, bucket, i, arraySize)
42         Call CollectElements(a, bucket)
43
44         If (i <> totalDigits) Then
45            Call ZeroBucket(bucket, arraySize)  ' Set all bucket contents to zero
46         End If
47
48      Next i
49   End Sub
50
51   ' Determine the number of digits in the largest number
52   Private Function NumberOfDigits(b() As Integer, arraySize As Integer)
53      Dim largest As Integer, digits As Integer, i As Integer
54
55      largest = b(0)
56
57      For i = 1 To arraySize
58
59         If (b(i) > largest) Then
60            largest = b(i)
61         End If
62
63      Next i
```

```
64
65      While (largest <> 0)
66         digits = digits + 1
67         largest = largest \ 10
68      Wend
69
70      NumberOfDigits = digits
71   End Function
72
73   ' Distribute elements into buckets based on specified digit
74   Private Sub DistributeElements(a() As Integer, _
75                                  buckets() As Integer, _
76                                  digit As Integer, _
77                                  arraySize As Integer)
78      Dim divisor As Integer, bucketNumber As Integer
79      Dim elementNumber As Integer, i As Integer
80
81      divisor = 10
82
83      For i = 1 To digit - 1              ' Determine the divisor
84         divisor = divisor * 10          ' used to get specific digit
85      Next i
86
87      For i = 0 To arraySize
88         ' BucketNumber example for hundreds digit:
89         ' (1234 Mod 1000 - 1234 Mod 100) \ 100 --> 2
90         bucketNumber = (a(i) Mod divisor - a(i) Mod _
91                        (divisor \ 10)) \ (divisor \ 10)
92
93         ' Retrieve value in buckets(bucketNumber, 0) to determine
94         ' which element of the row to store a(i) in.
95         buckets(bucketNumber, 0) = buckets(bucketNumber, 0) + 1
96         elementNumber = buckets(bucketNumber, 0)
97         buckets(bucketNumber, elementNumber) = a(i)
98      Next i
99
100  End Sub
101
102  ' Return elements to original array
103  Private Sub CollectElements(a() As Integer, buckets() As Integer)
104     Dim subscript As Integer, i As Integer, j As Integer
105
106     For i = 0 To 9
107
108        For j = 1 To buckets(i, 0)
109           a(subscript) = buckets(i, j)
110           subscript = subscript + 1
111        Next j
112
113     Next i
114
115  End Sub
116
117  ' Set all buckets to zero
118  Private Sub ZeroBucket(buckets() As Integer, arraySize As Integer)
119     Dim i As Integer, j As Integer
120
121     For i = 0 To 9
122
123        For j = 0 To arraySize
124           buckets(i, j) = 0
125        Next j
126
127     Next i
128
129  End Sub
```

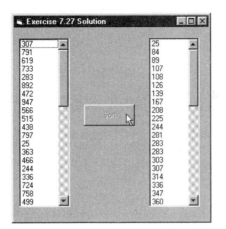

7.28   (*Quicksort*) In this chapter and previous exercises, we discussed the sorting techniques of bubble sort, bucket sort, and selection sort. We now present the recursive sorting technique called Quicksort. The basic algorithm for a one-dimensional array of values is as follows:

a) *Partitioning Step:* Take the first element of the unsorted array and determine its final location in the sorted array (i.e., all values to the left of the element in the array are less than the element, and all values to the right of the element in the array are greater than the element). We now have one element in its proper location and two unsorted subarrays.

b) *Recursive Step:* Perform step 1 on each unsorted subarray.

Each time step 1 is performed on a subarray, another element is placed in its final location of the sorted array, and two unsorted subarrays are created. When a subarray consists of one element, it must be sorted; therefore, that element is in its final location.

The basic algorithm seems simple enough, but how do we determine the final position of the first element of each subarray? As an example, consider the following set of values (the element in bold is the partitioning element—it will be placed in its final location in the sorted array):

37   2   6   4   89   8   10   12   68   45

a) Starting from the rightmost element of the array, compare each element to **37** until an element less than **37** is found, then swap **37** and that element. The first element less than **37** is 12, so **37** and 12 are swapped. The new array is:

12   2   6   4   89   8   10   **37**   68   45

Element 12 is in italic to indicate that it was just swapped with **37**.

b) Starting from the left of the array, but beginning with the element after 12, compare each element to **37** until an element greater than **37** is found, then swap **37** and that element. The first element greater than **37** is 89, so **37** and 89 are swapped. The new array is

12   2   6   4   **37**   8   10   *89*   68   45

c) Starting from the right, but beginning with the element before 89, compare each element to **37** until an element less than **37** is found, then swap **37** and that element. The first element less than **37** is 10, so **37** and 10 are swapped. The new array is

12   2   6   4   *10*   8   **37**   89   68   45

d) Starting from the left, but beginning with the element after 10, compare each element to **37** until an element greater than **37** is found, then swap **37** and that element. There are no more elements greater than **37**, so when we compare **37** to itself we know that **37** has been placed in its final location of the sorted array.

Once the partition has been applied on the above array, there are two unsorted subarrays. The subarray with values less than 37 contains 12, 2, 6, 4, 10 and 8. The subarray with values greater than 37 contains 89, 68 and 45. The sort continues with both subarrays being partitioned in the same manner as the original array.

Based on the preceding discussion, write recursive function **QuickSort** to sort a one-dimensional **Integer** array. The function should receive as arguments an **Integer** array, a starting index and an ending index. Function **Partition** should be called by **QuickSort** to perform the partitioning step.

ANS:

```
1   ' Exercise 7.28 Solution
2   Option Explicit
3   Option Base 1
4   Dim mArray(5000) As Integer
5
```

```
 6    Private Sub Form_Load()
 7       Dim r As Integer
 8
 9       Call Randomize
10
11       For r = 1 To 5000
12          mArray(r) = Int(Rnd() * 10000)
13          Call lstData.AddItem(mArray(r))
14       Next r
15
16    End Sub
17
18    Private Sub cmdSort_Click()
19       Dim r As Integer
20
21       Call QuickSort(mArray, LBound(mArray), UBound(mArray))
22
23       For r = 1 To 5000
24          Call lstSortedData.AddItem(mArray(r))
25       Next r
26
27       cmdSort.Enabled = False
28    End Sub
```

```
29    ' modQuickSort
30    Option Explicit
31
32    Public Sub QuickSort(a() As Integer, first As Integer, _
33                         last As Integer)
34
35       Dim currentLocation As Integer
36
37       If (first >= last) Then
38          Exit Sub
39       End If
40
41       ' Arguments are passed by the default call-by-reference
42       currentLocation = Partition(a, first, last)      ' Place an element
43       Call QuickSort(a, first, currentLocation - 1)  ' Sort left side
44       Call QuickSort(a, currentLocation + 1, last)    ' sort right side
45    End Sub
46
47    Private Function Partition(a() As Integer, ByVal leftSide As Integer, _
48                              ByVal rightSide As Integer) As Integer
49       Dim position As Integer
50
51       position = leftSide
52       While (True)
53
54          While (a(position) <= a(rightSide) And position <> rightSide)
55             rightSide = rightSide - 1
56          Wend
57
58          If (position = rightSide) Then
59             Partition = position
60             Exit Function
61          End If
62
63          If (a(position) > a(rightSide)) Then
64             Call Swap(a(position), a(rightSide))
65             position = rightSide
66          End If
67
68          While (a(leftSide) <= a(position) And leftSide <> position)
69             leftSide = leftSide + 1
70          Wend
```

```
71
72        If (position = leftSide) Then
73            Partition = position
74            Exit Function
75        End If
76
77        If (a(leftSide) > a(position)) Then
78            Call Swap(a(position), a(leftSide))
79            position = leftSide
80        End If
81
82    Wend
83
84 End Function
85
86 ' Each argument received is passed implicitly ByRef
87 Private Sub Swap(v As Integer, w As Integer)
88    Dim temp As Integer
89    temp = v
90    v = w
91    w = temp
92 End Sub
```

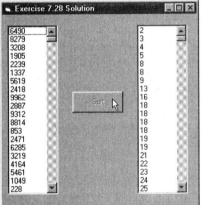

7.29   (*Turtle Graphics*) The Logo language, which is particularly popular among personal computer users, made the concept of turtle graphics famous. Imagine a mechanical turtle that walks around the room under the control of a Visual Basic program. The turtle holds a pen in one of two positions, up or down. While the pen is down, the turtle traces out shapes as it moves; while the pen is up, the turtle moves about freely without writing anything. In this problem you will simulate the operation of the turtle and create a computerized sketchbook as well.

Use a 20-by-20 array **floor** which is initialized to zeros. Read commands from an array that contains them. Keep track of the current position of the turtle at all times and whether the pen is currently up or down. Assume that the turtle always starts at position 0,0 of the floor with its pen up. The set of turtle commands your program must process are as follows:

Command	Meaning
1	Pen up
2	Pen down
3	Turn right
7	Turn left
5,10	Move forward *n* spaces (in this case 10)
6	Print the 20-by-20 array
9	End of data (sentinel)

Suppose that the turtle is somewhere near the center of the floor. The following "program" would draw and print a 12-by 12-square leaving the pen in the up position:

```
2
5,12
3
5,12
3
5,12
3
```

```
5,12
1
6
9
```

As the turtle moves with the pen down, set the appropriate elements of array **floor** to 1s. When the 6 command (print) is given, wherever there is a 1 in the array, display an asterisk, or some other character you choose. Wherever there is a zero display a blank. Write a program to implement the turtle graphics capabilities discussed here. Write several turtle graphics programs to draw interesting shapes. Add other commands to increase the power of your turtle graphics language.

7.30   [CD] Write a recursive version of the **LinearSearch** discussed in Fig. 7.8.
          ANS:

```
1   ' Exercise 7.30 Solution
2   Option Explicit
3   Option Base 1
4   Dim mArray(10) As Integer
5
6   Private Sub cmdSearch_Click()
7       Dim searchKey As Integer    ' Value to search for
8       Dim element As Integer      ' Index of Value
9
10      lblResult.Caption = ""
11      searchKey = txtKey.Text
12
13      ' Call LinearSearch and pass array and key
14      element = modLinearRecursive.LinearSearch(mArray(), LBound(mArray), searchKey)
15
16      If element <> -1 Then
17          lblResult.Caption = "Value was found."
18      Else
19          lblResult.Caption = "Value was not found."
20      End If
21  End Sub
22
23  Private Sub Form_Load()
24      Call lstData_Click
25  End Sub
26
27  Private Sub lstData_Click()
28      Dim x As Integer
29
30      Call Randomize
31      Call lstData.Clear
32      lblResult.Caption = ""
33
34      ' Generate some random data
35      For x = LBound(mArray) To UBound(mArray)
36          mArray(x) = 1 + Int(10000 * Rnd())
37          Call lstData.AddItem(mArray(x))
38      Next x
39
40  End Sub
41
42  Private Sub cmdExit_Click()
43      End
44  End Sub
```

```
46  ' Code module modLinearRecursive.bas
47  Option Explicit
48
49  Function LinearSearch(a() As Integer, b As Integer, key As Integer) As Integer
50      If b > UBound(a) Then
51          LinearSearch = -1  ' Value not found
52          Exit Function
```

```
53      ElseIf a(b) = key Then
54         LinearSearch = b    ' Return index
55         Exit Function
56      End If
57      LinearSearch = LinearSearch(a, b + 1, key)
58   End Function
```

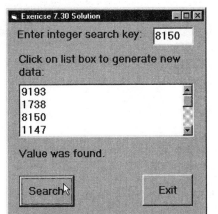

7.31   Write a recursive version of the **BinarySearch** discussed in Fig. 7.9.
       ANS:

```
1    ' Exercise 7.31 Solution
2    Option Explicit
3
4    Private Sub Form_Load()
5       Call Randomize
6       Print "Click the form to start..."
7    End Sub
8
9    Private Sub Form_Click()
10      Const MAXRANGE As Integer = 50
11      Dim values(10) As Integer, i As Integer, key As Integer
12
13      Call Cls
14
15      For i = LBound(values) To UBound(values)
16         values(i) = 1 + Int(Rnd() * MAXRANGE)
17         Print "  " & values(i);
18      Next i
19
20      Print
21      Print
22      key = 1 + Int(Rnd() * MAXRANGE)
23      Print "Searching for: " & key
24
25      If BinarySearch(values, LBound(values), key) = -1 Then
26         Print "The value " & key & " was not found."
27      Else
28         Print "The value was found."
29      End If
30
31   End Sub
```

```
32   ' modRecursiveBinary code module
33   Option Explicit
34
35   Public Function BinarySearch(a() As Integer, aIndex As Integer, _
36                                searchKey As Integer) As Integer
37
38      If aIndex = UBound(a) Then
39         BinarySearch = -1
```

```
40        ElseIf a(aIndex) = searchKey Then
41            BinarySearch = aIndex
42        Else
43            BinarySearch = BinarySearch(a, aIndex + 1, searchKey)
44        End If
45
46    End Function
```

7.32   [CD] The Fibonacci series

$$0, 1, 1, 2, 3, 5, 8, 13, 21, ...$$

begins with the terms 0 and 1 and has the property that each succeeding term is the sum of the two preceding terms. (a) Write a nonrecursive procedure **Fibonacci** that calculates the nth Fibonacci number. (b) Determine the largest Fibonacci number that can be calculated on your system. Use data type **Double**.

   ANS:

```
1    ' Exercise 7.32 Solution
2    ' Part A
3    Option Explicit
4
5    Private Sub Form_Load()
6        Dim x As Integer
7
8        ' 23 is the largest number that can be used
9        ' before an Overflow error occurs.
10       For x = 0 To 23
11           Call lstValues.AddItem(Fibonacci(x))
12       Next x
13
14   End Sub
15
16   Private Function Fibonacci(n As Integer)
17       Dim fibValues(23) As Integer, y As Integer
18
19       fibValues(0) = 0
20       fibValues(1) = 1
21
22       For y = 2 To n
23           fibValues(y) = fibValues(y - 1) + fibValues(y - 2)
24       Next y
25
26       Fibonacci = fibValues(n)
27   End Function
```

```
1    ' Exercise 7.32 Solution
2    ' Part B
3    Option Explicit
4
```

```
5   Private Sub Form_Load()
6      Dim x As Integer
7
8      ' 1476 is the largest Fibonacci supported on our systems
9      For x = 0 To 1476
10        Call lstValues.AddItem(Fibonacci(x))
11     Next x
12
13  End Sub
14
15  Private Function Fibonacci(n As Integer)
16     Dim fibValues(1476) As Double, y As Integer
17
18     fibValues(0) = 0
19     fibValues(1) = 1
20
21     For y = 2 To n
22        fibValues(y) = fibValues(y - 1) + fibValues(y - 2)
23     Next y
24
25     Fibonacci = fibValues(n)
26  End Function
```

Exercise 7.32 Solution

Chapter 8 Solutions
Strings, Dates and Times

8.3 Suppose that you are interested in determining how many commonly used three-letter words there are in the English language that begin with a particular letter. Write a program that obtains the first letter of the three-letter words from the user, and then generates all possible three-letter words beginning with the letter typed by the user. Use function **Mid$** to extract the individual letters from a string containing the alphabet.

ANS:

```
1   ' Exercise 8.3 Solution
2   Option Explicit
3   Dim mAlphabet As String
4
5   Private Sub Form_Load()
6       mAlphabet = "abcdefghijklmnopqrstuvwxyz"
7   End Sub
8
9   Private Sub cmdEnter_Click()
10      Dim b As Integer, c As Integer
11      Dim char As String
12
13      char = LCase$(txtInput.Text)
14      Call lstBox.Clear    ' Clear ListBox
15
16      For b = 1 To 26
17
18         For c = 1 To 26
19            Call lstBox.AddItem(char & Mid$(mAlphabet, b, 1) & _
20                            Mid$(mAlphabet, c, 1))
21         Next c
22
23      Next b
24   End Sub
```

8.4 Write a program that reads a five-letter word from the user and produces all possible three-letter words that can be derived from the letters of the five-letter word. For example, the three-letter words produced from the word "bathe" include the commonly used words

    ate   bat   bet   tab   hat   the   tea

8.5   Use the techniques for comparing strings developed in Section 8.5 and the techniques for sorting arrays developed in Chapter 7 to write a program that alphabetizes a list of strings. Use the names of 10 or 15 towns in your area as input data to your program.

ANS:

```
1    ' Exercise 8.5 Solution
2    Option Explicit
3    Option Base 1
4    Dim mStrings() As String
5    Dim mSize As Long
6
7    Private Sub cmdEnter_Click()
8       Dim a As Integer, b As Integer, c As Integer
9       Dim s As String
10
11      s = txtInput.Text
12      mSize = mSize + 1
13      ReDim Preserve mStrings(mSize)
14      mStrings(mSize) = s
15      Call modBubble2.BubbleSort(mStrings)
16      Call lstBox.Clear
17
18      For a = 1 To UBound(mStrings)
19         Call lstBox.AddItem(mStrings(a))
20      Next a
21   End Sub
```

```
23   ' Module modBubble2.bas
24   Option Explicit
25
26   Public Sub BubbleSort(theArray() As String)
27      Dim pass As Integer, compare As Integer
28      Dim hold As String
29
30      For pass = 1 To (UBound(theArray) - 1)
31         For compare = 1 To (UBound(theArray) - 1)
32            If theArray(compare) > theArray(compare + 1) Then
33               hold = theArray(compare)
34               theArray(compare) = theArray(compare + 1)
35               theArray(compare + 1) = hold
36            End If
37         Next compare
38      Next pass
39   End Sub
```

8.6   [CD] The chart in Appendix B shows the numeric code representations for the characters in the ANSI character set. Study this appendix carefully and then state whether each of the following is *true* or *false*.

a) The letter "A" comes before the letter "B."

ANS: True.

b) The digit "9" comes before the digit "0."

ANS: False.

c) The commonly used symbols for addition, subtraction, multiplication and division in Visual Basic all come before any of the digits.

ANS: True.

d) The digits come before the letters.
ANS: True.

e) If a sort program sorts strings into ascending sequence, the program will place the symbol for a right parenthesis before the symbol for a left parenthesis.
ANS: False. The right parenthesis,), is placed after the left parenthesis, (.

8.7   [CD] Write a program that reads a series of strings from the user and displays only those strings beginning with "b."
ANS:

```
1  ' Exericse 8.7 Solution
2  Option Explicit
3
4  Private Sub cmdEnter_Click()
5     Dim s As String
6
7     s = txtInput.Text
8
9     If Left$(s, 1) = "b" Then
10        Call lstDisplay.AddItem(s)
11    End If
12
13    txtInput.Text = ""
14  End Sub
```

8.8   Write a program that reads a series of strings from the user and prints only those strings that end with the letters "ED."
ANS:

```
1  ' Exericse 8.8 Solution
2  Option Explicit
3
4  Private Sub cmdEnter_Click()
5     Dim s As String
6
7     s = txtInput.Text
8
9     If Right$(s, 2) = "ED" Then
10        Call lstDisplay.AddItem(s)
11    End If
12
13    txtInput.Text = ""
14  End Sub
```

8.9   [CD] Write a program that generates all possible three-digit codes in the range 000 to 255 and attempts to print the corresponding characters using **Chr$**. What happens when this program is run?

ANS:

```
1   ' Exercise 8.9 Solution
2   Option Explicit
3
4   Private Sub Form_Load()
5      Dim r As Integer
6
7      Print Format$(Chr$(0), "@@@@");
8
9      For r = 1 To 255
10        Print Format$(Chr$(r), "@@@@");
11
12        If r Mod 10 = 0 Then
13           Print
14        End If
15
16     Next r
17
18  End Sub
```

NOTE: *Exercises 8.10 through 8.13 are reasonably challenging. Once you have done these problems, you ought to be able to implement most popular card games easily.*

8.10   Modify the program in Fig. 8.31 so that the card dealing method deals a five-card poker hand. Then write the following additional procedures:

    a) Determine if the hand contains a pair.
    b) Determine if the hand contains two pairs.
    c) Determine if the hand contains three of a kind (e.g., three jacks).
    d) Determine if the hand contains four of a kind (e.g., four aces).
    e) Determine if the hand contains a flush (i.e., all five cards of the same suit).
    f) Determine if the hand contains a straight (i.e., five cards of consecutive face values).
    g) Determine if the hand contains a full house (i.e., two cards of one face value and three cards of another face value).

ANS:

```
1   ' Exercise 8.10 Solution
2   Option Explicit
3   Dim mSuit(1 To 4) As String, mFace(1 To 13) As String
```

```vb
 4    Dim mDeck(1 To 4, 1 To 13) As Integer
 5    Dim mNumbers(1 To 13) As Integer
 6    Dim mHand(1 To 5) As String
 7
 8    Private Sub Form_Load()
 9       mSuit(1) = "Hearts"
10       mSuit(2) = "Diamonds"
11       mSuit(3) = "Clubs"
12       mSuit(4) = "Spades"
13
14       mFace(1) = "Ace"
15       mFace(2) = "Deuce"
16       mFace(3) = "Three"
17       mFace(4) = "Four"
18       mFace(5) = "Five"
19       mFace(6) = "Six"
20       mFace(7) = "Seven"
21       mFace(8) = "Eight"
22       mFace(9) = "Nine"
23       mFace(10) = "Ten"
24       mFace(11) = "Jack"
25       mFace(12) = "Queen"
26       mFace(13) = "King"
27
28       Call Randomize
29    End Sub
30
31    Private Sub cmdShuffle_Click()
32       Call lstOutput.Clear
33       Call lstResult.Clear
34       Call Shuffle
35       Call Deal
36       Call modCardProcedures.TotalHand(mFace, mHand, mNumbers)
37
38       If modCardProcedures.Flush(mHand) Then
39          Exit Sub
40       ElseIf modCardProcedures.Straight(mNumbers) Then
41          Exit Sub
42       ElseIf modCardProcedures.FourOfAKind(mFace, mNumbers) Then
43          Exit Sub
44       ElseIf modCardProcedures.FullHouse(mFace, mNumbers) Then
45          Exit Sub
46       ElseIf modCardProcedures.ThreeOfAKind(mFace, mNumbers) Then
47          Exit Sub
48       ElseIf modCardProcedures.Pair(mFace, mNumbers) Then
49          Exit Sub
50       End If
51
52    End Sub
53
54    Private Sub Shuffle()
55       Dim card As Integer, row As Integer, column As Integer
56
57       Call ZeroDeckArray
58
59       For card = 1 To 52
60
61          Do
62             row = 1 + Int(Rnd() * UBound(mSuit))
63             column = 1 + Int(Rnd() * UBound(mFace))
64          Loop While mDeck(row, column) <> 0
65
66          mDeck(row, column) = card
67       Next card
68
69    End Sub
70
```

```vb
71  Private Sub Deal()
72     Dim card As Integer, row As Integer, column As Integer
73     Dim length As Integer
74
75     For card = 1 To 5
76
77        For row = LBound(mSuit) To UBound(mSuit)
78
79           For column = LBound(mFace) To UBound(mFace)
80
81              If mDeck(row, column) = card Then
82
83                 ' First five characters are the face and
84                 ' the remaining characters are the suit
85                 length = Len(mFace(column))
86
87                 If length < 5 Then
88                    mHand(card) = mFace(column) & _
89                                     Space$(5 - length) & mSuit(row)
90                 Else
91                    mHand(card) = mFace(column) & mSuit(row)
92                 End If
93
94                 Call lstOutput.AddItem( _
95                         mFace(column) & " of " & mSuit(row))
96              End If
97
98           Next column
99
100       Next row
101
102    Next card
103
104 End Sub
105
106 Private Sub ZeroDeckArray()
107    Erase mDeck
108 End Sub
```

```vb
109 ' Module modBubble.bas
110 Option Explicit
111
112 Public Sub BubbleSort(theArray() As Integer)
113    Dim pass As Integer, compare As Integer
114    Dim hold As Integer
115
116    For pass = 1 To (UBound(theArray) - 1)
117
118       For compare = 1 To (UBound(theArray) - 1)
119
120          If theArray(compare) > theArray(compare + 1) Then
121             hold = theArray(compare)
122             theArray(compare) = theArray(compare + 1)
123             theArray(compare + 1) = hold
124          End If
125
126       Next compare
127    Next pass
128 End Sub
```

```vb
131 ' modCardProcedures.bas
132 Option Explicit
133 Dim mThreeFace As String
134 Dim mTwoFace As String
135 Dim mFirst As Boolean
136
```

```
137  Public Sub TotalHand(face() As String, _
138                       hand() As String, _
139                       numbers() As Integer)
140     Dim j As Integer, k As Integer
141
142     Erase numbers
143     mThreeFace = ""
144     mTwoFace = ""
145     mFirst = False
146
147     For j = LBound(hand) To UBound(hand)
148
149        For k = LBound(face) To UBound(face)
150
151           If RTrim$(Left$(hand(j), 5)) = face(k) Then
152              numbers(k) = numbers(k) + 1
153           End If
154
155        Next k
156
157     Next j
158  End Sub
159
160  Public Function Pair(face() As String, _
161                       numbers() As Integer) As Boolean
162     Dim j As Integer, found As Boolean
163
164     For j = LBound(face) To UBound(face)
165
166        If numbers(j) = 2 Then
167
168           If mFirst = False Then
169              Call frmCard.lstResult.AddItem("Pair of " & _
170                                              face(j) & "'s")
171           End If
172
173           found = True
174           mTwoFace = face(j)
175        End If
176
177     Next j
178
179     Pair = found
180  End Function
181
182  Public Function ThreeOfAKind(face() As String, _
183                       numbers() As Integer) As Boolean
184     Dim j As Integer
185
186     For j = LBound(face) To UBound(face)
187
188        If numbers(j) = 3 Then
189
190           If mFirst = False Then
191              Call frmCard.lstResult.AddItem("Three " & face(j) & "'s")
192           End If
193
194           mThreeFace = face(j)
195           ThreeOfAKind = True
196           Exit Function
197        End If
198
199     Next j
200
201     ThreeOfAKind = False
202  End Function
203
```

```
204  Public Function FourOfAKind(face() As String, _
205                         numbers() As Integer) As Boolean
206     Dim j As Integer
207
208     For j = LBound(face) To UBound(face)
209
210        If numbers(j) = 4 Then
211           Call frmCard.lstResult.AddItem("Four " & face(j) & "'s")
212           FourOfAKind = True
213           Exit Function
214        End If
215
216     Next j
217
218     FourOfAKind = False
219  End Function
220
221  Public Function FullHouse(face() As String, _
222                         numbers() As Integer) As Boolean
223     mFirst = True
224
225     If Pair(face, numbers) And ThreeOfAKind(face, numbers) Then
226
227        If mTwoFace <> mThreeFace Then
228           Call frmCard.lstResult.AddItem("Full House")
229           FullHouse = True
230           Exit Function
231        End If
232
233     End If
234
235     mFirst = False
236     FullHouse = False
237  End Function
238
239  Public Function Flush(hand() As String) As Boolean
240     Dim suit As String, j As Integer
241
242     suit = Mid$(hand(LBound(hand)), 6)
243
244     For j = (LBound(hand) + 1) To UBound(hand)
245
246        If Mid$(hand(j), 6) <> suit Then
247           Flush = False
248           Exit Function
249        End If
250
251     Next j
252
253     Call frmCard.lstResult.AddItem("Flush in " & suit)
254     Flush = True
255  End Function
256
257  Public Function Straight(numbers() As Integer) As Boolean
258     Dim locations(1 To 5) As Integer, j As Integer
259     Dim faceValue As Integer, c As Integer
260
261     c = LBound(locations)
262
263     For j = LBound(numbers) To UBound(numbers)
264
265        If numbers(j) = 1 Then
266           locations(c) = j
267           c = c + 1
268        End If
269
270     Next j
```

```
271
272       Call modBubble.BubbleSort(locations)
273       faceValue = locations(1)
274
275       For j = (LBound(locations) + 1) To UBound(locations)
276
277          If faceValue <> locations(j) - 1 Then
278             Straight = False
279             Exit Function
280          Else
281             faceValue = locations(j)
282          End If
283
284       Next j
285
286       Call frmCard.lstResult.AddItem("Straight")
287       Straight = True
288 End Function
```

8.11   Use the procedures developed in Exercise 8.10 to write a program that deals two five-card poker hands, evaluates each hand and determines which is the better hand.

   ANS:

```
1  ' Exercise 8.11 Solution
2  Option Explicit
3  Dim mSuit(1 To 4) As String, mFace(1 To 13) As String
4  Dim mDeck(1 To 4, 1 To 13) As Integer
5  Dim mNumbers(1 To 2, 1 To 13) As Integer
6  Dim mHand(1 To 2, 1 To 5) As String
7  Dim mHandStrength(1 To 2) As Integer
8
9  Private Sub Form_Load()
10    Call InitializeCards
11 End Sub
12
13 Private Sub cmdShuffle_Click()
14    Dim player As Integer, modifier As Integer
15
16    For player = 1 To 2
17       Call lstOutput(player).Clear
18       Call lstResult(player).Clear
19       mHandStrength(player) = 0
20    Next player
21
22    Call Randomize
23    Call Shuffle
24    Call Deal
25
```

```
26      For player = 1 To 2
27         Call modCardProcedures.TotalHand(mFace, mHand, _
28                                    mNumbers, player)
29
30         If modCardProcedures.Flush(mHand, player) Then
31            mHandStrength(player) = 600
32         ElseIf modCardProcedures.Straight(mNumbers, _
33                                    player, modifier) Then
34            mHandStrength(player) = modifier
35         ElseIf modCardProcedures.FourOfAKind(mFace, mNumbers, _
36                                    player, modifier) Then
37            mHandStrength(player) = modifier
38         ElseIf modCardProcedures.FullHouse(mFace, mNumbers, _
39                                    player, modifier) Then
40            mHandStrength(player) = modifier
41         ElseIf modCardProcedures.ThreeOfAKind(mFace, mNumbers, _
42                                    player, modifier) Then
43            mHandStrength(player) = modifier
44         ElseIf modCardProcedures.Pair(mFace, mNumbers, player, _
45                                 modifier) Then
46            mHandStrength(player) = modifier
47         End If
48
49      Next player
50
51      If mHandStrength(1) > mHandStrength(2) Then
52         Call lstResult(1).AddItem("Stronger hand.")
53      ElseIf mHandStrength(1) < mHandStrength(2) Then
54         Call lstResult(2).AddItem("Stronger hand.")
55      Else
56         Dim high1 As Integer, high2 As Integer
57
58         high1 = modCardProcedures.GetHighCard(mNumbers, 1)
59         high2 = modCardProcedures.GetHighCard(mNumbers, 2)
60
61         If high1 > high2 Then
62            Call lstResult(1).AddItem("Stronger hand.")
63         ElseIf high2 > high1 Then
64            Call lstResult(2).AddItem("Stronger hand.")
65         Else
66            Call lstResult(1).AddItem("Equal strength.")
67            Call lstResult(2).AddItem("Equal strength.")
68         End If
69
70      End If
71   End Sub
72
73   Private Sub Shuffle()
74      Dim card As Integer, row As Integer, column As Integer
75
76      Call ZeroDeckArray
77
78      For card = 1 To 52
79
80         Do
81            row = 1 + Int(Rnd() * UBound(mSuit))
82            column = 1 + Int(Rnd() * UBound(mFace))
83         Loop While (mDeck(row, column) <> 0)
84
85         mDeck(row, column) = card
86      Next card
87
88   End Sub
89
90   Private Sub Deal()
91      Dim card As Integer, row As Integer, column As Integer
92      Dim length As Integer, currentPlayer As Integer
```

```
93
94          For card = 1 To 10
95
96              For row = LBound(mSuit) To UBound(mSuit)
97
98                  For column = LBound(mFace) To UBound(mFace)
99
100                     If mDeck(row, column) = card Then
101
102                         ' First five characters are the face and
103                         ' the remaining characters are the suit
104                         length = Len(mFace(column))
105
106                         If card Mod 2 = 0 Then
107                             currentPlayer = 1
108                         Else
109                             currentPlayer = 2
110                         End If
111
112                         If length < 5 Then
113                             mHand(currentPlayer, (card Mod 5) + 1) = mFace(column) & _
114                                             Space$(5 - length) & mSuit(row)
115                         Else
116                             mHand(currentPlayer, (card Mod 5) + 1) = mFace(column) & _
117                                             mSuit(row)
118                         End If
119
120                         Call lstOutput(currentPlayer).AddItem( _
121                                 mFace(column) & " of " & mSuit(row))
122                     End If
123
124                 Next column
125
126             Next row
127
128         Next card
129
130     End Sub
131
132     Private Sub ZeroDeckArray()
133         Erase mDeck
134     End Sub
135
136     Private Sub InitializeCards()
137         mSuit(1) = "Hearts"
138         mSuit(2) = "Diamonds"
139         mSuit(3) = "Clubs"
140         mSuit(4) = "Spades"
141
142         mFace(1) = "Ace"
143         mFace(2) = "Deuce"
144         mFace(3) = "Three"
145         mFace(4) = "Four"
146         mFace(5) = "Five"
147         mFace(6) = "Six"
148         mFace(7) = "Seven"
149         mFace(8) = "Eight"
150         mFace(9) = "Nine"
151         mFace(10) = "Ten"
152         mFace(11) = "Jack"
153         mFace(12) = "Queen"
154         mFace(13) = "King"
155     End Sub


157     ' Module modBubble.bas
158     Option Explicit
```

```
159
160  Public Sub BubbleSort(theArray() As Integer)
161      Dim pass As Integer, compare As Integer
162      Dim hold As Integer
163
164      For pass = 1 To (UBound(theArray) - 1)
165
166          For compare = 1 To (UBound(theArray) - 1)
167
168              If theArray(compare) > theArray(compare + 1) Then
169                  hold = theArray(compare)
170                  theArray(compare) = theArray(compare + 1)
171                  theArray(compare + 1) = hold
172              End If
173
174          Next compare
175
176      Next pass
177
178  End Sub
```

```
179  ' modCardProcedures.bas
180  Option Explicit
181  Dim mThreeFace As String
182  Dim mTwoFace As String
183  Dim mFirst As Boolean
184
185  Public Sub TotalHand(face() As String, _
186                       hand() As String, _
187                       numbers() As Integer, _
188                       player As Integer)
189      Dim j As Integer, k As Integer
190
191      For j = LBound(numbers, 2) To UBound(numbers, 2)
192          numbers(player, j) = 0
193      Next j
194
195      mThreeFace = ""
196      mTwoFace = ""
197      mFirst = False
198
199      For j = LBound(hand, 2) To UBound(hand, 2)
200
201          For k = LBound(face) To UBound(face)
202
203              If RTrim$(Left$(hand(player, j), 5)) = face(k) Then
204                  numbers(player, k) = numbers(player, k) + 1
205              End If
206
207          Next k
208
209      Next j
210
211  End Sub
212
213  Public Function Pair(face() As String, _
214                       numbers() As Integer, _
215                       player As Integer, _
216                       modifier As Integer) As Boolean
217      Dim j As Integer, found As Boolean, count As Integer
218      Dim pairModifier(1 To 2) As Integer
219
220      For j = LBound(face) To UBound(face)
221
222          If numbers(player, j) = 2 Then
223              count = count + 1
```

```
224
225                If mFirst = False Then
226                    Call frmCard.lstResult(player).AddItem("Pair of " & _
227                                                  face(j) & "'s")
228                End If
229
230                If j = 1 Then
231                    pairModifier(count) = 14
232                Else
233                    pairModifier(count) = j
234                End If
235
236                found = True
237                mTwoFace = face(j)
238            End If
239
240        Next j
241
242        modifier = count * 105 + _
243                    IIf(pairModifier(1) > pairModifier(2), _
244                    pairModifier(1), pairModifier(2))
245        Pair = found
246    End Function
247
248    Public Function ThreeOfAKind(face() As String, _
249                            numbers() As Integer, _
250                            player As Integer, _
251                            modifier As Integer) As Boolean
252        Dim j As Integer
253
254        For j = LBound(face) To UBound(face)
255
256            If numbers(player, j) = 3 Then
257
258                If mFirst = False Then
259                    Call frmCard.lstResult(player).AddItem("Three " & _
260                                                  face(j) & "'s")
261                End If
262
263                mThreeFace = face(j)
264                modifier = 200 + GetHighCard(numbers, player)
265                ThreeOfAKind = True
266                Exit Function
267            End If
268
269        Next j
270
271        modifier = 0
272        ThreeOfAKind = False
273    End Function
274
275    Public Function FourOfAKind(face() As String, _
276                            numbers() As Integer, _
277                            player As Integer, _
278                            modifier As Integer) As Boolean
279        Dim j As Integer
280
281        For j = LBound(face) To UBound(face)
282
283            If numbers(player, j) = 4 Then
284                Call frmCard.lstResult(player).AddItem("Four " & _
285                                              face(j) & "'s")
286                modifier = 300 + GetHighCard(numbers, player)
287                FourOfAKind = True
288                Exit Function
289            End If
290        Next j
```

```
291
292        modifier = 0
293        FourOfAKind = False
294     End Function
295
296     Public Function FullHouse(face() As String, _
297                              numbers() As Integer, _
298                              player As Integer, _
299                              modifier As Integer) As Boolean
300        mFirst = True
301
302        ' Note: modifier is passed by value
303        If Pair(face, numbers, player, (modifier)) And _
304           ThreeOfAKind(face, numbers, player, (modifier)) Then
305
306           If mTwoFace <> mThreeFace Then
307              Call frmCard.1stResult(player).AddItem("Full House")
308              modifier = 400 + GetHighCard(numbers, player)
309              FullHouse = True
310              Exit Function
311           End If
312
313        End If
314
315        modifier = 0
316        mFirst = False
317        FullHouse = False
318     End Function
319
320     Public Function Flush(hand() As String, _
321                          player As Integer) As Boolean
322        Dim suit As String, j As Integer
323
324        suit = Mid$(hand(player, LBound(hand, 2)), 6)
325
326        For j = (LBound(hand, 2) + 1) To UBound(hand, 2)
327
328           If Mid$(hand(player, j), 6) <> suit Then
329              Flush = False
330              Exit Function
331           End If
332
333        Next j
334
335        Call frmCard.1stResult(player).AddItem("Flush in " & suit)
336        Flush = True
337     End Function
338
339     Public Function Straight(numbers() As Integer, _
340                             player As Integer, _
341                             modifier As Integer) As Boolean
342        Dim locations(1 To 5) As Integer, j As Integer
343        Dim faceValue As Integer, c As Integer
344
345        c = LBound(locations)
346
347        For j = LBound(numbers, 2) To UBound(numbers, 2)
348
349           If numbers(player, j) = 1 Then
350              locations(c) = j
351              c = c + 1
352           End If
353
354        Next j
355
356        Call modBubble.BubbleSort(locations)
357        faceValue = locations(1)
```

```
358
359        For j = (LBound(locations) + 1) To UBound(locations)
360
361           If faceValue <> locations(j) - 1 Then
362              modifier = 0
363              Straight = False
364              Exit Function
365           Else
366              faceValue = locations(j)
367           End If
368
369        Next j
370
371        modifier = 500 + GetHighCard(numbers, player)
372        Call frmCard.lstResult(player).AddItem("Straight")
373        Straight = True
374    End Function
375
376    Public Function GetHighCard(numbers() As Integer, _
377                               player As Integer) As Integer
378        Dim length As Integer, j As Integer
379
380        If numbers(player, 1) <> 0 Then
381           GetHighCard = 14
382           Exit Function
383        End If
384
385        length = UBound(numbers, 2)
386
387        For j = length To 2 Step -1
388
389           If numbers(player, j) <> 0 Then
390              GetHighCard = j
391              Exit Function
392           End If
393
394        Next j
395
396        GetHighCard = 99
397    End Function
```

8.12   Modify the program developed in Exercise 8.11 so that it can simulate the dealer. The dealer's five-card hand is dealt "face down" so the player cannot see it. The program should then evaluate the dealer's hand and, based on the quality of the hand, the dealer should draw one, two or three more cards to replace the corresponding number of unneeded cards in the original hand. The program should then reevaluate the dealer's hand. (*Caution:* This is a difficult problem!)

8.13   Modify the program developed in Exercise 8.12 so that it can handle the dealer's hand automatically, but the player is allowed to decide which cards of the player's hand to replace. The program should then evaluate both hands and determine who wins. Now use this new program to play 20 games against the computer. Who wins more games, you or the computer? Have one of your friends play 20 games against the computer. Who wins more games? Based on the results of these games, make appropriate modifications to refine your poker playing program (this, too, is a difficult problem). Play 20 more games. Does your modified program play a better game?

8.14   Write a program that uses random number generation to create sentences. Use four arrays of **String**s called **article**, **noun**, **verb** and **preposition**. Create a sentence by selecting a word at random from each array in the following order: **article**, **noun**, **verb**, **preposition**, **article** and **noun**. As each word is picked, concatenate it to the previous words in the sentence. The words should be separated by spaces. When the sentence is output, it should start with a capital letter and end with a period. The program should generate 20 sentences and output them to a **List**.

The arrays should be filled as follows: the **article** array should contain the articles **"the"**, **"a"**, **"one"**, **"some"** and **"any"**; the **noun** array should contain the nouns **"boy"**, **"girl"**, **"dog"**, **"town"** and **"car"**; the **verb** array should contain the verbs **"drove"**, **"jumped"**, **"ran"**, **"walked"** and **"skipped"**; the **preposition** array should contain the prepositions **"to"**, **"from"**, **"over"**, **"under"** and **"on"**.

After the preceding program is written, modify the program to produce a short story consisting of several of these sentences. (How about the possibility of a random story writer!)

ANS:

```
1   ' Exercise 8.14 Solution
2   Option Explicit
3
4   Private Sub Form_Load()
5      Dim article() As Variant, noun() As Variant
6      Dim verb() As Variant, preposition() As Variant
7      Dim sentence As String, k As Integer, firstWord As String
8      Dim j As Integer
9
10     article = Array("the", "a", "one", "some", "any")
11     noun = Array("boy", "girl", "dog", "town", "car")
12     verb = Array("drove", "jumped", "ran", "walked", "skipped")
13     preposition = Array("to", "from", "over", "under", "on")
14
15     Call Randomize
16
17     For k = 1 To 20
18        j = Int(Rnd() * 5)
19        firstWord = UCase$(Left$(article(j), 1)) & _
20                    Right$(article(j), Len(article(j)) - 1)
21        sentence = firstWord & " " & noun(Int(Rnd() * 5)) _
22                   & " " & verb(Int(Rnd() * 5)) & " " & _
23                   preposition(Int(Rnd() * 5)) & " " & _
24                   article(Int(Rnd() * 5)) & " " & _
25                   noun(Int(Rnd() * 5)) & "."
26        Call lstBox.AddItem(sentence)
27     Next k
28
29   End Sub
```

8.15   *(Limericks)* A limerick is a humorous five-line verse in which the first and second lines rhyme with the fifth, and the third line rhymes with the fourth. Using techniques similar to those developed in Exercise 8.14, write a program that produces random limericks. Polishing this program to produce good limericks is a challenging problem, but the result will be worth the effort!

8.16   **[CD]** Write a program that inputs a telephone number as a string in the form **(555) 555-5555**. The program should use functions **Mid$**, **Left$** and **Right$** to extract the area code, the first three digits of the phone number and the last four digits of the phone number. The seven digits of the phone number should be concatenated into one string. The program should convert the area code string and the phone number string to **Long**s. Both the area code and the phone number should be printed.

    ANS:

```
1   ' Exercise 8.16 Solution
2   ' Note: This solution does not validate the format.
3   Option Explicit
4
5   Private Sub cmdEnter_Click()
6      Dim s As String, phoneNumber As String
7      Dim areaCodeValue As Long, exchange As String
8      Dim areaCode As String, lineString As String
9      Dim lineValue As Long
10
11     Call lstDisplay.Clear
12     s = txtInput.Text
13     txtInput.Text = ""
14     Call lstDisplay.AddItem("Phone: " & s)
15
16     areaCode = Mid$(s, 2, 3)
17     Call lstDisplay.AddItem("Area Code: " & areaCode)
18
19     exchange = Mid$(s, 7, 3)
20     Call lstDisplay.AddItem("Exchange: " & exchange)
21
22     lineString = Right$(s, 4)
23     Call lstDisplay.AddItem("Line: " & lineString)
24
25     Call lstDisplay.AddItem("Concatenated: " & areaCode & exchange _
26                              & lineString)
27
28     areaCodeValue = CLng(areaCode)
29     lineValue = CLng(lineString)
30
31     Call lstDisplay.AddItem("Converted Area Code and Line: " & _
32                              areaCode & " " & lineValue)
33  End Sub
```

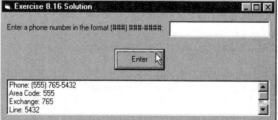

8.17   [CD] Write a program that inputs a line of text, breaks the string into substrings (called "tokenizing" the string) representing each word and outputs the substrings in reverse order.

    ANS:

```
1   ' Exercise 8.17 Solution
2   Option Explicit
3
4   Private Sub cmdSplit_Click()
5      Dim s As String, sentence As String
6      Dim x As Integer, token As String
7
8      Call lstDisplay.Clear
9      sentence = txtInput.Text
10     s = InStr(1, sentence, " ")          ' Find a space
11     Call Strtok(sentence, s)
12  End Sub
13
```

```
14  Private Sub Strtok(ByVal sentence As String, ByVal s As Long)
15     Dim token As String, newString As String, s2 As String
16
17     If s = 0 Then
18        Call lstDisplay.AddItem(sentence)
19     Else
20        token = Left$(sentence, s - 1)      ' Get "token"
21        newString = Right$(sentence, Len(sentence) - s)
22        s2 = InStr(1, newString, " ")
23        Call Strtok(newString, s2)
24        Call lstDisplay.AddItem(token)
25     End If
26
27  End Sub
```

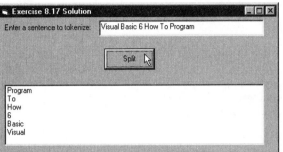

8.18   Rewrite the program of Exercise 8.17 using function **Split**. Function **Split** returns a one dimensional array of **String**s (starting at element 0) based on its two arguments—the string to be tokenized and the delimiter character. The delimiter character is the character that is used to determine where a "token" begins and ends. If the second argument is omitted, the default delimiter character is the space character.

    ANS:

```
1   ' Exercise 8.18 Solution
2   Option Explicit
3
4   Private Sub cmdSplit_Click()
5      Dim sentence As String
6
7      Call lstDisplay.Clear
8      sentence = txtInput.Text
9      Call PrintBackwards(sentence)
10  End Sub
11
12  Private Sub PrintBackwards(sentence As String)
13     Dim s() As String, j As Integer
14
15     s = Split(sentence)
16
17     For j = UBound(s) To LBound(s) Step -1
18        Call lstDisplay.AddItem(s(j))
19     Next j
20
21  End Sub
```

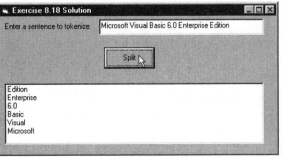

8.19   Write a program that inputs several lines of text and a search character, and uses function **InStr** to determine the number of occurrences of the character in the text.

ANS:

```
1    ' Exercise 8.19 Solution
2    Option Explicit
3
4    Private Sub cmdEnter_Click()
5       Dim counter As Integer, s As String
6       Dim char As String, current As Integer
7
8       Call lstList.Clear
9       s = txtString.Text
10      char = txtChar.Text
11      current = 1
12
13      current = InStr(current, s, char)
14
15      While current <> 0
16         counter = counter + 1
17         current = current + 1
18         current = InStr(current, s, char)
19      Wend
20
21      Call lstList.AddItem("Found " & counter & " " & _
22                           char & " characters.")
23   End Sub
```

8.20   Write a program based on the program of Exercise 8.19 that inputs several lines of text and uses function **InStr** to determine the total number of occurrences of each letter of the alphabet in the text. Uppercase and lowercase letters should be counted together. Store the totals for each letter in an array, and display the values in tabular format after the totals have been determined.

ANS:

```
1    ' Exercise 8.20 Solution
2    Option Explicit
3    Dim mCounters(97 To 122) As Integer
4    Dim mAlphabet As String
5
6    Private Sub Form_Load()
7       mAlphabet = "abcdefghijklmnopqrstuvwxyz"
8    End Sub
9
10   Private Sub cmdEnter_Click()
11      Dim s As String, current As Integer
12      Dim char As String, c As Integer
13
14      Call lstList.Clear
15      s = txtString.Text
16      s = LCase$(s)
17
18      For c = 1 To Len(mAlphabet)
19         current = 1
20         char = Mid$(mAlphabet, c, 1)
21         current = InStr(current, s, char)
22
23         While current <> 0
24            mCounters(Asc(char)) = mCounters(Asc(char)) + 1
```

```
25          current = current + 1
26          current = InStr(current, s, char)
27       Wend
28
29       Call lstList.AddItem("Found " & mCounters(Asc(char)) & " " & _
30                            char & " characters.")
31    Next c
32
33 End Sub
```

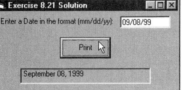

8.21   **[CD]** *(Printing Dates in Various Formats)* Dates are represented in several common formats. Two of the more common formats are:

07/21/55 and **July 21, 1955**

Write a program that reads a date in the first format and displays that date in the second format.

   ANS:

```
1  ' Exercise 8.21 Solution
2  Option Explicit
3
4  Private Sub cmdPrint_Click()
5     Dim d As Date, s As String, x As Integer
6
7     s = FormatDateTime(txtInput.Text, vbLongDate)
8     x = InStr(1, s, ",")
9     lblDisplay.Caption = Right$(s, Len(s) - x)
10 End Sub
```

8.22   *(Simple Encryption)* Some information on the Internet may be encrypted with a simple algorithm known as "rot13"—which rotates each character by 13 positions in the alphabet. Thus, **'a'** corresponds to **'n'**, **'x'** corresponds to **'k'**. Rot13 is an example of *symmetric key encryption*. With symmetric key encryption, both the encrypter and decrypter use the same key.
   a)   Write a program that encrypts a message using rot13.
   b)   Write a program that decrypts the scrambled message using 13 as the key.
   c)   After writing the programs of part (a) and part (b), briefly answer the following question: If you did not know the key for part (b), how difficult do you think it would be to break the code using any resources available? What if you had access to substantial computing power (e.g., Cray supercomputers)?
   ANS:

```
1  ' Exercise 8.22 Part A Solution
2  Option Explicit
3
4  Private Sub cmdEnter_Click()
5     Dim s As String, letter As String
6     Dim z As Integer, ascii As Byte
7
8     s = txtInput.Text
9     s = LCase$(s)          ' Convert to lowercase
```

```
10
11      For z = 1 To Len(s)
12
13         letter = Mid$(s, z, 1)
14
15         If letter <> " " Then
16            ascii = Asc(letter) + 13
17
18            If ascii > 122 Then
19               ascii = 96 + ascii - 122
20            End If
21
22            Mid$(s, z, 1) = Chr$(ascii)
23         End If
24
25      Next z
26
27      txtDisplay.Text = LCase$(s)
28   End Sub
```

Exercise 8.22 Solution

Enter a string:

The meeting is at nine pm in the old warehouse

Enter

gur zrrgvat vf ng avar cz va gur byq jnerubhfr

```
1    ' Exercise 8.22 Part B Solution
2    Option Explicit
3
4    Private Sub cmdEnter_Click()
5       Dim s As String, letter As String
6       Dim z As Integer, ascii As Byte
7
8       s = txtInput.Text
9       s = LCase$(s)          ' Convert to lowercase
10
11      For z = 1 To Len(s)
12
13         letter = Mid$(s, z, 1)
14
15         If letter <> " " Then
16            ascii = Asc(letter) - 13
17
18            If ascii < 97 Then
19               ascii = 123 - (97 - ascii)
20            End If
21
22            Mid$(s, z, 1) = Chr$(ascii)
23         End If
24
25      Next z
26
27      txtDisplay.Text = LCase$(s)
28   End Sub
```

Exercise 8.22 Solution

Enter a string:

gur zrrgvat vf ng avar cz va gur byq jnerubhfr

Enter

the meeting is at nine pm in the old warehouse

8.23   (*Hangman*) Write a program that plays the game of hangman. The program should pick a word (which is coded directly into the program) and display the following:

       Guess the word: XXXXXX

Each **X** represents a letter. If the user guesses correctly, the program should display

       Congratulations!!! You guessed my word. Play again? yes/no

The appropriate response **yes** or **no** should be input. If the user guesses incorrectly, display the appropriate body part.

After seven incorrect guesses, the user should be hung. The display should look like

```
      O
     /|\
      |
     / \
```

After each guess you want to display all their guesses.

     ANS:

```vb
1   ' Exercise 8.23 Solution
2   Option Explicit
3   Dim mWords(1 To 5) As String
4   Dim mCurrent As Integer
5   Dim mMask As String
6   Dim mBodyParts As String
7   Dim mCurrentBodyPart As Integer
8   Dim mGameMode As Boolean
9
10  Private Sub Form_Load()
11     mGameMode = True
12     mWords(1) = "yellow"
13     mWords(2) = "umbrella"
14     mWords(3) = "machine"
15     mWords(4) = "severe"
16     mWords(5) = "yam"
17     mBodyParts = "O/|\|/\"
18     Call SetWord
19  End Sub
20
21  Private Sub cmdEnter_Click()
22     Dim char As String, c As Integer, i As Integer
23     Dim dontAddBodyPart As Boolean, nextLine As Boolean
24     Dim done As Boolean
25
26     char = LCase$(txtInput.Text)
27
28     If mGameMode = True Then
29        lblGuesses.Caption = lblGuesses.Caption & char
30
31        For c = 1 To Len(mWords(mCurrent))
32
33           If char = Mid$(mWords(mCurrent), c, 1) Then
34              Mid$(mMask, c, 1) = char
35              lblDisplay.Caption = mMask
36              dontAddBodyPart = True
37           End If
38
39        Next c
40
41        done = True
42
43        For i = 1 To Len(mMask)
44           If Mid$(mMask, i, 1) = "X" Then
45              done = False
46              Exit For
47           End If
48        Next i
```

```
49
50          If done = True Then
51             Caption = "Congratulations!!! You guessed my word."
52             txtInput.MaxLength = 3
53             mGameMode = False
54             txtInput.Text = ""
55             lblPrompt2.Caption = "Play again?"
56          End If
57
58          If dontAddBodyPart = False Then
59             mCurrentBodyPart = mCurrentBodyPart + 1
60
61             If mCurrentBodyPart = 7 Then
62                Caption = "You have been hung."
63                txtInput.MaxLength = 3
64                lblDisplay.Caption = mWords(mCurrent)
65                mGameMode = False
66                lblPrompt2.Caption = "Try again?"
67                txtInput.Text = ""
68             End If
69
70             Call Cls
71
72             For i = 1 To mCurrentBodyPart
73
74                If i = 1 Or i = 5 Or i = 7 Then
75                   nextLine = True
76                   Print " ";
77                ElseIf i = 4 Then
78                   nextLine = True
79                Else
80                   nextLine = False
81                End If
82
83                Print Mid$(mBodyParts, i, 1);
84
85                If nextLine Then
86                   Print
87                End If
88
89             Next i
90
91          End If
92
93       Else
94
95          If char = "yes" Or char = "y" Then
96
97             If mCurrent = UBound(mWords) Then
98                Caption = "Sorry. I am out of words."
99                cmdEnter.Enabled = False
100               Exit Sub
101            End If
102
103            txtInput.MaxLength = 1
104            Call SetWord
105            mGameMode = True
106            txtInput.Text = ""
107            Caption = ""
108            lblPrompt2.Caption = "Enter Guess:"
109         Else
110            End
111         End If
112
113      End If
114 End Sub
115
```

```
116  Private Sub SetWord()
117     mCurrent = mCurrent + 1
118     mMask = String$(Len(mWords(mCurrent)), "X")
119     lblDisplay.Caption = mMask
120     lblGuesses.Caption = ""
121     mCurrentBodyPart = 0
122     Call Cls
123  End Sub
```

8.24 (*Cryptograms*) Write a program that creates a cryptogram out of a **String**. A cryptogram is a message or word, where each letter is replaced with another letter. For example, the **String**

     The birds name was squawk

might be scrambled to form

     xms kbypo zhqs fho obrhfu

Note that spaces are not scrambled. In this particular case, **T** was replaced with **x**, each **a** was replaced with **h**, etc. Uppercase letters and lowercase letters should be treated the same.

    ANS:

```
1   ' Exercise 8.24 Solution
2   Option Explicit
3
4   Private Sub cmdEnter_Click()
5      Dim s As String, offset As Integer, letter As String
6      Dim crypto As String, z As Integer
7      Dim alphabet As String, c As String
8
9      alphabet = "ABCDEFGHIJKLMNOPQRSTUVWXYZ"
10     s = txtInput.Text
11     s = LCase$(s)          ' Convert to lowercase
12     crypto = s             ' Copy String s
13     Call Randomize
14
15     ' Process whole String
16     For z = 1 To Len(s)
17
18        ' Pick a letter from the alphabet
19        ' asterisks, *, are placed in locations
20        ' where a letter is used.
21        Do
22           offset = 1 + Int(Rnd() * 26)
23           c = Mid$(alphabet, offset, 1)
24        Loop While c = "*"
```

```
25
26          ' Get the letter to replace
27          letter = Mid$(crypto, z, 1)
28
29          ' If it is a space do not replace it. Place
30          ' an asterisk in the alphabet string because
31          ' the character is now used. Replace all
32          ' occurances of the letter with the letter
33          ' chosen from alphabet.
34          If letter <> " " Then
35             Mid$(alphabet, offset, 1) = "*"
36             crypto = Replace(crypto, letter, c)
37          End If
38
39      Next z
40
41      ' Display the cryptogram
42      txtDisplay.Text = LCase$(crypto)
43   End Sub
```

```
Exercise 8.24 Solution                        _ □ X
Enter a string:
A giant parrot ate my homework

                  Enter

p rjpfq kpggiq pqe dm bideligc
```

8.25   Modify Exercise 8.24 to allow a user to solve the cryptogram by inputting two characters. The first character specifies the letter in the cryptogram, and the second letter specifies the user's guess. For example, if the user inputs **r g**, the user is guessing that the letter **r** is really a **g**.

8.26   Write a program that inputs a sentence and counts the number of palindromes in the sentence. A palindrome is a word that reads the same backwards and forwards. For example, **"tree"** is not a palindrome but **"noon"** is.

ANS:

```
1   ' Exercise 8.26 Solution
2   Option Explicit
3
4   Private Sub cmdPrintPal_Click()
5      Dim sentence As String
6
7      Call lstDisplay.Clear
8      sentence = txtInput.Text
9      Call Tokenize(sentence)
10  End Sub
11
12  Private Sub Tokenize(sentence As String)
13     Dim s() As String, j As Integer
14
15     s = Split(sentence)
16
17     For j = LBound(s) To UBound(s)
18
19        If IsPalindrome(s(j)) Then
20           Call lstDisplay.AddItem(s(j))
21        End If
22
23     Next j
24
25  End Sub
26
27  Private Function IsPalindrome(s As String) As Boolean
28     Dim length As Integer, j As Integer
29
30     length = Len(s)
```

```
31
32      If length = 1 Then
33         IsPalindrome = False
34         Exit Function
35      End If
36
37      For j = 1 To length
38
39         If Mid$(s, j, 1) <> Mid$(s, length, 1) Then
40            IsPalindrome = False
41            Exit Function
42         End If
43
44         length = length - 1
45      Next j
46
47      IsPalindrome = True
48   End Function
```

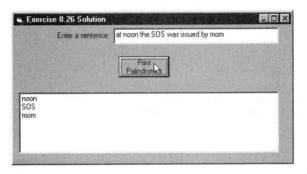

8.27   [CD] Write a program that inserts the characters `"*$$*"` in the middle of a **String**.
        ANS:

```
1    ' Exercise 8.27 Solution
2    Option Explicit
3
4    Private Sub Form_Load()
5       Print InsertChars("George Washington")
6       Print InsertChars("Thomas Jefferson")
7       Print InsertChars("John Adams")
8       Print InsertChars("Abraham Lincoln")
9       Print InsertChars("James K. Polk")
10   End Sub
11
12   Private Function InsertChars(s As String) As String
13      Dim length As Integer
14
15      length = Len(s)
16
17      If length >= 6 Then
18         Mid$(s, length \ 2 - 2, 4) = "*$$*"
19      End If
20
21      InsertChars = s
22   End Function
```

8.28   Write a program that generates from the string **"abcdefghijklmnopqrstuvwxyz{"** the following:

```
              a
             bcb
            cdedc
           defgfed
          efghihgfe
         fghijkjihgf
        ghijklmlkjihg
       hijklmnonmlkjih
      ijklmnopqponmlkji
     jklmnopqrsrqponmlkj
    klmnopqrstutsrqponmlk
   lmnopqrstuvwvutsrqponml
  mnopqrstuvwxyxwvutsrqponm
 nopqrstuvwxyz{zyxwvutsrqpon
```

ANS:

```
1    ' Exercise 8.28 Solution
2    Option Explicit
3    Dim mChars As String
4
5    Private Sub Form_Load()
6       Dim curPos As Integer, c As Integer
7       Dim decPos As Integer, s As String
8       Dim d As Integer, x As Integer, y As Integer
9
10      curPos = 1
11      mChars = "abcdefghijklmnopqrstuvwxyz{"
12
13      For c = 1 To 14
14         s = Space$(14 - c)
15         x = c
16
17         For d = 1 To c
18            s = s & Mid$(mChars, x, 1)
19            x = x + 1
20         Next d
21
22         y = x - 2
23
24         For d = 1 To c - 1
25            s = s & Mid$(mChars, y, 1)
26            y = y - 1
27         Next d
28
29         Call lstBox.AddItem(s)
30      Next c
31
32   End Sub
```

8.29   Modify Fig. 8.31 to **Deal** the cards more efficiently. Only rewrite **Deal** and use only the topics discussed in Chapters 1 through 8.

ANS:

```
1   ' Exercise 8.29 Solution
2   Option Explicit
3   Dim mSuit(1 To 4) As String, mFace(1 To 13) As String
4   Dim mDeck(1 To 4, 1 To 13) As Integer
5
6   Private Sub Form_Load()
7      mSuit(1) = "Hearts"
8      mSuit(2) = "Diamonds"
9      mSuit(3) = "Clubs"
10     mSuit(4) = "Spades"
11
12     mFace(1) = "Ace"
13     mFace(2) = "Deuce"
14     mFace(3) = "Three"
15     mFace(4) = "Four"
16     mFace(5) = "Five"
17     mFace(6) = "Six"
18     mFace(7) = "Seven"
19     mFace(8) = "Eight"
20     mFace(9) = "Nine"
21     mFace(10) = "Ten"
22     mFace(11) = "Jack"
23     mFace(12) = "Queen"
24     mFace(13) = "King"
25
26     Call Randomize
27  End Sub
28
29  Private Sub cmdShuffle_Click()
30     Call lstOutput.Clear
31     Call Shuffle
32     Call Deal
33  End Sub
34
35  Private Sub Shuffle()
36     Dim card As Integer, row As Integer, column As Integer
37
38     Call ZeroDeckArray
39
40     For card = 1 To 52
41        Do
42           row = 1 + Int(Rnd() * UBound(mSuit))
43           column = 1 + Int(Rnd() * UBound(mFace))
44        Loop While mDeck(row, column) <> 0
45
46        mDeck(row, column) = card
47     Next
48
49  End Sub
50
51  Private Sub Deal()
52     Dim card As Integer, row As Integer, column As Integer
53     Dim found As Boolean
54
55     For card = 1 To 52
56        row = 1
57        found = False
58
59        While row <= 4 And found = False
60           column = 1
61
62           While column <= 13 And found = False
63              If mDeck(row, column) = card Then
64                 Call lstOutput.AddItem(mFace(column) & " of " & mSuit(row))
```

```
65                    found = True
66                End If
67
68                column = column + 1
69            Wend
70
71            row = row + 1
72        Wend
73    Next card
74 End Sub
75
76 Private Sub ZeroDeckArray()
77    Dim row As Integer, column As Integer
78
79    For row = LBound(mSuit) To UBound(mSuit)
80
81        For column = LBound(mFace) To UBound(mFace)
82            mDeck(row, column) = 0
83        Next column
84
85    Next row
86
87 End Sub
```

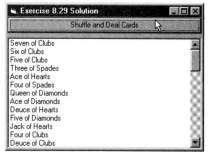

8.30   Law enforcement agencies often get partial descriptions of suspect license plate numbers and have to search for license plate numbers that match the description. Create a program that will allow a local law enforcement agency to determine how many license plate numbers match a partial description. Randomly create 500 6-character long license plate numbers and store them in an array. Allow the user to search for partial plate numbers of 3 or 4 digits. Note: License plate numbers can contain both digits and letters.

    ANS:

```
1  ' Exercise 8.30 Solution
2  Option Explicit
3  Dim mPlates(1 To 500) As String
4
5  Private Sub Form_Load()
6     Dim c As Integer, alphaNumeric As String, j As Integer
7
8     Call Randomize
9     alphaNumeric = "0123456789abcdefghijklmnopqrstuvwxyz"
10    Call lstPatterns.AddItem("  ?         Any one character")
11    Call lstPatterns.AddItem("  *         Multiple characters")
12    Call lstPatterns.AddItem("[chars]    Any one character " & _
13                       "in chars")
14    Call lstPatterns.AddItem("[!chars]   Any one character " & _
15                       "not in chars")
16
17    For c = 1 To 500
18
19        For j = 1 To 6
20            mPlates(c) = mPlates(c) & Mid$(alphaNumeric, _
21                      Int(Rnd() * Len(alphaNumeric)) + 1, 1)
22        Next j
23
24    Next c
25 End Sub
```

```
26
27  Private Sub cmdSearch_Click()
28     Dim i As Integer, b As Boolean
29
30     Call lstMatches.Clear
31
32     For i = 1 To 500
33
34        If mPlates(i) Like txtPattern.Text Then
35           Call lstMatches.AddItem(mPlates(i))
36           b = True
37        End If
38     Next i
39
40     If b = False Then
41        Call lstMatches.AddItem("No matches found.")
42     End If
43  End Sub
```

```
 Exercise 8.30 Solution                                           _ □ ×

  Pattern:                    Pattern descriptions:
  w[1-9]?"                     ?        Any one character
                              *        Multiple characters
  Matches:                   [chars]   Any one character in chars
  ┌──────────┐    ┌────────┐ [!chars]  Any one character not in chars
  │ w4anne   │    │ Search │
  │ w1mth5   │    └────────┘
  │ w8q2ay   │
  │ w87s3z   │
  └──────────┘
```

Special Section: Advanced String Manipulation Exercises

The preceding exercises are keyed to the text and designed to test the reader's understanding of fundamental string manipulation concepts. This section includes a collection of intermediate and advanced string manipulation exercises. The reader should find these problems challenging, yet entertaining. The problems vary considerably in difficulty. Some require an hour or two of program writing and implementation. Others are useful for lab assignments that might require two or three weeks of study and implementation. Some are challenging term projects.

8.31 *(Text Analysis)* The availability of computers with string manipulation capabilities has resulted in some rather interesting approaches to analyzing the writings of great authors. Much attention has been focused on whether William Shakespeare ever lived. Some scholars believe there is substantial evidence indicating that Christopher Marlowe or other authors actually penned the masterpieces attributed to Shakespeare. Researchers have used computers to find similarities in the writings of these two authors. This exercise examines three methods for analyzing texts with a computer.

   a) Write a program that reads several lines of text from the keyboard and displays a table indicating the number of occurrences of each letter of the alphabet in the text. For example, the phrase

   To be, or not to be: that is the question:

   contains one "a," two "b's," no "c's," etc.

   b) Write a program that reads several lines of text and displays a table indicating the number of one-letter words, two-letter words, three-letter words, etc. appearing in the text. For example, the phrase

   Whether 'tis nobler in the mind to suffer

   contains

Word length	Occurrences
1	0
2	2
3	1
4	2 (including 'tis)
5	0
6	2
7	1

c) Write a program that reads several lines of text and displays a table indicating the number of occurrences of each different word in the text. The first version of your program should include the words in the table in the same order in which they appear in the text. For example, the lines

> **To be, or not to be: that is the question:**
> **Whether 'tis nobler in the mind to suffer**

contain the words "to" three times, the word "be" two times, the word "or" once, etc. A more interesting (and useful) printout should then be attempted in which the words are sorted alphabetically.

ANS:

```
1   ' Exercise 8.31 Part A Solution
2   Option Explicit
3   Dim mCounters(97 To 122) As Integer
4   Dim mAlphabet As String
5
6   Private Sub Form_Load()
7       mAlphabet = "abcdefghijklmnopqrstuvwxyz"
8   End Sub
9
10  Private Sub cmdEnter_Click()
11      Dim s As String, current As Integer
12      Dim char As String, c As Integer
13
14      Call lstList.Clear
15      s = txtString.Text
16      s = LCase$(s)
17
18      For c = 1 To Len(mAlphabet)
19          current = 1
20          char = Mid$(mAlphabet, c, 1)
21          current = InStr(current, s, char)
22
23          While current <> 0
24              mCounters(Asc(char)) = mCounters(Asc(char)) + 1
25              current = current + 1
26              current = InStr(current, s, char)
27          Wend
28
29          Call lstList.AddItem("Found " & mCounters(Asc(char)) & " " & _
30                              char & " character(s).")
31      Next c
32
33  End Sub
```

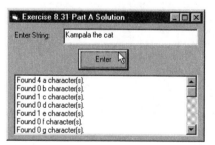

```
1   ' Exercise 8.31 Part B Solution
2   Option Explicit
3   Dim mCounters(1 To 10) As Integer
4
5   Private Sub cmdEnter_Click()
6       Dim s As String, length As Integer
7       Dim c As Integer, tokens() As String
8
9       Call lstList.Clear
10      s = txtString.Text
11      tokens = Split(LCase$(s))
```

```
12
13        For c = LBound(tokens) To UBound(tokens)
14           length = Len(tokens(c))
15
16           If length > 10 Then
17              Exit Sub
18           End If
19
20           mCounters(length) = mCounters(length) + 1
21        Next c
22
23        For c = 1 To 10
24           Call lstList.AddItem("Found " & mCounters(c) & _
25                                " word(s) of " & _
26                                c & " letter(s).")
27        Next c
28
29     End Sub
```

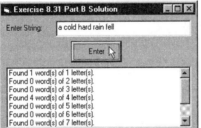

```
1     ' Exercise 8.31 Part C Solution
2     Option Explicit
3     Dim mCounters() As Integer
4     Dim mWords() As String
5     Dim mSize As Integer
6
7     Private Sub Form_Load()
8        mSize = 1
9        ReDim mWords(mSize)
10       mWords(mSize) = " "
11    End Sub
12
13    Private Sub cmdEnter_Click()
14       Dim s As String, tokens() As String
15       Dim result As Integer, c As Integer
16
17       Call lstList.Clear
18       s = txtString.Text
19       tokens = Split(LCase$(s))
20
21       For c = LBound(tokens) To UBound(tokens)
22          result = modLinear.LinearSearch(mWords, tokens(c))
23
24          If result = -1 Then
25             mSize = mSize + 1
26             ReDim Preserve mCounters(mSize)
27             ReDim Preserve mWords(mSize)
28             mWords(mSize) = tokens(c)
29             mCounters(mSize) = mCounters(mSize) + 1
30          Else
31             mCounters(result) = mCounters(result) + 1
32          End If
33
34       Next c
35
36       Call Display
37    End Sub
```

```
38
39   Public Sub Display()
40      Dim j As Integer
41
42      For j = (LBound(mWords) + 2) To UBound(mWords)
43         Call lstList.AddItem(mWords(j) & " appeared " & _
44                           mCounters(j) & " time(s).")
45      Next j
46
47   End Sub
```

```
48   ' Code module modLinear.bas
49   Option Explicit
50
51   Function LinearSearch(a() As String, key As String) As Integer
52      Dim x As Integer
53
54      For x = LBound(a) To UBound(a)
55
56         If a(x) = key Then
57            LinearSearch = x    ' Return index
58            Exit Function
59         End If
60
61      Next x
62
63      LinearSearch = -1         ' Value not found
64   End Function
```

8.32 *(Check Protection)* Computers are frequently employed in check-writing systems such as payroll applications and accounts payable applications. Many strange stories circulate regarding weekly paychecks being printed (by mistake) for amounts in excess of $1 million. Incorrect amounts are printed by computerized check-writing systems because of human error and/or machine failure. Systems designers build controls into their systems to prevent erroneous checks from being issued.

Another serious problem is the intentional alteration of a check amount by someone who intends to cash a check fraudulently. To prevent a dollar amount from being altered, most computerized check-writing systems employ a technique called *check protection.*

Checks designed for imprinting by computer contain a fixed number of spaces in which the computer may print an amount. Suppose a paycheck contains eight blank spaces in which the computer is supposed to print the amount of a weekly paycheck. If the amount is large, then all eight of those spaces will be filled, for example:

```
1,230.60 (check amount)
--------
12345678 (position numbers)
```

On the other hand, if the amount is less than $1000, then several of the spaces would ordinarily be left blank. For example,

```
   99.87
--------
12345678
```

contains three blank spaces. If a check is printed with blank spaces, it is easier for someone to alter the amount of the check. To prevent a check from being altered, many check-writing systems insert *leading asterisks* to protect the amount, as follows:

```
***99.87
--------
12345678
```

Write a program that inputs a dollar amount to be printed on a check, and then prints the amount in check-protected format with leading asterisks if necessary. Assume that nine spaces are available for printing the amount.

ANS:

```
1   ' Exercise 8.32 Solution
2   Option Explicit
3
4   Private Sub cmdEnter_Click()
5      Dim s As String, length As Integer
6
7      s = txtInput.Text
8      length = Len(s)
9
10     If length = 9 Then
11        lblDisplay.Caption = s
12     Else
13        lblDisplay.Caption = String$(9 - length, "*") & s
14     End If
15
16  End Sub
```

8.33 (*Writing the Word Equivalent of a Check Amount*) Continuing the discussion of Exercise 8.30, we reiterate the importance of designing check-writing systems to prevent alteration of check amounts. One common security method requires that the check amount be written both in numbers and "spelled out" in words as well. Even if someone is able to alter the numerical amount of the check, it is extremely difficult to change the amount in words.

Many computerized check-writing systems do not print the amount of the check in words. Perhaps the main reason for this omission is the fact that most high-level languages used in commercial applications do not contain adequate string manipulation features. Another reason is that the logic for writing word equivalents of check amounts is somewhat involved.

Write a program that inputs a numeric check amount and writes the word equivalent of the amount. For example, the amount 112.43 should be written as

ONE HUNDRED TWELVE and 43/100

ANS:

```
1   ' Exercise 8.33 Solution
2   ' Note: This solution only handles values upto $99.99
3   ' This program is easily modified to process larger values
4   Option Explicit
5   Option Base 1
6   Dim mDigits() As Variant
7   Dim mTeens() As Variant
8   Dim mTens() As Variant
9
10  Private Sub Form_Load()
11     mDigits = Array("ONE", "TWO", "THREE", "FOUR", "FIVE", _
12                     "SIX", "SEVEN", "EIGHT", "NINE")
13     mTeens = Array("TEN", "ELEVEN", "TWELVE", "THIRTEEN", _
14                    "FOURTEEN", "FIFTEEN", "SIXTEEN", _
15                    "SEVENTEEN", "EIGHTEEN", "NINETEEN")
16     mTens = Array("TEN", "TWENTY", "THIRTY", "FORTY", "FIFTY", _
17                   "SIXTY", "SEVENTY", "EIGHTY", "NINETY")
18  End Sub
19
20  Private Sub cmdEnter_Click()
21     Dim s As String, cents As Integer, dollars As Integer
22     Dim moneyString As String, digits1 As Integer
23     Dim digits2 As Integer
```

```
24
25      s = txtInput.Text
26      cents = Right$(s, 2)
27      dollars = Left$(s, InStr(s, ".") - 1)
28
29      If dollars < 10 Then
30         moneyString = mDigits(dollars)
31      ElseIf dollars < 20 Then
32         moneyString = mTeens(dollars - 10)
33      Else
34         digits1 = dollars \ 10
35         digits2 = (dollars Mod 10)
36
37         If digits2 = 0 Then
38            moneyString = mTens(digits1)
39         Else
40            moneyString = mTens(digits1) & "-" & mDigits(digits2)
41         End If
42
43      End If
44
45      lblDisplay.Caption = moneyString & " Dollars and " & cents & "/100"
46   End Sub
```

8.34   *(Morse Code)* Perhaps the most famous of all coding schemes is the Morse code, developed by Samuel Morse in 1832 for use with the telegraph system. The Morse code assigns a series of dots and dashes to each letter of the alphabet, each digit, and a few special characters (such as period, comma, colon, and semicolon). In sound-oriented systems, the dot represents a short sound and the dash represents a long sound. Other representations of dots and dashes are used with light-oriented systems and signal-flag systems.

Separation between words is indicated by a space, or, quite simply, the absence of a dot or dash. In a sound-oriented system, a space is indicated by a short period of time during which no sound is transmitted. The international version of the Morse code appears in Fig. 6.44.

Write a program that reads an English language phrase and encodes the phrase into Morse code. Also write a program that reads a phrase in Morse code and converts the phrase into the English language equivalent. Use one blank between each Morse-coded letter and three blanks between each Morse-coded word.

8.35   *(A Metric Conversion Program)* Write a program that will assist the user with metric conversions. Your program should allow the user to specify the names of the units as strings (i.e., centimeters, liters, grams, etc. for the metric system and inches, quarts, pounds, etc. for the English system) and should respond to simple questions such as

```
"How many inches are in 2 meters?"
"How many liters are in 10 quarts?"
```

Your program should recognize invalid conversions. For example, the question

```
"How many feet are there in 5 kilograms?"
```

is not a meaningful question because **"feet"** are units of length while **"kilograms"** are units of mass.

Special Section: Challenging String Manipulation Projects

8.36   *(Project: A Spelling Checker)* Many popular word processing software packages have built-in spell checkers.

In this project, you are asked to develop your own spell-checker utility. We make suggestions to help get you started. You should then consider adding more capabilities. Use a computerized dictionary (if you have access to one) as a source of words.

Why do we type so many words with incorrect spellings? In some cases, it is because we simply do not know the correct spelling, so we make a "best guess." In some cases, it is because we transpose two letters (e.g., "defualt" instead of "default"). Sometimes we double-type a letter accidentally (e.g., "hanndy" instead of "handy"). Sometimes we type a nearby key instead of the one we intended (e.g., "biryhday" instead of "birthday"). And so on.

Design and implement a spell-checker program in Visual Basic. Your program should maintain an array **wordList** of strings. Enable the user to enter these strings. Note: In Chapters 14, 15 and 19 we introduce file processing and networking. Once you have these capabilities, you can obtain the words for the spell checker from a computerized dictionary stored in a file.

Your program should ask a user to enter a word. The program should then look up that word in the **wordList** array. If the word is present in the array, your program should print "**Word is spelled correctly**."

If the word is not present in the array, your program should print "**word is not spelled correctly**." Then your program should try to locate other words in **wordList** that might be the word the user intended to type. For example, you can try all possible single transpositions of adjacent letters to discover that the word "default" is a direct match to a word in **wordList**. Of course, this implies that your program will check all other single transpositions, such as "edfault," "dfeault," "deafult," "defalut" and "defautl." When you find a new word that matches one in **wordList**, print that word in a message such as, "**Did you mean "default?"**"

Implement other tests, such as replacing each double letter with a single letter and any other tests you can develop to improve the value of your spell checker.

8.37   *(Project: A Crossword Puzzle Generator)* Most people have worked a crossword puzzle, but few have ever attempted to generate one. Generating a crossword puzzle is suggested here as a string manipulation project requiring substantial sophistication and effort.

There are many issues the programmer must resolve to get even the simplest crossword puzzle generator program working. For example, how does one represent the grid of a crossword puzzle inside the computer? Should one use a series of strings, or should double-subscripted arrays be used?

The programmer needs a source of words (i.e., a computerized dictionary) that can be directly referenced by the program. In what form should these words be stored to facilitate the complex manipulations required by the program?

The really ambitious reader will want to generate the "clues" portion of the puzzle, in which the brief hints for each "across" word and each "down" word are printed for the puzzle worker. Merely printing a version of the blank puzzle itself is not a simple problem.

Chapter 9 Solutions
Graphics

9.3 Fill in the blanks in each of the following:

a) The _____ property determines how "thick" a **Line** control line is.

ANS: BorderWidth.

b) The curved portion of a sector is an _____.

ANS: arc.

c) RGB is short for _____, _____ and _____.

ANS: red, green, blue.

d) Most graphical images are measured in units of _____.

ANS: pixels.

e) **Printer** method _____ kills a print job.

ANS: KillDoc.

9.4 [CD] State which of the following are *true* and which are *false*. If *false*, explain why.

a) A bit has a value of either 0 or 1.

ANS: True.

b) Visual Basic's default coordinate system is polar coordinates.

ANS: False.

c) **Line** controls are not affected by **AutoRedraw**.

ANS: True.

d) Method **Circle** can be used to draw sectors.

ANS: True.

e) **PictureBox** controls are simplified **Image** controls.

ANS: False. **PictureBox** controls contain more functionality than **Image** controls.

f) The pixel coordinate *(0, 0)* is located at the exact center of the screen.

ANS: False. *(0, 0)* represents the upper-left corner of the screen.

9.5 Write a program that draws a tetrahedron (i.e., a pyramid).

ANS:

```
1   ' Exercise 9.5 Solution
2   Option Explicit
3
4   Private Sub Form_load()
5      Scale (-200, 200)-(200, -200)
6
7      Line (0, 150)-(150, -85)
8      Line (0, 150)-(70, -100)
9      Line (0, 150)-(-150, -85)
10     Line (0, 150)-(-20, -75)
11     Line (-150, -85)-(-20, -75)
12     Line (70, -100)-(150, -85)
13     Line (150, -85)-(-20, -75)
14     Line (-150, -85)-(70, -100)
15  End Sub
```

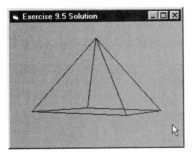

9.6   [CD] Write a program that draws a solid cube. Each of the visible faces should be a different color.
       ANS:

```
1   Private Sub Form_load()
2      Scale (-200, 200)-(200, -200)
3
4      ' Draw yellow face
5      ForeColor = vbYellow
6      FillColor = vbYellow
7      Line (0, 0)-(100, -100), , B
8
9      ' Draw blue face
10     ForeColor = vbBlue
11     Dim y As Integer, y2 As Integer
12
13     y2 = -100
14
15     For y = -50 To 50
16        Line (100, y2)-(150, y)
17        y2 = y2 + 1
18     Next y
19
20     ' Draw green face
21     ForeColor = vbGreen
22     Dim x As Integer, x2 As Integer
23
24     x2 = 0
25
26     For x = 50 To 150
27        Line (x2, 0)-(x, 50)
28        x2 = x2 + 1
29     Next x
30
31  End Sub
```

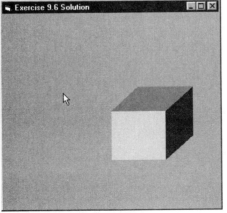

9.7   Write a program that displays four triangles of different sizes. Each triangle should be filled with a different color (or pattern).

ANS:

```
1   ' Exercise 9.7 Solution
2   Option Explicit
3
4   Private Sub Form_Load()
5      Dim x As Integer, y As Integer
6
7      Call Randomize
8      Scale (-100, 500)-(1000, -1000)
9
10     y = 490
11     For x = 400 To 0 Step -1
12        Line (y, 0)-(y, x), vbYellow
13        y = y - 1
14     Next x
15
16     y = 490
17     For x = 300 To 0 Step -1
18        Line (0, y)-(x, y), vbGreen
19        y = y - 1
20     Next x
21
22     y = -100
23     For x = 150 To 0 Step -1
24        Line (300 - x, y)-(x, y), vbWhite
25        y = y - 1
26     Next x
27
28     y = -400
29     For x = 200 To 0 Step -1
30        Line (400 - x, y)-(x, y), vbRed
31        y = y - 4    ' Make triangle steeper
32     Next x
33
34   End Sub
```

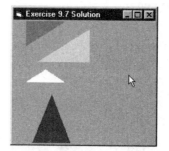

9.8   [CD] Write a program that draws a series of lines of different lengths in different colors.
       ANS:

```
1   ' Exercise 9.8 Solution
2   Option Explicit
3
4   Private Sub tmrTimer_Timer()
5      Call Cls
6      Call DrawLines
7   End Sub
8
9   Private Sub DrawLines()
10     Dim n As Integer
11
12     Call Randomize
13
14     For n = 1 To 10
15        Line (Rnd() * Width, Rnd() * Height)- _
```

```
16                (Rnd() * Width, Rnd() * Height), _
17                RGB(Rnd() * 256, Rnd() * 256, Rnd() * 256)
18       Next n
19
20   End Sub
```

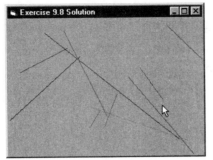

9.9   Write a program that draws a series of eight concentric circles each separated by 10 pixels.
       ANS:

```
1    ' Exercise 9.9 Solution
2    Option Explicit
3
4    Private Sub Form_Load()
5       Dim y As Integer
6
7       Scale (0, 0)-(300, 300)
8
9       For y = 1 To 8
10          Circle (ScaleWidth / 2, ScaleHeight / 2), y * 10
11      Next y
12   End Sub
```

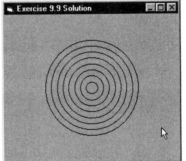

9.10   Write a program that reads four numbers from the user and graphs the numbers as a pie chart.
       ANS:

```
1    ' Exercise 9.10 Solution
2    Option Explicit
3
4    Private Sub Form_Load()
5       picPict.Scale (-10, 10)-(10, -10)
6    End Sub
7
8    Private Sub cmdGraph_Click()
9       Dim a(3) As Integer, i As Integer
10      Dim total As Integer, rads(3) As Double
11      Const PI As Double = 3.14159
12
13      Call picPict.Cls
14
15      For i = 0 To 3
16          a(i) = txtInput(i).Text
```

```
17          total = total + a(i)
18      Next i
19
20      For i = 0 To 3
21          rads(i) = a(i) / total * 2 * PI
22      Next i
23
24      picPict.ForeColor = vbYellow
25      picPict.Circle (0, 0), 4, , 0, -rads(0)
26
27      picPict.FillStyle = vbDownwardDiagonal
28      picPict.FillColor = vbBlue
29      picPict.Circle (0, 0), 4, , -rads(0), -(rads(0) + rads(1))
30
31      picPict.FillStyle = vbCross
32      picPict.FillColor = vbWhite
33      picPict.Circle (0, 0), 4, , -(rads(0) + rads(1)), _
34                                   -(rads(0) + rads(1) + rads(2))
35
36      picPict.FillStyle = vbHorizontalLine
37      picPict.FillColor = vbRed
38      picPict.Circle (0, 0), 4, , -(rads(1) + rads(2) + rads(0)), _
39                                   -(rads(2) + rads(3) + rads(0) + rads(1))
40  End Sub
```

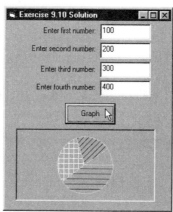

9.11 Modify Exercise 9.10 to graph the numbers as a bar graph.
ANS:

```
1   ' Exercise 9.11 Solution
2   Option Explicit
3
4   Private Sub cmdGraph_Click()
5       Dim a(3) As Integer, i As Integer
6       Dim total As Integer, x As Integer
7
8       Call picPict.Cls
9
10      For i = 0 To 3
11          a(i) = txtInput(i).Text
12          total = total + a(i)
13      Next i
14
15      picPict.Scale (0, total)-(200, 0)
16      picPict.ForeColor = vbYellow
17
18      picPict.Line (0, 0.25 * total)-(picPict.Width, 0.25 * total)
19      picPict.Line (0, 0.5 * total)-(picPict.Width, 0.5 * total)
20      picPict.Line (0, 0.75 * total)-(picPict.Width, 0.75 * total)
21
22      picPict.ForeColor = vbBlack
23      x = 40
```

```
24
25      For i = 0 To 3
26         picPict.FillColor = QBColor(i + 1)
27         picPict.Line (x + 2, a(i))-(x + 30, 0), , B
28         x = x + 30
29      Next i
30
31      picPict.ForeColor = vbBlack
32      picPict.CurrentX = 0
33      picPict.CurrentY = Int(0.25 * total) + 6
34      picPict.Print Int(0.25 * total)
35
36      picPict.CurrentY = Int(0.5 * total) + 5
37      picPict.Print Int(0.5 * total)
38      picPict.CurrentY = Int(0.75 * total) + 6
39      picPict.Print Int(0.75 * total)
40   End Sub
```

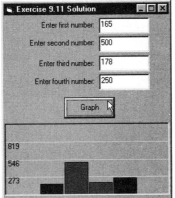

9.12   [CD] Write a program that flips a bitmap image horizontally.
        ANS:

```
1    ' Exercise 9.12 Solution
2    Option Explicit
3    Dim mPicture As IPictureDisp        ' Type that represents a picture
4
5    Private Sub Form_Load()
6       Set mPicture = LoadPicture("\vb_solutions\ch09\ex09_12\bird10.bmp")
7       Call PaintPicture(mPicture, 20, 20)
8    End Sub
9
10   Private Sub cmdFlip_Click()
11      Call PaintPicture(mPicture, 180, 20, -39)    ' 39 is the picture width
12      cmdFlip.Enabled = False
13   End Sub
```

9.13   Write a program that flips a bitmap image vertically.
        ANS:

```
1    ' Exercise 9.13 Solution
2    Option Explicit
3    Dim mPicture As IPictureDisp        ' Type that represents a picture
4
```

```
5   Private Sub Form_Load()
6      Set mPicture = LoadPicture("\vb_solutions\ch09\ex09_12\bird10.bmp")
7      Call PaintPicture(mPicture, 20, 20)
8   End Sub
9
10  Private Sub cmdFlip_Click()
11     Call PaintPicture(mPicture, 160, 60, , -39)
12     cmdFlip.Enabled = False
13  End Sub
```

9.14 Write a program that displays a linear gradient.
ANS:

```
1   ' Exercise 9.14 Solution
2   ' Program displays a red gradient
3   Option Explicit
4
5   Private Sub Form_Load()
6      Dim r As Integer, g As Integer, b As Integer
7      Dim x As Long
8
9      For x = 0 To ScaleWidth
10        Line (x, 0)-(x, ScaleHeight), RGB(r, g, b)
11        r = r + 1
12
13        If r = 255 Then
14           r = 0
15           g = g + 1
16
17           If g = 255 Then
18              g = 0
19              b = b + 1
20
21              If b = 255 Then
22                 b = 0
23              End If
24
25           End If
26
27        End If
28
29     Next x
30
31  End Sub
```

9.15 Write a program that displays a circular gradient.

ANS:

```
1    ' Exercise 9.15 Solution
2    ' Program displays a red gradient.
3    Option Explicit
4
5    Private Sub Form_Load()
6       Dim r As Integer, g As Integer, b As Integer
7       Dim x As Long
8
9       Scale (-285, 285)-(285, -285)
10
11      For x = 0 To ScaleWidth
12         Circle (0, 0), x, RGB(r, g, b)
13         r = r + 1
14
15         If r = 255 Then
16            r = 0
17            g = g + 1
18
19            If g = 255 Then
20               g = 0
21               b = b + 1
22
23               If b = 255 Then
24                  b = 0
25               End If
26
27            End If
28
29         End If
30
31      Next x
32
33   End Sub
```

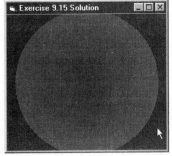

9.16 Write a program that draws a grid over an image displayed in a **PictureBox**. Provide a **CheckBox** that controls when the grid is visible.

ANS:

```
1    ' Exercise 9.16 Solution
2    Option Explicit
3    Dim mImage As IPictureDisp
4
5    Private Sub Form_Load()
6       Set mImage = LoadPicture("\vb_solutions\ch09\" & _
7                                "ex09_16\cool.jpg")
8
9       picPict.Picture = mImage
10   End Sub
11
```

```
12  Private Sub chkGrid_Click()
13     Dim x As Integer, y As Integer
14
15     If chkGrid.Value Then
16        For x = 0 To picPict.ScaleWidth Step 100
17
18           For y = 0 To picPict.ScaleHeight Step 100
19              picPict.Line (0, y)-(picPict.ScaleWidth, y)
20              picPict.Line (x, 0)-(x, picPict.ScaleHeight)
21           Next y
22
23        Next x
24     Else
25        picPict.Picture = mImage
26     End If
27  End Sub
```

9.17 Write a program that draws each **Shape** control shape with a different **BorderStyle**, **FillStyle** and **FillColor**.
ANS:

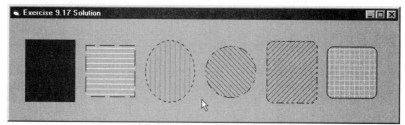

9.18 Write a program that displays a **Line** control line and allows the user to move the line by specifying values for **X1**, **Y1**, **X2** and **Y2**.
ANS:

```
1   ' Exercise 9.18 Solution
2   Option Explicit
3   Dim mX1 As Integer
4   Dim mX2 As Integer
5   Dim mY1 As Integer
6   Dim mY2 As Integer
7
8   Private Sub Form_Load()
9      picPict.Scale (-100, 100)-(100, -100)
10
11     mX1 = -100
12     mY1 = 100
13     mX2 = 100
14     mY2 = -100
15
16     Call Draw
17  End Sub
18
```

```
19    Private Sub cmdDraw_Click()
20       mX1 = txtInput(0).Text
21       mY1 = txtInput(1).Text
22       mX2 = txtInput(2).Text
23       mY2 = txtInput(3).Text
24       Call Draw
25    End Sub
26
27    Private Sub Draw()
28       Call picPict.Cls
29       picPict.Line (mX1, mY1)-(mX2, mY2)
30    End Sub
```

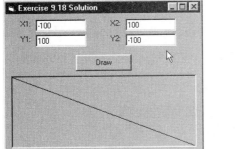

9.19   Modify either Fig. 9.9, 9.22, 9.25 or 9.29 to send the shape to the printer. If the example you are modifying uses a **Timer**, remove the **Timer** and replace it with a button. Each time the user presses the button, send the shape to the printer. Use the **Zoom** property to increase the size of the displayed image.

9.20   Although not discussed in line in the chapter, the **Common Dialog** control is capable of displaying a **Printer Common Dialog**. Modify Fig. 9.34 to display the **Printer Common Dialog** before information is sent to the printer. What is printed when the user changes the copies in the **Common Dialog** to an **Integer** value greater than 1?
         ANS:

```
1    ' Exercise 9.20 Solution
2    Option Explicit
3
4    Private Sub cmdPrint_Click()
5       Dim numberOfCopies As Integer, i As Integer
6
7       Call dlgPrinter.ShowPrinter
8       numberOfCopies = dlgPrinter.Copies
9       Printer.PrintQuality = vbPRPQDraft
10
11       For i = numberOfCopies To 0 Step -1
12          Call PrintForm        ' Print the form
13
14          ' Printing appears on a separate page
15          Printer.Print "Some Printer property values: "
16          Printer.Print "DriverName: " & Printer.DriverName
17          Printer.Print "Port: " & Printer.Port
18          Printer.Print "Copies: " & Printer.Copies
19          Printer.EndDoc        ' Send to printer
20       Next i
21    End Sub
```

9.21   Write a program that creates a tiled background (i.e., the same image repeated over the entire background) on the form using method **PaintPicture**.

ANS:

```
1   ' Exercise 9.21 Solution
2   Option Explicit
3   Dim mImage As IPictureDisp
4
5   Private Sub Form_Load()
6       Set mImage = LoadPicture("\vb_solutions\ch09\ex09_21\bird12.bmp")
7   End Sub
8
9   Private Sub Form_Resize()
10      Dim x As Integer, y As Integer
11
12      For x = 0 To Width Step mImage.Width \ 2
13          For y = 0 To Height Step mImage.Height \ 2
14              Call PaintPicture(mImage, x, y)
15          Next y
16      Next x
17  End Sub
```

9.22 Write a program that centers text input by the user on the form. Each time text is input, the background should be cleared before the centered text is drawn.

ANS:

```
1   ' Exercise 9.22 Solution
2   Option Explicit
3
4   Private Sub Form_Load()
5       lblDisplay.Visible = False
6
7       ' Size the Label to the text it displays
8       lblDisplay.AutoSize = True
9   End Sub
10
11  Private Sub cmdEnter_Click()
12      Dim s As String
13
14      lblDisplay.Caption = txtInput.Text
15      lblDisplay.Top = 0.5 * Height - 0.5 * lblDisplay.Height
16      lblDisplay.Left = 0.5 * Width - 0.5 * lblDisplay.Width
17      lblDisplay.Visible = True
18  End Sub
```

9.23   Write a program that draws a box, an oval, an arrow, and a diamond on the form.
           ANS:

```
1   ' Exercise 9.23 Solution
2   Option Explicit
3
4   Private Sub Form_Load()
5       Scale (-500, 100)-(500, -250)
6
7       Line (-400, 0)-(-200, -200), , B
8       Circle (-100, -100), 100, , , , 1.5
9
10      ' Diamond
11      Line (100, 50)-(150, -80)
12      Line (100, 50)-(50, -80)
13      Line (50, -80)-(100, -210)
14      Line (100, -210)-(150, -80)
15
16      ' Arrow
17      Line (250, -200)-(250, 0)
18      Line (250, 0)-(275, 0)
19      Line (275, 0)-(250, 50)
20      Line (250, 50)-(225, 0)
21      Line (225, 0)-(250, 0)
22  End Sub
```

9.24   (*Hangman*) Write a graphical version of Exercise 8.23. Use the drawing techniques discussed in this chapter to draw the person and the gallow.

9.25   Write a program that allows the user to demonstrate the various **RasterOp** constants used with **PaintPicture**. Consult the on-line documentation for the available **RasterOp** constants.

Chapter 10 Solutions
Basic Graphical User Interface Concepts

10.3   [CD] Fill in the blanks in each of the following:
   a)   _____ is the suggested prefix for a **Slider**.
   ANS: sld.
   b)   The _____ dialog is used to add ActiveX controls to the toolbox.
   ANS: Components.
   c)   Property _____ determines the style of a **ComboBox** or **ListBox**.
   ANS: Style.
   d)   _____ is the suggested prefix for a **MaskEdit** control.
   ANS: msk.
   e)   _____ is the suggested prefix for a **ComboBox**.
   ANS: cbo.

10.4   [CD] State which are *true* and which are *false*. If *false*, explain why.
   a)   **ListBox**es can only contain **String**s.
   ANS: True.
   b)   **Slider**s are considered to be intrinsic controls.
   ANS: False. **Slider**s are ActiveX controls.
   c)   A scrollbar's **Orientation** property determines if it is vertical or horizontal.
   ANS: False. Two separate controls represent the scrollbars.
   d)   Pop-up menus are displayed (i.e., visible) when method **DisplayPopup** is called.
   ANS: False. Method **PopupMenu** displays a pop up menu.
   e)   **MaskEdit** controls are considered to be ActiveX controls.
   ANS: True.

10.5   Write a statement or statements to accomplish each of the following:
   a)   Display a **MsgBox** containing an exclamation point icon, an **OK** button, "**Installation**" in the title bar, and "**Insert disk #8 and press OK**" as the prompt.
   ANS: Call MsgBox("Insert disk #8 and press OK", , "Installation")
   b)   Assign the text in **TextBox txtBx** to **String** variable **s**.
   ANS: s = txtBx.Text
   c)   Print the fifth **ListBox** item from **lstBx** on the form.
   ANS: Print lstBx.List(5)
   d)   In **ComboBox cboBx**, make the third item the selected item.
   ANS: cboBx.Text = cboBx.List(3)

10.6   Write a program that allows the user to understand the relationship between Fahrenheit temperatures and Celsius temperatures. Use a vertical **Slider** to scroll through a range of Fahrenheit temperatures. Use a **Label** to display the equivalent Celsius temperature. The **Label** should be updated as the **Slider**'s value changes. Use the following formula:

$$celsius = 5 / 9 \times (fahrenheit - 32)$$

   ANS:

```
1  ' Exercise 10.6 Solution
2  Option Explicit
```

```
3
4    Private Sub Form_Load()
5        Call sldFahrenheit_Change
6    End Sub
7
8    Private Sub sldFahrenheit_Change()
9        lblCelsius.Caption = "(" & sldFahrenheit.Value & Chr$(176) & _
10                             " F) is " & _
11                             Int(5 / 9 * (sldFahrenheit.Value - 32)) & _
12                             Chr$(176) & " C"
13       txtBox.Text = sldFahrenheit.Value
14   End Sub
15
16   Private Sub txtBox_Change()
17       Dim t As Integer
18
19       If txtBox.Text = "" Or txtBox.Text = "-" Then
20          Exit Sub
21       End If
22
23       t = txtBox.Text
24
25       If t < sldFahrenheit.Min Or t > sldFahrenheit.Max Then
26          Call MsgBox("Invalid input.")
27          Exit Sub
28       End If
29
30       sldFahrenheit.Value = t
31       Call sldFahrenheit_Change
32   End Sub
```

10.7   [CD] Write a program that displays the names of 15 states in a **ComboBox**. When an item is selected from the **ComboBox** remove it.

ANS:

```
1    ' Exercise 10.7 Solution
2    Option Explicit
3
4    Private Sub Form_Load()
5        Call cboStates.AddItem("Kansas")
6        Call cboStates.AddItem("Mississippi")
7        Call cboStates.AddItem("Ohio")
8        Call cboStates.AddItem("Texas")
9        Call cboStates.AddItem("Alaska")
10       Call cboStates.AddItem("North Dakota")
11       Call cboStates.AddItem("South Dakota")
12       Call cboStates.AddItem("Nevada")
13       Call cboStates.AddItem("Vermont")
14       Call cboStates.AddItem("Idaho")
15   End Sub
16
17   Private Sub cboStates_Click()
18       Call cboStates.RemoveItem(cboStates.ListIndex)
19   End Sub
```

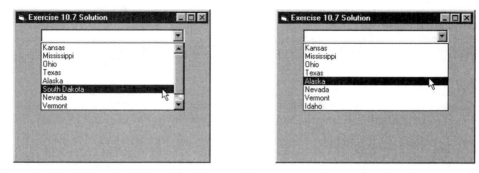

10.8   Modify your solution to Exercise 10.7 to add a **ListBox**. When the user selects an item from the **ComboBox**, remove the item from the **ComboBox** and add it to the **ListBox**. Your program should check to ensure that the **ComboBox** contains at least one item. If it does not, print a message using function **MsgBox** and terminate program execution.

ANS:

```
1   ' Exercise 10.8 Solution
2   Option Explicit
3
4   Private Sub Form_Load()
5      Call cboStates.AddItem("Iowa")
6      Call cboStates.AddItem("New Jersey")
7      Call cboStates.AddItem("Nebraska")
8      Call cboStates.AddItem("Delaware")
9      Call cboStates.AddItem("Colorado")
10     Call cboStates.AddItem("Illinois")
11     Call cboStates.AddItem("Wyoming")
12     Call cboStates.AddItem("Michigan")
13     Call cboStates.AddItem("Montana")
14     Call cboStates.AddItem("Kentucky")
15  End Sub
16
17  Private Sub cboStates_Click()
18     Call lstBox.AddItem(cboStates.List(cboStates.ListIndex))
19     Call cboStates.RemoveItem(cboStates.ListIndex)
20
21     If cboStates.ListCount = 0 Then
22        Call MsgBox("ComboBox is empty. Terminating.")
23        End
24     End If
25
26  End Sub
```

10.9   Write a program that allows the user to enter **String**s in a **TextBox**. Each **String** input is added to a **ListBox**. As each **String** is added to the **ListBox**, ensure that the **String**s are in sorted order. Any sorting routine used should be located in a separate code module (i.e., a standard module) for reuse purposes.

ANS:

```
1   ' Exercise 10.9 Solution
2   Option Explicit
3
4   Private Sub cmdAdd_Click()
5      ' lstBox's Sorted property has been set to True
```

```
6        Call lstBox.AddItem(txtInput.Text)
7    End Sub
```

10.10   Write a program that adds a series of social security numbers to a **ComboBox**. Use a **MaskEdit** control to input the social security numbers using a proper social security number format.

ANS:

```
1    ' Exercise 10.10 Solution
2    Option Explicit
3
4    Private Sub cmdAdd_Click()
5        cboSSN.Text = mskSSN.Text
6        Call cboSSN.AddItem(mskSSN.Text)
7    End Su
```

10.11   Write a program that plays "guess the number" as follows: Your program chooses the number to be guessed by selecting an **Integer** at random in the range 1-1000. The program then displays in a **Label**:

I have a number between 1 and 1000 can you guess my number?
Please enter your guess.

A **TextBox** is used to input the guess from the used. As each guess is input the **BackColor** should change to either red or blue. Red indicates that the user is getting "warmer" and blue indicates that the user is getting "colder." A second non-editable **TextBox** displays either "**Too High**" or "**Too Low**" to help the user zero in on the correct answer. When the users guesses correctly, "**Correct!**" is displayed and the input **TextBox** is disabled. Provide a button that allows the user to begin a new game.

ANS:

```
1    ' Exercise 10.11 Solution
2    Option Explicit
3    Dim mAnswer As Integer
4    Dim mGuess As Integer
5    Dim mGameOver As Boolean
6    Dim mLowest As Integer
7    Dim mHighest As Integer
8
9    Private Sub Form_Load()
10       Call GameSetUp
11       mLowest = 1
12       mHighest = 1000
13   End Sub
14
15   Private Sub cmdEnter_Click()
16
17       If mGameOver = False Then
18          mGuess = txtGuess.Text
19          Call CheckGuess
20       Else
21          Dim s As String
```

```vb
22
23          s = txtGuess.Text
24
25          If s = "Y" Or s = "y" Then
26             txtGuess.Text = ""
27             mGameOver = False
28             Call GameSetUp
29          Else
30             End
31          End If
32
33       End If
34
35    End Sub
36
37    Private Sub GameSetUp()
38       lblPrompt.Caption = "I have a number between 1 and 1000. " & _
39                           "Can you guess my number? Enter your guess."
40       mAnswer = GetNumber()
41    End Sub
42
43    Private Function GetNumber() As Integer
44       Call Randomize
45       GetNumber = 1 + Int(Rnd() * 1000)
46    End Function
47
48    Private Sub CheckGuess()
49
50       If mGuess = mAnswer Then
51          lblPrompt.Caption = "Excellent. You guessed the number! " & _
52                              "Would you like to play again (y or n)?"
53          BackColor = vbWhite
54          mLowest = 1000
55          mHighest = 0
56          mGameOver = True
57          Exit Sub
58       ElseIf mGuess < mAnswer Then
59          lblPrompt.Caption = "Too Low. Try again."
60
61          If mGuess < mLowest Then
62             BackColor = vbBlue
63          ElseIf mGuess > mLowest Then
64             mLowest = mGuess
65             BackColor = vbRed
66          End If
67
68       Else   ' mGuess > mAnswer
69          lblPrompt.Caption = "Too High. Try again."
70
71          If mGuess > mHighest Then
72             BackColor = vbBlue
73          ElseIf mGuess < mHighest Then
74             mHighest = mGuess
75             BackColor = vbRed
76          End If
77
78       End If
79
80    End Sub
```

10.12 **[CD]** Write a program that displays a circle of a random size and calculates and displays the area, radius, diameter and circumference. Use the following equations:

$$diameter = 2 \times radius$$
$$area = 3.14159 \times radius \wedge 2$$
$$circumference = 2 \times 3.14159 \times radius$$

All drawing should be done in a **PictureBox** and the results of the calculations should be displayed in a **ListBox**. Each time a button is pressed, a new circle should be displayed.

       ANS:

```
1   ' Exercise 10.12 Solution
2   Option Explicit
3
4   Private Sub Form_Load()
5      picDisplay.Scale (-50, 50)-(50, -50)
6   End Sub
7
8   Private Sub cmdDraw_Click()
9      Dim radius As Double
10
11     Call picDisplay.Cls
12     Call lstCircleData.Clear
13
14     radius = Rnd() * 50
15     picDisplay.Circle (0, 0), radius, vbWhite
16     Call lstCircleData.AddItem("Diameter: " & _
17                                Format$((2 * radius), _
18                                "Fixed"))
19     Call lstCircleData.AddItem("Area: " & _
20                                Format$((3.14159 * radius ^ 2), _
21                                "Fixed"))
22     Call lstCircleData.AddItem("Circumerence: " & _
23                                Format$((2 * 3.14159 * radius), _
24                                "Fixed"))
25  End Sub
```

10.13 Enhance your solution to Exercise 10.12 by allowing the user to alter the circle's radius with a scrollbar. The program should work for every radius in the range 100 to 200. As the radius changes, update the values in the **ListBox**. Set the initial radius to 150.

       ANS:

```
1   ' Exercise 10.13 Solution
2   Option Explicit
3
4   Private Sub Form_Load()
5      picDisplay.Scale (-550, 550)-(550, -550)
6      hsbScroll.TabStop = False
7      Call hsbScroll_Change
8   End Sub
9
```

```
10   Private Sub cmdDraw_Click()
11      Dim radius As Double
12
13      Call picDisplay.Cls
14      Call lstCircleData.Clear
15
16      radius = hsbScroll.Value
17      picDisplay.Circle (0, 0), radius, vbWhite
18      Call lstCircleData.AddItem("Diameter: " & _
19                                 Format$((2 * radius), _
20                                 "Fixed"))
21      Call lstCircleData.AddItem("Area: " & _
22                                 Format$((3.14159 * radius ^ 2), _
23                                 "Fixed"))
24      Call lstCircleData.AddItem("Circumerence: " & _
25                                 Format$((2 * 3.14159 * radius), _
26                                 "Fixed"))
27   End Sub
28
29   Private Sub hsbScroll_Change()
30      cmdDraw.ToolTipText = hsbScroll.Value
31      Call cmdDraw_Click
32   End Sub
33
34   Private Sub hsbScroll_Scroll()
35      Call hsbScroll_Change
36   End Sub
```

10.14   Write a program that uses several **MaskEdit** controls to exercise the **MaskEdit** control's formatting capabilities.

10.15   Write a program that contains the series of menus **File**, **Options** and **Help**. The **File** menu contains **Save**, **Print** and **Exit**. **Options** contains a submenu **Colors**. **Colors** contains two submenus **BackGround** and **ForeGround**. The **BackGround** menu contains the colors **white**, **red**, **green** and **blue**. The **ForeGround** menu contains the colors **black**, **yellow**, **cyan** and **gray**. The **Help** menu contains one command—**About**. Provide functionality only for the color commands, **About** and the **Exit** command. Use a **PictureBox** to test the colors. **About** displays a **MsgBox** informing the user that this is Exercise 10.15.
       ANS:

```
1    ' Exercise 10.15 Solution
2    Option Explicit
3
4    Private Sub Form_Load()
5       Call UpdatePictureBox
6    End Sub
7
8    Private Sub mnuitmAbout_Click()
9       Call MsgBox("This is Exercise 10.15", vbInformation, "VB 6")
10   End Sub
11
12   Private Sub mnuitmBackColors_Click(Index As Integer)
13
```

```
14       Select Case Index
15          Case 1
16             picPict.BackColor = vbWhite
17          Case 2
18             picPict.BackColor = vbRed
19          Case 3
20             picPict.BackColor = vbGreen
21          Case 4
22             picPict.BackColor = vbBlue
23       End Select
24
25       Call UpdatePictureBox
26    End Sub
27
28    Private Sub mnuitmExit_Click()
29       End
30    End Sub
31
32    Private Sub mnuitmForeColors_Click(Index As Integer)
33
34       Select Case Index
35          Case 1
36             picPict.ForeColor = vbBlack
37          Case 2
38             picPict.ForeColor = vbYellow
39          Case 3
40             picPict.ForeColor = vbCyan
41          Case 4
42             picPict.ForeColor = QBColor(8)
43       End Select
44
45       Call UpdatePictureBox
46    End Sub
47
48    Private Sub UpdatePictureBox()
49       picPict.CurrentX = 0
50       picPict.CurrentY = 0
51       picPict.Print "Visual Basic 6"
52    End Sub
```

10.16   Write program that allows the user to search a **ListBox** for a **String**. Populate the **ListBox** with animal names. When a **String** is found, highlight it. If a **String** is not found, display a **MsgBox** informing the user that the **String** was not found.
   ANS:

```
1    ' Exercise 10.16 Solution
2    Option Explicit
3    Option Base 1
4    Dim mArray() As String
5
6    Private Sub Form_Load()
7       Dim i As Integer
8
9       ReDim mArray(lstAnimals.ListCount)
10
11      For i = 1 To lstAnimals.ListCount
12         mArray(i) = lstAnimals.List(i)
13      Next i
14
15    End Sub
```

```
16
17   Private Sub cmdSearch_Click()
18       ' Data values in the ListBox were populated at design time
19       ' using ListBox property List in the Properties window
20       Dim key As String, result As Integer
21
22       key = txtInput.Text
23       result = modLinear.LinearSearch(mArray, key)
24
25       If result <> -1 Then
26           lstAnimals.Selected(result) = True
27       Else
28           Call MsgBox(key & " was not found.", vbExclamation, "VB")
29       End If
30
31   End Sub
```

```
32   ' Code module modLinear.bas
33   Option Explicit
34
35   Function LinearSearch(a() As String, key As String) As Integer
36       Dim x As Integer
37
38       For x = LBound(a) To UBound(a)
39
40           If a(x) = key Then
41               LinearSearch = x     ' Return index
42               Exit Function
43           End If
44
45       Next x
46
47       LinearSearch = -1            ' Value not found
48   End Function
```

10.17   Modify your solution to Exercise 10.16 to allow the user to search for **String**s that fit a specified pattern. For example, a user might want to know all the animal names that begin with the letter **c** or they might want to know how many names contain at least one **z**. Provide a second **ListBox** to store any names that match the description.

   ANS:

```
1    ' Exercise 10.17 Solution
2    Option Explicit
3    Option Base 1
4    Dim mArray() As String
5
6    Private Sub Form_Load()
7        Dim i As Integer
8
9        ReDim mArray(lstAnimals.ListCount)
10
11       For i = 1 To lstAnimals.ListCount
12           mArray(i) = lstAnimals.List(i)
13       Next i
14
15   End Sub
16
```

```
17    Private Sub cmdSearch_Click()
18        ' Data values in the ListBox were populated at design time
19        ' using ListBox property List in the Properties window
20        Dim key As String, i As Integer, min As Boolean
21
22        Call lstResults.Clear
23        key = txtInput.Text
24
25        For i = 1 To UBound(mArray)
26            If mArray(i) Like key Then
27                Call lstResults.AddItem(mArray(i))
28                min = True
29            End If
30        Next i
31
32        If min = False Then
33            Call lstResults.AddItem("No matches found.")
34        End If
35    End Sub
```

Special Section: Building Your Own Computer

In the next several problems, we take a temporary diversion away from the world of high-level language programming. We "peel open" a computer and look at its internal structure. We introduce machine language programming and write several machine language programs. To make this an especially valuable experience, we then build a computer (through the technique of software-based *simulation*) on which you can execute your machine language programs!

10.18   (*Machine-Language Programming*) Let us create a computer we will call the Simpletron. As its name implies, it is a simple machine, but, as we will soon see, a powerful one as well. The Simpletron runs programs written in the only language it directly understands, that is, Simpletron Machine Language, or SML for short.

The Simpletron contains an *accumulator*—a "special register" in which information is put before the Simpletron uses that information in calculations or examines it in various ways. All information in the Simpletron is handled in terms of *words*. A word is a signed decimal number such as **+3364**, **−1293**, **7**, **−1**, etc. Each word contains a maximum of four digits. The Simpletron is equipped with a 100-word memory and these words are referenced by their location numbers **00**, **01**, ..., **99**.

Before running an SML program, we must *load* or place the SML program into memory. The first instruction (or statement) of every SML program is always placed in memory location **00**. The simulator will start executing at this location.

Each instruction written in SML occupies one word of the Simpletron's memory (and hence instructions are signed four-digit decimal numbers). We assume that the sign of an SML instruction is always plus, but the sign of a data word may be either plus or minus. Each location in the Simpletron's memory may contain either an instruction, a data value used by a program or an unused (and hence undefined) area of memory. The first two digits of each SML instruction are the *operation code* specifying the operation to be performed. SML operation codes are summarized in Fig. 10.43. Each constant is part of **Enum OperationCodes**.

Operation code	Value	Meaning
Input/output operations:		
smlRead	10	Read a word from the keyword into a specific location in memory.
smlWrite	11	Write a word from a specific location in memory to the screen.

Fig. 10.43 Simpletron Machine Language (SML) operation codes (Part 1 of 2).

Operation code	Value	Meaning
Load/store operations:		
smlLoad	20	Load a word from a specific location in memory into the accumulator.
smlStore	21	Store a word from the accumulator into a specific location in memory.
Arithmetic operations:		
smlAdd	30	Add a word from a specific location in memory to the word in the accumulator (leave result in accumulator).
smlSubtract	31	Subtract a word from a specific location in memory from the word in the accumulator (leave result in accumulator).
smlDivide	32	Divide a word from a specific location in memory into the word in the accumulator (leave result in accumulator).
smlMultiply	33	Multiply a word from a specific location in memory by the word in the accumulator (leave result in accumulator).
Transfer of control operations:		
smlBranch	40	Branch to a specific location in memory.
smlBranchNegative	41	Branch to a specific location in memory if the accumulator is negative.
smlBranchZero	42	Branch to a specific location in memory if the accumulator is zero.
smlHalt	43	Halt—the program has completed its task.

Fig. 10.43 Simpletron Machine Language (SML) operation codes (Part 2 of 2).

The last two digits of an SML instruction are the *operand*—the memory location containing the word to which the operation applies. Let's consider several simple SML programs.

The first SML program (Example 1) reads two numbers from the keyboard and computes and prints their sum. The instruction **1007** reads the first number from the keyboard and places it into location **07** (which has been initialized to zero). Then instruction **1008** reads the next number into location **08**. The *load* instruction, **2007**, puts the first number into the accumulator, and the *add* instruction, **3008**, adds the second number to the number in the accumulator. *All SML arithmetic instructions leave their results in the accumulator.* The *store* instruction, **2109**, places the result in memory location **09** from which the *write* instruction, **1109**, takes the number and prints it (as a signed four-digit decimal number). The *halt* instruction, **4300**, terminates execution.

Example 1 Location	Number	Instruction
00	1007	(Read A)
01	1008	(Read B)
02	2007	(Load A)
03	3008	(Add B)
04	2109	(Store C)
05	1109	(Write C)
06	4300	(Halt)
07	0000	(Variable A)
08	0000	(Variable B)
09	0000	(Result C)

The second SML program reads two numbers from the keyboard and determines and prints the larger value. Note the use of the instruction **4107** as a conditional transfer of control, much the same as Visual Basic's **If** statement.

Example 2 Location	Number	Instruction
00	1009	(Read A)
01	1010	(Read B)

Example 2 Location	Number	Instruction
02	2009	(Load A)
03	3110	(Subtract B)
04	4107	(Branch negative to 07)
05	1109	(Write A)
06	4300	(Halt)
07	1110	(Write B)
08	4300	(Halt)
09	0000	(Variable A)
10	0000	(Variable B)

Now write SML programs to accomplish each of the following tasks.
a) Use a sentinel-controlled loop to read up to ten positive numbers and compute and print their sum. Input terminates when either ten positive numbers have been input or when a negative number is input.

ANS:
```
00  +1009        (Read Value)
01  +2009        (Load Value)
02  +4106        (Branch negative to 06)
03  +3008        (Add Sum)
04  +2108        (Store Sum)
05  +4000        (Branch 00)
06  +1108        (Write Sum)
07  +4300        (Halt)
08  +0000        (Storage for Sum)
09  +0000        (Storage for Value)
```

b) Use a counter-controlled loop to read seven numbers, some positive and some negative, and compute and print their average.

ANS:
```
00  +2018        (Load Counter)
01  +3121        (Subtract Termination)
02  +4211        (Branch zero to 11)
03  +2018        (Load Counter)
04  +3019        (Add Increment)
05  +2118        (Store Counter)
06  +1017        (Read Value)
07  +2016        (Load Sum)
08  +3017        (Add Value)
09  +2116        (Store Sum)
10  +4000        (Branch 00)
11  +2016        (Load Sum)
12  +3218        (Divide Counter)
13  +2120        (Store Result)
14  +1120        (Write Result)
15  +4300        (Halt)
16  +0000        (Variable Sum)
17  +0000        (Variable Value)
18  +0000        (Variable Counter)
19  +0001        (Variable Increment)
20  +0000        (Variable Result)
21  +0007        (Variable Termination)
```

c) Read a series of numbers and determine and print the largest number. The first number read indicates how many numbers should be processed.

ANS:
```
00  +1017        (Read Endvalue)
01  +2018        (Load Counter)
02  +3117        (Subtract Endvalue)
03  +4215        (Branch zero to 15)
04  +2018        (Load Counter)
05  +3021        (Add Increment)
06  +2118        (Store Counter)
```

```
07  +1019      (Read Value)
08  +2020      (Load Largest)
09  +3119      (Subtract Value)
10  +4112      (Branch negative to 12)
11  +4001      (Branch 01)
12  +2019      (Load Value)
13  +2120      (Store Largest)
14  +4001      (Branch 01)
15  +1120      (Write Largest)
16  +4300      (Halt)
17  +0000      (Variable EndValue)
18  +0000      (Variable Counter)
19  +0000      (Variable Value)
20  +0000      (Variable Largest)
21  +0001      (Variable Increment)
```

10.19 (*A Computer Simulator*) It may at first seem outrageous, but in this problem you are going to build your own computer. No, you will not be soldering components together. Rather, you will use the powerful technique of *software-based simulation* to create a *software model* of the Simpletron. You will not be disappointed. Your Simpletron simulator will turn the computer you are using into a Simpletron, and you will actually be able to run, test and debug the SML programs you wrote in Exercise 10.18. Figure 10.44 shows the initial Simpletron GUI at run time.

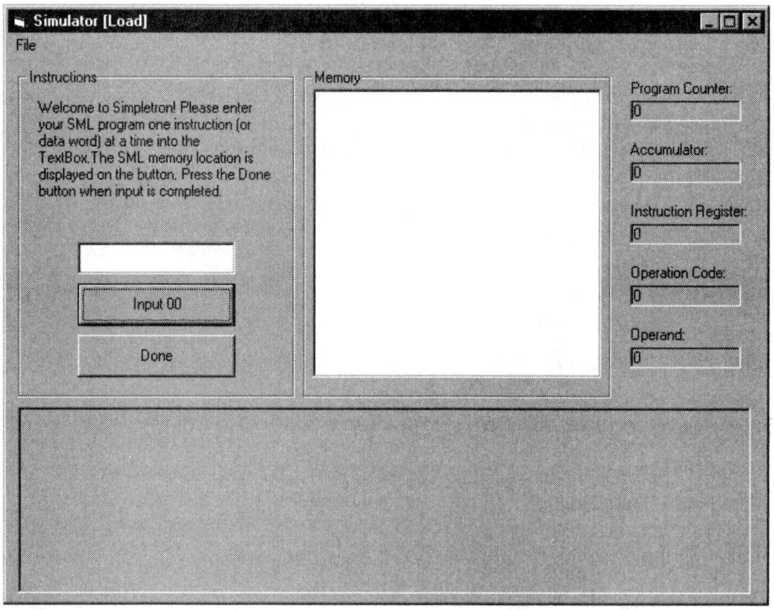

Fig. 10.44 Simpletron GUI.

When you run your Simpletron simulator, it should display:

> **Welcome to Simpletron! Please enter your SML program one
> instruction (or data word) at a time into the TextBox. The SML memory location is dis-
> played on the button. Press the Done button when input is completed.**

The program should display an input **TextBox** in which the user will type each instruction one at a time and a **Done** button for the user to press when the complete SML program has been entered. Simulate the memory of the Simpletron with a one-dimensional array **memory** that has 100 elements. Now assume that the simulator is running and let us examine the GUI as we enter the SML program from Example 2 of Exercise 10.18 (Fig. 10.45).

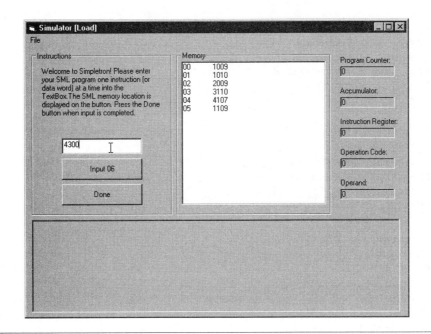

Fig. 10.45 Entering the program of Example 2.

Your program should use a **CommandButton**'s **Caption** property to display the memory location where the word will be loaded. Each word input by the user is loaded into **memory** and displayed (with its **memory** location) in a **ListBox**. When **Done** is pressed, the title bar displays:

Simulator [Execute]

The Simulator always displays its state in the title bar. Either **Load**, **Execute** or **Dump** is displayed in the square brackets.

The SML program has now been placed (or loaded) in array **memory**. The Simpletron should provide a **Timer** that—when its event is raised—calls **Execute** to execute one SML instruction. The **Timer** executes an instruction every three seconds (this allows you to see the execution of each instruction in the GUI as it occurs). Execution begins with the instruction in location **00** and, like Visual Basic, continues sequentially unless directed to some other part of the program by a transfer of control (these are discussed shortly). As an instruction is executed, it is highlighted in the **ListBox**.

Use the variable **accumulator** to represent the accumulator register. Use the variable **programCounter** to keep track of the location in **memory** that contains the instruction being performed. Use the variable **operationCode** to indicate the operation currently being performed, i.e., the left two digits of the instruction word. Use the variable **operand** to indicate the **memory** location on which the current instruction operates. Thus, **operand** is the rightmost two digits of the instruction currently being performed. Do not execute instructions directly from **memory**. Rather, transfer the next instruction to be performed from **memory** to a variable called **instructionRegister**. Then "pick off" the left two digits and place them in **operationCode** and "pick off" the right two digits and place them in **operand**. Each of the preceding registers should have a corresponding **Label** in which its current value is displayed at all times. When Simpletron begins execution, the special registers are all initialized to 0 and their corresponding **Label**s should display 0.

Now let us "walk through" the execution of the first SML instruction, **1009** in memory location **00**. This is called an *instruction execution cycle*.

The **programCounter** tells us the location of the next instruction to be performed. We *fetch* the contents of that location from **memory** by using the Visual Basic statement

```
instructionRegister = memory( programCounter )
```

The **operationCode** and the **operand** are extracted from the **instructionRegister** by the statements

```
operationCode = instructionRegister \ 100
operand = instructionRegister Mod 100
```

Now the Simpletron must determine that the **operationCode** is actually a *read* (versus a *write*, a *load*, etc.). A **Select Case** differentiates among the twelve SML operations.

In the **Select Case** structure, the behavior of various SML instructions is simulated as follows (each may require more code than that presented):

read: Display the prompt "**Enter an integer**." Enable the input **TextBox** so a value can be entered by the user. Read the value entered, convert it to an **Integer** and store it in location **memory(operand)**. See Fig. 10.46.

load: **accumulator = memory(operand)**

add: **accumulator = accumulator + memory(operand)**

branch: We will discuss the branch instructions shortly.

halt: This instruction prints the message
          *** Simpletron execution terminated ***

The other instructions are left to the reader to implement. When the SML program completes execution, the name and contents of each register as well as the complete contents of **memory** should be displayed. Such a printout is often called a *computer dump*. To help you program your **Dump** procedure, the dump format for Example 2 is shown in Fig. 10.47. Note that a dump after executing a Simpletron program shows the actual values of instructions and data values at the moment execution terminated. These values are displayed in a **PictureBox** in a **Courier** font.

     Let us proceed with the execution of our program's first instruction, namely the **1009** in location **00**. As we have indicated, the **Select Case** statement simulates this by prompting the user to enter a value into the input **TextBox**, reading the value, converting the value to an **Integer** and storing it in memory location **memory(operand)**. Because the Simpletron is event driven, it waits for the user to type a value into the input **TextBox** and press button **Enter**. The value is then read into location **09**.

     When the user presses **Enter**, simulation of the first instruction proceeds. All that remains is to prepare the Simpletron to execute the next instruction which is done by enabling the **Timer** (so it can raise new **Timer** events). Since the instruction just performed was not a transfer of control, we need merely increment the **programCounter** register as follows:

         programCounter = programCounter + 1

     This completes the simulated execution of the first instruction. When the **Timer** interval expires, the entire process (i.e., the instruction execution cycle) begins again with the fetch of the next instruction to be executed.

     Now let us consider how the branching instructions—the transfers of control—are simulated. All we need to do is adjust the value in the **programCounter** appropriately. Therefore, the *unconditional branch* instruction (**smlBranch**) is simulated in the **Select Case** as

         programCounter = operand

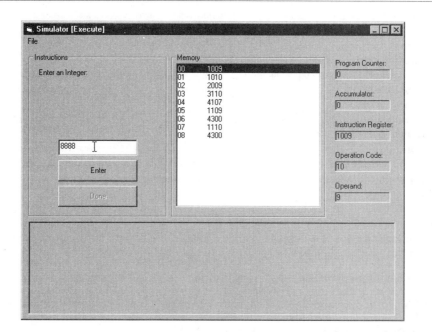

Fig. 10.46   Simpletron executing a read instruction.

     The conditional *branch if accumulator is zero* instruction is simulated as

```
If accumulator = 0 Then
   programCounter = operand
End If
```

At this point you should implement your Simpletron simulator and run each of the SML programs you wrote in Exercise 10.18. You may embellish SML with additional features and provide for these in your simulator. Figure 10.47 shows the GUI after the Simpletron program finishes executing.

Your simulator should only load and execute one set of instructions. Provide a **File** menu containing an **Exit** command to allow the user to terminate the program.

Your simulator should check for various types of errors. During the program loading phase, for example, each number the user types into the Simpletron's **memory** must be in the range **-9999** to **+9999**. Your simulator should test that each number entered is in this range, and, if not, display a **MsgBox** informing the user to enter a valid instruction.

During the execution phase, your simulator should check for various serious errors, such as attempts to divide by zero, attempts to execute invalid **operationCode**s, **accumulator** overflows (i.e., arithmetic operations resulting in values larger than **+9999** or smaller than **-9999**), and the like. Such serious errors are called *fatal errors*. When a fatal error is detected, your simulator should print an error message in a **MsgBox** such as:

```
*** Attempt to divide by zero ***
*** Simpletron execution abnormally terminated ***
```

and should print a full computer dump in the format we have discussed previously. This will help the user locate the error in the program. You will learn more about error handling in Chapter 13.

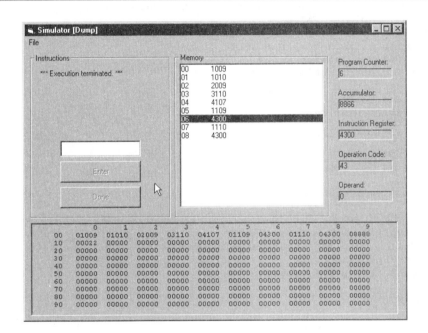

Fig. 10.47 Simulator GUI at the end of execution.

ANS:

```
1    ' Exercise 10.19 Solution
2    Option Explicit
3    Dim mProgramCounter As Integer
4    Dim mMemory(99) As Integer
5    Dim mInstructionRegister As Integer
6    Dim mOperationCode As Integer
7    Dim mOperand As Integer
8    Dim mAccumulator As Integer
9    Dim mMode As Integer
10
11   Enum Mode
12      smlLoadMemory
13      smlExecute
14      smlDump
15   End Enum
16
```

```
17   Enum OperationCodes
18       smlRead = 10
19       smlWrite = 11
20       smlLoad = 20
21       smlStore = 21
22       smlAdd = 30
23       smlSubtract = 31
24       smlDivide = 32
25       smlMultiply = 33
26       smlBranch = 40
27       smlBranchNegative = 41
28       smlBranchZero = 42
29       smlHalt = 43
30   End Enum
31
32   Private Sub Form_Load()
33       lblInstructions.Caption = "Welcome to Simpletron! Please enter " & _
34                                 "your SML program one instruction (or " & _
35                                 "data word) at a time into the TextBox." & _
36                                 "The SML memory location is displayed on " & _
37                                 "the button. Press the Done button when " & _
38                                 "input is completed."
39       tmrTimer.Enabled = False
40       mMode = smlLoadMemory
41       frmSimulator.Caption = "Simulator [Load]"
42       lblAccumulator.Caption = "0"
43       lblInstRegister.Caption = "0"
44       lblOpCode.Caption = "0"
45       lblOperand.Caption = "0"
46       lblProgramCounter.Caption = "0"
47   End Sub
48
49   Private Sub cmdCommand_Click()
50       Dim temp As Integer
51
52       If mMode = smlLoadMemory Then
53           temp = txtInput.Text
54
55           If IsValid(temp) = False Then
56               Call MsgBox("*** Load Overflow error ***", vbCritical)
57               txtInput.Text = ""
58               Call txtInput.SetFocus
59               Exit Sub
60           End If
61
62           mMemory(mProgramCounter) = temp
63           Call lstMemory.AddItem(Format$(mProgramCounter, "00") & vbTab & _
64                                 txtInput.Text, mProgramCounter)
65           mProgramCounter = mProgramCounter + 1
66           cmdCommand.Caption = "Input " & Format$(mProgramCounter, "00")
67           txtInput.Text = ""
68       ElseIf mMode = smlExecute Then
69           tmrTimer.Enabled = True
70       End If
71
72   End Sub
73
74   Private Sub cmdDone_Click()
75       txtInput.Enabled = False
76       cmdCommand.Enabled = False
77       cmdDone.Enabled = False
78       mProgramCounter = 0
79       tmrTimer.Enabled = True
80       mMode = smlExecute
81       frmSimulator.Caption = "Simulator [Execute]"
82   End Sub
83
```

```
84    Private Sub Execute()
85       Dim temp As Integer
86
87       lstMemory.Selected(mProgramCounter) = True
88       mInstructionRegister = mMemory(mProgramCounter)
89       mOperationCode = mInstructionRegister \ 100
90       mOperand = mInstructionRegister Mod 100
91
92       lblInstRegister.Caption = mInstructionRegister
93       lblOpCode.Caption = mOperationCode
94       lblOperand.Caption = mOperand
95       lblProgramCounter.Caption = mProgramCounter
96
97       Select Case mOperationCode
98          Case smlRead
99             lblInstructions.Caption = "Enter an Integer:"
100            txtInput.Enabled = True
101            Call txtInput.SetFocus
102            cmdCommand.Caption = "Enter"
103            cmdCommand.Enabled = True
104
105            If txtInput.Text = "" Then
106               tmrTimer.Enabled = False
107               Exit Sub
108            End If
109
110            mMemory(mOperand) = txtInput.Text
111            txtInput.Text = ""
112            mProgramCounter = mProgramCounter + 1
113            txtInput.Enabled = False
114            cmdCommand.Enabled = False
115         Case smlWrite
116            lblInstructions.Caption = "Memory " & _
117                        Format$(mProgramCounter, "00") & _
118                        ": " & Format$(mMemory(mOperand), "0000")
119            mProgramCounter = mProgramCounter + 1
120         Case smlLoad
121            mAccumulator = mMemory(mOperand)
122            lblAccumulator.Caption = mAccumulator
123            mProgramCounter = mProgramCounter + 1
124         Case smlStore
125            mMemory(mOperand) = mAccumulator
126            mProgramCounter = mProgramCounter + 1
127         Case smlAdd
128            temp = mAccumulator + mMemory(mOperand)
129
130            If IsValid(temp) = False Then
131               Call MsgBox("*** Overflow error ***", vbCritical)
132               Call ExecuteTermination
133               Exit Sub
134            End If
135
136            mAccumulator = temp
137            lblAccumulator.Caption = mAccumulator
138            mProgramCounter = mProgramCounter + 1
139         Case smlSubtract
140            temp = mAccumulator - mMemory(mOperand)
141
142            If IsValid(temp) = False Then
143               Call MsgBox("*** Overflow error ***", vbCritical)
144               Call ExecuteTermination
145               Exit Sub
146            End If
147
148            mAccumulator = temp
149            lblAccumulator.Caption = mAccumulator
150            mProgramCounter = mProgramCounter + 1
```

```
151            Case smlMultiply
152               temp = mAccumulator * mMemory(mOperand)
153
154               If IsValid(temp) = False Then
155                  Call MsgBox("*** Attempt to divide by zero ***", _
156                           vbCritical)
157                  Call ExecuteTermination
158                  Exit Sub
159               End If
160
161               mAccumulator = temp
162               lblAccumulator.Caption = mAccumulator
163               mProgramCounter = mProgramCounter + 1
164            Case smlDivide
165
166               If mMemory(mOperand) = 0 Then
167                  Call MsgBox("*** Attempt to divide by zero ***", vbCritical)
168                  Call ExecuteTermination
169                  Exit Sub
170               End If
171
172               mAccumulator = mAccumulator \ mMemory(mOperand)
173               lblAccumulator.Caption = mAccumulator
174               mProgramCounter = mProgramCounter + 1
175            Case smlBranch
176               mProgramCounter = mOperand
177            Case smlBranchNegative
178
179               If mAccumulator < 0 Then
180                  mProgramCounter = mOperand
181               Else
182                  mProgramCounter = mProgramCounter + 1
183               End If
184
185            Case smlBranchZero
186
187               If mAccumulator = 0 Then
188                  mProgramCounter = mOperand
189               Else
190                  mProgramCounter = mProgramCounter + 1
191               End If
192
193            Case smlHalt
194               lblInstructions.Caption = "*** Execution terminated. ***"
195               Call ExecuteTermination
196            Case Else
197               Call MsgBox("*** Invalid Instruction ***", vbCritical)
198               Call ExecuteTermination
199               Exit Sub
200         End Select
201
202   End Sub
203
204   Private Function IsValid(value As Integer) As Boolean
205
206      If value > 9999 Or value < -9999 Then
207         IsValid = False
208         Exit Function
209      End If
210
211      IsValid = True
212   End Function
213
214   Private Sub ExecuteTermination()
215      tmrTimer.Enabled = False
216      mMode = smlDump
217      frmSimulator.Caption = "Simulator [Dump]"
```

```
218        Call Dump
219   End Sub
220
221   Private Sub mnuitmExit_Click()
222        End
223   End Sub
224
225   Private Sub tmrTimer_Timer()
226        Call Execute
227   End Sub
228
229   Private Sub Dump()
230      Dim r As Integer, c As Integer
231
232      picOutput.Print Space$(14) & "0";
233
234      For r = 1 To 9
235         picOutput.Print Space$(6) & r;
236      Next r
237
238      picOutput.Print
239
240      For r = 0 To 9
241         picOutput.Print Space$(5) & Format$(r * 10, "00") & Space$(3);
242
243         For c = 0 To 9
244            picOutput.Print Format$(mMemory(r * 10 + c), _
245                                    "00000") & Space$(2);
246         Next c
247
248         picOutput.Print
249      Next r
250   End Sub
```

10.20   (*Modifications to the Simpletron Simulator*) In Exercise 10.19, you wrote a software simulation of a computer that executes programs written in Simpletron Machine Language (SML). In this exercise, we propose several modifications and enhancements to the Simpletron Simulator. Note: Some of these modifications may conflict with other modifications. For this reason you may choose to implement some of these separately.

    a) Extend the Simpletron Simulator's memory to contain 1000 memory locations.

    b) Add operation code **34** to allow the simulator to perform modulus calculations.

    b) Add operation code **35** to allow the simulator to perform exponential calculations.

    c) Modify the simulator to process floating-point values in addition to **Integer** values.

    d) Modify the simulator to display a leading **+** or **−** in front of data.

10.21   (*Simulation: The Tortoise and the Hare*) In this exercise you will recreate one of the truly great moments in history, namely the classic race of the tortoise and the hare.

    Our contenders begin the race at "square 1" of 70 squares. Each square represents a possible position along the race course. The finish line is at square 70. The first contender to reach or pass square 70 is rewarded with a pail of fresh carrots and lettuce. The course weaves its way up the side of a slippery mountain, so occasionally the contenders lose ground.

    There is a clock that ticks once per second implemented with a **Timer** object. With each tick, your program should randomly adjust the position of the animals according to the following rules:

Animal	Move type	% of the time	Actual move
Tortoise	Fast plod	50%	3 squares to the right
	Slip	20%	6 squares to the left
	Slow plod	30%	1 square to the right
Hare	Sleep	20%	No move at all
	Big hop	20%	9 squares to the right
	Big slip	10%	12 squares to the left
	Small hop	30%	1 square to the right
	Small slip	20%	2 squares to the left

Keep track of the positions of the animals (values from 1 to 70). Start each animal at position 1 (i.e., the "starting gate"). If an animal slips below position 1, move the animal back to position 1.

Generate the percentages in the preceding table by producing a random integer, i, in the range $1 \leq i \leq 10$. For the tortoise, perform a "fast plod" when $1 \leq i \leq 5$, a "slip" when $6 \leq i \leq 7$, or a "slow plod" when $8 \leq i \leq 10$. Use a similar technique to move the hare.

Begin the race by printing "**BANG!!!!! AND THEY'RE OFF!!!!!**" For each second, print a 70-position line showing the letter **T** in the position of the tortoise and the letter **H** in the position of the hare. Occasionally, the contenders will land on the same square. In this case, the tortoise bites the hare and your program should print **OUCH!!!** beginning at that position. All print positions other than the **T**, the **H**, or the **OUCH!!!** (in case of a tie) should be blank.

After each line is printed, test if either animal has reached or passed square 70. If so, then print the winner and terminate the simulation. If the tortoise wins, print **TORTOISE WINS!!! YAY!!!** If the hare wins, print **Hare wins. Yuch.** If both animals cross the finish line at the same time, you may want to favor the tortoise (the "underdog"), or you may want to print **It's a tie.** Remember to disable the **Timer** when the race finishes. If neither animal wins, continue the simulation. When you are ready to run your program, assemble a group of fans to watch the race. You'll be amazed at how involved your audience gets!

ANS:

```
1    ' Exercise 10.21 Solution
2    ' For graphical purposes the race has been extended to 300
3    Option Explicit
4    Dim mTortoise As Integer
5    Dim mHare As Integer
6    Dim mRaceFinished As Boolean
7    Dim mTime As Integer        ' Store approximate time of race in seconds
8
9    Private Sub Form_Load()
10       Picture = LoadPicture("\vb_solutions\ch10\ex10_21\background.gif")
11       mTortoise = 1
12       mHare = 1
13       ScaleLeft = -10
14       ScaleWidth = 400
15       ScaleHeight = 275
16       Caption = "BANG!!!!AND THEY'RE OFF!!!!!"
17    End Sub
18
19    Private Sub tmrTimer_Timer()
20       Call Cls
21       Call Randomize
22       Call MoveHare
23       Call MoveTortoise
24       Call DrawCurrentPositions
25       mTime = mTime + 1
26       lblDisplay(0).Caption = "Tortoise position: " & mTortoise
27       lblDisplay(1).Caption = "Hare position: " & mHare
28
29       If mRaceFinished Then
30          tmrTimer.Enabled = False
31       End If
32
33       lblTime.Caption = "Elapsed seconds: " & mTime
34    End Sub
35
36    Private Sub MoveTortoise()
37       Dim t As Integer
38
39       t = 1 + Int(Rnd() * 10)
40
41       ' Each move multiplied by 2 to speed up the race
42       If (t >= 1 And t <= 5) Then
43          mTortoise = mTortoise + 3 * 2  ' Fast plod
44       ElseIf (t = 6 Or t = 7) Then
45          mTortoise = mTortoise - 6 * 2  ' Slip
46       Else
47          mTortoise = mTortoise + 1 * 2  ' Slow plod
48       End If
```

```
49
50      If mTortoise < 0 Then
51          mTortoise = 0
52      ElseIf mTortoise >= 300 Then
53          mTortoise = 300
54          mRaceFinished = True
55          Caption = "TORTOISE WINS!!! YAY!!!"
56      End If
57  End Sub
58
59  Private Sub MoveHare()
60      Dim h As Integer
61
62      h = 1 + Int(Rnd() * 10)
63
64      ' Each move multiplied by 2 to speed up the race
65      If (h = 3 Or h = 4) Then
66          mHare = mHare + 9 * 2     ' Big hop
67      ElseIf (h = 5) Then
68          mHare = mHare - 12 * 2    ' Big slip
69      ElseIf (h >= 6 And h <= 8) Then
70          mHare = mHare + 1 * 2     ' Small hop
71      ElseIf (h > 8) Then
72          mHare = mHare - 2 * 2     ' Small slip
73      End If
74
75      If mHare < 0 Then
76          mHare = 0
77      ElseIf mHare >= 300 Then
78          mHare = 300
79          mRaceFinished = True
80          Caption = "Hare wins. Yuch."
81      End If
82  End Sub
83
84  Private Sub DrawCurrentPositions()
85      Dim yHare As Integer, yTortoise As Integer
86
87      ' Equation for a semi-circle to simulate climbing
88      yHare = 250 - Sqr(150 ^ 2 - (mHare - 150) ^ 2)
89      yTortoise = 250 - Sqr(150 ^ 2 - (mTortoise - 150) ^ 2)
90
91      If (yHare > ScaleHeight - 10) Then
92          yHare = ScaleHeight - 10
93      End If
94
95      If (yTortoise > ScaleHeight - 10) Then
96          yTortoise = ScaleHeight - 10
97      End If
98
99      If (yHare = yTortoise And mHare = mTortoise) Then
100         CurrentX = mHare
101         CurrentY = yHare - 60
102         Print "OUCH!!!"
103         CurrentX = mHare
104         CurrentY = yHare - 20
105         Print "H"                      ' The hare jumps
106     Else
107         CurrentX = mHare
108         CurrentY = yHare
109         Print "H"
110     End If
111
112     CurrentX = mTortoise
113     CurrentY = yTortoise
114     Print "T"
115 End Sub
```

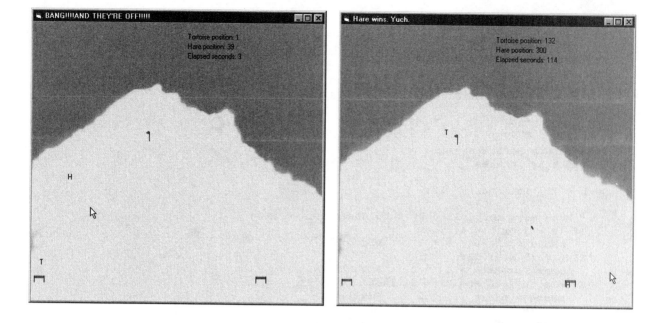

Chapter 11 Solutions

Advanced Graphical User Interface Concepts

11.5 [CD] Fill in the blanks in each of the following:

a) By default, Visual Basic programs are compiled to _____.

ANS: p-code.

b) **LoadPicture** returns type _____.

ANS: IPictureDisp.

c) The _____ statement provides a convenient syntax for setting multiple properties for a control.

ANS: With.

d) A _____ is a predefined form that is provided with Visual Basic.

ANS: template form (or form template).

e) **RichTextBox** property _____ determines the number and orientation of scrollbars.

ANS: Scrollbars.

11.6 State which of the following are *true* and which are *false*. If *false*, explain why.

a) An MDI parent window can contain multiple child windows.

ANS: True.

b) MDI is short for multiple document instance.

ANS: False. MDI is short for multiple document interface.

c) MDI child windows cannot have menus.

ANS: False. They may contain menus.

d) A **Image** control can be placed directly on an MDI parent window.

ANS: False. **Image** controls do not have an **Align** property.

e) An MDI child window can never be moved outside its MDI parent window.

ANS: True.

f) A form becomes an MDI child window when its **Child** property is set to **True**.

ANS: False. A form becomes an MDI child window when its **MDIChild** property is set to **True**.

g) In general, SDI applications are not as complex as MDI applications.

ANS: True.

h) MDI parent windows can have menus.

ANS: True.

11.7 Briefly explain the difference between an SDI application and an MDI application. Excluding the SDI and MDI applications discussed in the chapter, list 3 examples of an SDI application and list 3 examples of an MDI application.

ANS: SDI applications are narrow focused applications that typically only allow one document to be viewed at a time. MDI applications are much more complex than SDI. MDI applications typically allow multiple documents to be viewed simultaneously. SDI: Internet Explorer, Paint, Minesweeper. MDI: Visual Basic, Visual C++, Framemaker.

11.8 Briefly explain why a **Window** menu is important to an MDI parent window.

ANS: The **Window** menu allows the child windows to be graphically managed (tiled, cascaded, viewed, etc.).

11.9 Take any previous exercise you have solved and create a p-code executable file named **pcode.exe**. Now create a native code executable version (using **Optimize for Fast Code**) of the same program—name it **fast.exe**. How do the two file sizes compare? Now create two additional native code executables (one using **Optimize for Small Code** and the other using **No Optimization**) named **small.exe** and **no_op.exe**, respectively. How do these compare to each other and the other **.exe** files?

11.10   Write a program that begins decrementing a loop from 200000000 to 0 in decrements of –1 when a button is pressed. Use function **Timer** to determine how much time the loop required for execution. Although the time is approximate, the value is suitable for a basic performance test. Compile the program to a p-code executable. How much time did it take to execute?

ANS:

```
1    ' Exercise 11.10 Solution
2    Option Explicit
3
4    Private Sub cmdGo_Click()
5       Dim j As Long, t As Long
6
7       Screen.MousePointer = vbHourglass
8       t = Timer()
9
10      For j = 200000000 To 0 Step -1
11         ' Do nothing
12      Next j
13
14      lblResult.Caption = (Timer - t) & " seconds"
15      Screen.MousePointer = vbDefault
16   End Sub
```

11.11   Compile the program of Exercise 11.10 to a native code executable and time each optimization. Also test the **No Optimization** feature. How much execution time did each optimization take? Is this what you expected?

11.12   **[CD]** Write a small editor program that performs syntax color highlighting on ANSI C programming language keywords of Fig. 11.43. Each keyword should appear as green. Normal text should appear as black. Use the **RichTextBox** control. Consult the on-line documentation for additional **RichTextBox** properties, methods and events. Provide a button that when pressed changes every ANSI C keyword to green.

ANS:

```
1    ' Exercise 11.12 Solution
2    Option Explicit
3
4    Private Sub Form_Load()
5       Call rtfEditor.LoadFile("\vb_solutions\ch11\ex11_12\print.c")
6    End Sub
7
8    Private Sub cmdHighlight_Click()
9       Static location As Long           ' Location of a keyword
10      Dim indexValue As Integer         ' Index of keyword in ListBox
11      Dim keywordLength As Integer      ' Length of keyword
12      Dim lastCharPosition As Integer   ' Last position of text
13      Dim currentPosition As Integer    ' Current location in text
14
15      lastCharPosition = Len(rtfEditor.Text)
16
17      Do While (True)
18         location = rtfEditor.Find(lstKeywords.List(indexValue), _
19                               location + 1, , _
20                               rtfWholeWord Or rtfMatchCase)
21
22         ' Test if a keyword has been found
23         If location <> -1 Then
24            keywordLength = Len(lstKeywords.List(indexValue))
25            rtfEditor.SelLength = keywordLength    ' Select chars
26            rtfEditor.SelColor = vbGreen           ' Set color
27         End If
28
29         currentPosition = currentPosition + 1
30
31         ' Test for end of text
32         If currentPosition = lastCharPosition Then
33            indexValue = indexValue + 1
34            location = 0
```

```
35            currentPosition = 0
36         End If
37
38         ' Exit loop if we have searched for all keywords
39         If indexValue = lstKeywords.ListCount Then
40            Exit Do
41         End If
42
43         DoEvents    ' Allow other events to be processed
44      Loop
45
46      rtfEditor.HideSelection = True
47      Call cmdHighlight.SetFocus
48   End Sub
```

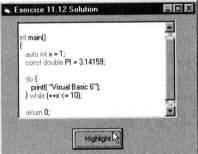

11.13   Modify the program of Fig. 11.24 to find the next occurrence of the text being searched for by the user. Display a **MsgBox** if the text is not found. Also display the current location (i.e., index) of the cursor. Consult the on-line documentation for additional **RichTextBox** properties, methods and events.

      ANS:

```
1    ' Exercise 11.13 Solution
2    Option Explicit
3    Dim mPos As Long
4
5    Private Sub Form_Load()
6       ' Load RTF file into Rich TextBox
7       Call rtfTextBox.LoadFile("\vb_solutions\" & _
8                         "ch11\ex11_13\sample.rtf", rtfRTF)
9
10      mPos = -1    ' Used in find operation
11
12      ' Allow selected text to be visible even
13      ' after user interacts with Rich TextBox
14      rtfTextBox.HideSelection = False
15   End Sub
16
17   Private Sub cmdFind_Click()
18      Dim options As Integer
19      Dim x As Integer, y As Integer
20
21      y = chkBoxes.LBound
22      For x = 1 To chkBoxes.Count
23
24         ' Sum the search options
25         If chkBoxes(y).Value Then
26            options = options + y
27         End If
28         y = y * 2    ' Adjust y for next control array element
29      Next x
30
31      ' Find text specified in TextBox
32      mPos = rtfTextBox.Find(txtKey.Text, mPos + 1, , options)
33
```

```
34        ' Not found - display a MsgBox
35        If mPos = -1 Then
36           Call MsgBox("Not found.")
37        End If
38
39     End Sub
40
41     Private Sub cmdSave_Click()
42        ' Save file to disk
43        Call rtfTextBox.SaveFile("\vb_solutions\" & _
44                         "ch11\ex11_13\sample.rtf", rtfRTF)
45     End Sub
46
47     Private Sub cmdBold_Click()
48        rtfTextBox.SelBold = Not rtfTextBox.SelBold
49     End Sub
50
51     Private Sub cmdItalic_Click()
52        rtfTextBox.SelItalic = Not rtfTextBox.SelItalic
53     End Sub
54
55     Private Sub cmdUnderline_Click()
56        rtfTextBox.SelUnderline = Not rtfTextBox.SelUnderline
57     End Sub
```

11.14   Modify the program of Fig. 11.24 by adding two additional buttons for subscripting and superscripting highlighted text. Also add three additional buttons for aligning the paragraphs. Use constants `rtfLeft`, `rtfRight` and `rtfCenter`. Consult the on-line documentation for additional **RichTextBox** properties, methods and events.

   ANS:

```
 1     ' Exercise 11.14 Solution
 2     Option Explicit
 3
 4     Private Sub Form_Load()
 5        ' Load RTF file into Rich TextBox
 6        Call rtfTextBox.LoadFile("\vb_solutions\" & _
 7                         "ch11\ex11_14\sample.rtf", rtfRTF)
 8
 9        ' Allow selected text to be visible even
10        ' after user interacts with Rich TextBox
11        rtfTextBox.HideSelection = False
12     End Sub
13
14     Private Sub cmdFind_Click()
15        Dim options As Integer
16        Dim x As Integer, y As Integer
17
18        y = chkBoxes.LBound
19        For x = 1 To chkBoxes.Count
20
```

```
21              ' Sum the search options
22              If chkBoxes(y).Value Then
23                  options = options + y
24              End If
25              y = y * 2    ' Adjust y for next control array element
26          Next x
27
28          ' Find text specified in TextBox
29          Call rtfTextBox.Find(txtKey.Text, , , options)
30      End Sub
31
32      Private Sub cmdSave_Click()
33          ' Save file to disk
34          Call rtfTextBox.SaveFile("\vb_solutions\" & _
35                              "ch11\ex11_14\sample.rtf", rtfRTF)
36      End Sub
37
38      Private Sub cmdBold_Click()
39          rtfTextBox.SelBold = Not rtfTextBox.SelBold
40      End Sub
41
42      Private Sub cmdItalic_Click()
43          rtfTextBox.SelItalic = Not rtfTextBox.SelItalic
44      End Sub
45
46      Private Sub cmdUnderline_Click()
47          rtfTextBox.SelUnderline = Not rtfTextBox.SelUnderline
48      End Sub
49
50      Private Sub cmdSuper_Click()
51          rtfTextBox.SelCharOffset = 50
52      End Sub
53
54      Private Sub cmdSub_Click()
55          rtfTextBox.SelCharOffset = -50
56      End Sub
57
58      Private Sub cmdAlign_Click(Index As Integer)
59          ' Buttons in control array cmdAlign have
60          ' rtfLeft, rtfRight and rtfCenter for their
61          ' Index property value.
62          rtfTextBox.SelAlignment = Index
63      End Sub
```

11.15 Modify your solution to Exercise 11.13 to provide a find and replace feature. Consult the on-line documentation for additional **RichTextBox** properties, methods and events.

11.16 Rewrite the Craps program of Exercise 6.24 to use an **ImageList** control to manage the images.

ANS:

```
1   ' Exercise 11.16 Solution
2   Option Explicit        ' General declaration
3
4   ' Declare module variables
5   Dim mMyPoint As Integer
6   Dim mDie1 As Integer
7   Dim mDie2 As Integer
8   Dim mBankBalance As Currency
9   Dim mWager As Currency
10  Const mWIN As Integer = 1
11  Const mLOSE As Integer = 2
12
13  Enum Names
14      snakeEyes = 2    ' Explicitly assign 2
15      trey             ' Implicitly assign 3
16      [yo leven] = 11  ' Explicitly assign 11
17      boxCars          ' Implicitly assign 12
18  End Enum
19
20  Private Sub Form_Load()
21      Icon = ilsImages.ListImages(7).Picture
22      cmdPlay.Enabled = False
23      mBankBalance = 1000
24      txtBankBalance.Text = Format$(mBankBalance, "Currency")
25  End Sub
26
27  Private Sub cmdPlay_Click()
28      Call Craps
29  End Sub
30
31  Private Sub cmdEnter_Click()
32      mWager = txtWager.Text
33      Caption = ""
34
35      If ValidateWager = True Then
36          cmdEnter.Enabled = False
37          cmdPlay.Enabled = True
38      Else
39          Caption = "You must enter a valid wager."
40      End If
41
42  End Sub
43
44  Private Sub Craps()
45      Dim sum As Integer
46
47      ' initialization
48      mMyPoint = 0
49      fraPoint.Caption = "Point"
50      lblStatus.Caption = ""
51      imgPointDie1.Picture = LoadPicture("")
52      imgPointDie2.Picture = LoadPicture("")
53      Call Randomize
54
55      sum = RollDice()        ' Invoke rollDice
56
57      ' Determine outcome of first roll
58      Select Case sum
59          Case 7, [yo leven]
60              cmdRoll.Enabled = False    ' Disable Roll button
61              cmdPlay.Enabled = False
62              cmdEnter.Enabled = True
63              lblStatus.Caption = "You Win!!!"
64              Call UpdateBank(mWIN)
```

```
65          Case snakeEyes, trey, boxCars
66              cmdRoll.Enabled = False
67              lblStatus.Caption = "Sorry. You lose."
68              Call UpdateBank(mLOSE)
69          Case Else
70              Call Chatter
71              mMyPoint = sum
72              fraPoint.Caption = "Point is " & sum
73              lblStatus.Caption = "Roll Again."
74              Call DisplayDie(imgPointDie1, mDie1)
75              Call DisplayDie(imgPointDie2, mDie2)
76              cmdPlay.Enabled = False    ' Disable Play button
77              cmdRoll.Enabled = True     ' Enable Roll button
78      End Select
79
80  End Sub
81
82  Private Sub cmdRoll_Click()
83      Dim sum As Integer
84
85      sum = RollDice()              ' Invoke rollDice
86
87      ' Check for a win or loss
88      If sum = mMyPoint Then          ' Win
89          lblStatus.Caption = "You Win!!!"
90          cmdRoll.Enabled = False
91          cmdPlay.Enabled = False
92          cmdEnter.Enabled = True
93          Call UpdateBank(mWIN)
94      ElseIf sum = 7 Then             ' Loss
95          lblStatus.Caption = "Sorry. You lose."
96          cmdRoll.Enabled = False
97          cmdPlay.Enabled = False
98          cmdEnter.Enabled = True
99          Call UpdateBank(mLOSE)
100     End If
101
102 End Sub
103
104 Private Sub DisplayDie(imgDie As Image, face As Integer)
105     imgDie.Picture = ilsImages.ListImages(face).Picture
106 End Sub
107
108 Private Sub UpdateBank(result As Integer)
109
110     If result = mWIN Then
111         mBankBalance = mBankBalance + mWager
112     Else  ' mLOSE
113         mBankBalance = mBankBalance - mWager
114
115         If mBankBalance = 0 Then
116             cmdRoll.Enabled = False
117             cmdPlay.Enabled = False
118             cmdEnter.Enabled = False
119             Caption = "SORRY. YOU BUSTED!"
120         End If
121
122     End If
123
124     txtBankBalance.Text = Format$(mBankBalance, "Currency")
125 End Sub
126
127 Private Function RollDice() As Integer
128     Dim die1 As Integer, die2 As Integer, dieSum As Integer
129     Dim a As Integer, b As Integer
130
131     die1 = 1 + Int(6 * Rnd())       ' Roll die1
```

```
132     die2 = 1 + Int(6 * Rnd())        ' Roll die2
133
134     Call DisplayDie(imgDie1, die1) ' Draw die image
135     Call DisplayDie(imgDie2, die2) ' Draw die image
136     Call Chatter
137
138     mDie1 = die1                      ' Store die1 value
139     mDie2 = die2                      ' Store die2 value
140     dieSum = die1 + die2             ' Sum dice
141     RollDice = dieSum                ' Return dieSum to caller
142 End Function
143
144 Private Function ValidateWager() As Boolean
145
146     If mWager <= 0 Or mWager > mBankBalance Then
147         ValidateWager = False
148         Exit Function
149     End If
150
151     ValidateWager = True
152 End Function
153
154 Private Sub Chatter()
155
156     Select Case Int(Rnd() * 10)
157         Case 0
158             Caption = "Oh, you're going for broke, huh?"
159         Case 1
160             Caption = "Aw cmon, take a chance!"
161         Case 2
162             Caption = "You're up big. Now's the time to cash in your chips!"
163         Case 3
164             Caption = "Way to lucky! Must be a cheat!!"
165         Case 4
166             Caption = "Shooter is hot!"
167         Case 5
168             Caption = "Hey! Keep your hands away from my chips!"
169         Case 6
170             Caption = "Bet it all! Bet it all!"
171         Case 7
172             Caption = "Pass me those lucky dice."
173         Case 8
174             Caption = "Can I borrow a few chips?"
175         Case 9
176             Caption = "I gonna make some money tonight!"
177     End Select
178
179 End Sub
```

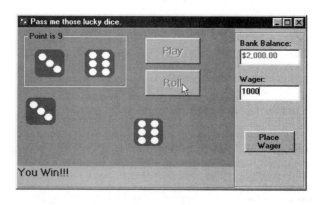

11.17   Create a simple animation using a **PictureBox** control and images from an **ImageList** control.

ANS:

```
1   ' Exercise 11.17 Solution
2   Option Explicit
3   Dim mCurrent As Integer
4
5   Private Sub tmrTimer_Timer()
6      mCurrent = (mCurrent Mod 9) + 1
7
8      picPict.Picture = ilsImages.ListImages(mCurrent).Picture
9   End Sub
```

C keywords			
auto	break	case	char
const	continue	default	do
double	else	enum	extern
float	for	goto	if
int	long	register	return
short	signed	sizeof	static
struct	switch	typedef	union
unsigned	void	volatile	while

Fig. 11.43   ANSI C programming language keywords.

11.18 Create a simple animation using method **PaintPicture**.
ANS:

```
1    ' Exercise 11.18 Solution
2    Option Explicit
3    Dim mX As Double
4    Dim mPicture As IPictureDisp
5
6    Private Sub Form_Load()
7       Set mPicture = LoadPicture("\vb_solutions\ch11\ex11_18\bird9.bmp")
8    End Sub
9
10   Private Sub tmrTimer_Timer()
11      Call Cls
12      Call PaintPicture(mPicture, mX, 0)
13
14      mX = mX + 39
```

```
15
16      If mX >= ScaleWidth Then
17          mX = 0
18      End If
19
20  End Sub
```

 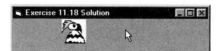

11.19   Modify Fig. 11.10 to provide password protection. Use the template form **Login**.
ANS:

```
1   ' Exercise 11.19 Solution
2   Option Explicit
3
4   Public Sub Main()
5      Call frmLogin.Show
6   End Sub
```

```
7   Option Explicit        ' General declaration mdiParent
8
9   Private Sub MDIForm_Load()
10      Call Load(frmForm3)      ' Load child frmForm3
11      Call Load(frmForm2)      ' Load child frmForm2
12      Call Load(frmForm1)      ' Load child frmForm1
13  End Sub
14
15  Private Sub mnuItem_Click(Index As Integer)
16      Call mdiParent.Arrange(Index)   ' Arrange children
17  End Sub
18
19  Private Sub mnuC_Click()
20      Call frmForm1.Show     ' Show child frmForm1
21  End Sub
22
23  Private Sub mnuCpp_Click()
24      Call frmForm2.Show     ' Show child frmForm2
25  End Sub
26
27  Private Sub mnuJava_Click()
28      Call frmForm3.Show     ' Show child frmForm3
29  End Sub
30
31  Private Sub mnuExit_Click()
32      Call Unload(frmForm1) ' Unload child frmForm1
33      Call Unload(frmForm2) ' Unload child frmForm2
34      Call Unload(frmForm3) ' Unload child frmForm3
35      End                   ' Terminate execution
36  End Sub
```

```
37  ' frmLogin
38  Option Explicit
39  Public LoginSucceeded As Boolean
40
41  Private Sub Form_Load()
42      Caption = Caption & " (password is: password)"     'ADDED CODE
43  End Sub
44
45  Private Sub cmdCancel_Click()
46      'set the global var to false
47      'to denote a failed login
48      LoginSucceeded = False
49      Me.Hide
```

```
50
51         End          ' ADDED CODE
52    End Sub
53
54    Private Sub cmdOK_Click()
55         'check for correct password
56         If txtPassword = "password" Then
57              'place code to here to pass the
58              'success to the calling sub
59              'setting a global var is the easiest
60              LoginSucceeded = True
61              Me.Hide
62              Call mdiParent.Show     ' ADDED CODE
63         Else
64              MsgBox "Invalid Password, try again!", , "Login"
65              txtPassword.SetFocus
66              SendKeys "{Home}+{End}"
67         End If
68    End Sub
```

```
69    ' Form frmForm1
70    Option Explicit     ' General declaration frmForm1
71
72    Private Sub Form_Load()
73        imgImage.Picture = LoadPicture("\vb_solutions\ch11\" & _
74                                "ex11_19\chtp2.gif")
75    End Sub
```

```
76    ' Form frmForm2
77    Option Explicit     ' General declaration frmForm2
78
79    Private Sub Form_Load()
80        imgImage.Picture = LoadPicture("\vb_solutions\ch11\" & _
81                                "ex11_19\cpphtp2.gif")
82    End Sub
```

```
83    ' Form frmForm3
84    Option Explicit        ' General declaration frmForm3
85
86    Private Sub Form_Load()
87        imgImage.Picture = LoadPicture("\vb_solutions\ch11\" & _
88                                "ex11_19\jhtp2.gif")
89    End Sub
90
91    Private Sub mnuGray_Click()
92        BackColor = QBColor(7)
93    End Sub
94
95    Private Sub mnuWhite_Click()
96        BackColor = vbWhite
97    End Sub
```

11.20   Using method **PaintPicture** to display on the form two **.bmp** images—one flipped horizontally and the other flipped vertically. (Hint: Passing negative values for the fourth and/or fifth arguments flips an image.)

ANS:

```
1   ' Exercise 11.20 Solution
2   Option Explicit
3   Dim mPicture As IPictureDisp      ' Type that represents a picture
4
5   Private Sub Form_Load()
6      Set mPicture = LoadPicture("\vb_solutions\ch11\ex11_20\bird10.bmp")
7      Call PaintPicture(mPicture, 20, 20)
8   End Sub
9
10  Private Sub cmdFlip_Click()
11     Call PaintPicture(mPicture, 100, 60, , -39) ' 39 is the picture height
12     Call PaintPicture(mPicture, 180, 20, -39)   ' 39 is the picture width
13     cmdFlip.Enabled = False
14  End Sub
```

11.21 Write a program that plays the game of concentration. Use a series of **PictureBox** controls to display the images. When the user **Click**s on a **PictureBox**, the image associated with that **PictureBox** is displayed. Clicking a second **PictureBox** displays the image associated with the second **PictureBox**. If the images match, they remain displayed. If they do not match, both images should be hidden.

ANS:

```
1   ' Exercise 11.21 Solution
2   Option Explicit
3   Dim mImages(1 To 10) As IPictureDisp
4   Dim mSelectedCount As Integer
5   Dim mSelected(1 To 2) As PictureBox
6
7   Private Sub Form_Load()
8      Dim j As Integer
9
10     Call Setup
11
12     ' Cover all images
13     For j = 1 To 10
14        picImages(j).Line (0, 0)-(picImages(j).ScaleWidth, _
15                          picImages(j).ScaleHeight), vbYellow, BF
16     Next j
17
18  End Sub
19
20  Private Sub Setup()
21     Dim j As Integer, c As Integer, k As Integer
22     Dim used(1 To 10) As Boolean
23
24     Call Randomize
25
26     ' Place all 5 images from ImageList control
27     For j = 1 To 5
28
29        ' Each image needs to be placed twice
30        For k = 1 To 2
31
32           ' Keep looping until an unused PictureBox
33           ' has been found.
```

```
34                  Do
35                      c = Int(Rnd() * 10) + 1
36                  Loop While used(c) <> False
37
38                  ' Draw image in PictureBox and keep track of
39                  ' which image it is.
40                  used(c) = True
41                  picImages(c).Picture = ilsImages.ListImages(j).Picture
42                  Set mImages(c) = ilsImages.ListImages(j).Picture
43              Next k
44
45          Next j
46
47      End Sub
48
49      Private Sub picImages_Click(Index As Integer)
50          Dim j As Long
51
52          mSelectedCount = mSelectedCount + 1
53
54          picImages(Index).Picture = mImages(Index)
55          Set mSelected(mSelectedCount) = picImages(Index)
56
57          ' Check that two images are selected
58          If mSelectedCount = 2 Then
59              mSelectedCount = 0
60
61              ' Create a delay such that 2nd image is visible
62              For j = 1 To 20000
63                  DoEvents
64              Next j
65
66              ' Check for a match--if not a match then cover
67              If mSelected(1).Picture <> mSelected(2).Picture Then
68                  mSelected(1).Line (0, 0)-(mSelected(1).ScaleWidth, _
69                              mSelected(1).ScaleHeight), vbYellow, BF
70                  mSelected(2).Line (0, 0)-(mSelected(2).ScaleWidth, _
71                              mSelected(2).ScaleHeight), vbYellow, BF
72              End If
73
74          End If
75
76      End Sub
```

11.22   Modify the program of Fig. 11.16 to use template form **Dialog** instead of function **MsgBox**.
    ANS:

```
1   ' Exercise 11.23 Solution
2   Option Explicit
3
4   Private Sub Main()
5       Call frmStarter.Show      ' Display frmStarter
6       Call Load(frmForm1)       ' Load frmForm1 into memory
7       Call Load(frmForm2)       ' Load frmForm2 into memory
8       Call Load(frmForm3)       ' Load frmForm3 into memory
9       Call Load(frmDialog)      ' Load frmDialog into memory
10  End Sub
```

```
11   ' Form frmStarter
12   Option Explicit
13   Option Base 1
14   Dim mImagesArray(3) As IPictureDisp
15   Dim mExit As Boolean
16
17   Private Sub Form_Load()
18       Set mImagesArray(1) = LoadPicture("\vb_solutions\ch11\" & _
19                                        "\ex11_22\chtp2.gif")
20       Set mImagesArray(2) = LoadPicture("\vb_solutions\ch11\" & _
21                                        "\ex11_22\cpphtp2.gif")
22       Set mImagesArray(3) = LoadPicture("\vb_solutions\ch11\" & _
23                                        "\ex11_22\jhtp2.gif")
24   End Sub
25
26   Private Sub cmdC_Click()
27       frmForm1.imgImage.Picture = mImagesArray(1)
28       Call frmForm1.Show(vbModal)   ' Display the form
29   End Sub
30
31   Private Sub cmdCpp_Click()
32       frmForm2.imgImage.Picture = mImagesArray(2)
33       Call frmForm2.Show(vbModal)     ' Display the form
34   End Sub
35
36   Private Sub cmdJava_Click()
37       frmForm3.imgImage.Picture = mImagesArray(3)
38       Call frmForm3.Show(vbModal)     ' Display the form
39   End Sub
40
41   Private Sub Form_QueryUnload(Cancel As Integer, UnloadMode As Integer)
42       Call frmDialog.Show(vbModal)
43
44       If mExit = True Then
45           Cancel = True     ' Allow Form_Unload to be called
46       End If
47
48   End Sub
49
50   Private Sub Form_Unload(Cancel As Integer)
51           Call Unload(frmForm1)       ' Unload frmForm1
52           Call Unload(frmForm2)       ' Unload frmForm2
53           Call Unload(frmForm3)       ' Unload frmForm3
54   End Sub
55
56   Public Sub SetExit(c As Boolean)
57       mExit = c
58   End Sub
```

```
59   ' frmDialog
60   Option Explicit
61   Private Sub cmdNo_Click()
62       Call frmStarter.SetExit(True)
63       Call Hide
64   End Sub
65   Private Sub cmdYes_Click()
66       Call frmStarter.SetExit(False)
67       Call Unload(Me)     ' Unload this form (Me)
68   End Sub
```

11.23   A company pays its employees as managers (who receive a fixed weekly salary), hourly workers (who receive a fixed hourly wage for up to the first 40 hours they work and "time-and-a-half," i.e., 1.5 times their hourly wage, for overtime hours worked), commission workers (who receive a $250 plus 5.7% of their gross weekly sales), or pieceworkers (who receive a fixed amount of money per item for each of the items they produce—each pieceworker in this company works on only one type of item). Write a program to compute the weekly pay for each employee. You do not know the number of employees in advance. Each type of employee has its own pay code: Managers have paycode 1, hourly workers have code 2, commission workers have code 3 and pieceworkers have code 4. Enter the appropriate facts your program needs to calculate each employee's pay based on that employee's paycode. Each employee type should be handled as a separate form.

ANS:

```
1   ' Exercise 11.23 Solution
2   Option Explicit
3   Dim mFirst As Boolean
4
5   Private Sub Form_Load()
6      mFirst = True
7      Call Load(frmManager)
8      Call Load(frmHourly)
9      Call Load(frmCommission)
10     Call Load(frmPiece)
11  End Sub
12
13  Private Sub optEmployee_Click(Index As Integer)
14
15     If mFirst = True Then
16        mFirst = False
17        Exit Sub
18     End If
19
20     Select Case Index
21        Case 1
22           Call frmManager.Show(vbModal)
23        Case 2
24           Call frmHourly.Show(vbModal)
25        Case 3
26           Call frmCommission.Show(vbModal)
27        Case 4
28           Call frmPiece.Show(vbModal)
29     End Select
30
31  End Sub
32
33  Private Sub Form_Unload(Cancel As Integer)
34     Call Unload(frmManager)
35     Call Unload(frmHourly)
36     Call Unload(frmCommission)
37     Call Unload(frmPiece)
38  End Sub
```

```
39  ' frmManager
40  Option Explicit
41
42  Private Sub cmdEnter_Click()
43     Call MsgBox("Salary is " & Format$(txtInput.Text, "currency"))
44     Call Hide
45  End Sub
```

```
46  ' frmCommission
47  Option Explicit
48
49  Private Sub cmdEnter_Click()
50     Dim g As Currency
51
52     g = txtInput.Text
```

```
53      Call MsgBox("Salary is " & _
54                  Format$(250 + 0.057 * g, "currency"))
55      Call Hide
56   End Sub
```

```
57   ' frmHourly
58   Option Explicit
59
60   Private Sub cmdEnter_Click()
61      Dim h As Single, w As Currency
62
63      h = txtHours.Text
64      w = txtAmount.Text
65
66      If h > 40 Then
67         Call MsgBox("Salary is " & _
68                     Format$((40 * w + (h - 40) * 1.5 * w), _
69                     "Currency"))
70      Else
71         Call MsgBox("Salary is " & Format$(h * w, "Currency"))
72      End If
73
74      Call Hide
75   End Sub
```

```
76   ' frmPiece
77   Option Explicit
78
79   Private Sub cmdEnter_Click()
80      Dim n As Integer, a As Currency
81
82      n = txtItems.Text
83      a = txtAmount.Text
84
85      Call MsgBox("Salary is " & Format$(n * a, "Currency"))
86      Call Hide
87   End Sub
```

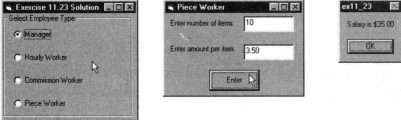

11.24   Modify the Simpletron Simulator of Exercise 10.19 to use MDI. The user should be able to independently display windows for loading an SML program, executing the instructions of an SML program and the dump display. Provide checked menu items that allow the user to select which windows are displayed at any time.

Chapter 12 Solutions

Mouse and Keyboard

12.4 Fill in the blanks in each of the following:

a) The _____ event is triggered when a pressed mouse button is released.
ANS: MouseUp.

b) The process of moving an object with the mouse to another location is called _____.
ANS: drag and drop.

c) The **DragMode** property is either _____ or _____.
ANS: manual, automatic.

d) Movement of the mouse triggers the _____ event.
ANS: MouseMove.

e) The **MousePointer** property can have _____ different values.
ANS: 17.

12.5 [CD] State which of the following are *true* and which are *false*. If *false*, explain why.

a) The mouse pointer can be changed using the **MousePointer** property.
ANS: True.

b) Visual Basic allows animated cursors to be used for the mouse pointer.
ANS: False. Visual Basic does not allow animated cursors to be used.

c) Method **Move** must be used with manual drag-and-drop.
ANS: False. Method **Move** is not required for a manual drag-and-drop operation.

d) Operator **And** is often used in bit manipulation for masking.
ANS: True.

e) The status of the *Shift*, *Ctrl* and *Alt* keys is stored in the most significant bits of the **Shift** bit field.
ANS: False. The status is stored in the least significant bits of bit field **Shift**.

f) The status of mouse buttons is stored in the least significant bits of the **Button** bit field.
ANS: True.

12.6 (*Towers of Hanoi*) Modify your solution to Exercise 6.32 to allow the user to drag-and-drop a disk from one tower to another.
ANS:

```
1   ' Exercise 12.6 Solution
2   Option Explicit
3   Dim mDiskLocations(1 To 3, 1 To 4) As Integer
4   Dim mHasDisk(1 To 3) As Boolean
5   Dim mCurrentDisk As Integer
6   Const mGRAPH_ADJUST = 140    ' Adjustment to place disks graphically
7                                ' on bottom of pole
8
9   Private Sub Form_Load()
10      Dim i As Integer, cursorImage As IPictureDisp
11      Dim poleImage As IPictureDisp
12
13      For i = 1 To 4
14         mDiskLocations(1, i) = 1    ' All disks on left pole
15      Next i
16
17      mHasDisk(1) = True              ' Left pole contains at least one disk
18      mCurrentDisk = 1               ' Current disk to move is the smallest
```

```
19
20        Set cursorImage = LoadPicture("\vb_solutions\ch12\ex12_06\towers2.cur")
21        Set poleImage = LoadPicture("\vb_solutions\ch12\ex12_06\post.gif")
22
23        For i = 1 To 3
24           picPole(i).Picture = poleImage
25           picPole(i).DragIcon = cursorImage
26        Next i
27
28    End Sub
29
30    Private Sub picPole_MouseDown(Index As Integer, Button As Integer, _
31                             Shift As Integer, X As Single, Y As Single)
32        Dim c As Integer
33
34        ' Check to see if we have at least one disk on this pole
35        If mHasDisk(Index) = False Then
36           Exit Sub     ' Exit - pole does not contain a disk
37        End If
38
39        ' For this pole determine the disk to move
40        For c = 1 To 4
41
42           If mDiskLocations(Index, c) = 1 Then
43              mCurrentDisk = c
44              Exit For
45           End If
46
47        Next c
48
49        ' Begin the drag operation
50        Call picPole(Index).Drag(vbBeginDrag)
51    End Sub
52
53    Private Sub picPole_DragDrop(Index As Integer, Source As Control, _
54                             X As Single, Y As Single)
55
56        Dim k As Integer, h As Single, j As Integer
57
58        ' If drop is on same pole exit
59        If Index = Source.Index Then
60           Exit Sub
61        End If
62
63        ' Check to see if a larger disk is being placed on top of a
64        ' smaller disk and if so exit the procedure
65        For k = 1 To 4
66
67           If mDiskLocations(Index, k) <> 0 And k < mCurrentDisk Then
68              Call MsgBox("You cannot place a larger disk on a smaller disk")
69              Exit Sub
70           End If
71
72        Next k
73
74        ' Disk has moved--but not graphically yet
75        mDiskLocations(Source.Index, mCurrentDisk) = 0
76
77        ' This pole now has at least one disk
78        mHasDisk(Index) = True
79
80        ' Place disk on pole
81        Set shpDisk(mCurrentDisk).Container = picPole(Index)
82
83        ' Get graphical height of pole
84        h = picPole(Index).Height
85
```

```
86      ' Determine how many disks are on pole
87      ' and add up their heights
88      For j = 4 To 1 Step -1
89
90         If mDiskLocations(Index, j) = 1 Then
91            h = h - shpDisk(j).Height
92         End If
93
94      Next j
95
96      ' Adjust h for the height of the disk we are going
97      ' to draw
98      h = h - shpDisk(mCurrentDisk).Height
99
100     ' Determine where to draw the disk on the pole
101     ' Center disks and draw at proper elevation
102     For k = 4 To 1 Step -1
103
104        If mDiskLocations(Index, k) = 0 Then
105
106           Call shpDisk(mCurrentDisk).Move(0.5 * _
107                    picPole(Index).Width - 0.5 * _
108                    shpDisk(mCurrentDisk).Width, _
109                    h - mGRAPH_ADJUST)
110           Exit For
111
112        End If
113
114     Next k
115
116     ' Update disk location
117     mDiskLocations(Index, mCurrentDisk) = 1
118
119     ' Determine if the Pole where disk was located still
120     ' contains at least one disk.
121     For k = 1 To 4
122
123        If mDiskLocations(Source.Index, k) = 1 Then
124           mHasDisk(Source.Index) = True
125           Exit Sub
126        End If
127
128     Next k
129
130     mHasDisk(Source.Index) = False
131
132     ' If disk was placed on right pole check for solution
133     If Index = 3 Then
134
135        If IsSolved Then
136           Call MsgBox("You did it!")
137
138           For k = 1 To 3
139              picPole(k).Enabled = False
140           Next k
141
142           tmrTimer.Enabled = True
143        End If
144
145     End If
146
147  End Sub
148
149  Private Function IsSolved() As Boolean
150     Dim i As Integer
151
```

```
152       ' Check for all 4 disks on right pole
153       For i = 1 To 4
154
155          If mDiskLocations(3, i) = 0 Then
156             IsSolved = False
157             Exit Function
158          End If
159
160       Next i
161
162       IsSolved = True
163    End Function
164
165    Private Sub tmrTimer_Timer()
166       Dim i As Integer
167
168       Call Randomize
169
170       For i = 1 To 4
171          shpDisk(i).FillColor = RGB(Rnd() * 256, Rnd() * 256, Rnd() * 256)
172       Next i
173
174    End Sub
```

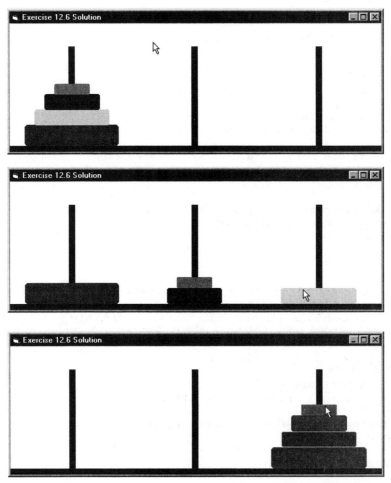

12.7　(*Knight's Tour*) Modify your solution to Exercise 7.19 to use the graphical features of Fig. 12.10. As the knight leaves a square, the appropriate move number should be displayed on the square.

　　　ANS:

```
1    ' Exercise 12.7 Solution
2    Option Explicit
3    Dim mCurrentCell As Integer
```

```
4    Dim mBlackBoard As IPictureDisp
5    Dim mWhiteBoard As IPictureDisp
6    Dim mWhiteKnight As IPictureDisp
7    Dim mBlackKnight As IPictureDisp
8
9    Private Sub Form_Load()
10       Dim x As Integer
11
12       Set mBlackBoard = LoadPicture("\vb_solutions\ch12\" & _
13                                     "ex12_07\b_marble.jpg")
14       Set mWhiteBoard = LoadPicture("\vb_solutions\ch12\" & _
15                                     "ex12_07\w_marble.jpg")
16       Set mBlackKnight = LoadPicture("\vb_solutions\ch12\" & _
17                                      "ex12_07\b_knight.jpg")
18       Set mWhiteKnight = LoadPicture("\vb_solutions\ch12\" & _
19                                      "ex12_07\w_knight.jpg")
20
21       mCurrentCell = Int(Rnd() * 64) + 1
22
23       For x = 1 To 64
24
25          If x Mod 2 Then
26             picSquare(x).Picture = mBlackBoard
27          Else
28             picSquare(x).Picture = mWhiteBoard
29          End If
30
31          With picSquare(x)
32             .FontSize = 14
33             .ForeColor = vbRed
34             .FontBold = True
35          End With
36
37       Next x
38
39       Call modKnightAccess.FirstMove
40    End Sub
41
42    Public Sub TranslateMove(s As String)
43       Dim i As Integer
44
45       For i = 1 To 64
46
47          ' The Tag property can be used by programmers to
48          ' store any type of data. Each picSquare Tag
49          ' property contains strings such as "00", "24", etc.
50          ' that allow the move board to map to the graphical
51          ' display.
52          If picSquare(i).Tag = s Then
53
54             If i Mod 2 Then
55                picSquare(i).Picture = mBlackKnight
56             Else
57                picSquare(i).Picture = mWhiteKnight
58             End If
59
60             Exit Sub
61          End If
62
63       Next i
64
65    End Sub
66
67    Public Sub ClearLastImage(s As String, n As Integer)
68       Dim i As Integer
69
```

```
70        For i = 1 To 64
71
72            If picSquare(i).Tag = s Then
73
74                ' Clear the image
75                If i Mod 2 Then
76                    picSquare(i).Picture = mBlackBoard
77                Else
78                    picSquare(i).Picture = mWhiteBoard
79                End If
80
81                picSquare(i).Print n    ' Print the move number
82                Exit Sub
83            End If
84
85        Next i
86
87    End Sub
88
89    Private Sub tmrTimer_Timer()
90        Call modKnightAccess.Tour
91    End Sub
```

```
92    ' modKnightAccess
93    Option Explicit
94    Dim mMoveNumber As Integer
95    Dim mBoard(7, 7) As Integer
96    Dim mAccess(7) As Variant
97    Dim mHorizontal As Variant
98    Dim mVertical As Variant
99    Dim mCurrentRow As Integer
100   Dim mCurrentColumn As Integer
101
102   Public Sub FirstMove()
103       Call Randomize
104       Call KnightTourAccess
105   End Sub
106
107   Private Sub KnightTourAccess()
108       mHorizontal = Array(2, 1, -1, -2, -2, -1, 1, 2)
109       mVertical = Array(-1, -2, -2, -1, 1, 2, 2, 1)
110
111       Call CreateAccess
112       Call BeginTour
113   End Sub
114
115   Private Sub CreateAccess()
116       ' mAccess is an array of Variants. Each element of the array
117       ' is an array. To access an individual element of mAccess the
118       ' syntax:
119       '     mAccess(r)(c)
120       ' is used.
121       mAccess(0) = Array(2, 3, 4, 4, 4, 4, 3, 2)
122       mAccess(1) = Array(3, 4, 6, 6, 6, 6, 4, 3)
123       mAccess(2) = Array(4, 6, 8, 8, 8, 8, 6, 4)
124       mAccess(3) = Array(4, 6, 8, 8, 8, 8, 6, 4)
125       mAccess(4) = Array(4, 6, 8, 8, 8, 8, 6, 4)
126       mAccess(5) = Array(4, 6, 8, 8, 8, 8, 6, 4)
127       mAccess(6) = Array(3, 4, 6, 6, 6, 6, 4, 3)
128       mAccess(7) = Array(2, 3, 4, 4, 4, 4, 3, 2)
129   End Sub
130
131   Private Function ConvertMove(r As Integer, c As Integer) As String
132       ' Create and return a string such as "46", "70", etc. that is
133       ' used to determine which picSquare picturebox is maps to
134       ' mBoard.
```

```vb
135      ConvertMove = r & c
136  End Function
137
138  Private Sub BeginTour()
139      ' Randomly place knight on the board
140      mCurrentRow = Int(Rnd() * 8)
141      mCurrentColumn = Int(Rnd() * 8)
142      mMoveNumber = mMoveNumber + 1
143      mBoard(mCurrentRow, mCurrentColumn) = mMoveNumber
144      Call frmChecker.TranslateMove(ConvertMove(mCurrentRow, _
145                               mCurrentColumn))
146      frmChecker.tmrTimer.Enabled = True
147  End Sub
148
149  Public Sub Tour()
150      Dim testRow As Integer, testColumn As Integer
151      Dim minRow As Integer, minColumn As Integer, minAccess As Integer
152      Dim accessNumber As Integer, done As Boolean, moveType As Integer
153
154      minAccess = 9      ' Set initial value to an out of range value
155
156      ' Perform the tour based upon the first move
157      accessNumber = minAccess
158
159      ' Test all possible moves based on the current position
160      ' Moves include those that are off the board
161      For moveType = 0 To 7
162          testRow = mCurrentRow + mVertical(moveType)
163          testColumn = mCurrentColumn + mHorizontal(moveType)
164
165          ' Test for a valid move
166          If (ValidMove(testRow, testColumn)) Then
167
168              ' If the access is lower than the current accessNumber
169              ' then remember it
170              If (mAccess(testRow)(testColumn) < accessNumber) Then
171                  accessNumber = mAccess(testRow)(testColumn)
172                  minRow = testRow
173                  minColumn = testColumn
174              End If
175
176              ' Reduce the accessibility for locations we can move to
177              mAccess(testRow)(testColumn) = mAccess(testRow)(testColumn) - 1
178          End If
179
180      Next moveType
181
182      ' If we did find a move then move there and update the
183      ' current position
184      If (accessNumber = minAccess) Then
185          frmChecker.tmrTimer.Enabled = False
186      Else
187          Call frmChecker.ClearLastImage(ConvertMove(mCurrentRow, _
188                               mCurrentColumn), mMoveNumber)
189          mCurrentRow = minRow
190          mCurrentColumn = minColumn
191          mMoveNumber = mMoveNumber + 1
192          mBoard(mCurrentRow, mCurrentColumn) = mMoveNumber
193          Call frmChecker.TranslateMove(ConvertMove(mCurrentRow, _
194                               mCurrentColumn))
195      End If
196
197  End Sub
198
199  Private Function ValidMove(row As Integer, col As Integer) As Boolean
200
201      If ((row >= 0 And row < 8) And (col >= 0 And col < 8)) Then
```

```
202
203          ' Visual Basic logical operators do not short circuit
204          ' therefore this is written as a separate condition
205          If (mBoard(row, col) = 0) Then
206             ValidMove = True
207             Exit Function
208          End If
209       End If
210
211       ValidMove = False
212    End Function
```

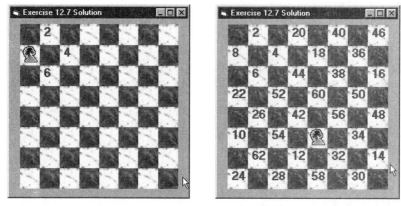

12.8   (*Knight's Tour*) Modify your solution to Exercise 12.7 to provide a **Hint** button. When **Hint** is pressed, display an asterisk on the square with the lowest accessibility. If the user can no longer make any moves or if the tour is successfully completed, disable the **Hint** button.

ANS:

```
1    ' Exercise 12.8 Solution
2    Option Explicit
3    Dim mCurrentCell As Integer
4    Dim mBlackBoard As IPictureDisp
5    Dim mWhiteBoard As IPictureDisp
6    Dim mWhiteKnight As IPictureDisp
7    Dim mBlackKnight As IPictureDisp
8    Dim mKnightCursor As IPictureDisp
9    Dim mKnightFinal As IPictureDisp
10   Dim mKnightFinal2 As IPictureDisp
11   Dim mValidMoves() As String
12
13   Private Sub Form_Load()
14      Dim x As Integer
15
16      Set mBlackBoard = LoadPicture("\vb_solutions\ch12\" & _
17                                 "ex12_08\b_marble.jpg")
18      Set mWhiteBoard = LoadPicture("\vb_solutions\ch12\" & _
19                                 "ex12_08\w_marble.jpg")
20      Set mBlackKnight = LoadPicture("\vb_solutions\ch12\" & _
21                                  "ex12_08\b_knight.jpg")
22      Set mWhiteKnight = LoadPicture("\vb_solutions\ch12\" & _
23                                  "ex12_08\w_knight.jpg")
24      Set mKnightCursor = LoadPicture("\vb_solutions\ch12\" & _
25                                   "ex12_08\knight.cur")
26
27      mCurrentCell = Int(Rnd() * 64) + 1
28
29      For x = 1 To 64
30
31         If x Mod 2 Then
32            picSquare(x).Picture = mBlackBoard
33         Else
34            picSquare(x).Picture = mWhiteBoard
35         End If
```

```
36
37            With picSquare(x)
38               .FontSize = 14
39               .ForeColor = vbRed
40               .FontBold = True
41               .DragIcon = mKnightCursor
42               .AutoRedraw = True
43            End With
44
45        Next x
46
47        Call modKnightAccess.FirstMove
48    End Sub
49
50    Public Sub TranslateMove(s As String)
51        Dim i As Integer
52
53        For i = 1 To 64
54
55            ' The Tag property can be used by programmers to
56            ' store any type of data. Each picSquare Tag
57            ' property contains strings such as "00", "24", etc.
58            ' that allow the move board to map to the graphical
59            ' display.
60            If picSquare(i).Tag = s Then
61
62                If i Mod 2 Then
63                    picSquare(i).Picture = mBlackKnight
64                Else
65                    picSquare(i).Picture = mWhiteKnight
66                End If
67
68                mCurrentCell = i
69                Exit Sub
70            End If
71
72        Next i
73
74    End Sub
75
76    Private Sub cmdHint_Click()
77        Dim k As Integer, s As String
78
79        s = modKnightAccess.GetHint
80
81        For k = 1 To 64
82
83            If picSquare(k).Tag = s Then
84                picSquare(k).Print "*"
85                picSquare(k).CurrentX = 0
86                picSquare(k).CurrentY = 0
87                Exit Sub
88            End If
89
90        Next k
91    End Sub
92
93    Private Sub picSquare_MouseDown(Index As Integer, _
94                                   Button As Integer, _
95                                   Shift As Integer, _
96                                   x As Single, Y As Single)
97        ' If on the PictureBox displaying the image
98        ' then enable dragging.
99        If Index = mCurrentCell Then
100           Call picSquare(mCurrentCell).Drag(vbBeginDrag)
101       End If
102   End Sub
```

```vb
103
104  Private Function IsValidMove(idx As Integer) As Boolean
105     Dim c As Integer
106
107     For c = LBound(mValidMoves) To UBound(mValidMoves)
108
109        If picSquare(idx).Tag = mValidMoves(c) Then
110           Call modKnightAccess.UpdatePosition( _
111                              Left$(picSquare(idx).Tag, _
112                              1), Right$(picSquare(idx).Tag, 1))
113           IsValidMove = True
114           Exit Function
115        End If
116     Next c
117
118     IsValidMove = False
119  End Function
120
121  Private Sub picSquare_DragDrop(Index As Integer, _
122                              Source As Control, _
123                              x As Single, Y As Single)
124     Erase mValidMoves
125     mValidMoves = modKnightAccess.GetValidMoves
126
127     If IsValidMove(Index) = False Then
128        Call MsgBox("Invalid Move.")
129        Exit Sub
130     End If
131
132     ' Draw image at new position
133     If Index Mod 2 Then
134        picSquare(Index).Picture = mBlackKnight
135     Else
136        picSquare(Index).Picture = mWhiteKnight
137     End If
138
139     ' Remove last image only if the drop is at
140     ' a different location.
141     If mCurrentCell <> Index Then
142        If Source.Index Mod 2 Then
143           Source.Picture = mBlackBoard
144           Source.Print modKnightAccess.GetMoveNumber
145        Else
146           Source.Picture = mWhiteBoard
147           Source.Print modKnightAccess.GetMoveNumber
148        End If
149     End If
150
151     ' Update current image position
152     mCurrentCell = Index
153
154     Call modKnightAccess.IncrementMoveNumber
155
156     If modKnightAccess.IsFinished Then
157        Call GameOver
158
159        If modKnightAccess.GetMoveNumber = 64 Then
160           Caption = "Congratulations. You did it!!!"
161
162           If Index Mod 2 Then
163              Set mKnightFinal = LoadPicture("\vb_solutions\ch12\" & _
164                              "ex12_08\b_knight_f.jpg")
165              Set mKnightFinal2 = LoadPicture("\vb_solutions\ch12\" & _
166                              "ex12_08\w_knight.jpg")
167           Else
168              Set mKnightFinal = LoadPicture("\vb_solutions\ch12\" & _
169                              "ex12_08\w_knight_f.jpg")
```

```
170              Set mKnightFinal2 = LoadPicture("\vb_solutions\ch12\" & _
171                                          "ex12_08\w_knight.jpg")
172          End If
173
174          tmrTimer.Enabled = True
175       Else
176          Call MsgBox("Game Over.")
177          Caption = "Game Over."
178       End If
179
180    End If
181 End Sub
182
183 Public Sub GameOver()
184    Dim c As Integer
185
186    For c = 1 To 64
187       picSquare(c).Enabled = False
188    Next c
189
190    cmdHint.Enabled = False
191 End Sub
192
193 Private Sub tmrTimer_Timer()
194    Static c As Boolean
195
196    If c = False Then
197       picSquare(mCurrentCell).Picture = mKnightFinal
198    Else
199       picSquare(mCurrentCell).Picture = mKnightFinal2
200    End If
201
202    c = Not c
203 End Sub
```

```
210 ' modKnightAccess
211 Option Explicit
212 Dim mMoveNumber As Integer
213 Dim mBoard(7, 7) As Integer
214 Dim mAccess(7) As Variant
215 Dim mHorizontal As Variant
216 Dim mVertical As Variant
217 Dim mCurrentRow As Integer
218 Dim mCurrentColumn As Integer
219 Dim mValidMoves() As String
220 Dim mLength As Integer
221
222 Public Sub FirstMove()
223    Call Randomize
224    Call KnightTourAccess
225 End Sub
226
227 Private Sub KnightTourAccess()
228    mHorizontal = Array(2, 1, -1, -2, -2, -1, 1, 2)
229    mVertical = Array(-1, -2, -2, -1, 1, 2, 2, 1)
230
231    Call CreateAccess
232    Call BeginTour
233 End Sub
234
235 Private Sub CreateAccess()
236    ' mAccess is an array of Variants. Each element of the array
237    ' is an array. To access an individual element of mAccess the
238    ' syntax:
239    '     mAccess(r)(c)
240    ' is used.
```

```
241        mAccess(0) = Array(2, 3, 4, 4, 4, 4, 3, 2)
242        mAccess(1) = Array(3, 4, 6, 6, 6, 6, 4, 3)
243        mAccess(2) = Array(4, 6, 8, 8, 8, 8, 6, 4)
244        mAccess(3) = Array(4, 6, 8, 8, 8, 8, 6, 4)
245        mAccess(4) = Array(4, 6, 8, 8, 8, 8, 6, 4)
246        mAccess(5) = Array(4, 6, 8, 8, 8, 8, 6, 4)
247        mAccess(6) = Array(3, 4, 6, 6, 6, 6, 4, 3)
248        mAccess(7) = Array(2, 3, 4, 4, 4, 4, 3, 2)
249    End Sub
250
251    Private Function ConvertMove(r As Integer, c As Integer) As String
252        ' Create and return a string such as "46", "70", etc. that is
253        ' used to determine which picSquare picturebox maps to mBoard.
254        ConvertMove = r & c
255    End Function
256
257    Private Sub BeginTour()
258
259        ' Randomly place knight on the board
260        mCurrentRow = Int(Rnd() * 8)
261        mCurrentColumn = Int(Rnd() * 8)
262        mMoveNumber = 1
263        mBoard(mCurrentRow, mCurrentColumn) = mMoveNumber
264        Call frmChecker.TranslateMove(ConvertMove(mCurrentRow, mCurrentColumn))
265    End Sub
266
267    Public Function GetValidMoves() As String()
268        Dim testRow As Integer, testColumn As Integer
269        Dim accessNumber As Integer, moveType As Integer
270
271        Erase mValidMoves
272        mLength = 0
273
274        ' Test all possible moves based on the current position
275        ' Moves include those that are off the board
276        For moveType = 0 To 7
277            testRow = mCurrentRow + mVertical(moveType)
278            testColumn = mCurrentColumn + mHorizontal(moveType)
279
280            ' Test for a valid move
281            If (ValidMove(testRow, testColumn)) Then
282                mLength = mLength + 1
283                ReDim Preserve mValidMoves(mLength)
284
285                mValidMoves(mLength) = ConvertMove(testRow, testColumn)
286
287                ' If the access is lower than the current accessNumber
288                ' then remember it
289                If (mAccess(testRow)(testColumn) < accessNumber) Then
290                    accessNumber = mAccess(testRow)(testColumn)
291                End If
292
293                ' Reduce the accessibility for locations we can move to
294                mAccess(testRow)(testColumn) = mAccess(testRow)(testColumn) - 1
295            End If
296        Next moveType
297
298        GetValidMoves = mValidMoves
299    End Function
300
301    Public Function IsFinished() As Boolean
302        Dim m As Integer, testRow As Integer
303        Dim testColumn As Integer, invalidMoves As Integer
304
305        For m = 0 To 7
306            testRow = mCurrentRow + mVertical(m)
307            testColumn = mCurrentColumn + mHorizontal(m)
```

```
308
309          ' Test for a valid move
310          If (ValidMove(testRow, testColumn) = False) Then
311              invalidMoves = invalidMoves + 1
312          End If
313
314      Next m
315
316      ' If there are no more moves based upon where the knight
317      ' currently is then end the session.
318      If invalidMoves = 8 Then
319          IsFinished = True
320          Exit Function
321      End If
322
323      IsFinished = False
324  End Function
325
326  Private Function ValidMove(row As Integer, col As Integer) As Boolean
327
328      If ((row >= 0 And row < 8) And (col >= 0 And col < 8)) Then
329          ' Visual Basic logical operators do not short circuit
330          ' therefore this is written as a separate condition
331          If (mBoard(row, col) = 0) Then
332              ValidMove = True
333              Exit Function
334          End If
335
336      End If
337
338      ValidMove = False
339  End Function
340
341  Public Sub UpdatePosition(r As Integer, c As Integer)
342      mCurrentRow = r
343      mCurrentColumn = c
344      mBoard(r, c) = mMoveNumber
345  End Sub
346
347  Public Function GetHint() As String
348      Dim mt As Integer, testRow As Integer
349      Dim testColumn As Integer, hint As String
350      Dim accessNumber As Integer
351
352      accessNumber = 9
353
354      For mt = 0 To 7
355          testRow = mCurrentRow + mVertical(mt)
356          testColumn = mCurrentColumn + mHorizontal(mt)
357
358          ' Test for a valid move
359          If (ValidMove(testRow, testColumn)) Then
360
361              ' If the access is lower than the current accessNumber
362              ' then remember it
363              If (mAccess(testRow)(testColumn) < accessNumber) Then
364                  accessNumber = mAccess(testRow)(testColumn)
365                  hint = ConvertMove(testRow, testColumn)
366              End If
367
368          End If
369
370      Next mt
371
372      GetHint = hint
373  End Function
```

```
374
375  Public Sub IncrementMoveNumber()
376      mMoveNumber = mMoveNumber + 1
377  End Sub
378
379  Public Function GetMoveNumber() As Integer
380      GetMoveNumber = mMoveNumber
381  End Function
```

12.9 (*Eight Queens*) Modify your solution to Exercise 7.22 to allow the user to drag-and-drop each queen on the board. Use the graphical features of Fig. 12.10. Provide eight queen images to the right of the board from which the user can drag-and-drop onto the board. When a queen is dropped on the board, its corresponding image to the left should not be visible.

ANS:

```
1   ' Exercise 12.9 Solution
2   Option Explicit
3   Option Base 1
4   Dim mCurrentCell As Integer
5   Dim mBlackQueenImage As IPictureDisp
6   Dim mWhiteQueenImage As IPictureDisp
7   Dim mBlackCell As IPictureDisp
8   Dim mWhiteCell As IPictureDisp
9   Dim mQueenLocations(8) As Integer
10  Dim mCorrect As Boolean
11
12  Private Sub Form_Load()
13      Dim k As Integer, queenImage As IPictureDisp
14      Dim queenCursor As IPictureDisp
15
16      mCorrect = True
17      Call ClearBoard     ' Clear mBoard
18
19      ' Necessary although access features not used in this
20      ' solution. You may consider using the access features
21      ' to enhance this solution to allow the user to receive
22      ' hints on possible moves.
23      Call CreateAccess
24
25      Set queenCursor = LoadPicture("\vb_solutions\ch12\" & _
26                                "ex12_09\queen.cur")
27
28      Set mBlackCell = LoadPicture("\vb_solutions\ch12\" & _
29                                "ex12_09\b_marble.jpg")
30
31      Set mWhiteCell = LoadPicture("\vb_solutions\ch12\" & _
32                                "ex12_09\w_marble.jpg")
33
34      For k = 1 To 64
35          If k Mod 2 Then
36              picSquare(k).Picture = mWhiteCell
```

```
37              Else
38                  picSquare(k).Picture = mBlackCell
39              End If
40          Next k
41
42          Set mBlackQueenImage = LoadPicture("\vb_solutions\ch12\" & _
43                                      "ex12_09\b_queen.jpg")
44          Set mWhiteQueenImage = LoadPicture("\vb_solutions\ch12\" & _
45                                      "ex12_09\w_queen.jpg")
46
47          Set queenImage = LoadPicture("\vb_solutions\ch12\ex12_09" & _
48                                      "\queen.jpg")
49          For k = 1 To 8
50              picQueen(k).Picture = queenImage
51              picQueen(k).DragIcon = queenCursor
52          Next k
53      End Sub
54
55      Private Sub picQueen_MouseDown(Index As Integer, Button As Integer, _
56                                  Shift As Integer, x As Single, Y As Single)
57
58          Call picQueen(Index).Drag(vbBeginDrag)
59      End Sub
60
61      Private Sub picSquare_DragDrop(Index As Integer, _
62                                  Source As Control, _
63                                  x As Single, Y As Single)
64
65          Dim row As Integer, col As Integer, done As Boolean
66          Dim count As Integer, c As Integer
67
68          mQueenLocations(Source.Index) = Index
69
70          ' Draw image at new position
71          If Index Mod 2 Then
72              picSquare(Index).Picture = mWhiteQueenImage
73          Else
74              picSquare(Index).Picture = mBlackQueenImage
75          End If
76
77          ' Hide queen where drag originated
78          Source.Visible = False
79
80          ' Get the row and col where queen is dropped.
81          ' Each picSquare element stores a two-digit number in its
82          ' Tag property describing its location relative to array
83          ' mBoard. The first digit specifies the row and the
84          ' second digit specifies the column. The Tag property
85          ' is available for storing any type of data the programmer
86          ' needs in a program.
87          row = picSquare(Index).Tag \ 10
88          col = picSquare(Index).Tag Mod 10
89
90          ' Place queen in mBoard and determine if any conflicts are
91          ' present with the placement of the queen.
92          mBoard(row, col) = 81
93          mCorrect = XconflictSquares(row, col)
94
95          ' Notify the user that a conflict has occured.
96          If mCorrect = False Then
97              Caption = "Sorry. At least one conflict."
98
99              ' Disable all queen images.
100             For c = 1 To 8
101                 picQueen(c).Enabled = False
102             Next c
103
```

```
104        Call MsgBox("Game Over!")
105    End If
106
107    ' Check if 8 queens have been placed on board
108    For c = 1 To 8
109
110        If mQueenLocations(c) = 0 Then
111            count = count + 1
112            Exit Sub
113        End If
114
115    Next c
116
117    ' Check for a correct solution
118    If mCorrect = True And count = 0 Then
119        Caption = "CONGRATULATIONS!!! You did it."
120    End If
121
122 End Sub
```

```
1  ' modQueensAccess
2  Option Explicit
3  Dim mQueens As Integer
4  Dim mDone As Boolean
5  Dim mAccess(7)
6  Public mBoard(7, 7) As Integer
7
8  Public Sub Setup()
9      Call Randomize
10     Call CreateAccess
11     Call ClearBoard
12     Call FirstMove
13     Call PlaceQueens
14 End Sub
15
16 Public Sub CreateAccess()
17     ' mAccess is an array of Variants. Each element of the array
18     ' is an array. To access an individual element of mAccess the
19     ' syntax:
20     '      mAccess(r)(c)
21     ' is used.
22     mAccess(0) = Array(22, 22, 22, 22, 22, 22, 22, 22)
23     mAccess(1) = Array(22, 24, 24, 24, 24, 24, 24, 22)
24     mAccess(2) = Array(22, 24, 26, 26, 26, 26, 24, 22)
25     mAccess(3) = Array(22, 24, 26, 28, 28, 26, 24, 22)
26     mAccess(4) = Array(22, 24, 26, 28, 28, 26, 24, 22)
27     mAccess(5) = Array(22, 24, 26, 26, 26, 26, 24, 22)
28     mAccess(6) = Array(22, 24, 24, 24, 24, 24, 24, 22)
29     mAccess(7) = Array(22, 22, 22, 22, 22, 22, 22, 22)
30 End Sub
31
32 Public Sub ClearBoard()
33     Dim a As Integer, b As Integer
34
35     mQueens = 0
36
37     For a = 0 To 7
38
39         For b = 0 To 7
40             mBoard(a, b) = 32    ' ASCII value for a space
41         Next b
42
43     Next a
44
45 End Sub
46
```

```
47   Private Sub FirstMove()
48      Dim rowMove As Integer, colMove As Integer
49
50      mQueens = 0
51      mDone = False
52      rowMove = Int(Rnd() * 8)
53      colMove = Int(Rnd() * 8)
54      mBoard(rowMove, colMove) = 81   ' ASCII value for Q
55      Call XconflictSquares(rowMove, colMove)
56      mQueens = mQueens + 1
57      Call NewAccess
58   End Sub
59
60   Private Sub PlaceQueens()
61
62      While (Not mDone)
63         Call NextMove
64      Wend
65
66   End Sub
67
68   Private Sub NextMove()
69      Dim lowestAccess As Integer, currentRow As Integer
70      Dim currentCol As Integer, rowMove As Integer, colMove As Integer
71
72      lowestAccess = 100   ' Assign a value greater than the highest access
73      mDone = True
74
75      For currentRow = 0 To 7
76         For currentCol = 0 To 7
77
78            If mBoard(currentRow, currentCol) = 32 Then
79               mDone = False
80
81               If mAccess(currentRow)(currentCol) < lowestAccess Then
82                  lowestAccess = mAccess(currentRow)(currentCol)
83                  rowMove = currentRow
84                  colMove = currentCol
85               End If
86
87            End If
88
89         Next currentCol
90      Next currentRow
91
92      If mDone Then
93         Exit Sub
94      End If
95
96      mBoard(rowMove, colMove) = 81   ' ASCII value for Q
97      Call XconflictSquares(rowMove, colMove)
98      mQueens = mQueens + 1
99      Call NewAccess
100  End Sub
101
102  Private Sub NewAccess()
103     Dim r As Integer, c As Integer
104
105     For r = 0 To 7
106        For c = 0 To 7
107           If (mBoard(r, c) = 32) Then
108              Call UpdateAccess(r, c)
109           End If
110        Next c
111     Next r
112  End Sub
113
```

```
114  Private Sub UpdateAccessDiagonals(r As Integer, c As Integer, _
115                                   rowAdjust As Integer, _
116                                   colAdjust As Integer, _
117                                   row As Integer, col As Integer)
118      Dim a As Integer
119
120      While (a < 8 And ValidMove(r, c))
121         If mAccess(r)(c) = 0 Then
122            mAccess(row)(col) = mAccess(row)(col) - 1
123         End If
124
125         r = r + rowAdjust
126         c = c + colAdjust
127         a = a + 1
128      Wend
129
130  End Sub
131
132  Private Sub UpdateAccess(row As Integer, col As Integer)
133      Call UpdateAccessDiagonals(row - 1, col - 1, -1, -1, row, col)
134      Call UpdateAccessDiagonals(row - 1, col + 1, -1, 1, row, col)
135      Call UpdateAccessDiagonals(row + 1, col - 1, 1, -1, row, col)
136      Call UpdateAccessDiagonals(row + 1, col + 1, 1, 1, row, col)
137      Call UpdateAccessRowsAndCols(row, col)
138  End Sub
139
140  Private Sub UpdateAccessRowsAndCols(row As Integer, col As Integer)
141      Dim a As Integer
142
143      For a = 0 To 7
144         If (mAccess(row)(a) = 0) Then
145            mAccess(row)(col) = mAccess(row)(col) - 1
146         End If
147
148         If (mAccess(a)(col) = 0) Then
149            mAccess(row)(col) = mAccess(row)(col) - 1
150         End If
151      Next a
152  End Sub
153
154  Private Function ValidMove(row As Integer, col As Integer) As Boolean
155      ValidMove = (row >= 0 And row < 8 And col >= 0 And col < 8)
156  End Function
157
158  Public Function AvailableSquare() As Boolean
159      Dim r As Integer, c As Integer
160      For r = 0 To 7
161         For c = 0 To 7
162            If mBoard(r, c) = 32 Then
163               AvailableSquare = False   ' At least one open square is available
164               Exit Function
165            End If
166         Next c
167      Next r
168
169      AvailableSquare = True
170  End Function
171
172  Public Function XconflictSquares(row As Integer, col As Integer) As Boolean
173      Dim a As Integer, queensInRow As Integer, queensInCol As Integer
174
175      For a = 0 To 7
176
177         ' Place a 35 in the row occupied by the queen
178         If (mBoard(row, a) = 32) Then
179            mBoard(row, a) = 35      ' ASCII value for #
180            mAccess(row)(a) = 0
```

```
181            ElseIf mBoard(row, a) = 81 Then
182                queensInRow = queensInRow + 1
183            End If
184
185            If queensInRow > 1 Then
186                XconflictSquares = False
187                Exit Function
188            End If
189
190            ' Place a 35 in the col occupied by the queen
191            If (mBoard(a, col) = 32) Then
192                mBoard(a, col) = 35
193                mAccess(a)(col) = 0
194            ElseIf mBoard(a, col) = 81 Then
195                queensInCol = queensInCol + 1
196            End If
197
198            If queensInCol > 1 Then
199                XconflictSquares = False
200                Exit Function
201            End If
202
203        Next a
204
205        ' Place a 35 in the diagonals occupied by the queen
206        XconflictSquares = Xdiagonals(row, col)
207  End Function
208
209  Private Function Xdiagonals(row As Integer, col As Integer) As Boolean
210
211        If XdiagonalHelper(row - 1, col - 1, -1, -1) = False Then
212            Xdiagonals = False
213            Exit Function
214        ElseIf XdiagonalHelper(row - 1, col + 1, -1, 1) = False Then
215            Xdiagonals = False
216            Exit Function
217        ElseIf XdiagonalHelper(row + 1, col - 1, 1, -1) = False Then
218            Xdiagonals = False
219            Exit Function
220        ElseIf XdiagonalHelper(row + 1, col + 1, 1, 1) = False Then
221            Xdiagonals = False
222            Exit Function
223        End If
224
225        Xdiagonals = True
226  End Function
227
228  Private Function XdiagonalHelper(r As Integer, c As Integer, rAdjust As Integer, _
229                         cAdjust As Integer) As Boolean
230        Dim a As Integer
231
232        While (a < 8 And ValidMove(r, c))
233
234            If mBoard(r, c) = 81 Then
235                XdiagonalHelper = False
236                Exit Function
237            End If
238
239            mBoard(r, c) = 35
240            mAccess(r)(c) = 0
241            r = r + rAdjust
242            c = c + cAdjust
243            a = a + 1
244        Wend
245
246        XdiagonalHelper = True
247  End Function
```

```
248
249  Public Sub PrintBoard(f As Form)
250     Dim queens As Integer, r As Integer, c As Integer
251
252     Call f.Cls
253
254     ' Header for columns
255     f.Print "   0 1 2 3 4 5 6 7"
256
257     For r = 0 To 7
258        f.Print Format$(r, "@@") & " ";
259        For c = 0 To 7
260
261           ' Function Chr$ prints the ASCII character
262           ' representation of an Integer.
263           f.Print Chr$(mBoard(r, c)) & " ";
264
265           If (mBoard(r, c) = 81) Then
266              queens = queens + 1
267           End If
268
269        Next c
270
271        f.Print
272     Next r
273
274     f.Print
275     f.Print queens & " Queens were placed on the board."
276  End Sub
```

12.10   [CD] Write a program that uses the mouse to draw a square on the form. The upper-left coordinate should be the location where the user first pressed the mouse button, and the lower-right coordinate should be the location where the user releases the mouse button. Also display the area in twips in the **Caption**.

ANS:

```
1   ' Exercise 12.10 Solution
2   Option Explicit
3   Dim mUpperX As Single
4   Dim mUpperY As Single
5
6   Private Sub Form_MouseDown(Button As Integer, Shift As Integer, _
7                              X As Single, Y As Single)
8      mUpperX = X
9      mUpperY = Y
10  End Sub
11
12  Private Sub Form_MouseUp(Button As Integer, Shift As Integer, _
13                           X As Single, Y As Single)
14     Line (mUpperX, mUpperY)-(X, Y), , B
15     Caption = "Area: " & (Abs(mUpperX - X) * Abs(mUpperY - Y)) & _
16               " Twips"
17  End Sub
```

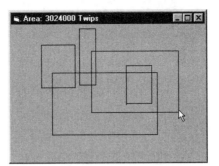

12.11 Modify your solution to Exercise 12.10 to allow the user to draw different shapes. As a minimum, the user should be allowed to choose from an oval, circle, line and rectangle. Allow the user to select the shape type from a menu.

ANS:

```
1    ' Exercise 12.11 Solution
2    Option Explicit
3    Dim mX1 As Single
4    Dim mY1 As Single
5    Dim mShape As Integer
6
7    Enum ShapeType
8       shptypLINE
9       shptypOVAL
10      shptypCIRCLE
11      shptypRECTANGLE
12   End Enum
13
14   Private Sub Form_MouseDown(Button As Integer, Shift As Integer, _
15                              X As Single, Y As Single)
16      mX1 = X
17      mY1 = Y
18   End Sub
19
20   Private Sub Form_MouseUp(Button As Integer, Shift As Integer, _
21                            X As Single, Y As Single)
22
23      Call DrawShape(X, Y)
24   End Sub
25
26   Private Sub DrawShape(X As Single, Y As Single)
27      Dim temp As Single
28
29      Select Case mShape
30         Case shptypLINE
31            Line (mX1, mY1)-(X, Y)
32            Caption = "Line"
33         Case shptypOVAL
34            Call SetMaxPoint(X, Y)
35            Circle (X - Abs(mX1 - X) / 2, Y - Abs(mY1 - Y) / 2), _
36                   Abs(mX1 - X) / 2, , , , 0.5
37            Caption = "Oval"
38         Case shptypCIRCLE
39            Call SetMaxPoint(X, Y)
40            Circle (X - Abs(mX1 - X) / 2, Y - Abs(mY1 - Y) / 2), Abs(mX1 - X) / 2
41            Caption = "Circle"
42         Case shptypRECTANGLE
43            Line (mX1, mY1)-(X, Y), , B
44            Caption = "Area: " & (Abs(mX1 - X) * _
45                      Abs(mY1 - Y)) & " Twips"
46      End Select
47
48   End Sub
49
```

```
50   Private Sub SetMaxPoint(X As Single, Y As Single)
51      Dim temp As Single
52
53      If mX1 > X Then
54         temp = X
55         X = mX1
56         mX1 = temp
57      End If
58
59      If mY1 > Y Then
60         temp = Y
61         Y = mY1
62         mY1 = temp
63      End If
64   End Sub
65
66   Private Sub mnuShape_Click(Index As Integer)
67      mShape = Index
68   End Sub
```

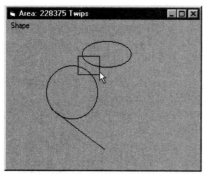

12.12   Modify your solution to Exercise 12.11 to allow the user to specify the shape using the keyboard. The shape drawn should be determined by the following keys: *o* for oval, *c* for circle, *r* for rectangle, *O* for a solid oval, *C* for a solid circle, *R* for a solid rectangle and *L* for line. All drawing is done in the color blue. The initial shape defaults to a circle.

   ANS:

```
1    ' Exercise 12.12 Solution
2    Option Explicit
3    Dim mX1 As Single
4    Dim mY1 As Single
5    Dim mShape As Integer
6    Dim mFilled As Boolean
7
8    Enum ShapeType
9       shptypLINE
10      shptypOVAL
11      shptypCIRCLE
12      shptypRECTANGLE
13   End Enum
14
15   Private Sub Form_Load()
16      mShape = shptypCIRCLE
17   End Sub
18
19   Private Sub Form_Keypress(KeyCode As Integer)
20
21      Select Case KeyCode
22         Case Asc("o")
23            mShape = shptypOVAL
24            mFilled = False
25         Case Asc("r")
26            mShape = shptypRECTANGLE
27            mFilled = False
28         Case Asc("c")
29            mShape = shptypCIRCLE
```

```
30              mFilled = False
31          Case Asc("C")
32              mShape = shptypCIRCLE
33              mFilled = True
34          Case Asc("R")
35              mShape = shptypRECTANGLE
36              mFilled = True
37          Case Asc("O")
38              mShape = shptypOVAL
39              mFilled = True
40          Case Asc("L")
41              mShape = shptypLINE
42              mFilled = False
43      End Select
44  End Sub
45
46  Private Sub Form_MouseDown(Button As Integer, Shift As Integer, _
47                            X As Single, Y As Single)
48      mX1 = X
49      mY1 = Y
50  End Sub
51
52  Private Sub Form_MouseUp(Button As Integer, Shift As Integer, _
53                          X As Single, Y As Single)
54      Call DrawShape(X, Y)
55  End Sub
56
57  Private Sub DrawShape(X As Single, Y As Single)
58      Dim temp As Single
59
60      If mFilled Then
61          FillStyle = vbFSSolid
62      Else
63          FillStyle = vbFSTransparent
64      End If
65
66      Select Case mShape
67          Case shptypLINE
68              Line (mX1, mY1)-(X, Y)
69              Caption = "Line"
70          Case shptypOVAL
71              Call SetMaxPoint(X, Y)
72              Circle (X - Abs(mX1 - X) / 2, Y - Abs(mY1 - Y) / 2), _
73                      Abs(mX1 - X) / 2, , , , 0.5
74              Caption = "Oval"
75          Case shptypCIRCLE
76              Call SetMaxPoint(X, Y)
77              Circle (X - Abs(mX1 - X) / 2, Y - Abs(mY1 - Y) / 2), Abs(mX1 - X) / 2
78              Caption = "Circle"
79          Case shptypRECTANGLE
80              Line (mX1, mY1)-(X, Y), , B
81              Caption = "Area: " & (Abs(mX1 - X) * _
82                      Abs(mY1 - Y)) & " Twips"
83      End Select
84  End Sub
85
86  Private Sub SetMaxPoint(X As Single, Y As Single)
87      Dim temp As Single
88
89      If mX1 > X Then
90          temp = X
91          X = mX1
92          mX1 = temp
93      End If
94
95      If mY1 > Y Then
96          temp = Y
```

```
97           Y = mY1
98           mY1 = temp
99        End If
100 End Sub
101
102 Private Sub mnuShape_Click(Index As Integer)
103     mShape = Index
104 End Sub
```

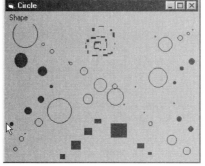

12.13   Modify your solution to Exercise 12.10 or Exercise 12.11 to provide a "rubber-banding" effect. As the user drags the mouse, the user should be able to see the current size of the rectangle to know exactly what the rectangle will look like when the mouse button is released.

ANS:

```
1  ' Exercise 12.13 Solution
2  Option Explicit
3  Dim mUpperX As Single
4  Dim mUpperY As Single
5
6  Private Sub Form_MouseDown(Button As Integer, Shift As Integer, _
7                             X As Single, Y As Single)
8     mUpperX = X
9     mUpperY = Y
10 End Sub
11
12 Private Sub Form_MouseMove(Button As Integer, Shift As Integer, _
13                            X As Single, Y As Single)
14
15    If Button = vbLeftButton Then
16       Call Cls
17       Line (mUpperX, mUpperY)-(X, Y), , B
18    End If
19
20 End Sub
21
22 Private Sub Form_MouseUp(Button As Integer, Shift As Integer, _
23                          X As Single, Y As Single)
24    Line (mUpperX, mUpperY)-(X, Y), , B
25    Caption = "Area: " & (Abs(mUpperX - X) * Abs(mUpperY - Y)) & _
26            " Twips"
27 End Sub
```

12.14   Modify your solution to Exercise 11.12 to change the ANSI C keywords to green after the word is typed. Remove the button from your solution.

12.15   [**CD**] *(Drawing program)* Write a program that allows the user to draw "free-hand" images with the mouse in a **Picture-Box**. Provide a button that allows the user to clear the **PictureBox**.

ANS:

```
1   ' Exercise 12.15 Solution
2   Option Explicit
3
4   Private Sub Form_Load()
5      picPicture.Scale (0, 0)-(400, 400)
6      picPicture.FillStyle = vbFSSolid
7   End Sub
8
9   Private Sub cmdClear_Click()
10     Call picPicture.Cls
11  End Sub
12
13  Private Sub picPicture_MouseMove(Button As Integer, Shift As Integer, _
14                               X As Single, Y As Single)
15     If Button = vbLeftButton Then
16        picPicture.Circle (X, Y), 3
17     End If
18
19  End Sub
```

12.16   Modify Exercise 12.15 to allow the user to select the drawing color and the pen size.

ANS:

```
1   ' Exercise 12.16 Solution
2   Option Explicit
3
4   Private Sub Form_Load()
5      picPicture.Scale (0, 0)-(400, 400)
6      picPicture.FillStyle = vbFSSolid
7      picPicture.ForeColor = vbBlack
8      picPicture.FillColor = vbBlack
9   End Sub
10
11  Private Sub cmdClear_Click()
12     Call picPicture.Cls
13  End Sub
14
15  Private Sub optColor_Click(Index As Integer)
16     picPicture.ForeColor = optColor.Item(Index).BackColor
```

```
17
18        ' Ensure that drawing is done in a uniform color
19        picPicture.FillColor = optColor.Item(Index).BackColor
20    End Sub
21
22    Private Sub picPicture_MouseMove(Button As Integer, Shift As Integer, _
23                                    X As Single, Y As Single)
24
25        If Button = vbLeftButton Then
26            picPicture.Circle (X, Y), cboPen.Text
27        End If
28
29    End Sub
```

Chapter 13 Solutions
Error Handling and Debugging

13.3 **[CD]** Fill in the blanks in each of the following:
    a) Either _____ or _____ disables an active error handler.
    ANS: **On Error GoTo 0** or exiting a procedure. Note: Activating an error handler also disables any previously active error handler.
    b) The sequence of calls generated to reach a procedure or function is called the _____.
    ANS: call stack.
    c) The _____ object is the error object.
    ANS: **Err**.

13.4 State which of the following are *true* and which are *false*. If *false*, explain why.
    a) The **Resume** statement can be placed anywhere a line of executable code is permitted.
    ANS: True.
    b) An active error handler is always said to be enabled.
    ANS: True.
    c) The statement **On Error Goto -1** disables an error handler.
    ANS: False. The statement **On Error Goto 0** disables an error handler.
    d) Error handlers can be disabled when using the debugger.
    ANS: True.

13.5 **[CD]** List three common errors.
    ANS: Overflow, Type mismatch, Divide by Zero.

13.6 Explain what happens when an error is raised in a procedure that does not contain an error handler.
    ANS: The error propagates to the calling procedure.

13.7 **[CD]** Why are error handlers typically preceded by **Exit Sub** or **Exit Function**?
    ANS: **Exit Sub/Exit Function** is typically used to prevent the error handling code from being executed accidently.

13.8 Briefly describe the three IDE modes.
    ANS: Design: The developer is using the IDE to create a program.
             Break: The program is running in a suspended state. Debugging features can be used to trace the flow of logic.
             Run: The program is executing.

13.9 Modify the program of Fig. 13.9 to allow the user to set the procedure where the error is raised.

13.10 Modify the Simpletron Simulator of Exercise 10.19 to handle the various errors that can occur (i.e., replace your **MsgBox** function calls with **On Error** statements).
    ANS:

```
1   ' Exercise 13.10 Solution
2   Option Explicit
3   Dim mProgramCounter As Integer
4   Dim mMemory(99) As Integer
5   Dim mInstructionRegister As Integer
6   Dim mOperationCode As Integer
7   Dim mOperand As Integer
8   Dim mAccumulator As Integer
9   Dim mMode As Integer
10
```

```
11    Enum Mode
12        smlLoadMemory
13        smlExecute
14        smlDump
15    End Enum
16
17    Enum OperationCodes
18        smlRead = 10
19        smlWrite = 11
20        smlLoad = 20
21        smlStore = 21
22        smlAdd = 30
23        smlSubtract = 31
24        smlDivide = 32
25        smlMultiply = 33
26        smlBranch = 40
27        smlBranchNegative = 41
28        smlBranchZero = 42
29        smlHalt = 43
30    End Enum
31
32    Private Sub Form_Load()
33        lblInstructions.Caption = "Welcome to Simpletron! Please enter " & _
34                                  "your SML program one instruction (or " & _
35                                  "data word) at a time into the TextBox." & _
36                                  "The SML memory location is displayed on " & _
37                                  "the button. Press the Done button when " & _
38                                  "input is completed."
39        tmrTimer.Enabled = False
40        mMode = smlLoadMemory
41        frmSimulator.Caption = "Simulator [Load]"
42        lblAccumulator.Caption = "0"
43        lblInstRegister.Caption = "0"
44        lblOpCode.Caption = "0"
45        lblOperand.Caption = "0"
46        lblProgramCounter.Caption = "0"
47    End Sub
48
49    Private Sub cmdCommand_Click()
50        Dim temp As Integer
51
52        On Error GoTo errorHandler
53
54        If mMode = smlLoadMemory Then
55            temp = txtInput.Text
56
57            If IsValid(temp) = False Then
58                Call Err.Raise(65000)
59            End If
60
61            mMemory(mProgramCounter) = temp
62            Call lstMemory.AddItem(Format$(mProgramCounter, "00") & vbTab & _
63                                   txtInput.Text, mProgramCounter)
64            mProgramCounter = mProgramCounter + 1
65            cmdCommand.Caption = "Input " & Format$(mProgramCounter, "00")
66            txtInput.Text = ""
67        ElseIf mMode = smlExecute Then
68            tmrTimer.Enabled = True
69        End If
70
71        Exit Sub
72
73    errorHandler:
74
75        If Err.Number = 65000 Then
76            Call MsgBox("*** Load Overflow error ***", vbCritical)
77            txtInput.Text = ""
```

```
78          Call txtInput.SetFocus
79       End If
80
81    End Sub
82
83    Private Sub cmdDone_Click()
84       txtInput.Enabled = False
85       cmdCommand.Enabled = False
86       cmdDone.Enabled = False
87       mProgramCounter = 0
88       tmrTimer.Enabled = True
89       mMode = smlExecute
90       frmSimulator.Caption = "Simulator [Execute]"
91    End Sub
92
93    Private Sub Execute()
94       Dim temp As Integer
95
96       On Error GoTo errorHandler
97
98       lstMemory.Selected(mProgramCounter) = True
99       mInstructionRegister = mMemory(mProgramCounter)
100      mOperationCode = mInstructionRegister \ 100
101      mOperand = mInstructionRegister Mod 100
102
103      lblInstRegister.Caption = mInstructionRegister
104      lblOpCode.Caption = mOperationCode
105      lblOperand.Caption = mOperand
106      lblProgramCounter.Caption = mProgramCounter
107
108      Select Case mOperationCode
109         Case smlRead
110            lblInstructions.Caption = "Enter an Integer:"
111            txtInput.Enabled = True
112            Call txtInput.SetFocus
113            cmdCommand.Caption = "Enter"
114            cmdCommand.Enabled = True
115
116            If txtInput.Text = "" Then
117               tmrTimer.Enabled = False
118               Exit Sub
119            End If
120
121            mMemory(mOperand) = txtInput.Text
122            txtInput.Text = ""
123            mProgramCounter = mProgramCounter + 1
124            txtInput.Enabled = False
125            cmdCommand.Enabled = False
126         Case smlWrite
127            lblInstructions.Caption = "Memory " & _
128                        Format$(mProgramCounter, "00") & _
129                        ": " & Format$(mMemory(mOperand), "0000")
130            mProgramCounter = mProgramCounter + 1
131         Case smlLoad
132            mAccumulator = mMemory(mOperand)
133            lblAccumulator.Caption = mAccumulator
134            mProgramCounter = mProgramCounter + 1
135         Case smlStore
136            mMemory(mOperand) = mAccumulator
137            mProgramCounter = mProgramCounter + 1
138         Case smlAdd
139            temp = mAccumulator + mMemory(mOperand)
140
141            If IsValid(temp) = False Then
142               Call Err.Raise(65001)
143            End If
144
```

```
145            mAccumulator = temp
146            lblAccumulator.Caption = mAccumulator
147            mProgramCounter = mProgramCounter + 1
148        Case smlSubtract
149            temp = mAccumulator - mMemory(mOperand)
150
151            If IsValid(temp) = False Then
152                Call Err.Raise(65001)
153            End If
154
155            mAccumulator = temp
156            lblAccumulator.Caption = mAccumulator
157            mProgramCounter = mProgramCounter + 1
158        Case smlMultiply
159            temp = mAccumulator * mMemory(mOperand)
160
161            If IsValid(temp) = False Then
162                Call Err.Raise(65002)
163            End If
164
165            mAccumulator = temp
166            lblAccumulator.Caption = mAccumulator
167            mProgramCounter = mProgramCounter + 1
168        Case smlDivide
169
170            If mMemory(mOperand) = 0 Then
171                Call Err.Raise(65003)
172            End If
173
174            mAccumulator = mAccumulator \ mMemory(mOperand)
175            lblAccumulator.Caption = mAccumulator
176            mProgramCounter = mProgramCounter + 1
177        Case smlBranch
178            mProgramCounter = mOperand
179        Case smlBranchNegative
180
181            If mAccumulator < 0 Then
182                mProgramCounter = mOperand
183            Else
184                mProgramCounter = mProgramCounter + 1
185            End If
186
187        Case smlBranchZero
188
189            If mAccumulator = 0 Then
190                mProgramCounter = mOperand
191            Else
192                mProgramCounter = mProgramCounter + 1
193            End If
194
195        Case smlHalt
196            lblInstructions.Caption = "*** Execution terminated. ***"
197            Call ExecuteTermination
198        Case Else
199            Call Err.Raise(65004)
200    End Select
201
202    Exit Sub
203
204 errorHandler:
205
206    Select Case Err.Number
207        Case 65001
208            Call MsgBox("*** Overflow error ***", vbCritical)
209        Case 65002
210            Call MsgBox("*** Attempt to divide by zero ***", _
211                        vbCritical)
```

```
212         Case 65003
213            Call MsgBox("*** Attempt to divide by zero ***", _
214                        vbCritical)
215         Case 65004
216            Call MsgBox("*** Invalid Instruction ***", vbCritical)
217         Case Else
218            Call MsgBox("Unexpected error " & Err.Number & _
219                        ". Terminating.")
220            Call mnuitmExit_Click
221      End Select
222
223      Call ExecuteTermination
224   End Sub
225
226   Private Function IsValid(value As Integer) As Boolean
227
228      If value > 9999 Or value < -9999 Then
229         IsValid = False
230         Exit Function
231      End If
232
233      IsValid = True
234   End Function
235
236   Private Sub ExecuteTermination()
237      tmrTimer.Enabled = False
238      mMode = smlDump
239      frmSimulator.Caption = "Simulator [Dump]"
240      Call Dump
241   End Sub
242
243   Private Sub mnuitmExit_Click()
244      End
245   End Sub
246
247   Private Sub tmrTimer_Timer()
248      Call Execute
249   End Sub
250
251   Private Sub Dump()
252      Dim r As Integer, c As Integer
253
254      picOutput.Print Space$(14) & "0";
255
256      For r = 1 To 9
257         picOutput.Print Space$(6) & r;
258      Next r
259
260      picOutput.Print
261
262      For r = 0 To 9
263         picOutput.Print Space$(5) & Format$(r * 10, "00") & Space$(3);
264
265         For c = 0 To 9
266            picOutput.Print Format$(mMemory(r * 10 + c), _
267                                    "00000") & Space$(2);
268         Next c
269
270         picOutput.Print
271      Next r
272
273   End Sub
```

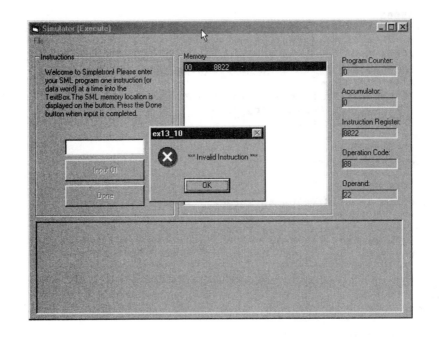

Chapter 14 Solutions
Sequential File Processing

14.4 [CD] Fill in the blanks in each of the following:

a) Computers store large amounts of data on secondary storage devices as _____.

ANS: files.

b) A_____ is composed of several fields.

ANS: record.

c) A field that may contain only digits, letters and blanks is called an _____ field.

ANS: alphanumeric.

d) Method _____ closes a file.

ANS: Close.

e) A group of related characters that conveys meaning is called a _____ .

ANS: field.

14.5 State which of the following are *true* and which are *false*. If *false*, explain why.

a) Each statement that processes a **File** in a program explicitly refers to that **File** by name.

ANS: False. Either a **File** object or a **FileSystemObject** is used.

b) Data items represented in computers form a data hierarchy in which data items become larger and more complex as we progress from fields to characters to bits, etc.

ANS: False. Data items processed by a computer form a data hierarchy in which data items become larger and more complex as we progress from bits to characters to fields, etc.

14.6 Write a program that reads in a series of **Integer**s from a file named **data.dat** and sorts them in descending order with a quick sort.

ANS:

```
1   ' Exercise 14.6 Solution
2   Option Explicit
3   Dim mFileSysObj As New FileSystemObject
4   Dim mFile As File
5   Dim mTxtStream As TextStream
6   Dim mNumbers() As Integer
7   Dim mCurrent As Integer
8
9   Private Sub Form_Load()
10      Set mFile = mFileSysObj.GetFile("\vb_solutions\ch14\" & _
11                            "ex14_06\data.dat")
12      Set mTxtStream = mFile.OpenAsTextStream(ForReading)
13  End Sub
14
15  Private Sub cmdRead_Click()
16      Dim s As String, j As Integer
17
18      On Error GoTo handler
19
20      Do
21         mCurrent = mCurrent + 1
22         ReDim Preserve mNumbers(mCurrent)
```

```
23              mNumbers(mCurrent) = mTxtStream.ReadLine
24       Loop While mTxtStream.AtEndOfStream = False
25
26       Call mTxtStream.Close
27       cmdRead.Enabled = False
28
29       Call modQuickSort.QuickSort(mNumbers, LBound(mNumbers), _
30                                   UBound(mNumbers))
31       For j = UBound(mNumbers) To LBound(mNumbers) Step -1
32          Call lstList.AddItem(mNumbers(j))
33       Next j
34
35       Exit Sub
36
37    handler:
38       Call MsgBox("Error #: " & Err.Number & "   " & Err.Description)
39    End Sub
```

```
40    ' modQuickSort
41    Option Explicit
42
43    Public Sub QuickSort(a() As Integer, first As Integer, _
44                         last As Integer)
45
46       Dim currentLocation As Integer
47       If (first >= last) Then
48          Exit Sub
49       End If
50
51       ' Arguments are passed by the default call-by-reference
52       currentLocation = Partition(a, first, last)     ' Place an element
53       Call QuickSort(a, first, currentLocation - 1)   ' Sort left side
54       Call QuickSort(a, currentLocation + 1, last)    ' sort right side
55    End Sub
56
57    Private Function Partition(a() As Integer, ByVal leftSide As Integer, _
58                              ByVal rightSide As Integer) As Integer
59       Dim position As Integer
60
61       position = leftSide
62
63       While (True)
64
65          While (a(position) <= a(rightSide) And position <> rightSide)
66             rightSide = rightSide - 1
67          Wend
68
69          If (position = rightSide) Then
70             Partition = position
71             Exit Function
72          End If
73
74          If (a(position) > a(rightSide)) Then
75             Call Swap(a(position), a(rightSide))
76             position = rightSide
77          End If
78
79          While (a(leftSide) <= a(position) And leftSide <> position)
80             leftSide = leftSide + 1
81          Wend
82
83          If (position = leftSide) Then
84             Partition = position
85             Exit Function
86          End If
87
```

```
88              If (a(leftSide) > a(position)) Then
89                  Call Swap(a(position), a(leftSide))
90                  position = leftSide
91              End If
92
93          Wend
94
95      End Function
96
97      ' Each argument received is passed implicitly ByRef
98      Private Sub Swap(v As Integer, w As Integer)
99          Dim temp As Integer
100         temp = v
101         v = w
102         w = temp
103     End Sub
```

14.7   Modify Exercise 14.6 to write the sorted values to a file called **data.out**.
           ANS:

```
1       ' Exercise 14.7 Solution
2       Option Explicit
3       Dim mFileSysObj As New FileSystemObject
4       Dim mFile As File
5       Dim mTxtStream As TextStream
6       Dim mNumbers() As Integer
7       Dim mCurrent As Integer
8
9       Private Sub Form_Load()
10          Set mFile = mFileSysObj.GetFile("\vb_solutions\ch14\" & _
11                                      "ex14_07\data.dat")
12          Set mTxtStream = mFile.OpenAsTextStream(ForReading)
13      End Sub
14
15      Private Sub cmdRead_Click()
16          Dim s As String, j As Integer
17
18          On Error GoTo handler
19
20          Do
21              mCurrent = mCurrent + 1
22              ReDim Preserve mNumbers(mCurrent)
23              mNumbers(mCurrent) = mTxtStream.ReadLine
24          Loop While mTxtStream.AtEndOfStream = False
25
26          Call mTxtStream.Close
27          cmdRead.Enabled = False
28          Call mFileSysObj.CreateTextFile("\vb_solutions\ch14\" & _
29                                      "ex14_07\data.out")
30          Set mFile = mFileSysObj.GetFile("\vb_solutions\ch14\" & _
31                                      "ex14_07\data.out")
32          Set mTxtStream = mFile.OpenAsTextStream(ForWriting)
33
34          Call modQuickSort.QuickSort(mNumbers, LBound(mNumbers), _
35                                      UBound(mNumbers))
36
```

```
37        For j = UBound(mNumbers) To LBound(mNumbers) Step -1
38           Call mTxtStream.WriteLine(mNumbers(j))
39           Call lstList.AddItem(mNumbers(j))
40        Next j
41
42        Call mTxtStream.Close
43        Exit Sub
44
45   handler:
46        Call MsgBox("Error #: " & Err.Number & "    " & Err.Description)
47   End Sub
```

```
48   ' modQuickSort
49   Option Explicit
50
51   Public Sub QuickSort(a() As Integer, first As Integer, last As Integer)
52
53        Dim currentLocation As Integer
54
55        If (first >= last) Then
56           Exit Sub
57        End If
58
59        ' Arguments are passed by the default call-by-reference
60        currentLocation = Partition(a, first, last)     ' Place an element
61        Call QuickSort(a, first, currentLocation - 1)   ' Sort left side
62        Call QuickSort(a, currentLocation + 1, last)    ' sort right side
63   End Sub
64
65   Private Function Partition(a() As Integer, ByVal leftSide As Integer, _
66                            ByVal rightSide As Integer) As Integer
67        Dim position As Integer
68
69        position = leftSide
70
71        While (True)
72
73           While (a(position) <= a(rightSide) And position <> rightSide)
74              rightSide = rightSide - 1
75           Wend
76
77           If (position = rightSide) Then
78              Partition = position
79              Exit Function
80           End If
81
82           If (a(position) > a(rightSide)) Then
83              Call Swap(a(position), a(rightSide))
84              position = rightSide
85           End If
86
87           While (a(leftSide) <= a(position) And leftSide <> position)
88              leftSide = leftSide + 1
89           Wend
90
91           If (position = leftSide) Then
92              Partition = position
93              Exit Function
94           End If
95
96           If (a(leftSide) > a(position)) Then
97              Call Swap(a(position), a(leftSide))
98              position = leftSide
99           End If
100      Wend
101  End Function
```

```
102
103   ' Each argument received is passed implicitly ByRef
104   Private Sub Swap(v As Integer, w As Integer)
105      Dim temp As Integer
106
107      temp = v
108      v = w
109      w = temp
110   End Sub
```

14.8 *(Telephone Number Word Generator)* Standard telephone keypads contain the digits 0 through 9. The numbers 2 through 9 each have three letters associated with them, as indicated in the Fig. 14.21.

Many people find it difficult to memorize phone numbers, so they use the correspondence between digits and letters to develop seven-letter words that correspond to their phone numbers. For example, a person whose telephone number is 686-2377 might use the correspondence indicated in the above table to develop the seven-letter word "NUMBERS."

Each seven-letter word corresponds to exactly one seven-digit telephone number. The restaurant wishing to increase its takeout business could surely do so with the number 825-3688 (i.e., "TAKEOUT").

Each seven-letter phone number corresponds to many separate seven-letter words. Unfortunately, most of these represent unrecognizable juxtapositions of letters. It is possible, however, that the owner of a barber shop would be pleased to know that the shop's telephone number, 424-7288, corresponds to "HAIRCUT." The owner of a liquor store would, no doubt, be delighted to find that the store's number, 233-7226, corresponds to "BEERCAN." A veterinarian with the phone number 738-2273 would be pleased to know that the number corresponds to the letters "PETCARE." An automotive dealership would be pleased to know that the dealership number, 639-2277, corresponds to "NEWCARS."

Write a program that, given a seven-digit number, writes to a file every possible seven-letter word combination corresponding to that number. There are 2187 (3^7) such words. Avoid phone numbers with the digits 0 and 1.

　　　ANS:

```
1    ' Exercise 14.8 Solution
2    Option Explicit
3    Dim mFileSysObj As New FileSystemObject
4    Dim mFile As File
5    Dim mTxtStream As TextStream
6    Dim mPhoneLetters(2 To 9) As String
7
8    Private Sub Form_Load()
9       Dim k As Integer, m As Integer
10      Dim c As Integer, s As String
11
12      c = 65
13
14      For k = 2 To 9
15         For m = 1 To 3
16            If c = Asc("Q") Then
17               c = c + 1
18            End If
19
20            s = s & Chr$(c)
21            c = c + 1
22         Next m
23
24         mPhoneLetters(k) = s
25         s = ""
26      Next k
27
```

```
28         Call mFileSysObj.CreateTextFile("\vb_solutions\ch14\" & _
29                                         "ex14_08\phone.dat")
30
31         Set mFile = mFileSysObj.GetFile("\vb_solutions\ch14\" & _
32                                         "ex14_08\phone.dat")
33
34         Set mTxtStream = mFile.OpenAsTextStream(ForWriting)
35     End Sub
36
37     Private Sub cmdWrite_Click()
38         Dim a As Integer, b As Integer, c As Integer
39         Dim d As Integer, e As Integer, f As Integer
40         Dim g As Integer, x As String, counter As Integer
41         Dim s As String
42
43         Screen.MousePointer = vbHourglass
44         s = txtInput.Text
45         s = Left$(s, 3) & Right$(s, 4)
46
47         For a = 1 To 3
48            For b = 1 To 3
49               For c = 1 To 3
50                  For d = 1 To 3
51                     For e = 1 To 3
52                        For f = 1 To 3
53                           For g = 1 To 3
54                              x = Mid$(mPhoneLetters(Mid$(s, 1, 1)), a, 1) & _
55                                  Mid$(mPhoneLetters(Mid$(s, 2, 1)), b, 1) & _
56                                  Mid$(mPhoneLetters(Mid$(s, 3, 1)), c, 1) & _
57                                  Mid$(mPhoneLetters(Mid$(s, 4, 1)), d, 1) & _
58                                  Mid$(mPhoneLetters(Mid$(s, 5, 1)), e, 1) & _
59                                  Mid$(mPhoneLetters(Mid$(s, 6, 1)), f, 1) & _
60                                  Mid$(mPhoneLetters(Mid$(s, 7, 1)), g, 1)
61                              Call mTxtStream.Write(x & " ")
62                              counter = counter + 1
63
64                              If counter Mod 9 = 0 Then
65                                 Call mTxtStream.WriteLine
66                              End If
67
68                           Next g
69                        Next f
70                     Next e
71                  Next d
72               Next c
73            Next b
74         Next a
75
76         Call mTxtStream.Close      ' Close the text stream
77         Screen.MousePointer = vbDefault
78     End Sub
```

14.9   Modify the program of Fig. 14.4 to provide a **ComboBox** that acts as a filter for the files displayed in the **FileListBox**. Provide as a minimum the following filters in the **ComboBox**:

```
All Files (*.*)
Text Files (*.txt)
Executable Files (*.exe)
```

Use the **FileListBox Pattern** property.

ANS:

```
1   ' Exercise 14.9 Solution
2   Option Explicit
3
4   Private Sub Form_Load()
5       Call cboFilter.AddItem("All Files (*.*)")
6       Call cboFilter.AddItem("Text Files (*.txt)")
7       Call cboFilter.AddItem("Executable Files (*.exe)")
8       cboFilter.Text = cboFilter.List(0)
9   End Sub
10
11  Private Sub dirDirBox_Change()
12
13      ' Update the file path to the directory path
14      filFileBox.Path = dirDirBox.Path
15  End Sub
16
17  Private Sub drvDriveBox_Change()
18      On Error GoTo errorhandler
19
20      ' Update the directory path to the drive
21      dirDirBox.Path = drvDriveBox.Drive
22      Exit Sub
23
24  errorhandler:
25      Dim message As String
26
27      ' Check for device unavailable error
28      If Err.Number = 68 Then
29          Dim r As Integer
30
31          message = "Drive is not available."
32          r = MsgBox(message, vbRetryCancel + vbCritical, _
33                  "VBHTP: Chapter 14")
34
35          ' Determine where control should resume
36          If r = vbRetry Then
37              Resume
38          Else    ' Cancel was pressed.
39              drvDriveBox.Drive = drvDriveBox.List(1)
40              Resume Next
41          End If
42
43      Else
44          Call MsgBox(Err.Description, vbOKOnly + vbExclamation)
45          Resume Next
46      End If
47
48  End Sub
49
50  Private Sub cboFilter_Click()
51      Dim p As String
52
53      p = Mid$(cboFilter.Text, InStr(cboFilter.Text, "*"))
54      p = Left$(p, Len(p) - 1)
55      filFileBox.Pattern = p
56  End Sub
```

14.10   Modify the program of Fig. 14.4 to allow the user to drag-and-drop files from one folder into another.

14.11   Modify the program of Fig. 14.4 to allow the user to drag-and-drop a subfolder from one folder into another.

14.12   **[CD]** Error handing is an important part of file processing. Modify the Credit Inquiry Program of Fig. 14.20 to prevent a run-time error from occurring if the program attempts to read from an empty file.

      ANS:

```
1    ' Fig. 14.20
2    ' Credit inquiry program
3    Option Explicit                    ' General declaration
4    Dim mFso As New FileSystemObject   ' General declaration
5    Dim mType As Integer               ' General declaration
6    Const mCREDIT = 0, mDEBIT = 1, mZERO = 2  ' General declaration
7
8    Private Sub cmdButton_Click(Index As Integer)
9      mType = Index    ' Assign cmdButton control array index
10     Call openAndReadFile  ' Open and read file
11   End Sub
12
13   Private Sub openAndReadFile()
14      Dim txtStream As TextStream, s As String
15      Dim balance As Currency, pos As Long
16
17      txtDisplay.Text = "Accounts:"
18
19      On Error GoTo filehandler      ' Set error trap
20
21      ' Get "clients.dat" and open a TextStream for reading
22      Set txtStream = mFso.GetFile("\vb_solutions\ch14\ex14_12\clients.dat"). _
23                 OpenAsTextStream(ForReading)
24
25      ' Loop until end of stream is found
26      Do
27        s = txtStream.ReadLine    ' Read one line
28
29        ' Find the position of the second space
30        pos = InStr(InStr(1, s, " ", vbTextCompare) + 1, s, " ", _
31                 vbTextCompare)
32
33        ' Extract the String that contains the balance
34        balance = Trim$(Mid$(s, pos, Len(s) - pos))
35
36        ' Determine what if anything should be displayed
37        If (mType = mCREDIT And balance < 0) Then
38           txtDisplay.Text = txtDisplay.Text & vbNewLine & s
39        ElseIf (mType = mDEBIT And balance > 0) Then
40           txtDisplay.Text = txtDisplay.Text & vbNewLine & s
41        ElseIf (mType = mZERO And balance = 0) Then
42           txtDisplay.Text = txtDisplay.Text & vbNewLine & s
43        End If
44
45      Loop While (txtStream.AtEndOfStream = False)
```

```
46
47      Call txtStream.Close       ' Close TextStream
48      Exit Sub
49
50  filehandler:
51
52      If Err.Number = 62 Then
53          Call MsgBox("File does not contain data.", vbExclamation)
54      End If
55
56  End Sub
```

Digit	Letters
2	A B C
3	D E F
4	G H I
5	J K L
6	M N O
7	P R S
8	T U V
9	W X Y

Fig. 14.21 Telephone keypad digits and letters.

Chapter 15 Solutions
Records and Random-Access Files

15.5 [CD] Fill in the blanks in each of the following:

a) When opening a file for random access, the _____ specifies the record size.

ANS: `Len =`.

b) The _____ access specifier is used to specify that a random-access file is to be opened in read mode.

ANS: `Read`.

c) The _____ statement is used to read data randomly from a file.

ANS: `Get`.

d) The _____ access specifier states that a random-access file can be read from and written to.

ANS: `Read Write`.

15.6 State which of the following are *true* and which are *false*. If *false*, explain why.

a) It is not necessary to search through all the records in a randomly accessed file to find a specific record.

ANS: True.

b) Random-access files are always referred to by name in a program.

ANS: False. A number is used.

c) When a program creates a file, the file is automatically retained by the computer for future reference.

ANS: True.

d) A program must explicitly close a random-access file before the program terminates.

ANS: False. Although it is a good practice to do so.

e) Fixed-length records should be used with random-access files.

ANS: True.

f) Unlike sequential-access files, random-access files store information as bytes.

ANS: True.

g) A random-access file always has the same size as a sequential-access file.

ANS: False. Random-access files are typically much larger than sequential-access files.

h) The `Get` statement always takes three arguments.

ANS: False. The second argument is optional.

i) Random-access files must end with the `.rnd` extension.

ANS: False. Extension `.rnd` is recommended but not required.

15.7 Find the error and show how to correct it in each of the following.

a) `Get #6, udtCarInformation   ' Store data in record`

ANS: The second argument is missing. Possible corrections are

```
Get #6, , udtCarInformation   ' Store data in record
```
or
```
Get #6, recordNumber, udtCarInformation   ' Store data in record
```

b) `Open #99 For Random Access Append Len = 140`

ANS: A string specifying the file name an location should follow the **Open** keyword. **Append** should be **Read Write**. Missing **As #** before keyword **Len**. A corrected statement might read:

```
Open "c:\filepath\filename.rnd" For Random Access Read Write As #99 Len = 140
```

c) `Put #33, 15, inventory%     ' inventory is an array name`

ANS: `inventory` should be a **Variant**.

d)
```
' Open a file for reading and writing
Open "c:\customer.rnd" Access Read+
```
ANS: `Open "c:\customer.rnd" For Random Access Read Write As #234 Len = 55`

15.8   Exercise 15.3 asked the reader to write a series of single statements. Actually, these statements form the core of an important type of file processing program, namely, a file-matching program. In commercial data processing, it is common to have several files in each application system. In an accounts receivable system, for example, there is generally a master file containing detailed information about each customer, such as the customer's name, address, telephone number, outstanding balance, credit limit, discount terms, contract arrangements, and possibly a condensed history of recent purchases and cash payments.

As transactions occur (i.e., sales are made and cash payments arrive in the mail), they are entered into a file. At the end of each business period (i.e., a month for some companies, a week for others and a day in some cases) the file of transactions (called **"trans.dat"** in Exercise 15.3) is applied to the master file (called **"oldmast.rnd"** in Exercise 15.3), thus updating each account's record of purchases and payments. During an updating run, the master file is rewritten as a new file (**"newmast.rnd"**), which is then used at the end of the next business period to begin the updating process again.

File-matching programs must deal with certain problems that do not exist in single-file programs. For example, a match does not always occur. A customer on the master file may not have made any purchases or cash payments in the current business period, and therefore no record for this customer will appear on the transaction file. Similarly, a customer who did make some purchases or cash payments may have just moved to this community, and the company may not have had a chance to create a master record for this customer.

Use the statements written in Exercise 15.3 as a basis for writing a complete file-matching accounts receivable program. Use the account number on each file as the record key for matching purposes. Assume each file is a sequential file with records stored in increasing order by account number.

When a match occurs (i.e., records with the same account number appear on both the master file and the transaction file), add the dollar amount on the transaction file to the current balance on the master file, and write the **"newmast.rnd"** record. (Assume that purchases are indicated by positive amounts on the transaction file, and that payments are indicated by negative amounts.) When there is a master record for a particular account but no corresponding transaction record, merely write the master record to **"newmast.rnd"**. When there is a transaction record but no corresponding master record, print the message **"Unmatched transaction record for account number …"** (fill in the account number from the transaction record).

   ANS: NOTE: THIS SOLUTION INCLUDES SOLUTIONS TO **15.9**, **15.10** AND **15.11**. The first code listing generates the old.rnd file. The second code listing does the updating.

```
1   ' Exercise 15.8 Solution
2   ' Write Customer information to "old.rnd"
3   Option Explicit
4   Option Base 1
5
6   Private Type Customer
7      account As Integer
8      firstName As String * 10
9      lastName As String * 10
10     balance As Currency
11  End Type
12
13  Private Sub Form_Load()
14     Dim udtPerson As Customer, j As Integer
15     Dim firstNames() As Variant, lastNames() As Variant
16     Dim fileName As String
17
18     fileName = "\vb_solutions\ch15\ex15_08\old.rnd"
19     firstNames = Array("Bob", "Sue", "Mike", "Kim", "Erin")
20     lastNames = Array("Black", "White", "Brown", "Green", "Blue")
21     Call Randomize
22
23     On Error GoTo handler
24     Open fileName For Random Access Write As #8 Len = Len(udtPerson)
25
26     ' Write empty records to disk
27     For j = 100 To 500
28        Put #8, j, udtPerson
29     Next j
30
31     Call lstBox.AddItem("Generating data...")
32
33     ' Write some data
34     For j = 100 To 500 Step 100
35
36        With udtPerson
37           .account = j
```

```
38                    .firstName = firstNames(j / 100)
39                    .lastName = lastNames(j / 100)
40                    .balance = 500 - Rnd() * 1000
41              End With
42
43              Call lstBox.AddItem(udtPerson.account & " " & _
44                               Trim$(udtPerson.firstName) & " " & _
45                               Trim$(udtPerson.lastName) & " " & _
46                               Format$(udtPerson.balance, "Currency"))
47           Put #8, j, udtPerson
48       Next j
49
50       Exit Sub
51
52   handler:
53       Call MsgBox(Err.Description & vbTab & Err.Number)
54   End Sub
```

```
GENERATING DATA...
100 BOB BLACK $326.54
200 SUE WHITE ($20.32)
300 MIKE BROWN $53.03
400 KIM GREEN $297.15
500 ERIN BLUE $484.78
```

```
1    ' Exercise 15.8 Solution
2    ' Note: Step 1 must be executed before executing this
3    ' solution.
4    Option Explicit
5
6    Private Type Customer
7        account As Integer
8        firstName As String * 10
9        lastName As String * 10
10       balance As Currency
11   End Type
12
13   Private Sub Form_Load()
14       Dim inOldMaster As String, inTran As String
15       Dim fso As New FileSystemObject, t As TextStream
16       Dim outNewMaster As String
17       Dim udtPerson As Customer, acct As Integer
18       Dim transAmount As Currency, s As String
19       Dim loc As Integer
20
21       loc = 100
22       Call lstOld.AddItem("Contents of old.rnd")
23       Call lstNew.AddItem("Contents of new.rnd")
24       Call lstTrans.AddItem("Contents of trans.dat")
25       inOldMaster = "\vb_solutions\ch15\ex15_08\old.rnd"
26       outNewMaster = "\vb_solutions\ch15\ex15_08\new.rnd"
27       inTran = "\vb_solutions\ch15\ex15_08\trans.dat"
28       Call fso.CopyFile(inOldMaster, outNewMaster)
29
30       Open inOldMaster For Random Access Read As #8 Len = Len(udtPerson)
31       Open outNewMaster For Random Access Read Write As #10 Len = Len(udtPerson)
32       Set t = fso.OpenTextFile(inTran, ForReading)
33
34       ' Read all the "old.dat" records and update ListBox
35       Do
36          Get #8, loc, udtPerson
37
```

```
38          If udtPerson.account <> 0 Then
39              Call lstOld.AddItem(udtPerson.account & " " & _
40                              Trim$(udtPerson.firstName) & " " & _
41                              Trim$(udtPerson.lastName) & " " & _
42                              Format$(udtPerson.balance, "currency"))
43          End If
44
45          loc = loc + 1
46      Loop Until EOF(8)
47
48      ' Write to "new.dat" the "old.dat" updated with "trans.dat"
49      While t.AtEndOfStream = False
50          s = Trim$(t.ReadLine)
51          Call lstTrans.AddItem(s)
52          acct = Left$(s, 3)
53          transAmount = Mid$(s, 5)
54
55          Get #10, acct, udtPerson
56
57          If udtPerson.account <> 0 Then
58              udtPerson.balance = udtPerson.balance + transAmount
59              Put #10, udtPerson.account, udtPerson
60          Else
61              Call lstOutput.AddItem("Unmatched transaction " & _
62                              "for account number " & acct)
63          End If
64
65      Wend
66
67      loc = 100
68
69      Do
70          Get #10, loc, udtPerson
71
72          If udtPerson.account <> 0 Then
73              Call lstNew.AddItem(udtPerson.account & " " & _
74                              Trim$(udtPerson.firstName) & " " & _
75                              Trim$(udtPerson.lastName) & " " & _
76                              Format$(udtPerson.balance, "currency"))
77          End If
78
79          loc = loc + 1
80      Loop Until EOF(10)
81
82      ' Close files
83      Close #8
84      Close #10
85      Call t.Close
86  End Sub
```

```
Exercise 15.8 Solution

Contents of old.rnd          Contents of trans.dat      Contents of new.rnd
100 Bob Black $326.54        100 9.33                   100 Bob Black $361.20
200 Sue White ($20.32)       300 122.54                 200 Sue White ($20.32)
300 Mike Brown $53.03        333 99.33                  300 Mike Brown $175.57
400 Kim Green $297.15        400 800.04                 400 Kim Green $1,170.07
500 Erin Blue $484.78        100 25.33                  500 Erin Blue $484.78
                             400 72.88

Unmatched transaction for account number 333
```

15.9   After writing the program of Exercise 15.8, write a simple program to create some test data for checking out the program. Use the following sample account data:

Master file account number	Name	Balance
100	Alan Jones	348.17
300	Mary Smith	27.19
500	Sam Sharp	0.00
700	Suzy Green	-14.22

Transaction file account number	Transaction amount
100	27.14
300	62.11
400	100.56
900	82.17

15.10   Run the program of Exercise 15.8 using the files of test data created in Exercise 15.9. Print the new master file. Check that the accounts have been updated correctly.

15.11   It is possible (actually common) to have several transaction records with the same record key. This occurs because a particular customer might make several purchases and cash payments during a business period. Rewrite your accounts receivable file-matching program of Exercise 15.8 to provide for the possibility of handling several transaction records with the same record key. Modify the test data of Exercise 15.9 to include the following additional transaction records:

Account number	Dollar amount
300	83.89
700	80.78
700	1.53

15.12   **[CD]** Write a series of statements that accomplish each of the following. Assume that the record

```
Type person
   lastName As String * 15
   firstName As String * 15
   age As String * 3
End Type
```

has been defined, and that the random-access file has been opened properly.

a) Initialize the file **"nameage.dat"** with 100 records containing **lastName = "unassigned"**, **firstName = ""**, and **age = "0"**.

ANS:

```
Dim mPersonRecord as person, mCurrentRecord as Integer

Private Sub InitializeRecord()
   Dim x as Integer

   mPersonRecord.lastName = "unassigned"
   mPersonRecord.firstName = ""
   mPersonRecord.age = "0"

   For x = 1 To 100

      Put #1, x, mPersonRecord  ' Write records
   Next x
End Sub
```

b) Input 10 last names, first names and ages, and write them to the file.
ANS:

```
Private Sub cmdInput_Click()
   Static counter as Integer

   If counter = 10 Then
      cmdInput.Enabled = False
      Exit Sub
   End If

   mPersonRecord.lastName = txtLastName.Text
   mPersonRecord.firstName = txtFirstName.Text
   mPersonRecord.age = txtAge.Text

   Put #1, counter + 1, mPersonRecord   ' Write record
   counter = counter + 1
End Sub
```

c) Update a record that has information in it, and if there is none tell the user "No info."
ANS:

```
Private Sub cmdLoadRecord_Click()
   mCurrentRecord = Val(txtRecordLocation.Text)
   Get #1, mCurrentRecord, mPersonRecord
   txtLastName.Text = mPersonRecord.lastName
   txtFirstName.Text = mPersonRecord.firstName
   txtAge.Text = mPersonRecord.age
End Sub

Private Sub cmdUpdate_Click()
   If mPersonRecord.lastName = "unassigned" Then
      txtLastName.Text = mPersonRecord.lastName
      txtFirstName.Text = "No info"
      txtAge.Text = "No info"
   Else
      mPersonRecord.lastName = txtLastName.Text
      mPersonRecord.firstName = txtFirstName.Text
      mPersonRecord.age = txtAge.Text
      Put #1, mCurrentRecord, mPersonRecord   ' Write record
   End If
End Sub
```

d) Delete a record that has information by reinitializing that particular record.
ANS:

```
Private Sub cmdDelete_Click()
   mPersonRecord.lastName = "unassigned"
   mPersonRecord.firstName = ""
   mPersonRecord.age = "0"
   Put #1, mCurrentRecord, mPersonRecord   ' Write record
End Sub
```

15.13   You are the owner of a hardware store and need to keep an inventory that can tell you what different tools you have, how many of each you have on hand and the cost of each one. Write a program that initializes the random-access file **"hardware.dat"** to one hundred empty records, lets you input the data concerning each tool, enables you to list all your tools, lets you delete a record for a tool that you no longer have and lets you update *any* information in the file. The tool identification number should be the record number. Use the following information to start your file:

Record number	Tool name	Quantity	Cost
3	Electric sander	7	57.98
17	Hammer	76	11.99

Record number	Tool name	Quantity	Cost
24	Jigsaw	21	11.00
39	Lawn mower	3	79.50
56	Power saw	18	99.99
68	Screwdriver	106	6.99
77	Sledgehammer	11	21.50
83	Wrench	34	7.50

ANS:

```
1   ' Exercise 15.13 Solution
2   ' Part 1--creates the random access file
3   Option Explicit
4   Option Base 1
5
6   Private Type Tool
7      recordNumber As Integer
8      toolName As String * 25
9      quantity As Integer
10     cost As Currency
11  End Type
12
13  Private Sub Form_Load()
14     Dim udtTools As Tool, fileName As String, j As Integer
15     Dim recordNumbers() As Variant, toolNames() As Variant
16     Dim quantities() As Variant, costs() As Variant
17
18     recordNumbers = Array(3, 17, 24, 39, 56, 68, 77, 83)
19     toolNames = Array("Electric sander", "Hammer", "Jigsaw", _
20                     "Lawn mower", "Power saw", "Screwdriver", _
21                     "Sledgehammer", "Wrench")
22     quantities = Array(7, 76, 21, 3, 18, 106, 11, 34)
23     costs = Array(57.98, 11.99, 11, 79.5, 99.99, 6.99, 21.5, 7.5)
24     fileName = "\vb_solutions\ch15\ex15_13\hardware.rnd"
25
26     Open fileName For Random Access Read Write As #44 Len = Len(udtTools)
27
28     ' Write 100 blank records
29     For j = 1 To 100
30        Put #44, j, udtTools
31     Next j
32
33     Call lstBox.AddItem("Creating the records...")
34
35     ' Write starter data to file
36     For j = LBound(recordNumbers) To UBound(recordNumbers)
37
38        With udtTools
39           .recordNumber = recordNumbers(j)
40           .toolName = toolNames(j)
41           .quantity = quantities(j)
42           .cost = costs(j)
43           Put #44, .recordNumber, udtTools
44           Call lstBox.AddItem(.recordNumber & vbTab & _
45                          .toolName & vbTab & .quantity _
46                          & vbTab & Format$(.cost, "currency"))
47        End With
48     Next j
49
50     Close #44
51  End Sub
```

```
1    ' Exercise 15.13 Solution
2    ' Part 1 should be executed before running this program.
3    Option Explicit
4
5    Private Type Tool
6       recordNumber As Integer
7       toolName As String * 25
8       quantity As Integer
9       cost As Currency
10   End Type
11
12   Dim mUdtTools As Tool     ' User defined type
13
14   Private Sub Form_Load()
15      tabOperations.Enabled = False
16   End Sub
17
18   Sub cmdOpenFile_Click()
19      Dim recordLength As Long, fileName As String
20
21      ' Determine number of bytes in a ClientRecord object
22      recordLength = Len(mUdtTools)
23
24      Call dlgOpen.ShowOpen
25      fileName = dlgOpen.fileName
26
27      If dlgOpen.FileTitle <> "" Then
28         ' Open file for writing
29         Open fileName For Random Access Read Write As #1 _
30                                       Len = recordLength
31         cmdOpenFile.Enabled = False
32         cmdCloseFile.Enabled = True
33         tabOperations.Enabled = True
34      Else
35         Call MsgBox("You must specify a file name")
36      End If
37
38   End Sub
39
40   ' Create a text file representation of the random-access file
41   Private Sub cmdTextFile_Click()
42      Dim fso As New FileSystemObject, t As TextStream
43      Dim fileName As String, costString As String, r As Integer
44
45      r = 1
46      On Error Resume Next
47      Call dlgTextFile.ShowOpen
48      fileName = dlgTextFile.fileName
49
50      If dlgTextFile.FileTitle <> "" Then
51         Call fso.CreateTextFile(fileName)
52         Set t = fso.OpenTextFile(fileName, ForWriting)
53
54         Call t.WriteLine("Record" & vbTab & "Tool Name" & _
55                          vbTab & vbTab & "Quantity" & vbTab & _
56                          "Cost")
57
```

```
58          Get #1, r, mUdtTools    ' Read first record
59
60          While Not EOF(1)
61
62              If mUdtTools.recordNumber <> 0 Then
63                  Call t.WriteLine(mUdtTools.recordNumber & vbTab & _
64                                   mUdtTools.toolName & vbTab & _
65                                   mUdtTools.quantity & vbTab & _
66                                   Format$(mUdtTools.cost, "Currency"))
67              End If
68
69              r = r + 1
70              Get #1, r, mUdtTools  ' Read next record
71          Wend
72
73          Call t.Close
74      Else
75          Call MsgBox("You must specify a file name")
76      End If
77
78  End Sub
79
80  ' Add a new record to the file
81  Private Sub cmdAddNew_Click()
82
83      If txtRecordNumber.Text <> "" Then
84          Get #1, Val(txtRecordNumber), mUdtTools  ' Read record
85
86          If mUdtTools.recordNumber = 0 Then
87              mUdtTools.recordNumber = Val(txtRecordNumber)
88              mUdtTools.toolName = txtToolName.Text
89              mUdtTools.quantity = txtQuantity.Text
90              mUdtTools.cost = txtCost.Text
91              Put #1, mUdtTools.recordNumber, mUdtTools
92              Call MsgBox("Record " & mUdtTools.recordNumber & _
93                          " has been added to the file")
94          Else
95              Call MsgBox("Record already exists")
96          End If
97
98      Else
99          Call MsgBox("You must enter an account number")
100     End If
101
102 End Sub
103
104 Private Sub cmdUpdate_Click()
105     mUdtTools.recordNumber = txtUpdateRecord.Text
106     mUdtTools.toolName = txtUpdateToolName.Text
107     mUdtTools.quantity = txtUpdateQuantity.Text
108     mUdtTools.cost = txtUpdateCost.Text
109     Put #1, mUdtTools.recordNumber, mUdtTools
110     txtUpdateRecord.Text = ""
111     txtUpdateToolName.Text = ""
112     txtUpdateQuantity.Text = ""
113     txtUpdateCost.Text = ""
114     cmdUpdate.Enabled = False
115 End Sub
116
117 ' Update an existing record
118 Private Sub cmdLocate_Click()
119     Dim r As Integer
120     On Error Resume Next
121
122     r = Val(InputBox("Enter record number"))
123     Get #1, r, mUdtTools  ' Read record
124
```

```
125      If mUdtTools.recordNumber <> 0 Then
126         txtUpdateRecord.Text = mUdtTools.recordNumber
127         txtUpdateToolName.Text = mUdtTools.toolName
128         txtUpdateQuantity.Text = mUdtTools.quantity
129         txtUpdateCost.Text = mUdtTools.cost
130         cmdUpdate.Enabled = True
131      Else
132         Call MsgBox("Record " & r & " does not exist")
133      End If
134
135 End Sub
136
137 ' Delete the specified record
138 Private Sub cmdDelete_Click()
139      Dim blankRecord As Tool
140
141      On Error Resume Next
142
143      Get #1, Val(txtDelete.Text), mUdtTools  ' Read record
144
145      If mUdtTools.recordNumber <> 0 Then
146         Put #1, mUdtTools.recordNumber, blankRecord
147         Call MsgBox("Record # " & mUdtTools.recordNumber & _
148                      " has been deleted")
149      Else
150         Call MsgBox("Record does not exist")
151      End If
152
153 End Sub
154
155 Sub cmdCloseFile_Click()
156      Close #1
157      cmdOpenFile.Enabled = True
158      cmdCloseFile.Enabled = False
159 End Sub
160
161 Private Sub cmdExit_Click()
162      Close
163      Call Unload(Me)
164 End Sub
```

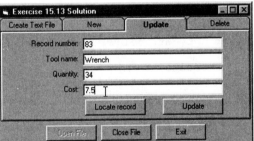

15.14 Modify the card shuffling and dealing program of Fig. 8.31 to use a user-defined type to represent a card (i.e., a face **String** and a suit **String**). Rewrite the shuffling and dealing algorithms to be more efficient. For the shuffling algorithm, make one pass of the array of card objects and swap the current card with a randomly chosen card in the deck. For the dealing algorithm, simply "walk through" the array of cards and display each card.

   ANS:

```
1  ' Exercise 15.14 Solution
2  Option Explicit
3  Option Base 0
4
5  Private Type Card
6     face As String
7     suit As String
8  End Type
```

```
9
10   Dim mSuit(), mFace()
11   Dim mDeck(51) As Card
12
13   Private Sub Form_Load()
14      mSuit = Array("Hearts", "Clubs", "Diamonds", "Spades")
15      mFace = Array("Ace", "Deuce", "Three", "Four", "Five", "Six", _
16                    "Seven", "Eight", "Nine", "Ten", "Jack", "Queen", _
17                    "King")
18      Call FillDeck
19      Call Randomize
20   End Sub
21
22   Private Sub FillDeck()
23      Dim x As Integer
24
25      For x = LBound(mDeck) To UBound(mDeck)
26         mDeck(x).face = mFace(x Mod 13)
27         mDeck(x).suit = mSuit(x \ 13)
28      Next x
29
30      Call Deal
31   End Sub
32
33   Private Sub cmdShuffle_Click()
34      Call lstOutput.Clear
35      Call Shuffle
36      Call Deal
37   End Sub
38
39   Private Sub Shuffle()
40      Dim i As Integer, j As Integer, tempCard As Card
41
42      For i = LBound(mDeck) To UBound(mDeck)
43         j = 1 + Int(Rnd() * UBound(mDeck))
44         tempCard = mDeck(j)
45         mDeck(j) = mDeck(i)
46         mDeck(i) = tempCard
47      Next i
48
49   End Sub
50
51   Private Sub Deal()
52      Dim c As Integer, row As Integer, column As Integer
53
54      For c = LBound(mDeck) To UBound(mDeck)
55         Call lstOutput.AddItem(mDeck(c).face & " of " & mDeck(c).suit)
56      Next c
57
58   End Sub
```

Exercise 15.14 Solution		Exercise 15.14 Solution
Shuffle and Deal Cards		Shuffle and Deal Cards
Ace of Hearts		Three of Spades
Deuce of Hearts		King of Spades
Three of Hearts		Five of Hearts
Four of Hearts		Four of Hearts
Five of Hearts		Eight of Clubs
Six of Hearts		Ace of Clubs
Seven of Hearts		Six of Spades
Eight of Hearts		Jack of Diamonds
Nine of Hearts		Ten of Clubs
Ten of Hearts		Seven of Hearts
Jack of Hearts		Six of Diamonds
Queen of Hearts		Three of Clubs
King of Hearts		Eight of Hearts

Chapter 16 Solutions
Object-Oriented Programming

16.3 Consider the class **CBicycle**. Given your knowledge of some common components of bicycles, show a class hierarchy in which the class **CBicycle** inherits from other classes, which, in turn, inherit from yet other classes. Discuss the instantiation of various objects of class **CBicycle**. Discuss inheritance from class **CBicycle** for other closely related subclasses.

    ANS: Possible classes are displayed in bold.
Bicycle composed of:
HandleBars
Seat
Frame
Wheels composed of:
   Tires
   Rims
   Spokes
Pedals
Chain composed of:
   Links
Brakes composed of:
   Wires
   BrakePads
   BrakeHandles
Classes such as **Tricycle** and **Unicycle** could inherit from **Bicycle**.

16.4 Define each of the following terms: class, **Implements**, interface, superclass and subclass.
    ANS: A class is a reusable module that does not have a graphical user interface and is used in the instantiation of one or more objects. **Implements** is a Visual Basic keyword that allows one class to inherit the interface of another class. An interface is a class that is implemented by another class. Superclass is the class being inherited from. Subclass is the class that inherits from another class.

16.5 [CD] Distinguish between single inheritance and multiple inheritance. What feature of Visual Basic helps realize the benefits of multiple inheritance?
    ANS: Single inheritance indicates that a class inherits from exactly one class. Multiple inheritance indicates that a class inherits from two or more classes. Interface inheritance allows Visual Basic to realize the benefits of multiple inheritance.

16.6 (True/False) A subclass is generally smaller than its superclass.
    ANS: False. A subclass is usually larger than it superclass because it adds additional attributes and behaviors.

16.7 [CD] (True/False) A subclass object is also an object of that subclass's superclass.
    ANS: True.

16.8 How is it that polymorphism enables you to program "in the general" rather than "in the specific." Discuss the key advantages of programming "in the general."
    ANS: Polymorphism enables the programmer to concentrate on the processing of common operations that are applied to all data types in a class hierarchy without knowledge of the individual details of each data type. The general processing capabilities are separated from the internal details of each type. Programming in the general enables you to write more maintainable and modifyable systems. New data types can be added into the system as long as they belong to the portion of the class hierarchy being polymorphically processed.

16.9 Discuss the problems of programming with **Select Case** logic. Why is polymorphism an effective alternative to using **Select Case** logic.

ANS: The main problem with programming using the **Select Case** structure is the extensibility and maintainability of the program. A program containing many **Select Case** structures is difficult to modify. All the structures must be modified to handle the processing of an additional type or of one less type. Polymorphism determines the type of an object automatically, so it is not necessary to determine the type of an object to process the object in a generic manner.

16.10   How does polymorphism promote extensibility?

ANS: Polymorphism makes programs more extensible by making all method calls generic. When a new class type with the appropriate methods is added to the hierarchy, no changes need to be made to the generic method calls to enable processing of the new data type.

16.11   You have been asked to develop a flight simulator that will have elaborate graphical outputs. Explain why polymorphic programming would be especially effective for a problem of this nature.

16.12   Study the inheritance hierarchy of Fig. 16.7. For each class, indicate some common attributes and behaviors consistent with the hierarchy. Add some other classes (i.e., **CUndergraduateStudent**, **CGraduateStudent**, **CFreshman**, **CSophomore**, **CJunior**, **CSenior**, etc., to enrich the hierarchy).

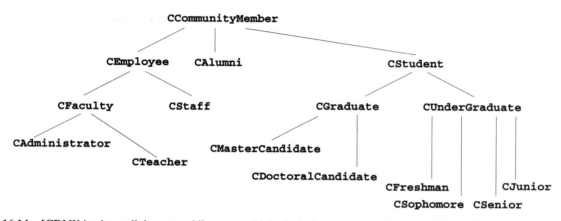

16.14   [CD] Write down all the automobile you can think of—both passenger and commercial—and form those shapes into a hierarchy. Your hierarchy should have superclass **IAutomobile** from which class **IPassenger** and class **ICommercial** are derived. Once you have developed the hierarchy, define each of the classes in the hierarchy.

ANS:

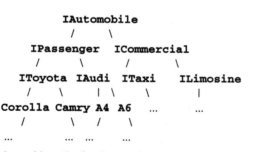

16.15   Write an inheritance hierarchy for classes **IQuadrilateral**, **CTrapezoid**, **CParallelogram**, **CRectangle** and **CSquare**. Use **IQuadrilateral** as the superclass of the hierarchy. Make the hierarchy as deep (i.e., as many levels) as possible. Write a program that instantiates and uses objects of each of these classes.

ANS:

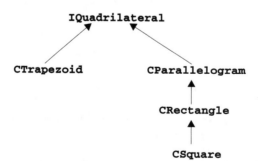

16.16   [CD] Create a **CDate2** class that can output the date in multiple formats such as

```
MM/DD/YY
June 14, 1992
DDD YYYY
```

ANS:

```
1    ' Exercise 16.15 Solution
2    Option Explicit
3
4    Private Sub Form_Load()
5        Dim d As New CDate2
6
7        Call d.SetDate(8, 9, 1972)
8
9        Print d.FormatMMDDYY
10       Print d.formatDDDYYYY
11       Print d.FormatStandard
12       Print
13
14       Call d.SetDate(19, 12, 1994)
15
16       Print d.FormatMMDDYY
17       Print d.formatDDDYYYY
18       Print d.FormatStandard
19
20       Set d = Nothing
21   End Sub
```

```
22   ' Class CDate2 definition
23   Option Explicit
24   Private mMonth As Integer
25   Private mDay As Integer
26   Private mYear As Integer
27   Private mDaysPerMonth()
28
29   Private Sub Class_Initialize()
30       mDay = 1
31       mMonth = 1
32       mYear = 1900
33       mDaysPerMonth = Array(0, 31, 28, 31, 30, 31, 30, 31, 31, _
34                           30, 31, 30, 31)
35   End Sub
36
37   Public Function FormatMMDDYY() As String
38       FormatMMDDYY = Format$(mMonth, "00") & "/" & _
39                   Format$(mDay, "00") & "/" & _
40                   Format$(mYear Mod 100, "00")
41   End Function
42
43   Public Function formatDDDYYYY() As String
44       Dim c As Integer, totalDays As Integer
45
46       For c = 1 To (mMonth - 1)
47          totalDays = totalDays + mDaysPerMonth(c)
48       Next c
49
50       formatDDDYYYY = Format$(totalDays + mDay, "000") & " " & mYear
51   End Function
52
53   Public Function FormatStandard() As String
54       Dim months()
55
56       months = Array("", "January", "February", "March", "April", "May", "June", _
57                   "July", "August", "September", "October", "November", _
58                   "December")
59
60       FormatStandard = months(mMonth) & " " & Format$(mDay, "00") & ", " & mYear
61   End Function
62
```

```
63  Public Property Get Day() As Integer
64      Day = mDay
65  End Property
66
67  Public Property Let Day(ByVal dy As Integer)
68      mDay = ValidateDay(dy)
69  End Property
70
71  Public Property Get Month() As Integer
72      Month = mMonth
73  End Property
74
75  Public Property Let Month(ByVal mth As Integer)
76      mMonth = ValidateMonth(mth)
77  End Property
78
79  Public Property Get year() As Integer
80      year = mYear
81  End Property
82
83  Public Property Let year(ByVal yr As Integer)
84      mYear = yr    ' Could also be validated by programmer
85  End Property
86
87  Public Function ToString() As String
88      ToString = mMonth & "/" & mDay & "/" & mYear
89  End Function
90
91  Public Sub SetDate(ByVal dy As Integer, ByVal mth As Integer, _
92                     ByVal yr As Integer)
93      mMonth = ValidateMonth(mth)
94      mDay = ValidateDay(dy)
95      mYear = yr
96  End Sub
97
98  Private Function ValidateMonth(ByVal mth As Integer) As Integer
99      ValidateMonth = IIf((mth > 0 And mth <= 12), mth, 1)
100 End Function
101
102 Private Function ValidateDay(ByVal dy As Integer) As Integer
103
104     If dy > 0 And dy <= mDaysPerMonth(mMonth) Then
105        ValidateDay = dy
106        Exit Function
107     End If
108
109     If mMonth = 2 And dy = 29 And (mYear Mod 400 = 0 Or _
110                                    mYear Mod 4 = 0 And _
111                                    mYear Mod 100 <> 0) Then
112        ValidateDay = dy
113        Exit Function
114     End If
115
116     ' An invalid day was passed to ValidateDay
117     ' Set the day to a default value of 1
118     ValidateDay = 1
119 End Function
```

Exercise 16.15 Solution
09/08/72
251 1972
September 08, 1972

12/19/94
353 1994
December 19, 1994

16.17 Create a class called **CComplex** for performing arithmetic with complex numbers. Write a program to test your class.

Complex numbers have the form

   realPart + imaginaryPart ∞ *i*

where *i* is

$$\sqrt{-1}$$

Use floating-point variables to represent the **Private** data of the class. Provide **Public** methods for each of the following:

a) Addition of two **CComplex** numbers: The real parts are added together and the imaginary parts are added together.

b) Subtraction of two **CComplex** numbers: The real part of the right operand is subtracted from the real part of the left operand and the imaginary part of the right operand is subtracted from the imaginary part of the left operand.

c) Printing **CComplex** numbers in the form **(A, B)**, where **A** is the real part and **B** is the imaginary part.

ANS:

```
1   ' Exercise 16.16 Solution
2   Option Explicit
3
4   Private Sub Form_Load()
5      Dim a As New CComplex, b As New CComplex
6
7      a.Real = 9.9
8      a.Imaginary = 7.7
9      b.Real = 1.2
10     b.Imaginary = 3.1
11
12     Print "a = " & a.ToString
13     Print "b = " & b.ToString
14     Print "a + b = " & a.Add(b).ToString
15     Print "a - b = " & a.Subtract(b).ToString
16  End Sub
```

```
17  ' Class CComplex
18  Option Explicit
19  Private mReal As Double
20  Private mImaginary As Double
21
22  Public Function Add(r As CComplex) As CComplex
23     Dim complex As New CComplex
24
25     complex.Real = mReal + r.Real
26     complex.Imaginary = mImaginary + r.Imaginary
27     Set Add = complex
28  End Function
29
30  Public Function Subtract(r As CComplex) As CComplex
31     Dim complex As New CComplex
32
33     complex.Real = mReal - r.Real
34     complex.Imaginary = mImaginary - r.Imaginary
35     Set Subtract = complex
36  End Function
37
38  Public Function ToString() As String
39     ToString = "(" & mReal & ", " & mImaginary & ")"
40  End Function
41
42  Public Property Get Real() As Double
43     Real = mReal
44  End Property
45
46  Public Property Let Real(r As Double)
47     mReal = r
48  End Property
49
50  Public Property Get Imaginary() As Double
```

```
51        Imaginary = mImaginary
52   End Property
53
54   Public Property Let Imaginary(i As Double)
55        mImaginary = i
56   End Property
```

Exercise 16.16 Solution
A = (9.9, 7.7)
B = (1.2, 3.1)
A + B = (11.1, 10.8)
A - B = (8.7, 4.6)

16.18   Create a class called **CRational** for performing arithmetic with fractions. Write a program to test your class.

Use **Integer** variables to represent the **Private** instance variables of the class—**mNumerator** and **mDenominator**. The class should store the fraction in reduced form (i.e., the fraction

2/4

would be stored in the object as 1 in the **mNumerator** and 2 in the **mDenominator**). Provide **Public** methods for each of the following:

    a) Addition of two **CRational** numbers. The result is stored in reduced form.

    b) Subtraction of two **CRational** numbers. The result is stored in reduced form.

    c) Multiplication of two **CRational** numbers. The result is stored in reduced form.

    d) Division of two **CRational** numbers. The result is stored in reduced form.

    e) Returning **CRational** numbers in the form **mNumerator/mDenominator** (i.e., a **String** with this format).

    f) Returning **CRational** numbers in floating-point format. (Consider providing formatting capabilities that enable the user of the class to specify the number of digits of precision to the right of the decimal point.)

ANS:

```
1    ' Exercise 16.17 Solution
2    Option Explicit
3
4    Private Sub Form_Load()
5        Dim a As New CRational, b As New CRational
6        Dim c As CRational
7
8        a.Numerator = 4
9        a.Denominator = 8
10       b.Numerator = 16
11       b.Denominator = 3
12
13       Print "a + b = " & a.Add(b).ToString()
14       Print "a - b = " & a.Subtract(b).ToString()
15       Print "a * b = " & a.Multiply(b).ToString()
16       Print "a / b = " & a.Divide(b).ToString()
17
18       Print "a + b = " & a.Add(b).ToFloatString()
19       Print "a - b = " & a.Subtract(b).ToFloatString()
20       Print "a * b = " & a.Multiply(b).ToFloatString()
21       Print "a / b = " & a.Divide(b).ToFloatString(3)
22   End Sub
```

```
23   ' Class CRational
24   Option Explicit
25   Private mNumerator As Integer
26   Private mDenominator As Integer
27
28   Public Function Add(r As CRational) As CRational
29       Dim rational As New CRational
```

```
30       Dim d As Integer, n As Integer
31
32       d = mDenominator * r.Denominator
33       n = mNumerator * r.Denominator + r.Numerator * mDenominator
34
35       rational.Denominator = d
36       rational.Numerator = n
37       Call Reduce(rational)
38       Set Add = rational
39   End Function
40
41   Public Function Subtract(r As CRational) As CRational
42       Dim rational As New CRational
43       Dim d As Integer, n As Integer
44
45       d = mDenominator * r.Denominator
46       n = mNumerator * r.Denominator - r.Numerator * mDenominator
47
48       rational.Denominator = d
49       rational.Numerator = n
50       Call Reduce(rational)
51       Set Subtract = rational
52   End Function
53
54   Public Function Multiply(r As CRational) As CRational
55       Dim rational As New CRational
56       Dim d As Integer, n As Integer
57
58       n = mNumerator * r.Numerator
59       d = mDenominator * r.Denominator
60
61       rational.Denominator = d
62       rational.Numerator = n
63       Call Reduce(rational)
64       Set Multiply = rational
65   End Function
66
67   Public Function Divide(r As CRational) As CRational
68       Dim rational As New CRational
69       Dim d As Integer, n As Integer
70
71       n = mNumerator * r.Denominator
72       d = mDenominator * r.Numerator
73
74       rational.Denominator = d
75       rational.Numerator = n
76       Call Reduce(rational)
77       Set Divide = rational
78   End Function
79
80   Public Function ToString() As String
81       ToString = mNumerator & "/" & mDenominator
82   End Function
83
84   Public Function ToFloatString(Optional precision As Integer = 2) As String
85       ToFloatString = FormatNumber$(mNumerator / mDenominator, precision)
86   End Function
87
88   Private Sub Reduce(r As CRational)
89       Dim gcd As Integer, smaller As Integer, k As Integer
90
91       smaller = r.Numerator
92
93       If r.Denominator < smaller Then
94           smaller = r.Denominator
95       End If
96
```

```
97         smaller = Abs(smaller)
98
99         For k = 2 To smaller
100
101            If (r.Numerator Mod k = 0 And r.Denominator Mod k = 0) Then
102               gcd = k
103            End If
104
105         Next k
106
107         If gcd <> 0 Then
108            r.Numerator = r.Numerator \ gcd
109            r.Denominator = r.Denominator \ gcd
110         End If
111   End Sub
112
113   Public Property Get Numerator() As Integer
114         Numerator = mNumerator
115   End Property
116
117   Public Property Let Numerator(n As Integer)
118         mNumerator = n
119   End Property
120
121   Public Property Get Denominator() As Integer
122         Denominator = mDenominator
123   End Property
124
125   Public Property Let Denominator(d As Integer)
126         mDenominator = d
127   End Property
```

16.19   Modify class **CTime2** (Fig. 16.4) to include method **Tick** which increments the time stored in a **CTime2** object by one second. Name the new class **CTime3**. Also provide method **IncrementMinute** to increment **mMinute** and method **IncrementHour** to increment **mHour**. The **CTime3** object should always remain in a consistent state. Write a program that tests method **Tick**, method **IncrementMinute** and method **IncrementHour** to ensure that they work correctly. Be sure to test the following cases:

    a) Incrementing into the next **mMinute**.
    b) Incrementing into the next **mHour**.
    c) Incrementing into the next day (i.e., 11:59:59 PM to 12:00:00 AM).
    ANS:

```
1    ' Exercise 16.18 Solution
2    Option Explicit
3    Private mTime As CTime3
4
5    Private Sub Form_Load()
6       Set mTime = New CTime3
7       Call mTime.SetTime(txtHour.Text, txtMinute.Text, _
8                      txtSecond.Text)
9       Call UpdateDisplay
10   End Sub
11
12   Private Sub cmdEnter_Click()
```

```
13       mTime.Hour = txtHour.Text
14       mTime.Minute = txtMinute.Text
15       mTime.Second = txtSecond.Text
16       Call UpdateDisplay
17    End Sub
18
19    Private Sub cmdAdd_Click()
20       Call mTime.Tick
21       Call UpdateDisplay
22    End Sub
23
24    Private Sub UpdateDisplay()
25       lblDisplay.Caption = Space$(12) & "Standard: " & _
26                            mTime.ToStandardTime() & _
27                            "    Universal: " & _
28                            mTime.ToUniversalTime()
29    End Sub
30
31    Private Sub Form_Terminate()
32       Set mTime = Nothing
33    End Sub
```

```
34    ' Class definition for CTime3
35    Option Explicit
36    Private mHour As Integer
37    Private mMinute As Integer
38    Private mSecond As Integer
39
40    Public Sub IncrementMinute()
41       mMinute = ValidateMinute(mMinute + 1)
42    End Sub
43
44    Public Sub IncrementHour()
45       mHour = ValidateHour(mHour + 1)
46    End Sub
47
48    Public Sub Tick()
49       mSecond = ValidateSecond(mSecond + 1)
50
51       If mSecond = 0 Then
52          Call IncrementMinute
53
54          If mMinute = 0 Then
55             Call IncrementHour
56          End If
57
58       End If
59
60    End Sub
61
62    Public Sub SetTime(ByVal h As Integer, ByVal m As Integer, _
63                       ByVal s As Integer)
64
65       mHour = ValidateHour(h)
66       mMinute = ValidateMinute(m)
67       mSecond = ValidateSecond(s)
68    End Sub
69
70    Public Function ToUniversalTime() As String
71       ToUniversalTime = Format$(mHour, "00") & ":" & _
72                         Format$(mMinute, "00") & ":" & _
73                         Format$(mSecond, "00")
74    End Function
75
76    Public Function ToStandardTime() As String
77       Dim h As Integer
```

```
78
79      h = IIf((mHour = 12 Or mHour = 0), 12, mHour Mod 12)
80
81      ToStandardTime = h & ":" & _
82                         Format$(mMinute, "00") & ":" & _
83                         Format$(mSecond, "00") & " " & _
84                         IIf(mHour < 12, "AM", "PM")
85   End Function
86
87   Public Property Get Hour() As Integer
88      Hour = mHour
89   End Property
90
91   Public Property Let Hour(ByVal h As Integer)
92      mHour = ValidateHour(h)
93   End Property
94
95   Public Property Get Minute() As Integer
96      Minute = mMinute
97   End Property
98
99   Public Property Let Minute(ByVal m As Integer)
100     mMinute = ValidateMinute(m)
101  End Property
102
103  Public Property Get Second() As Integer
104     Second = mSecond
105  End Property
106
107  Public Property Let Second(ByVal s As Integer)
108     mSecond = ValidateSecond(s)
109  End Property
110
111  Private Function ValidateHour(ByVal h As Integer)
112     ValidateHour = IIf((h >= 0 And h < 24), h, 0)
113  End Function
114
115  Private Function ValidateMinute(ByVal m As Integer)
116     ValidateMinute = IIf((m >= 0 And m < 60), m, 0)
117  End Function
118
119  Private Function ValidateSecond(ByVal s As Integer)
120     ValidateSecond = IIf((s >= 0 And s < 60), s, 0)
121  End Function
```

16.20   Modify class **CDate1** (Fig. 16.5) to perform error checking on the initializer values for instance variables **mMonth**, **mDay** and **mYear**. Name the new class **CDate2**. Also, provide a method **NextDay** to increment the day by one. The **CDate2** object should always remain in a consistent state. Write a program that tests method **NextDay** in a loop that prints the date during each iteration of the loop to illustrate that method **NextDay** works correctly. Be sure to test the following cases:

   a) Incrementing into the next **mMonth**.
   b) Incrementing into the next **mYear**.
   ANS:

```
1    ' Exercise 16.19 Solution
2    Option Explicit
3
4    Private Sub Form_Load()
5       Dim d As New CDate2, j As Integer
6       Call d.SetDate(2, 10, 1998)
7
8       For j = 1 To 160
9          Call lstBox.AddItem(d.ToString())
10         Call d.NextDay
11      Next j
12   End Sub
```

```
15   ' Class CDate2 definition
16   Option Explicit
17   Private mMonth As Integer
18   Private mDay As Integer
19   Private mYear As Integer
20
21   Private Sub Class_Initialize()
22      mDay = 1
23      mMonth = 1
24      mYear = 1900
25   End Sub
26
27   Public Property Get Day() As Integer
28      Day = mDay
29   End Property
30
31   Public Property Let Day(ByVal dy As Integer)
32      mDay = ValidateDay(dy)
33   End Property
34
35   Public Property Get Month() As Integer
36      Month = mMonth
37   End Property
38
39   Public Property Let Month(ByVal mth As Integer)
40      mMonth = ValidateMonth(mth)
41   End Property
42
43   Public Property Get year() As Integer
44      year = mYear
45   End Property
46
47   Public Property Let year(ByVal yr As Integer)
48      mYear = yr    ' Could also be validated by programmer
49   End Property
50
51   Public Function ToString() As String
52      ToString = mMonth & "/" & mDay & "/" & mYear
53   End Function
54
55   Public Sub NextDay()
56      mDay = ValidateDay(mDay + 1)
57      If mDay = 1 Then
58         mMonth = ValidateMonth(mMonth + 1)
59
60         If mMonth = 1 Then
61            mYear = mYear + 1
62         End If
63      End If
64   End Sub
65
66   Public Sub SetDate(ByVal dy As Integer, ByVal mth As Integer, _
```

```
67                     ByVal yr As Integer)
68      mMonth = ValidateMonth(mth)
69      mDay = ValidateDay(dy)
70      mYear = yr
71   End Sub
72
73   Private Function ValidateMonth(ByVal mth As Integer) As Integer
74      ValidateMonth = IIf((mth > 0 And mth <= 12), mth, 1)
75   End Function
76
77   Private Function ValidateDay(ByVal dy As Integer) As Integer
78      Dim daysPerMonth() As Variant
79
80      daysPerMonth = Array(0, 31, 28, 31, 30, 31, 30, 31, 31, 30, 31, 30, 31)
81
82      If dy > 0 And dy <= daysPerMonth(mMonth) Then
83         ValidateDay = dy
84         Exit Function
85      End If
86
87      If mMonth = 2 And dy = 29 And (mYear Mod 400 = 0 Or _
88                                mYear Mod 4 = 0 And _
89                                mYear Mod 100 <> 0) Then
90         ValidateDay = dy
91         Exit Function
92      End If
93
94      ' An invalid day was passed to ValidateDay
95      ' Set the day to a default value of 1
96      ValidateDay = 1
97   End Function
```

```
Exercise 16.19 Solution
10/29/1998
10/30/1998
10/31/1998
11/1/1998
11/2/1998
```

16.21   Combine the **CTime3** class of Exercise 16.18 and the **CDate2** class of Exercise 16.19 into one class called **CDateAnd-Time**. Modify method **Tick** to call method **NextDay** if the time is incremented into the next **mDay**. Modify methods **ToStan-dardTime** and **ToUniversalTime** to output the date in addition to the time. Write a program to test the new class **CDateAndTime**. Specifically test incrementing the time to the next **mDay**.

   ANS:

```
1    ' Exercise 16.20 Solution
2    Option Explicit
3    Private mTimeDate As CDateAndTime
4
5    Private Sub Form_Load()
6       Set mTimeDate = New CDateAndTime
7       Call mTimeDate.SetDate(31, 1, 1999)
8       Call mTimeDate.SetTime(txtHour.Text, txtMinute.Text, _
9                       txtSecond.Text)
10      Call UpdateDisplay
11   End Sub
12
13   Private Sub cmdEnter_Click()
14      mTimeDate.Hour = txtHour.Text
15      mTimeDate.Minute = txtMinute.Text
16      mTimeDate.Second = txtSecond.Text
17      Call UpdateDisplay
18   End Sub
19
20   Private Sub cmdAdd_Click()
```

```
21          Call mTimeDate.Tick
22          Call UpdateDisplay
23      End Sub
24
25      Private Sub UpdateDisplay()
26          lblDisplay.Caption = Space$(12) & "Standard: " & _
27                               mTimeDate.ToStandardTime() & _
28                               "    Universal: " & _
29                               mTimeDate.ToUniversalTime()
30      End Sub
31
32      Private Sub Form_Terminate()
33          Set mTimeDate = Nothing
34      End Sub
```

```
35      ' Class CDateAndTime definition
36      Option Explicit
37      Private mMonth As Integer
38      Private mDay As Integer
39      Private mYear As Integer
40      Private mHour As Integer
41      Private mMinute As Integer
42      Private mSecond As Integer
43
44      Private Sub Class_Initialize()
45          mDay = 1
46          mMonth = 1
47          mYear = 1900
48      End Sub
49
50      Public Property Get Day() As Integer
51          Day = mDay
52      End Property
53
54      Public Property Let Day(ByVal dy As Integer)
55          mDay = ValidateDay(dy)
56      End Property
57
58      Public Property Get Month() As Integer
59          Month = mMonth
60      End Property
61
62      Public Property Let Month(ByVal mth As Integer)
63          mMonth = ValidateMonth(mth)
64      End Property
65
66      Public Property Get year() As Integer
67          year = mYear
68      End Property
69
70      Public Property Let year(ByVal yr As Integer)
71          mYear = yr     ' Could also be validated by programmer
72      End Property
73
74      Public Function ToString() As String
75          ToString = mMonth & "/" & mDay & "/" & mYear
76      End Function
77
78      Public Sub NextDay()
79          mDay = ValidateDay(mDay + 1)
80
81          If mDay = 1 Then
82              mMonth = ValidateMonth(mMonth + 1)
83
84              If mMonth = 1 Then
85                  mYear = mYear + 1
```

```
86           End If
87
88       End If
89
90   End Sub
91
92   Public Sub SetDate(ByVal dy As Integer, ByVal mth As Integer, _
93                       ByVal yr As Integer)
94       mMonth = ValidateMonth(mth)
95       mDay = ValidateDay(dy)
96       mYear = yr
97   End Sub
98
99   Private Function ValidateMonth(ByVal mth As Integer) As Integer
100      ValidateMonth = IIf((mth > 0 And mth <= 12), mth, 1)
101  End Function
102
103  Private Function ValidateDay(ByVal dy As Integer) As Integer
104      Dim daysPerMonth() As Variant
105
106      daysPerMonth = Array(0, 31, 28, 31, 30, 31, 30, 31, 31, _
107                            30, 31, 30, 31)
108
109      If dy > 0 And dy <= daysPerMonth(mMonth) Then
110         ValidateDay = dy
111         Exit Function
112      End If
113
114      If mMonth = 2 And dy = 29 And (mYear Mod 400 = 0 Or _
115                                     mYear Mod 4 = 0 And _
116                                     mYear Mod 100 <> 0) Then
117         ValidateDay = dy
118         Exit Function
119      End If
120
121      ' An invalid day was passed to ValidateDay
122      ' Set the day to a default value of 1
123      ValidateDay = 1
124  End Function
125
126  Public Sub IncrementMinute()
127      mMinute = ValidateMinute(mMinute + 1)
128  End Sub
129
130  Public Sub IncrementHour()
131      mHour = ValidateHour(mHour + 1)
132  End Sub
133
134  Public Sub Tick()
135      mSecond = ValidateSecond(mSecond + 1)
136
137      If mSecond = 0 Then
138         Call IncrementMinute
139
140         If mMinute = 0 Then
141            Call IncrementHour
142
143            If mHour = 0 Then
144               Call NextDay
145            End If
146
147         End If
148
149      End If
150  End Sub
```

```
151
152  Public Sub SetTime(ByVal h As Integer, ByVal m As Integer, _
153                      ByVal s As Integer)
154
155      mHour = ValidateHour(h)
156      mMinute = ValidateMinute(m)
157      mSecond = ValidateSecond(s)
158  End Sub
159
160  Public Function ToUniversalTime() As String
161      ToUniversalTime = Format$(mHour, "00") & ":" & _
162                        Format$(mMinute, "00") & ":" & _
163                        Format$(mSecond, "00") & _
164                        Space$(4) & ToString()
165  End Function
166
167  Public Function ToStandardTime() As String
168      Dim h As Integer
169
170      h = IIf((mHour = 12 Or mHour = 0), 12, mHour Mod 12)
171
172      ToStandardTime = h & ":" & _
173                        Format$(mMinute, "00") & ":" & _
174                        Format$(mSecond, "00") & " " & _
175                        IIf(mHour < 12, "AM", "PM") & _
176                        Space$(4) & ToString()
177  End Function
178
179  Public Property Get Hour() As Integer
180      Hour = mHour
181  End Property
182
183  Public Property Let Hour(ByVal h As Integer)
184      mHour = ValidateHour(h)
185  End Property
186
187  Public Property Get Minute() As Integer
188      Minute = mMinute
189  End Property
190
191  Public Property Let Minute(ByVal m As Integer)
192      mMinute = ValidateMinute(m)
193  End Property
194
195  Public Property Get Second() As Integer
196      Second = mSecond
197  End Property
198
199  Public Property Let Second(ByVal s As Integer)
200      mSecond = ValidateSecond(s)
201  End Property
202
203  Private Function ValidateHour(ByVal h As Integer)
204      ValidateHour = IIf((h >= 0 And h < 24), h, 0)
205  End Function
206
207  Private Function ValidateMinute(ByVal m As Integer)
208      ValidateMinute = IIf((m >= 0 And m < 60), m, 0)
209  End Function
210
211  Private Function ValidateSecond(ByVal s As Integer)
212      ValidateSecond = IIf((s >= 0 And s < 60), s, 0)
213  End Function
```

16.22 [CD] Create a class **CRectangle** that has attributes **mLength** and **mWidth**, each of which defaults to 1. **CRectangle** has methods that calculate the rectangle's **Perimeter** and **Area**. It has *set* and *get* methods for both **mLength** and **mWidth**. The *set* methods should verify that **mLength** and **mWidth** are each numbers larger than 0.0 and less than 20.0.

ANS:

```
1   ' Exercise 16.21 Solution
2   Option Explicit
3   Private WithEvents mRectangle As CRectangle
4
5   Private Sub Form_Load()
6       Set mRectangle = New CRectangle
7   End Sub
8
9   Private Sub cmdEnter_Click()
10      lblMessage.Caption = ""
11      mRectangle.Length = txtLength
12      mRectangle.Width = txtWidth
13      lblLengthDisplay.Caption = "Area: " & mRectangle.Area
14      lblWidthDisplay.Caption = "Perimeter: " & _
15                              mRectangle.Perimeter
16  End Sub
17
18  ' This event procedure is called when class CRectangle's
19  ' RaiseEvent statement is executed.
20  Private Sub mRectangle_DefaultValue(s As String, id As String)
21      lblMessage.Caption = s
22
23      If id = "width" Then
24          txtWidth.Text = 1
25      Else
26          txtLength.Text = 1
27      End If
28
29  End Sub
30
31  Private Sub Form_Terminate()
32      Set mRectangle = Nothing
33  End Sub
```

```
34  ' Class CRectangle definition
35  Option Explicit
36
37  ' Instance variables
38  Private mLength As Double
39  Private mWidth As Double
40
41  ' Event class is capable of raising
42  Public Event DefaultValue(s As String, id As String)
43
44  Private Sub Class_Initialize()
45      mLength = 1
```

```
46        mWidth = 1
47    End Sub
48
49    Public Property Let Length(ByVal lengthValue As Double)
50        Call ValidateValue(lengthValue, mLength, "length")
51    End Property
52
53    Public Property Let Width(ByVal widthValue As Double)
54        Call ValidateValue(widthValue, mWidth, "width")
55    End Property
56
57    Public Function Area() As Double
58        Area = mLength * mWidth
59    End Function
60
61    Public Function Perimeter() As Double
62        Perimeter = 2 * mLength + 2 * mWidth
63    End Function
64
65    Private Sub ValidateValue(n As Double, _
66                              modVar As Double, id As String)
67
68        If n > 0 And n < 20 Then
69            modVar = n
70        Else
71            modVar = 1    ' Set to default
72
73            ' Raise the event to let the users of the class know
74            ' that the setting was rejected.
75            RaiseEvent DefaultValue("Invalid setting. Using default " & _
76                                    "value of 1.", id)
77        End If
78    End Sub
```

```
 Exercise 16.21 Solution

Enter Width of rectangle:   5
Enter Length of rectangle:  8

            Enter

Perimeter: 26

Area: 40
```

16.23   Create a more sophisticated **CRectangle** class than the one you created in Exercise 16.21. This class stores only the Cartesian coordinates of the four corners of the rectangle. Verify that each set of coordinates is in the first quadrant with no single *x* or *y* coordinate larger than 20.0. Also verify that the supplied coordinates do, in fact, specify a rectangle. Methods calculate the **Length**, **Width**, **Perimeter** and **Area**. The length is the larger of the two dimensions. Include a predicate method **IsSquare** which determines if the rectangle is a square.

     ANS:

```
1    ' Exercise 16.22 Solution
2    Option Explicit
3
4    Private Sub Form_Load()
5        Dim r As New CRectangle2, r2 As New CRectangle2
6
7        Call r.SetPoints(0, 0, 20, 0, 0, 10, 20, 10)
8        Call r2.SetPoints(5, 10, 50, 70, 4, 33, 12, 8)
9
10       Print "Length = " & r.Length
11       Print "Width = " & r.Width
12       Print "Perimeter = " & r.Perimeter()
13       Print "Area = " & r.Area()
```

```
14        Print "IsSquare = " & r.IsSquare()
15        Print
16        Print "Length = " & r2.Length
17        Print "Width = " & r2.Width
18        Print "Perimeter = " & r2.Perimeter()
19        Print "Area = " & r2.Area()
20        Print "IsSquare = " & r2.IsSquare()
21    End Sub
```

```
22    ' Class CPoint
23    Option Explicit
24    Private mX As Integer
25    Private mY As Integer
26
27    Public Property Get X() As Integer
28        X = mX
29    End Property
30
31    Public Property Let X(xValue As Integer)
32        mX = xValue
33    End Property
34
35    Public Property Get Y() As Integer
36        Y = mY
37    End Property
38
39    Public Property Let Y(yValue As Integer)
40        mY = yValue
41    End Property
```

```
42    ' Class CRectangle2
43    Option Explicit
44    Private mPoint(1 To 4) As CPoint
45    Private mLength As Integer
46    Private mWidth As Integer
47    Private mSquare As Boolean
48
49    Private Sub Class_Initialize()
50        Dim j As Integer
51
52        For j = 1 To 4
53            Set mPoint(j) = New CPoint
54        Next j
55    End Sub
56
57    Public Property Get Length() As Integer
58        Length = mLength
59    End Property
60
61    Public Property Let Length(m As Integer)
62        mLength = m
63    End Property
64
65    Public Property Get Width() As Integer
66        Width = mWidth
67    End Property
68
69    Public Property Let Width(w As Integer)
70        mWidth = w
71    End Property
72
```

```vb
73   ' Arguments are assumed to be passed in the order
74   '   x1,y1--------------x2,y2
75   '      |                |
76   '      |                |
77   '   x3,y3--------------x4,y4
78   '
79   Public Sub SetPoints(uplx As Integer, uply As Integer, _
80                        uprx As Integer, upry As Integer, _
81                        blx As Integer, bly As Integer, _
82                        brx As Integer, bry As Integer)
83      mPoint(1).X = IIf(uplx >= 0 And uplx <= 20, uplx, 1)
84      mPoint(1).Y = IIf(uply >= 0 And uply <= 20, uply, 1)
85      mPoint(2).X = IIf(uprx >= 0 And uprx <= 20, uprx, 1)
86      mPoint(2).Y = IIf(upry >= 0 And upry <= 20, upry, 1)
87      mPoint(3).X = IIf(blx >= 0 And blx <= 20, blx, 1)
88      mPoint(3).Y = IIf(bly >= 0 And bly <= 20, bly, 1)
89      mPoint(4).X = IIf(brx >= 0 And brx <= 20, brx, 1)
90      mPoint(4).Y = IIf(bry >= 0 And bry <= 20, bry, 1)
91
92      ' If points do not form a rectangle set them to defaults
93      If (mPoint(1).Y <> mPoint(2).Y Or mPoint(3).Y <> mPoint(4).Y Or _
94          mPoint(1).X <> mPoint(3).X Or mPoint(2).X <> mPoint(4).X) Then
95         mPoint(1).X = 0
96         mPoint(1).Y = 0
97         mPoint(2).X = 10
98         mPoint(2).Y = 0
99         mPoint(3).X = 0
100        mPoint(3).Y = 10
101        mPoint(4).X = 10
102        mPoint(4).Y = 10
103        mSquare = True
104     End If
105
106     Dim temp As Integer, temp2  As Integer
107
108     temp = mPoint(2).X - mPoint(1).X
109     temp2 = mPoint(3).Y - mPoint(1).Y
110
111     If (temp > temp2) Then
112        mLength = temp
113        mWidth = temp2
114     Else
115        mLength = temp2
116        mWidth = temp
117     End If
118
119   End Sub
120
121   Public Function Perimeter() As Integer
122      Perimeter = 2 * mLength + 2 * mWidth
123   End Function
124
125   Public Function Area() As Integer
126      Area = mLength * mWidth
127   End Function
128
129   Public Function IsSquare() As Boolean
130      IsSquare = (mLength = mWidth)
131   End Function
132
133   Private Sub Class_Terminate()
134      Dim j As Integer
135
136      For j = 1 To 4
137         Set mPoint(j) = Nothing
138      Next j
139   End Sub
```

16.24   Create a class **CHugeInteger** which uses a 40-element array of digits to store **Integer**s as large as 40-digits each. Provide methods **InputHugeInteger**, **OutputHugeInteger**, **AddHugeIntegers** and **SubtractHugeIntegers**. For comparing **CHugeInteger** objects provide methods **IsEqualTo**, **IsNotEqualTo**, **IsGreaterThan**, **IsLessThan**, **IsGreaterThanOrEqualTo** and **IsLessThanOrEqualTo**—each of these is a "predicate" method that simply returns **True** if the relationship holds between the two **CHugeInteger**s and returns **False** if the relationship does not hold. Provide a predicate method **IsZero**. If you feel ambitious, also provide the method **MultiplyHugeIntegers**, the method **DivideHugeIntegers** and the method **ModulusHugeIntegers**.

   ANS:

```
1   ' Exercise 16.23 Solution
2   Option Explicit
3
4   Private Sub Form_Load()
5      Dim n As New CHugeInteger, m As New CHugeInteger
6
7      n.Number = "7654321"
8      m.Number = "7891234"
9      Print "a = " & n.Number
10     Print "b = " & m.Number
11     Print "a + b = " & n.Add(m).Number
12     Print
13     n.Number = "9999999999999999999999999993"
14     m.Number = "9999999"
15     Print "c = " & n.Number
16     Print "d = " & m.Number
17     Print "c - d = " & n.Subtract(m).Number
18     Print
19     Print "c = d is " & n.IsEqualTo(m)
20     Print "c <> d is " & n.IsNotEqualTo(m)
21     Print "c > d is " & n.IsGreaterThan(m)
22     Print "c >= d is " & n.IsGreaterThanOrEqualTo(m)
23     Print "c < d is " & n.IsLessThan(m)
24     Print "c <= d is " & n.IsLessThanOrEqualTo(m)
25     Print
26     n.Number = "55555555555"
27     m.Number = "55555555555"
28     Print "e = " & n.Number
29     Print "f = " & m.Number
30     Print
31     Print "e = f is " & n.IsEqualTo(m)
32     Print "e <> f is " & n.IsNotEqualTo(m)
33     Print "e > f is " & n.IsGreaterThan(m)
34     Print "e >= f is " & n.IsGreaterThanOrEqualTo(m)
35     Print "e < f is " & n.IsLessThan(m)
36     Print "e <= f is " & n.IsLessThanOrEqualTo(m)
37  End Sub

38  ' Class CHugeInteger
39  ' Note: Negative numbers are not supported in this solution.
40  Option Explicit
41  Private mIntArray(1 To 40) As Integer
42
```

```
43    Public Function GetArray() As Integer()
44       GetArray = mIntArray
45    End Function
46
47    Public Property Get Number() As String
48       Number = ConvertToString(mIntArray)
49    End Property
50
51    Public Property Let Number(num As String)
52       Dim j As Integer, k As Integer, length As Integer
53
54       Erase mIntArray
55       length = Len(num)
56       j = 40
57
58       If length > 40 Then
59          Call MsgBox("Only 40 or fewer digits are supported.")
60          Exit Property
61       End If
62
63       For k = length To 1 Step -1
64          mIntArray(j) = Mid$(num, k, 1)
65          j = j - 1
66       Next k
67
68    End Property
69
70    Public Function Add(r As CHugeInteger) As CHugeInteger
71       Dim temp As New CHugeInteger, carry As Integer
72       Dim j As Integer, rArray() As Integer, tArray(1 To 40) As Integer
73
74       rArray = r.GetArray()
75
76       For j = 40 To 1 Step -1
77          tArray(j) = mIntArray(j) + rArray(j) + carry
78
79          If tArray(j) > 9 Then
80             tArray(j) = tArray(j) Mod 10
81             carry = 1
82          Else
83             carry = 0
84          End If
85
86       Next j
87
88       temp.Number = temp.ConvertToString(tArray)
89       Set Add = temp
90    End Function
91
92    ' Note: Subtract is written such that mIntArray is assumed to be
93    ' larger than r's mIntArray.
94    Public Function Subtract(r As CHugeInteger) As CHugeInteger
95       Dim temp As New CHugeInteger, tArray(1 To 40) As Integer
96       Dim j As Integer, rArray() As Integer, c() As Integer
97
98       rArray = r.GetArray()
99       c = mIntArray
100
101      For j = 40 To 1 Step -1
102
103         If c(j) < rArray(j) Then
104            c(j - 1) = c(j - 1) - 1
105            c(j) = c(j) + 10
106         End If
107
108         tArray(j) = c(j) - rArray(j)
109      Next j
```

```
110
111    temp.Number = temp.ConvertToString(tArray)
112    Set Subtract = temp
113 End Function
114
115 Public Function IsEqualTo(r As CHugeInteger) As Boolean
116    Dim a() As Integer, j As Integer, thisLowIndex As Integer
117    Dim aLowIndex As Integer
118
119    a = r.GetArray()
120    thisLowIndex = GetLowestUsedIndex(mIntArray)
121    aLowIndex = GetLowestUsedIndex(a)
122
123    If thisLowIndex <> aLowIndex Then
124       IsEqualTo = False
125       Exit Function
126    End If
127
128    For j = thisLowIndex To 40
129       If a(j) <> mIntArray(j) Then
130          IsEqualTo = False
131          Exit Function
132       End If
133    Next j
134
135    IsEqualTo = True
136 End Function
137
138 Public Function IsNotEqualTo(r As CHugeInteger) As Boolean
139    Dim a() As Integer, j As Integer, thisLowIndex As Integer
140    Dim aLowIndex As Integer
141
142    a = r.GetArray()
143    thisLowIndex = GetLowestUsedIndex(mIntArray)
144    aLowIndex = GetLowestUsedIndex(a)
145
146    If thisLowIndex <> aLowIndex Then
147       IsNotEqualTo = True
148       Exit Function
149    End If
150
151    For j = thisLowIndex To 40
152       If a(j) <> mIntArray(j) Then
153          IsNotEqualTo = True
154          Exit Function
155       End If
156    Next j
157
158    IsNotEqualTo = False
159 End Function
160
161 Public Function IsGreaterThan(r As CHugeInteger) As Boolean
162    Dim a() As Integer, thisLowIndex As Integer
163    Dim aLowIndex As Integer
164
165    a = r.GetArray()
166    thisLowIndex = GetLowestUsedIndex(mIntArray)
167    aLowIndex = GetLowestUsedIndex(a)
168
169    If thisLowIndex < aLowIndex Then
170       IsGreaterThan = True
171       Exit Function
172    ElseIf thisLowIndex > aLowIndex Then
173       IsGreaterThan = False
174       Exit Function
175    End If
176 End Function
```

```
177
178  Public Function IsLessThan(r As CHugeInteger) As Boolean
179      Dim a() As Integer, thisLowIndex As Integer
180      Dim aLowIndex As Integer
181
182      a = r.GetArray()
183      thisLowIndex = GetLowestUsedIndex(mIntArray)
184      aLowIndex = GetLowestUsedIndex(a)
185
186      If thisLowIndex > aLowIndex Then
187         IsLessThan = True
188         Exit Function
189      ElseIf thisLowIndex < aLowIndex Then
190         IsLessThan = False
191         Exit Function
192      End If
193  End Function
194
195  Public Function IsGreaterThanOrEqualTo(r As CHugeInteger) As Boolean
196      Dim a() As Integer, j As Integer, thisLowIndex As Integer
197      Dim aLowIndex As Integer
198
199      a = r.GetArray()
200      thisLowIndex = GetLowestUsedIndex(mIntArray)
201      aLowIndex = GetLowestUsedIndex(a)
202
203      If thisLowIndex < aLowIndex Then
204         IsGreaterThanOrEqualTo = True
205         Exit Function
206      ElseIf thisLowIndex > aLowIndex Then
207         IsGreaterThanOrEqualTo = False
208         Exit Function
209      End If
210
211      For j = thisLowIndex To 40
212         If mIntArray(j) > a(j) Then
213            IsGreaterThanOrEqualTo = True
214            Exit Function
215         ElseIf mIntArray(j) < a(j) Then
216            IsGreaterThanOrEqualTo = False
217            Exit Function
218         End If
219      Next j
220
221      IsGreaterThanOrEqualTo = True
222  End Function
223
224  Public Function IsLessThanOrEqualTo(r As CHugeInteger) As Boolean
225      Dim a() As Integer, thisLowIndex As Integer
226      Dim aLowIndex As Integer, j As Integer
227
228      a = r.GetArray()
229      thisLowIndex = GetLowestUsedIndex(mIntArray)
230      aLowIndex = GetLowestUsedIndex(a)
231
232      If thisLowIndex > aLowIndex Then
233         IsLessThanOrEqualTo = True
234         Exit Function
235      ElseIf thisLowIndex < aLowIndex Then
236         IsLessThanOrEqualTo = False
237         Exit Function
238      End If
239
240      For j = thisLowIndex To 40
241         If mIntArray(j) < a(j) Then
242            IsLessThanOrEqualTo = True
243            Exit Function
```

```
244            ElseIf mIntArray(j) > a(j) Then
245                IsLessThanOrEqualTo = False
246                Exit Function
247            End If
248        Next j
249
250        IsLessThanOrEqualTo = True
251    End Function
252
253    Private Function GetLowestUsedIndex(a() As Integer) As Integer
254        Dim j As Integer
255
256        For j = 1 To 40
257            If a(j) <> 0 Then
258                GetLowestUsedIndex = j
259                Exit Function
260            End If
261        Next j
262
263        GetLowestUsedIndex = -1
264    End Function
265
266    Public Function ConvertToString(a() As Integer) As String
267        Dim j As Integer, s As String
268
269        For j = GetLowestUsedIndex(a) To 40
270            s = s & a(j)
271        Next j
272
273        ConvertToString = s
274    End Function
```

```
Exercise 16.23 Solution                                    _ □ ✕
a = 7654321
b = 7891234
a + b = 15545555


c = 99999999999999999999999999993
d = 9999999
c - d = 99999999999999999999989999994

c = d is False
c <> d is True
c > d is True
c >= d is True
c < d is False
c <= d is False

e = 55555555555
f = 55555555555

e = f is True
e <> f is False
e > f is False
e >= f is True
e < f is False
e <= f is True
```

16.25   Create class **CSavingsAccount**. Variable **mAnnualInterestRate** stores the interest rate for each of the savers. Each object of the class contains a **Private** instance variable **mSavingsBalance** indicating the amount the saver currently has on deposit. Provide method **CalculateMonthlyInterest** to calculate the monthly interest by multiplying **mSavingsBalance** by **mAnnualInterestRate** divided by 12; this interest should be added to **mSavingsBalance**. Provide method **ModifyInterestRate** that sets the **mAnnualInterestRate** to a new value.

Write a program to test class **CSavingsAccount**. Instantiate two different **CSavingsAccount** objects, **saver1** and **saver2**, with balances of $2000.00 and $3000.00, respectively. Set **mAnnualInterestRate** to 4%, then calculate the monthly interest and print the new balances for each of the savers. Then set the **mAnnualInterestRate** to 5% and calculate the next month's interest and print the new balances for each of the savers.

ANS:

```
1   ' Exercise 16.24 Solution
2   Option Explicit
3
4   Private Sub Form_Load()
5       Dim saver1 As New CSavingsAccount
6       Dim saver2 As New CSavingsAccount
7
8       saver1.SavingsBalance = 2000
9       saver1.AnnualInterestRate = 4
10      saver2.SavingsBalance = 3000
11      saver2.AnnualInterestRate = 4
12
13      Print "Interest rate set to 4%"
14      saver1.SavingsBalance = saver1.CalculateMonthlyInterest() + _
15                              saver1.SavingsBalance
16      Print "Saver1's balance is " & _
17            Format$(saver1.SavingsBalance, "Currency")
18      saver2.SavingsBalance = saver2.CalculateMonthlyInterest() + _
19                              saver2.SavingsBalance
20      Print "Saver2's balance is " & _
21            Format$(saver2.SavingsBalance, "Currency")
22      Print
23      Print "Interest rate set to 5%"
24      saver1.AnnualInterestRate = 5
25      saver2.AnnualInterestRate = 5
26      saver1.SavingsBalance = saver1.CalculateMonthlyInterest() + _
27                              saver1.SavingsBalance
28      Print "Saver1's balance is " & _
29            Format$(saver1.SavingsBalance, "Currency")
30      saver2.SavingsBalance = saver2.CalculateMonthlyInterest() + _
31                              saver2.SavingsBalance
32      Print "Saver2's balance is " & _
33            Format$(saver2.SavingsBalance, "Currency")
34  End Sub
```

```
35  ' Class CSavingsAccount
36  Option Explicit
37  Private mAnnualInterestRate As Integer
38  Private mSavingsBalance As Currency
39
40  Public Function CalculateMonthlyInterest() As Currency
41      CalculateMonthlyInterest = mSavingsBalance * (mAnnualInterestRate / 100) / 12
42  End Function
43
44  Public Property Get AnnualInterestRate() As Integer
45      AnnualInterestRate = mAnnualInterestRate
46  End Property
47
48  Public Property Let AnnualInterestRate(rate As Integer)
49      If rate > 0 And rate < 100 Then
50          mAnnualInterestRate = rate
51      End If
52  End Property
```

```
53
54   Public Property Get SavingsBalance() As Currency
55       SavingsBalance = mSavingsBalance
56   End Property
57
58   Public Property Let SavingsBalance(balance As Currency)
59       mSavingsBalance = balance
60   End Property
```

16.26   Create class **CIntegerSet**. Each object of the class can hold **Integer**s in the range 0 through 100. A set is represented internally as an array of ones and zeros. Array element **a(i)** is 1 if **Integer** i is in the set. Array element **a(j)** is 0 if **Integer** j is not in the set.

Provide the following methods: Method **UnionOfIntegerSets** creates a third set which is the set-theoretic union of two existing sets (i.e., an element of the third set's array is set to 1 if that element is 1 in either or both of the existing sets; otherwise, the element of the third set is set to 0). Method **IntersectionOfIntegerSets** creates a third set which is the set-theoretic intersection of two existing sets (i.e., an element of the third set's array is set to 0 if that element is 0 in either or both of the existing sets; otherwise, the element of the third set is set to 1). Method **InsertElement** inserts a new **Integer** k into a set (by setting **a(k)** to 1). Method **DeleteElement** deletes **Integer** m (by setting **a(m)** to 0). Method **ToString** returns a **String** containing a set as a list of numbers separated by spaces and prints only those elements that are present in the set or **---** for an empty set. Method **IsEqualTo** determines if two sets are equal. Write a program to test your **CIntegerSet** class. Instantiate several **CIntegerSet** objects. Test that all your methods work properly.

ANS:

```
1    ' Exercise 16.25 Solution
2    Option Explicit
3
4    Private Sub Form_Load()
5        Dim a As New CIntegerSet, b As New CIntegerSet
6        Dim i As CIntegerSet, u As CIntegerSet
7
8        Call a.InsertElement(1)
9        Call a.InsertElement(2)
10       Call a.InsertElement(3)
11       Call a.InsertElement(4)
12
13       Call b.InsertElement(3)
14       Call b.InsertElement(4)
15       Call b.InsertElement(9)
16       Call b.InsertElement(22)
17       Print "A is " & a.ToString
18       Print "B is " & b.ToString
19
20       Set u = a.UnionOfIntegerSets(b)
21       Print "A union B is " & u.ToString
22
23       Set i = a.IntersectionOfIntegerSets(b)
24       Print "A intersection B is " & i.ToString
25
26       Print "Removing 22 from B..."
27       Call b.DeleteElement(22)
28
29       Print "B is " & b.ToString
30   End Sub
```

```
31   ' Class CIntegerSet
32   Option Explicit
33   Dim mIntegerSet(100) As Integer
34
35   Public Function UnionOfIntegerSets(r As CIntegerSet) As CIntegerSet
36      Dim t As New CIntegerSet, j As Integer, s() As Integer
37
38      s = r.IntegerSet
39
40      For j = 0 To 100
41
42         If mIntegerSet(j) = 1 Or s(j) = 1 Then
43            Call t.InsertElement(j)
44         End If
45
46      Next j
47
48      Set UnionOfIntegerSets = t
49   End Function
50
51   Public Function IntersectionOfIntegerSets(r As CIntegerSet) As CIntegerSet
52      Dim t As New CIntegerSet, j As Integer, s() As Integer
53
54      s = r.IntegerSet
55
56      For j = 0 To 100
57
58         If mIntegerSet(j) = 1 And s(j) = 1 Then
59            Call t.InsertElement(j)
60         End If
61
62      Next j
63
64      Set IntersectionOfIntegerSets = t
65   End Function
66
67   Public Sub InsertElement(m As Integer)
68
69      If IsValid(m) Then
70         mIntegerSet(m) = 1
71      Else
72         Call MsgBox("Invalid Insertion Attempted.")
73      End If
74
75   End Sub
76
77   Public Sub DeleteElement(m As Integer)
78
79      If IsValid(m) Then
80         mIntegerSet(m) = 0
81      Else
82         Call MsgBox("Invalid Deletion Attempted.")
83      End If
84
85   End Sub
86
87   Public Function IsEqualTo(r As CIntegerSet) As Boolean
88      Dim k As Integer, s() As Integer
89
90      s = r.IntegerSet
91
92      For k = 0 To 100
93         If mIntegerSet(k) <> s(k) Then
94            IsEqualTo = False
95            Exit Function
96         End If
97      Next k
```

```
98
99        IsEqualTo = True
100  End Function
101
102  Public Function ToString() As String
103      Dim k As Integer, b As Boolean
104      Dim s As String
105
106      b = True
107
108      s = "{"
109
110      For k = 0 To 100
111
112          If mIntegerSet(k) <> 0 Then
113              b = False
114              s = s & Format$(k, "@@@@")
115          End If
116
117      Next k
118
119      If b Then
120          s = s & "---"
121      End If
122
123      ToString = s & "    }"
124  End Function
125
126  Public Sub EmptySet()
127      Erase mIntegerSet
128  End Sub
129
130  Private Function IsValid(i As Integer) As Boolean
131      IsValid = (i >= 0 And i <= 100)
132  End Function
133
134  Public Property Get IntegerSet() As Integer()
135      IntegerSet = mIntegerSet
136  End Property
```

16.27 It would be perfectly reasonable for the **CTime1** class of Fig. 16.2 to represent the time internally as the number of seconds since midnight rather than the three **Integer** values **mHour**, **mMinute** and **mSecond**. Clients could use the same **Public** methods and get the same result. Modify class **CTime1** class to implement the time as the number of seconds since midnight and show that there is no visible change to the clients of the class. Name the new class **CTime4**.

16.28 Many programs written with inheritance could be solved with composition instead and vice versa. Discuss the relative merits of these approaches in the context of the **CPoint**, **CCircle**, **CCylinder** class hierarchy in this chapter. Rewrite the program of Fig. 16.11 (and the supporting classes) to use composition rather than inheritance. After you do this, reassess the relative merits of the two approaches both for the **CPoint**, **CCircle**, **CCylinder** problem and for object-oriented programs in general.

  ANS:

```
1  ' Exercise 16.27 Solution
2  Option Explicit
3  Option Base 1
4
5  Private Sub Form_Load()
6      Dim k As Integer
```

```
7       Dim p As New CPoint, c As New CCircle
8       Dim cy As New CCylinder
9
10      p.X = 333          ' Set X via Property Let
11      p.Y = 444          ' Set Y via Property Let
12
13      c.Radius = 10      ' Set Radius via Property Let
14      c.X = 55           ' Set X via Property Let
15      c.Y = 9            ' Set Y via Property Let
16
17      cy.Radius = 2      ' Set Radius via Property Let
18      cy.Height = 6      ' Set Height via Property Let
19      cy.X = 20          ' Set X via Property Let
20      cy.Y = 88          ' Set Y via Property Let
21
22      Print p.GetName() & " " & p.ToString()
23      Print c.GetName() & " " & c.ToString()
24      Print cy.GetName() & " " & cy.ToString()
25   End Sub
```

```
26   ' CPoint definition
27   Option Explicit
28   Private mX As Integer
29   Private mY As Integer
30
31   Public Function GetName() As String
32      GetName = "Point"
33   End Function
34
35   Public Function ToString() As String
36      ToString = "[" & mX & ", " & mY & "]"
37   End Function
38
39   Public Property Let X(ByVal newX As Integer)
40      mX = newX
41   End Property
42
43   Public Property Get X() As Integer
44      X = mX
45   End Property
46
47   Public Property Let Y(ByVal newY As Integer)
48      mY = newY
49   End Property
50
51   Public Property Get Y() As Integer
52      Y = mY
53   End Property
```

```
54   ' CCircle class definition
55   Option Explicit
56   Private mRadius As Double
57   Private mCenter As CPoint
58
59   Private Sub Class_Initialize()
60      Set mCenter = New CPoint
61   End Sub
62
63   Public Function Area() As Double
64      Area = 3.14159 * mRadius ^ 2
65   End Function
66
67   Public Function GetName() As String
68      GetName = "Circle"
69   End Function
70
```

```
71  Public Function ToString() As String
72      ToString = "[" & mCenter.X & ", " & mCenter.Y & "], " & "Radius: " & mRadius
73  End Function
74
75  Public Property Let X(ByVal xValue As Integer)
76      mCenter.X = xValue
77  End Property
78
79  Public Property Get X() As Integer
80      X = mCenter.X
81  End Property
82
83  Public Property Let Y(ByVal yValue As Integer)
84      mCenter.Y = yValue
85  End Property
86
87  Public Property Get Y() As Integer
88      Y = mCenter.Y
89  End Property
90
91  Public Property Let Radius(ByVal radiusValue As Double)
92      mRadius = radiusValue
93  End Property
94
95  Public Property Get Radius() As Double
96      Radius = mRadius
97  End Property
98
99  Private Sub Class_Terminate()
100     Set mCenter = Nothing
101 End Sub
```

```
103 ' CCylinder class definition
104 Option Explicit
105 Private mHeight As Double
106 Private mCircle As CCircle
107
108 Private Sub Class_Initialize()
109     Set mCircle = New CCircle
110 End Sub
111
112 Public Function Volume() As Double
113     Volume = 3.14159 * mCircle.Radius ^ 2 * mHeight
114 End Function
115
116 Public Function Area() As Double
117     Area = 2 * 3.14159 * mCircle.Radius ^ 2 + 2 * 3.14159 * mCircle.Radius * mHeight
118 End Function
119
120 Public Function GetName() As String
121     GetName = "Cylinder"
122 End Function
123
124 Public Function ToString() As String
125     ToString = "[" & mCircle.X & ", " & mCircle.Y & "], " & _
126                 "Radius: " & mCircle.Radius & ", Height: " & _
127                 mHeight
128 End Function
129
130 Public Property Let X(ByVal xValue As Integer)
131     mCircle.X = xValue
132 End Property
133
134 Public Property Get X() As Integer
135     X = mCircle.X
136 End Property
```

```
137
138  Public Property Let Y(ByVal yValue As Integer)
139     mCircle.Y = yValue
140  End Property
141
142  Public Property Get Y() As Integer
143     Y = mCircle.Y
144  End Property
145
146  Public Property Let Radius(ByVal radiusValue As Double)
147     mCircle.Radius = radiusValue
148  End Property
149
150  Public Property Get Radius() As Double
151     Radius = mCircle.Radius
152  End Property
153
154  Public Property Let Height(ByVal h As Double)
155     mHeight = h
156  End Property
157
158  Public Property Get Height() As Double
159     Height = mHeight
160  End Property
161
162  Private Sub Class_Terminate()
163     Set mCircle = Nothing
164  End Sub
```

```
 Exercise 16.27 Solution                    _ □ ×
Point [333, 444]
Circle [55, 9], Radius: 10
Cylinder [20, 88], Radius: 2, Height: 6
```

16.29   Rewrite the **CPoint**, **CCircle**, **CCylinder** program of Fig. 16.11 as a **CPoint**, **CSquare**, **CCube** program. Do this two ways—with inheritance and with composition.

16.30   Modify the payroll system of Fig. 16.10 to add **Private** instance variables **mBirthDate** (use class **CDate1** from Fig. 16.5) and **mDepartmentCode** (an **Integer**) to class **IEmployee** (name this new class **IEmployee3**) Assume this payroll is processed once per month. Then, as your program calculates the payroll for each **IEmployee3** (polymorphically), add a $100.00 bonus to the person's payroll amount if this is the month in which the **IEmployee3**'s birthday occurs.

      ANS:

```
1    ' Form module to exercise IEmployee3,
2    ' CBoss, CComissionWorker, CHourlyWorker,
3    ' and CPieceWorker
4    Option Explicit
5    Private mEmployeeRef As IEmployee3
6    Private mBoss As New CBoss
7    Private mCommissionWorker As New CCommissionWorker
8    Private mHourlyWorker As New CHourlyWorker
9    Private mPieceWorker As New CPieceWorker
10
11   Private Sub Form_Load()
12
13      With mBoss
14         .FirstName = "John"
15         .LastName = "Smith"
16         .WeeklySalary = 800
17      End With
18
19      Set mEmployeeRef = mBoss
20      mEmployeeRef.DepartmentCode = 357
21      Call mEmployeeRef.BirthDate.SetDate(3, 8, 1944)
22      Call Display(mBoss)
23
```

```
24      With mCommissionWorker
25          .FirstName = "Sue"
26          .LastName = "Jones"
27          .Quantity = 150
28          .Commission = 3
29          .Salary = 400
30      End With
31
32      Set mEmployeeRef = mCommissionWorker
33      mEmployeeRef.DepartmentCode = 1793
34      Call mEmployeeRef.BirthDate.SetDate(1, 1, 1957)
35      Call Display(mCommissionWorker)
36
37      With mHourlyWorker
38          .FirstName = "Karen"
39          .LastName = "Price"
40          .Hours = 40
41          .Wage = 13.75
42      End With
43
44      Set mEmployeeRef = mHourlyWorker
45      mEmployeeRef.DepartmentCode = 853
46      Call mEmployeeRef.BirthDate.SetDate(9, 27, 1949)
47      Call Display(mHourlyWorker)
48
49      With mPieceWorker
50          .FirstName = "Bob"
51          .LastName = "Lewis"
52          .Quantity = 200
53          .WagePerPiece = 2.5
54      End With
55
56      Set mEmployeeRef = mPieceWorker
57      mEmployeeRef.DepartmentCode = 731
58      Call mEmployeeRef.BirthDate.SetDate(13, 11, 1953)
59      Call Display(mPieceWorker)
60  End Sub
61
62  Private Sub Display(e As IEmployee3)
63      Dim bonus As Integer
64
65      If Month(Now) = e.BirthDate.Month Then
66          Print "Happy Birthday ";
67          bonus = 100
68      End If
69
70      Print e.ToString & " earned " & FormatCurrency(e.Earnings() + bonus) & _
71              " Dept: " & e.DepartmentCode & " Born: " & e.BirthDate.ToString()
72  End Sub
```

```
75  ' Interface IEmployee definition
76  Option Explicit
77  Private mBirthDate As CDate1
78  Private mDepartmentCode As Integer
79
80  Private Sub Class_Initialize()
81      Set mBirthDate = New CDate1
82  End Sub
83
84  Public Function Earnings() As Double
85  End Function
86
87  Public Function ToString() As String
88  End Function
89
```

```
90   Public Property Get BirthDate() As CDate1
91      Set BirthDate = mBirthDate
92   End Property
93
94   Public Property Get DepartmentCode() As Integer
95      DepartmentCode = mDepartmentCode
96   End Property
97
98   Public Property Let BirthDate(bDate As CDate1)
99      mBirthDate = bDate
100  End Property
101
102  Public Property Let DepartmentCode(code As Integer)
103     mDepartmentCode = code
104  End Property
105
106  Private Sub Class_Terminate()
107     Set mBirthDate = Nothing
108  End Sub
109
110  Private Sub Form_Terminate()
111     Set mBoss = Nothing
112     Set mCommissionWorker = Nothing
113     Set mPieceWorker = Nothing
114     Set mHourlyWorker = Nothing
115     Set mEmployeeRef = Nothing
116  End Sub
```

```
117  ' Class CDate1 definition
118  Option Explicit
119  Private mMonth As Integer
120  Private mDay As Integer
121  Private mYear As Integer
122
123  Private Sub Class_Initialize()
124     mDay = 1
125     mMonth = 1
126     mYear = 1900
127  End Sub
128
129  Public Property Get Day() As Integer
130     Day = mDay
131  End Property
132
133  Public Property Let Day(ByVal dy As Integer)
134     mDay = ValidateDay(dy)
135  End Property
136
137  Public Property Get Month() As Integer
138     Month = mMonth
139  End Property
140
141  Public Property Let Month(ByVal mth As Integer)
142     mMonth = ValidateMonth(mth)
143  End Property
144
145  Public Property Get year() As Integer
146     year = mYear
147  End Property
148
149  Public Property Let year(ByVal yr As Integer)
150     mYear = yr    ' Could also be validated by programmer
151  End Property
152
```

```vb
153 Public Function ToString() As String
154     ToString = mMonth & "/" & mDay & "/" & mYear
155 End Function
156
157 Public Sub SetDate(ByVal dy As Integer, ByVal mth As Integer, _
158                    ByVal yr As Integer)
159     mMonth = ValidateMonth(mth)
160     mDay = ValidateDay(dy)
161     mYear = yr
162 End Sub
163
164 Private Function ValidateMonth(ByVal mth As Integer) As Integer
165     ValidateMonth = IIf((mth > 0 And mth <= 12), mth, 1)
166 End Function
167
168 Private Function ValidateDay(ByVal dy As Integer) As Integer
169     Dim daysPerMonth()
170
171     daysPerMonth = Array(0, 31, 28, 31, 30, 31, 30, 31, 31, _
172                          30, 31, 30, 31)
173
174     If dy > 0 And dy <= daysPerMonth(mMonth) Then
175         ValidateDay = dy
176         Exit Function
177     End If
178
179     If mMonth = 2 And dy = 29 And (mYear Mod 400 = 0 Or _
180                                    mYear Mod 4 = 0 And _
181                                    mYear Mod 100 <> 0) Then
182         ValidateDay = dy
183         Exit Function
184     End If
185
186     ' An invalid day was passed to ValidateDay
187     ' Set the day to a default value of 1
188     ValidateDay = 1
189 End Function
```

```vb
190 ' CBoss definition
191 Option Explicit
192 Implements IEmployee3
193 Private mFirstName As String
194 Private mLastName As String
195 Private mWeeklySalary As Currency
196 Private mEmployee As IEmployee3
197
198 Public Sub Class_Initialize()
199     Set mEmployee = New IEmployee3
200 End Sub
201
202 Public Property Let WeeklySalary(ByVal wg As Currency)
203     mWeeklySalary = IIf(wg > 0, wg, 0)
204 End Property
205
206 Public Property Get WeeklySalary() As Currency
207     WeeklySalary = mWeeklySalary
208 End Property
209
210 Public Property Let FirstName(ByVal fName As String)
211     mFirstName = fName
212 End Property
213
214 Public Property Get FirstName() As String
215     FirstName = mFirstName
216 End Property
217
```

```
218  Public Property Let LastName(ByVal name As String)
219     mLastName = name
220  End Property
221
222  Public Property Get LastName() As String
223     LastName = mLastName
224  End Property
225
226  Private Property Let IEmployee3_BirthDate(bDate As CDate1)
227     mEmployee.BirthDate = bDate
228  End Property
229
230  Private Property Get IEmployee3_BirthDate() As CDate1
231     Set IEmployee3_BirthDate = mEmployee.BirthDate
232  End Property
233
234  Private Property Let IEmployee3_DepartmentCode(code As Integer)
235     mEmployee.DepartmentCode = code
236  End Property
237
238  Private Property Get IEmployee3_DepartmentCode() As Integer
239     IEmployee3_DepartmentCode = mEmployee.DepartmentCode
240  End Property
241
242  Private Function IEmployee3_Earnings() As Double
243     IEmployee3_Earnings = mWeeklySalary
244  End Function
245
246  Private Function IEmployee3_ToString() As String
247     IEmployee3_ToString = "Boss: " & mFirstName & " " & mLastName
248  End Function
249
250  Private Sub Class_Terminate()
251     Set mEmployee = Nothing
252  End Sub
```

```
254  ' CCommissionWorker definition
255  Option Explicit
256  Implements IEmployee3
257  Private mFirstName As String
258  Private mLastName As String
259  Private mSalary As Currency
260  Private mCommission As Currency
261  Private mQuantity As Long
262  Private mEmployee As IEmployee3
263
264  Public Sub Class_Initialize()
265     Set mEmployee = New IEmployee3
266  End Sub
267
268  Public Property Let FirstName(ByVal fName As String)
269     mFirstName = fName
270  End Property
271
272  Public Property Get FirstName() As String
273     FirstName = mFirstName
274  End Property
275
276  Public Property Let LastName(ByVal name As String)
277     mLastName = name
278  End Property
279
280  Public Property Get LastName() As String
281     LastName = mLastName
282  End Property
283
```

```
284   Private Property Let IEmployee3_BirthDate(bDate As CDate1)
285      mEmployee.BirthDate = bDate
286   End Property
287
288   Private Property Get IEmployee3_BirthDate() As CDate1
289      Set IEmployee3_BirthDate = mEmployee.BirthDate
290   End Property
291
292   Private Property Let IEmployee3_DepartmentCode(code As Integer)
293      mEmployee.DepartmentCode = code
294   End Property
295
296   Private Property Get IEmployee3_DepartmentCode() As Integer
297      IEmployee3_DepartmentCode = mEmployee.DepartmentCode
298   End Property
299
300   Public Property Let Salary(ByVal wg As Currency)
301      mSalary = IIf(wg > 0, wg, 0)
302   End Property
303
304   Public Property Get Salary() As Currency
305      Salary = mSalary
306   End Property
307
308   Public Property Let Commission(ByVal com As Currency)
309      mCommission = IIf(com > 0, com, 0)
310   End Property
311
312   Public Property Get Commission() As Currency
313      Commission = mCommission
314   End Property
315
316   Public Property Let Quantity(ByVal qty As Long)
317      mQuantity = IIf(qty > 0, qty, 0)
318   End Property
319
320   Public Property Get Quantity() As Long
321      Quantity = mQuantity
322   End Property
323
324   Private Function IEmployee3_Earnings() As Double
325      IEmployee3_Earnings = mSalary + mCommission * mQuantity
326   End Function
327
328   Private Function IEmployee3_ToString() As String
329      IEmployee3_ToString = "Commission worker: " & mFirstName & _
330                            " " & mLastName
331   End Function
332
333   Private Sub Class_Terminate()
334      Set mEmployee = Nothing
335   End Sub
```

```
336   ' CHourlyWorker definition
337   Option Explicit
338   Implements IEmployee3
339   Private mFirstName As String
340   Private mLastName As String
341   Private mWage As Currency
342   Private mHours As Integer
343   Private Const mHoursInAWeek As Integer = 168
344   Private mEmployee As IEmployee3
345
346   Public Sub Class_Initialize()
347      Set mEmployee = New IEmployee3
348   End Sub
```

```
349
350 Public Property Let FirstName(ByVal fName As String)
351    mFirstName = fName
352 End Property
353
354 Public Property Get FirstName() As String
355    FirstName = mFirstName
356 End Property
357
358 Public Property Let LastName(ByVal name As String)
359    mLastName = name
360 End Property
361
362 Public Property Get LastName() As String
363    LastName = mLastName
364 End Property
365
366 Private Property Let IEmployee3_BirthDate(bDate As CDate1)
367    mEmployee.BirthDate = bDate
368 End Property
369
370 Private Property Get IEmployee3_BirthDate() As CDate1
371    Set IEmployee3_BirthDate = mEmployee.BirthDate
372 End Property
373
374 Private Property Let IEmployee3_DepartmentCode(code As Integer)
375    mEmployee.DepartmentCode = code
376 End Property
377
378 Private Property Get IEmployee3_DepartmentCode() As Integer
379    IEmployee3_DepartmentCode = mEmployee.DepartmentCode
380 End Property
381
382 Public Property Let Wage(ByVal wg As Currency)
383    mWage = IIf(wg > 0, wg, 0)
384 End Property
385
386 Public Property Get Wage() As Currency
387    Wage = mWage
388 End Property
389
390 Public Property Let Hours(ByVal hrs As Integer)
391    mHours = IIf((hrs >= 0 And hrs < mHoursInAWeek), hrs, 0)
392 End Property
393
394 Public Property Get Hours() As Integer
395    Hours = mHours
396 End Property
397
398 Private Function IEmployee3_Earnings() As Double
399    If mHours > 40 Then
400       Dim otHours As Integer
401
402       otHours = mHours - 40
403       IEmployee3_Earnings = otHours * 1.5 * mWage + mWage * 40
404    Else
405       IEmployee3_Earnings = mWage * mHours
406    End If
407 End Function
408
409 Private Function IEmployee3_ToString() As String
410    IEmployee3_ToString = "Hourly worker: " & mFirstName & " " & mLastName
411 End Function
412
413 Private Sub Class_Terminate()
414    Set mEmployee = Nothing
415 End Sub
```

```
416   ' CPieceWorker definition
417   Option Explicit
418   Implements IEmployee3
419   Private mFirstName As String
420   Private mLastName As String
421   Private mWagePerPiece As Currency
422   Private mQuantity As Long
423   Private mEmployee As IEmployee3
424
425   Public Sub Class_Initialize()
426       Set mEmployee = New IEmployee3
427   End Sub
428
429   Public Property Let WagePerPiece(ByVal wg As Currency)
430       mWagePerPiece = IIf(wg > 0, wg, 0)
431   End Property
432
433   Public Property Get WagePerPiece() As Currency
434       WagePerPiece = mWagePerPiece
435   End Property
436
437   Public Property Let FirstName(ByVal fName As String)
438       mFirstName = fName
439   End Property
440
441   Public Property Get FirstName() As String
442       FirstName = mFirstName
443   End Property
444
445   Public Property Let LastName(ByVal name As String)
446       mLastName = name
447   End Property
448
449   Public Property Get LastName() As String
450       LastName = mLastName
451   End Property
452
453   Private Property Let IEmployee3_BirthDate(bDate As CDate1)
454       mEmployee.BirthDate = bDate
455   End Property
456
457   Private Property Get IEmployee3_BirthDate() As CDate1
458       Set IEmployee3_BirthDate = mEmployee.BirthDate
459   End Property
460
461   Private Property Let IEmployee3_DepartmentCode(code As Integer)
462       mEmployee.DepartmentCode = code
463   End Property
464
465   Private Property Get IEmployee3_DepartmentCode() As Integer
466       IEmployee3_DepartmentCode = mEmployee.DepartmentCode
467   End Property
468
469   Public Property Let Quantity(ByVal qty As Long)
470       mQuantity = IIf(qty > 0, qty, 0)
471   End Property
472
473   Public Property Get Quantity() As Long
474       Quantity = mQuantity
475   End Property
476
477   Private Function IEmployee3_Earnings() As Double
478       IEmployee3_Earnings = mWagePerPiece * mQuantity
479   End Function
480
```

```
481  Private Function IEmployee3_ToString() As String
482     IEmployee3_ToString = "Piece worker: " & mFirstName & " " & mLastName
483  End Function
484
485  Private Sub Class_Terminate()
486     Set mEmployee = Nothing
487  End Sub
```

```
Exercise 16.29 Solution                                                _ □ ×
Boss: John Smith earned $800.00 Dept: 357 Born: 8/3/1944
Happy Birthday Commission worker: Sue Jones earned $950.00 Dept: 1793 Born: 1/1/1957
Happy Birthday Hourly worker: Karen Price earned $650.00 Dept: 853 Born: 1/9/1949
Piece worker: Bob Lewis earned $500.00 Dept: 731 Born: 11/13/1953
```

16.31   Develop a basic graphics package. Use the **IShape** class inheritance hierarchy from Fig. 16.8. Limit yourself to two-dimensional shapes such as squares, rectangles, triangles and circles. Interact with the user. Let the user specify the position, size, shape and fill characters to be used in drawing each shape. The user can specify many items of the same shape. As you create each shape, place a **IShape** reference to each new **IShape** object into an array. Each class has its own **Draw** method. Write a polymorphic screen manager that walks through the array sending **Draw** messages to each object in the array to form a screen image. Redraw the screen image each time the user specifies an additional shape.

16.32   Create a class **CTicTacToe** that will enable you to write a complete program to play the game of tic-tac-toe. The class contains as **Private** data a 3-by-3 array of **Integer**s. The array stores 0 for an empty location, 1 for an X location and 2 for a O location. Allow two human players to play the game. Wherever the first player moves, place a 1 in the specified square; place a 2 wherever the second player moves. Each move must be to an empty square. After each move determine if the game has been won, or if the game is a draw.

ANS:

```
1   ' Exercise 16.31 Solution
2   Option Explicit
3   Dim mImages(1 To 2) As IPictureDisp
4   Dim mGame As CTicTacToe
5
6   Private Sub Form_Load()
7      Set mImages(1) = LoadPicture("\vb_solutions\ch16\ex16_31\x.jpg")
8      Set mImages(2) = LoadPicture("\vb_solutions\ch16\ex16_31\o.jpg")
9      Set mGame = New CTicTacToe
10  End Sub
11
12  Private Sub picSquare_Click(Index As Integer)
13     Dim player As Integer, j As Integer
14
15     player = mGame.CurrentPlayer
16
17     If mGame.IsValid(picSquare(Index).Tag) = False Then
18        Call MsgBox("Invalid move")
19        Exit Sub
20     End If
21
22     picSquare(Index).Picture = mImages(player)
23
24     If mGame.XOMove() = True Then
25        Caption = "Game Over"
26
27        For j = 0 To 8
28           picSquare(j).Enabled = False
29        Next j
30     End If
31  End Sub
```

```
34  ' Class CTicTacToe
35  Option Explicit
36  Private mBoard(2, 2) As Integer
37  Private mCurrentPlayer As Integer
38  Private mRow As Integer
```

```
39   Private mCol As Integer
40
41   Public Enum tttResult
42       tttWIN
43       tttLOSE
44       tttCONTINUE
45       tttDRAW
46   End Enum
47
48   Private Sub Class_Initialize()
49       mCurrentPlayer = 1
50   End Sub
51
52   Private Function GameStatus() As tttResult
53       Dim r As Integer, c As Integer
54
55       ' Check for a win on diagonals
56       If (mBoard(0, 0) <> 0 And mBoard(0, 0) = mBoard(1, 1) And _
57           mBoard(0, 0) = mBoard(2, 2)) Then
58          GameStatus = tttWIN
59          Exit Function
60       ElseIf (mBoard(2, 0) <> 0 And mBoard(2, 0) = _
61               mBoard(1, 1) And mBoard(2, 0) = mBoard(0, 2)) Then
62          GameStatus = tttWIN
63          Exit Function
64       End If
65
66       ' Check for win in rows
67       For r = 0 To 2
68          If (mBoard(r, 0) <> 0 And mBoard(r, 0) = mBoard(r, 1) And _
69              mBoard(r, 0) = mBoard(r, 2)) Then
70             GameStatus = tttWIN
71             Exit Function
72          End If
73       Next r
74
75       ' Check for win in columns
76       For r = 0 To 2
77          If (mBoard(0, r) <> 0 And mBoard(0, r) = mBoard(1, r) And _
78              mBoard(0, r) = mBoard(2, r)) Then
79             GameStatus = tttWIN
80             Exit Function
81          End If
82       Next r
83
84       ' Check for a completed game
85       For r = 0 To 2
86          For c = 0 To 2
87              If (mBoard(r, c) = 0) Then
88                  GameStatus = tttCONTINUE
89                  Exit Function
90              End If
91          Next c
92       Next r
93
94       GameStatus = tttDRAW   ' Game is a draw
95   End Function
96
97   Public Function XOMove() As Boolean
98       Dim x As Integer, xoStatus As tttResult
99
100      mBoard(mRow, mCol) = mCurrentPlayer
101      xoStatus = GameStatus()
102
103      If (xoStatus = tttWIN) Then
104          Call MsgBox(IIf(mCurrentPlayer = 1, "X", "O") & " wins!")
105          XOMove = True
```

```
106        ElseIf (xoStatus = tttDRAW) Then
107           Call MsgBox("Game is a draw.")
108           XOMove = True
109        Else    ' tttCONTINUE
110           XOMove = False
111        End If
112
113        mCurrentPlayer = 1 + (mCurrentPlayer Mod 2)
114     End Function
115
116     Public Function IsValid(location As String) As Boolean
117        mRow = CInt(Left$(location, 1))
118        mCol = CInt(Right$(location, 1))
119        IsValid = (mBoard(mRow, mCol) = 0)
120     End Function
121
122     Public Property Get CurrentPlayer() As Integer
123        CurrentPlayer = mCurrentPlayer
124     End Property
```

16.33   If you feel ambitious, modify your solution to Exercise 16.31 so that the computer makes the moves for one of the players automatically. Also, allow the player to specify whether he or she wants to go first or second. If you feel exceptionally ambitious, develop a program that will play three-dimensional tic-tac-toe on a 4-by-4-by-4 board (Note: This is a challenging project that could take many weeks of effort!).

Chapter 17 Solutions
ActiveX

17.4   [CD] Write a program that verifies the order in which events (discussed in Section 17.4) occur for the **UserControl**. Use **Debug.Print** statements to display the name of each event as it occurs.

ANS:

```
1   ' Exercise 17.4 Solution
2   Option Explicit
3
4   Private Sub UserControl_Initialize()
5      Debug.Print "UserControl_Initialize"
6   End Sub
7
8   Private Sub UserControl_InitProperties()
9      Debug.Print "UserControl_InitProperties"
10  End Sub
11
12  Private Sub UserControl_ReadProperties(PropBag As PropertyBag)
13     Debug.Print "UserControl_ReadProperties"
14  End Sub
15
16  Private Sub UserControl_Resize()
17     Debug.Print "UserControl_Resize"
18  End Sub
19
20  Private Sub UserControl_Show()
21     Debug.Print "UserControl_Show"
22  End Sub
23
24  Private Sub UserControl_Terminate()
25     Debug.Print "UserControl_Terminate"
26  End Sub
27
28  Private Sub UserControl_WriteProperties(PropBag As PropertyBag)
29     Debug.Print "UserControl_WriteProperties"
30  End Sub
```

17.5   Modify the **Clock** ActiveX control of Section 17.7 to display the current date as a tool tip when the mouse pointer rests on the control.

17.6   Modify the **Clock** ActiveX control of Section 17.7 to add a custom property called **TimeFormat**. The **TimeFormat** property should allow either a setting of **0 - 24 Hour** or **1 - 12 Hour**. These settings should be part of an enumeration. The **1 - 12 Hour** format should display either **AM** or **PM**. Also write a second custom property called **DisplaySeconds**. The **DisplaySeconds** property, when **True**, results in the control displaying seconds. When **False**, seconds are not displayed.

ANS:

```
1   ' Exercise 17.6 Solution
2   Option Explicit
3   Private mFormatValue As clkFormatSettings
```

```
 4    Private mDisplaySeconds As Boolean
 5
 6    Public Enum clkFormatSettings
 7        [24 Hour]      ' Value of 0
 8        [12 Hour]      ' Value of 1
 9    End Enum
10
11    ''''''''''''''''''''''''''''''''''
12    ' UserControl event procedures    '
13    ''''''''''''''''''''''''''''''''''
14    Private Sub UserControl_Initialize()
15        mDisplaySeconds = True
16    End Sub
17
18    Private Sub UserControl_Show()
19        BackColor = Ambient.BackColor
20    End Sub
21
22    Private Sub UserControl_AmbientChanged(PropertyName As String)
23        If PropertyName = "BackColor" Then
24            BackColor = Ambient.BackColor
25        End If
26    End Sub
27
28    Private Sub UserControl_Resize()
29        Font.Size = ScaleY(ScaleHeight, vbPixels, vbPoints)
30        If Width < 3.95 * Height Then
31            Width = 4 * Height
32        End If
33    End Sub
34
35    Private Sub UserControl_WriteProperties(PropBag As PropertyBag)
36        Call PropBag.WriteProperty("ForeColor", ForeColor, vbBlack)
37        Call PropBag.WriteProperty("TimeFormat", mFormatValue, 0)
38        Call PropBag.WriteProperty("DisplaySeconds", mDisplaySeconds, True)
39    End Sub
40
41    Private Sub UserControl_ReadProperties(PropBag As PropertyBag)
42        UserControl.ForeColor = PropBag.ReadProperty("ForeColor", vbBlack)
43        TimeFormat = PropBag.ReadProperty("TimeFormat", 0)
44        DisplaySeconds = PropBag.ReadProperty("DisplaySeconds", True)
45    End Sub
46
47    ''''''''''''''''''''''''''''''''''
48    ' UserControl property methods    '
49    ''''''''''''''''''''''''''''''''''
50    Public Property Get ForeColor() As OLE_COLOR
51        ForeColor = UserControl.ForeColor
52    End Property
53
54    Public Property Let ForeColor(ByVal c As OLE_COLOR)
55        UserControl.ForeColor = c
56        Call PropertyChanged("ForeColor")
57    End Property
58
59    Public Property Get TimeFormat() As clkFormatSettings
60        TimeFormat = mFormatValue
61    End Property
62
63    Public Property Let TimeFormat(ByVal value As clkFormatSettings)
64        mFormatValue = value
65        Call PropertyChanged("TimeFormat")
66    End Property
67
68    Public Property Get DisplaySeconds() As Boolean
69        DisplaySeconds = mDisplaySeconds
70    End Property
```

```
71
72  Public Property Let DisplaySeconds(b As Boolean)
73     mDisplaySeconds = b
74     Call PropertyChanged("DisplaySeconds")
75  End Property
76
77  '''''''''''''''''''''''''''''''''
78  ' Timer event procedure         '
79  '''''''''''''''''''''''''''''''''
80  Private Sub tmrTimer_Timer()
81     Dim t As Integer
82
83     t = Hour(Now)
84     Call Cls
85
86     If mFormatValue = [24 Hour] Then
87        Print Trim$(t);
88        Print ":" & Format$(Minute(Now), "00");
89     Else
90        Print Trim$(IIf(t < 12, t, t - 12));
91        Print ":" & Format$(Minute(Now), "00");
92     End If
93
94     If mDisplaySeconds Then
95        Print ":" & Format$(Second(Now), "00");
96     End If
97
98     If mFormatValue = [12 Hour] Then
99        Print IIf(t < 12, " AM", " PM")
100    End If
101 End Sub
```

17.7 Write a user-drawn control that displays an analog clock. Use the **Circle** and **Line** methods to graphically draw the clock and its hands. Do not use the ActiveX control creation wizard.

17.8 [CD] Write a user-drawn control that allows the user to draw "freehand" pictures with the mouse.
ANS:

```
1   ' Exercise 17.8 Solution
2   Option Explicit
3
4   ''''''''''''''''''''''''''''''''
5   ' UserControl event procedures  '
6   ''''''''''''''''''''''''''''''''
7   Private Sub UserControl_Initialize()
8      UserControl.Scale (0, 0)-(400, 400)
9      UserControl.FillStyle = vbFSSolid
10     UserControl.BackColor = vbWhite
11  End Sub
12
13  Private Sub UserControl_MouseMove(Button As Integer, Shift As Integer, _
14                                    X As Single, Y As Single)
15     If Button = vbLeftButton Then
16        UserControl.Circle (X, Y), 3
17     End If
18  End Sub
19
```

```
20  Private Sub UserControl_WriteProperties(PropBag As PropertyBag)
21     Call PropBag.WriteProperty("ForeColor", ForeColor, vbBlack)
22     Call PropBag.WriteProperty("BackColor", BackColor, vbWhite)
23     Call PropBag.WriteProperty("AutoRedraw", AutoRedraw, False)
24  End Sub
25
26  Private Sub UserControl_ReadProperties(PropBag As PropertyBag)
27     UserControl.ForeColor = PropBag.ReadProperty("ForeColor", vbBlack)
28     UserControl.BackColor = PropBag.ReadProperty("BackColor", vbWhite)
29     UserControl.AutoRedraw = PropBag.ReadProperty("AutoRedraw", False)
30  End Sub
31
32  '''''''''''''''''''''''''''''''''''
33  ' UserControl property methods     '
34  '''''''''''''''''''''''''''''''''''
35  Public Property Get BackColor() As OLE_COLOR
36     BackColor = UserControl.BackColor
37  End Property
38
39  Public Property Let BackColor(ByVal c As OLE_COLOR)
40     UserControl.BackColor = c
41     Call PropertyChanged("BackColor")
42  End Property
43
44  Public Property Get AutoRedraw() As Boolean
45     AutoRedraw = UserControl.AutoRedraw
46  End Property
47
48  Public Property Let AutoRedraw(bool As Boolean)
49     UserControl.AutoRedraw = bool
50  End Property
51
52  Public Property Get ForeColor() As OLE_COLOR
53     ForeColor = UserControl.ForeColor
54  End Property
55
56  Public Property Let ForeColor(ByVal c As OLE_COLOR)
57     UserControl.ForeColor = c
58     Call PropertyChanged("ForeColor")
59  End Property
```

17.9 Create a property page for the **Clock** ActiveX control of Exercise 17.6.
ANS:

```
1   ' Exercise 17.6 Solution
2   Option Explicit
3   Private mFormatValue As clkFormatSettings
4   Private mDisplaySeconds As Boolean
5
6   Public Enum clkFormatSettings
7      [24 Hour]     ' Value of 0
8      [12 Hour]     ' Value of 1
9   End Enum
10
11  '''''''''''''''''''''''''''''''''''
12  ' UserControl event procedures     '
13  '''''''''''''''''''''''''''''''''''
```

```
14   Private Sub UserControl_Initialize()
15      mDisplaySeconds = True
16   End Sub
17
18   Private Sub UserControl_Show()
19      BackColor = Ambient.BackColor
20   End Sub
21
22   Private Sub UserControl_AmbientChanged(PropertyName As String)
23
24      If PropertyName = "BackColor" Then
25         BackColor = Ambient.BackColor
26      End If
27
28   End Sub
29
30   Private Sub UserControl_Resize()
31      Font.Size = ScaleY(ScaleHeight, vbPixels, vbPoints)
32
33      If Width < 3.95 * Height Then
34         Width = 4 * Height
35      End If
36
37   End Sub
38
39   Private Sub UserControl_WriteProperties(PropBag As PropertyBag)
40      Call PropBag.WriteProperty("ForeColor", ForeColor, vbBlack)
41      Call PropBag.WriteProperty("TimeFormat", mFormatValue, 0)
42      Call PropBag.WriteProperty("DisplaySeconds", mDisplaySeconds, True)
43   End Sub
44
45   Private Sub UserControl_ReadProperties(PropBag As PropertyBag)
46      UserControl.ForeColor = PropBag.ReadProperty("ForeColor", vbBlack)
47      TimeFormat = PropBag.ReadProperty("TimeFormat", 0)
48      DisplaySeconds = PropBag.ReadProperty("DisplaySeconds", True)
49   End Sub
50
51   '''''''''''''''''''''''''''''''''''''
52   ' UserControl property methods     '
53   '''''''''''''''''''''''''''''''''''''
54   Public Property Get ForeColor() As OLE_COLOR
55      ForeColor = UserControl.ForeColor
56   End Property
57
58   Public Property Let ForeColor(ByVal c As OLE_COLOR)
59      UserControl.ForeColor = c
60      Call PropertyChanged("ForeColor")
61   End Property
62
63   Public Property Get TimeFormat() As clkFormatSettings
64      TimeFormat = mFormatValue
65   End Property
66
67   Public Property Let TimeFormat(ByVal value As clkFormatSettings)
68      mFormatValue = value
69      Call PropertyChanged("TimeFormat")
70   End Property
71
72   Public Property Get DisplaySeconds() As Boolean
73      DisplaySeconds = mDisplaySeconds
74   End Property
75
76   Public Property Let DisplaySeconds(b As Boolean)
77      mDisplaySeconds = b
78      Call PropertyChanged("DisplaySeconds")
79   End Property
80
```

```
81   ''''''''''''''''''''''''''''''''''
82   ' Timer event procedure          '
83   ''''''''''''''''''''''''''''''''''
84   Private Sub tmrTimer_Timer()
85      Dim t As Integer
86
87      t = Hour(Now)
88      Call Cls
89
90      If mFormatValue = [24 Hour] Then
91         Print Trim$(t);
92         Print ":" & Format$(Minute(Now), "00");
93      Else
94         Print Trim$(IIf(t < 12, t, t - 12));
95         Print ":" & Format$(Minute(Now), "00");
96      End If
97
98      If mDisplaySeconds Then
99         Print ":" & Format$(Second(Now), "00");
100     End If
101
102     If mFormatValue = [12 Hour] Then
103        Print IIf(t < 12, " AM", " PM")
104     End If
105
106  End Sub
```

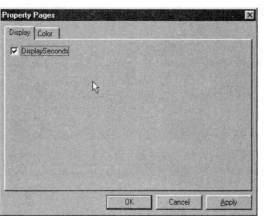

17.10 Create a control that "ties" together constituent controls **DirListBox**, **DriveListBox** and **FileListBox**.

17.11 Modify the **LabelScrollbar** control (Section 17.6) to provide a toolbox icon and attribute descriptions for properties **Min**, **Max**, **SmallChange**, **LargeChange** and **Value**.

   ANS:

```
1    ' Exercise 17.11 Solution
2    Option Explicit
3    Public Event Change()
4
5    ''''''''''''''''''''''''''''''''''''
6    ' Event procedures for UserControl '
7    ''''''''''''''''''''''''''''''''''''
8    Private Sub UserControl_InitProperties()
9       With hsbScroll
10         .Min = 0
11         .Max = 32767
12         .Value = (.Min + .Max) / 2
13         .SmallChange = 1
14         .LargeChange = 5
15      End With
16
17      lblDisplay.Caption = hsbScroll.Value
18   End Sub
```

```
19
20   Private Sub UserControl_ReadProperties(PropBag As PropertyBag)
21      With hsbScroll
22         .Value = PropBag.ReadProperty("Value", (.Min + .Max) \ 2)
23         .Min = PropBag.ReadProperty("Min", 0)
24         .Max = PropBag.ReadProperty("Max", 32767)
25         .LargeChange = PropBag.ReadProperty("LargeChange", 5)
26         .SmallChange = PropBag.ReadProperty("SmallChange", 1)
27      End With
28
29      lblDisplay.Caption = PropBag.ReadProperty("Caption", _
30                                              (hsbScroll.Min + _
31                                               hsbScroll.Max) \ 2)
32   End Sub
33
34   Private Sub UserControl_WriteProperties(PropBag As PropertyBag)
35      Call PropBag.WriteProperty("Value", hsbScroll.Value, _
36                              (hsbScroll.Min + hsbScroll.Max) \ 2)
37      Call PropBag.WriteProperty("Caption", hsbScroll.Value, _
38                              (hsbScroll.Min + hsbScroll.Max) \ 2)
39      Call PropBag.WriteProperty("Min", hsbScroll.Min, 0)
40      Call PropBag.WriteProperty("Max", hsbScroll.Max, 32767)
41      Call PropBag.WriteProperty("SmallChange", _
42                              hsbScroll.SmallChange, 1)
43      Call PropBag.WriteProperty("LargeChange", _
44                              hsbScroll.LargeChange, 5)
45   End Sub
46
47   Private Sub UserControl_Resize()
48      With hsbScroll
49         .Left = lblDisplay.Width
50         .Width = ScaleWidth - hsbScroll.Left
51         .Height = ScaleHeight
52      End With
53
54      lblDisplay.Height = ScaleHeight
55   End Sub
56
57   ''''''''''''''''''''''''''''''''''''''''
58   ' Event procedures for hsbScroll       '
59   ''''''''''''''''''''''''''''''''''''''''
60   Private Sub hsbScroll_Change()
61      lblDisplay.Caption = hsbScroll.Value
62      RaiseEvent Change
63   End Sub
64
65   ''''''''''''''''''''''''''''''''''''''''
66   ' Property methods for hsbScroll       '
67   ''''''''''''''''''''''''''''''''''''''''
68   Public Property Get Value() As Long
69      Value = hsbScroll.Value
70   End Property
71
72   Public Property Let Value(ByVal v As Long)
73      hsbScroll.Value = v
74      Call UserControl.PropertyChanged("Value")
75   End Property
76
77   Public Property Get Max() As Integer
78      Max = hsbScroll.Max
79   End Property
80
81   Public Property Let Max(ByVal m As Integer)
82      hsbScroll.Max = m
83      Value = (hsbScroll.Min + hsbScroll.Max) \ 2
84      Call UserControl.PropertyChanged("Max")
85   End Property
```

```
86
87  Public Property Get Min() As Integer
88     Min = hsbScroll.Min
89  End Property
90
91  Public Property Let Min(ByVal m As Integer)
92     hsbScroll.Min = m
93     Value = (hsbScroll.Min + hsbScroll.Max) \ 2
94     Call UserControl.PropertyChanged("Min")
95  End Property
96
97  Public Property Get LargeChange() As Integer
98     LargeChange = hsbScroll.LargeChange
99  End Property
100
101  Public Property Let LargeChange(ByVal c As Integer)
102     hsbScroll.LargeChange = c
103     Call UserControl.PropertyChanged("LargeChange")
104  End Property
105
106  Public Property Get SmallChange() As Integer
107     SmallChange = hsbScroll.SmallChange
108  End Property
109
110  Public Property Let SmallChange(ByVal c As Integer)
111     hsbScroll.SmallChange = c
112     Call UserControl.PropertyChanged("SmallChange")
113  End Property
```

17.12 Enhance your solution to Exercise 17.11 to add a custom property called **Spacing**. Property **Spacing** determines how much space is between the **Label** and the scrollbar. **Spacing** is a design-time property.

   ANS:

```
1  ' Exercise 17.12 Solution
2  ' Note: This solution does not allow the control to be
3  ' resized by the developer.
4  Option Explicit
5  Public Event Change()
6  Private mSpacing As Integer
7
8  ''''''''''''''''''''''''''''''''''''
9  ' Event procedures for UserControl  '
10  ''''''''''''''''''''''''''''''''''''
11  Private Sub UserControl_InitProperties()
12
13     With hsbScroll
14        .Width = 200
15        .Left = 42
16        .Min = 0
17        .Max = 32767
```

```
18           .Value = (.Min + .Max) / 2
19           .SmallChange = 1
20           .LargeChange = 5
21           lblDisplay.Caption = .Value
22       End With
23
24       UserControl.Width = ScaleX(lblDisplay.Width, vbPixels, vbTwips) + _
25                            ScaleX(hsbScroll.Width, vbPixels, vbTwips)
26   End Sub
27
28   Private Sub UserControl_ReadProperties(PropBag As PropertyBag)
29       With hsbScroll
30           .Value = PropBag.ReadProperty("Value", (.Min + .Max) \ 2)
31           .Min = PropBag.ReadProperty("Min", 0)
32           .Max = PropBag.ReadProperty("Max", 32767)
33           .LargeChange = PropBag.ReadProperty("LargeChange", 5)
34           .SmallChange = PropBag.ReadProperty("SmallChange", 1)
35           .Left = PropBag.ReadProperty("Left", 42)
36           lblDisplay.Caption = PropBag.ReadProperty("Caption", _
37                                                   (.Min + .Max) \ 2)
38       End With
39
40       mSpacing = PropBag.ReadProperty("Spacing", 0)
41       Width = PropBag.ReadProperty("Width", 242)
42   End Sub
43
44   Private Sub UserControl_WriteProperties(PropBag As PropertyBag)
45       Call PropBag.WriteProperty("Value", hsbScroll.Value, _
46                                 (hsbScroll.Min + hsbScroll.Max) \ 2)
47       Call PropBag.WriteProperty("Caption", hsbScroll.Value, _
48                                 (hsbScroll.Min + hsbScroll.Max) \ 2)
49       Call PropBag.WriteProperty("Min", hsbScroll.Min, 0)
50       Call PropBag.WriteProperty("Max", hsbScroll.Max, 32767)
51       Call PropBag.WriteProperty("SmallChange", _
52                                 hsbScroll.SmallChange, 1)
53       Call PropBag.WriteProperty("LargeChange", _
54                                 hsbScroll.LargeChange, 5)
55       Call PropBag.WriteProperty("Spacing", _
56                                 mSpacing, 0)
57       Call PropBag.WriteProperty("Left", _
58                                 hsbScroll.Left, 42)
59       Call PropBag.WriteProperty("Width", Width, 200)
60   End Sub
61
62   Private Sub UserControl_Resize()
63
64       Width = ScaleX(lblDisplay.Width, vbPixels, vbTwips) + _
65               ScaleX(hsbScroll.Width, vbPixels, vbTwips) + _
66               ScaleX(mSpacing, vbPixels, vbTwips)
67       hsbScroll.Left = lblDisplay.Width + mSpacing
68       hsbScroll.Height = ScaleHeight
69       Call UserControl.PropertyChanged("Width")
70       Call UserControl.PropertyChanged("Left")
71       lblDisplay.Height = ScaleHeight
72   End Sub
73
74   ''''''''''''''''''''''''''''''''''''''
75   ' Event procedures for hsbScroll      '
76   ''''''''''''''''''''''''''''''''''''''
77   Private Sub hsbScroll_Change()
78       lblDisplay.Caption = hsbScroll.Value
79       RaiseEvent Change
80   End Sub
81
82   ''''''''''''''''''''''''''''''''''''''
83   ' Property methods for hsbScroll      '
84   ''''''''''''''''''''''''''''''''''''''
```

```
85   Public Property Get Value() As Long
86       Value = hsbScroll.Value
87   End Property
88
89   Public Property Let Value(ByVal v As Long)
90       hsbScroll.Value = v
91       Call UserControl.PropertyChanged("Value")
92   End Property
93
94   Public Property Get Max() As Integer
95       Max = hsbScroll.Max
96   End Property
97
98   Public Property Let Max(ByVal m As Integer)
99       hsbScroll.Max = m
100      Value = (hsbScroll.Min + hsbScroll.Max) \ 2
101      Call UserControl.PropertyChanged("Max")
102  End Property
103
104  Public Property Get Min() As Integer
105      Min = hsbScroll.Min
106  End Property
107
108  Public Property Let Min(ByVal m As Integer)
109      hsbScroll.Min = m
110      Value = (hsbScroll.Min + hsbScroll.Max) \ 2
111      Call UserControl.PropertyChanged("Min")
112  End Property
113
114  Public Property Get LargeChange() As Integer
115      LargeChange = hsbScroll.LargeChange
116  End Property
117
118  Public Property Let LargeChange(ByVal c As Integer)
119      hsbScroll.LargeChange = c
120      Call UserControl.PropertyChanged("LargeChange")
121  End Property
122
123  Public Property Get SmallChange() As Integer
124      SmallChange = hsbScroll.SmallChange
125  End Property
126
127  Public Property Let SmallChange(ByVal c As Integer)
128      hsbScroll.SmallChange = c
129      Call UserControl.PropertyChanged("SmallChange")
130  End Property
131
132  '''''''''''''''''''''''''''''''''''''''''''
133  ' Property methods for UserControl    '
134  '''''''''''''''''''''''''''''''''''''''''''
135  Public Property Get Spacing() As Integer
136      Spacing = mSpacing
137  End Property
138
139  Public Property Let Spacing(ByVal s As Integer)
140
141      ' Allow property to be set only at design time
142      If Ambient.UserMode = False Then
143         mSpacing = s
144         Call UserControl.PropertyChanged("Spacing")
145         Call UserControl_Resize
146      End If
147
148  End Property
```

17.13   Enhance your solution to Exercise 17.12 to add a **BackColor** property. The **BackColor** property specifies the color of the spacing that appears between the **Label** and the scrollbar.

ANS:

```
1   ' Exercise 17.13 Solution
2   ' Note: This solution does not allow the control to be
3   ' resized by the developer.
4   Option Explicit
5   Public Event Change()
6   Private mSpacing As Integer
7
8   ''''''''''''''''''''''''''''''''''''''''''
9   ' Event procedures for UserControl    '
10  ''''''''''''''''''''''''''''''''''''''''''
11  Private Sub UserControl_InitProperties()
12
13     With hsbScroll
14        .Width = 200
15        .Left = 42
16        .Min = 0
17        .Max = 32767
18        .Value = (.Min + .Max) / 2
19        .SmallChange = 1
20        .LargeChange = 5
21        lblDisplay.Caption = .Value
22     End With
23
24     UserControl.Width = ScaleX(lblDisplay.Width, vbPixels, vbTwips) + _
25                         ScaleX(hsbScroll.Width, vbPixels, vbTwips)
26  End Sub
27
28  Private Sub UserControl_ReadProperties(PropBag As PropertyBag)
29
30     With hsbScroll
31        .Value = PropBag.ReadProperty("Value", (.Min + .Max) \ 2)
32        .Min = PropBag.ReadProperty("Min", 0)
33        .Max = PropBag.ReadProperty("Max", 32767)
34        .LargeChange = PropBag.ReadProperty("LargeChange", 5)
35        .SmallChange = PropBag.ReadProperty("SmallChange", 1)
36        .Left = PropBag.ReadProperty("Left", 42)
37        lblDisplay.Caption = PropBag.ReadProperty("Caption", _
38                                                  (.Min + .Max) \ 2)
39     End With
40
41     mSpacing = PropBag.ReadProperty("Spacing", 0)
42     Width = PropBag.ReadProperty("Width", 242)
43     BackColor = PropBag.ReadProperty("BackColor", QBColor(8))
44  End Sub
45
46  Private Sub UserControl_WriteProperties(PropBag As PropertyBag)
47     Call PropBag.WriteProperty("Value", hsbScroll.Value, _
48                                (hsbScroll.Min + hsbScroll.Max) \ 2)
49     Call PropBag.WriteProperty("Caption", hsbScroll.Value, _
50                                (hsbScroll.Min + hsbScroll.Max) \ 2)
```

```
51    Call PropBag.WriteProperty("Min", hsbScroll.Min, 0)
52    Call PropBag.WriteProperty("Max", hsbScroll.Max, 32767)
53    Call PropBag.WriteProperty("SmallChange", hsbScroll.SmallChange, 1)
54    Call PropBag.WriteProperty("LargeChange",hsbScroll.LargeChange, 5)
55    Call PropBag.WriteProperty("Spacing", mSpacing, 0)
56    Call PropBag.WriteProperty("Left", hsbScroll.Left, 42)
57    Call PropBag.WriteProperty("Width", Width, 200)
58    Call PropBag.WriteProperty("BackColor", BackColor, QBColor(8))
59 End Sub
60
61 Private Sub UserControl_Resize()
62    Width = ScaleX(lblDisplay.Width, vbPixels, vbTwips) + _
63            ScaleX(hsbScroll.Width, vbPixels, vbTwips) + _
64            ScaleX(mSpacing, vbPixels, vbTwips)
65    hsbScroll.Left = lblDisplay.Width + mSpacing
66    hsbScroll.Height = ScaleHeight
67    Call UserControl.PropertyChanged("Width")
68    Call UserControl.PropertyChanged("Left")
69    lblDisplay.Height = ScaleHeight
70 End Sub
71
72 ''''''''''''''''''''''''''''''''''''''
73 ' Event procedures for hsbScroll     '
74 ''''''''''''''''''''''''''''''''''''''
75 Private Sub hsbScroll_Change()
76    lblDisplay.Caption = hsbScroll.Value
77    RaiseEvent Change
78 End Sub
79
80 ''''''''''''''''''''''''''''''''''''''
81 ' Property methods for hsbScroll      '
82 ''''''''''''''''''''''''''''''''''''''
83 Public Property Get Value() As Long
84    Value = hsbScroll.Value
85 End Property
86
87 Public Property Let Value(ByVal v As Long)
88    hsbScroll.Value = v
89    Call UserControl.PropertyChanged("Value")
90 End Property
91
92 Public Property Get Max() As Integer
93    Max = hsbScroll.Max
94 End Property
95
96 Public Property Let Max(ByVal m As Integer)
97    hsbScroll.Max = m
98    Value = (hsbScroll.Min + hsbScroll.Max) \ 2
99    Call UserControl.PropertyChanged("Max")
100 End Property
101
102 Public Property Get Min() As Integer
103    Min = hsbScroll.Min
104 End Property
105
106 Public Property Let Min(ByVal m As Integer)
107    hsbScroll.Min = m
108    Value = (hsbScroll.Min + hsbScroll.Max) \ 2
109    Call UserControl.PropertyChanged("Min")
110 End Property
111
112 Public Property Get LargeChange() As Integer
113    LargeChange = hsbScroll.LargeChange
114 End Property
115
116 Public Property Let LargeChange(ByVal c As Integer)
117    hsbScroll.LargeChange = c
```

```
118        Call UserControl.PropertyChanged("LargeChange")
119    End Property
120
121    Public Property Get SmallChange() As Integer
122        SmallChange = hsbScroll.SmallChange
123    End Property
124
125    Public Property Let SmallChange(ByVal c As Integer)
126        hsbScroll.SmallChange = c
127        Call UserControl.PropertyChanged("SmallChange")
128    End Property
129
130    '''''''''''''''''''''''''''''''''''''''''''
131    ' Property methods for UserControl   '
132    '''''''''''''''''''''''''''''''''''''''''''
133    Public Property Get Spacing() As Integer
134        Spacing = mSpacing
135    End Property
136
137    Public Property Let Spacing(ByVal s As Integer)
138
139        ' Allow property to be set only at design time
140        If Ambient.UserMode = False Then
141            mSpacing = s
142            Call UserControl.PropertyChanged("Spacing")
143            Call UserControl_Resize
144        End If
145    End Property
146
147    Public Property Get BackColor() As OLE_COLOR
148        BackColor = UserControl.BackColor
149    End Property
150
151    Public Property Let BackColor(color As OLE_COLOR)
152        UserControl.BackColor = color
153        Call PropertyChanged("BackColor")
154    End Property
```

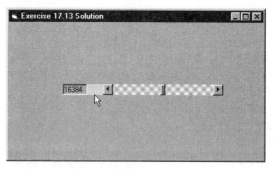

17.14   Write an ActiveX DLL that contains procedures for converting hexadecimal to octal, decimal to binary, octal to hexadecimal, binary to hexadecimal, etc.

17.15   Modify the **Clock** ActiveX control to raise an **OnHour** event every time the clock "strikes" the hour.
         ANS:

```
1    ' Exercise 17.15 Solution
2    Option Explicit
3    Public Event OnHour()
4    Private mFormatTime As clkFormatSettings
5    Private mDisplaySeconds As Boolean
6
7    Public Enum clkFormatSettings
8        [24 Hour]    ' Value of 0
9        [12 Hour]    ' Value of 1
10   End Enum
11
```

```
12   ''''''''''''''''''''''''''''''''''
13   ' UserControl event procedures     '
14   ''''''''''''''''''''''''''''''''''
15   Private Sub UserControl_Initialize()
16      mDisplaySeconds = True
17   End Sub
18
19   Private Sub UserControl_Show()
20      BackColor = Ambient.BackColor
21   End Sub
22
23   Private Sub UserControl_AmbientChanged(PropertyName As String)
24      If PropertyName = "BackColor" Then
25         BackColor = Ambient.BackColor
26      End If
27   End Sub
28
29   Private Sub UserControl_Resize()
30      Font.Size = ScaleY(ScaleHeight, vbPixels, vbPoints)
31
32      If Width < 3.95 * Height Then
33         Width = 4 * Height
34      End If
35   End Sub
36
37   Private Sub UserControl_WriteProperties(PropBag As PropertyBag)
38      Call PropBag.WriteProperty("ForeColor", ForeColor, vbBlack)
39      Call PropBag.WriteProperty("TimeFormat", mFormatTime, 0)
40      Call PropBag.WriteProperty("DisplaySeconds", mDisplaySeconds, True)
41   End Sub
42
43   Private Sub UserControl_ReadProperties(PropBag As PropertyBag)
44      UserControl.ForeColor = PropBag.ReadProperty("ForeColor", vbBlack)
45      TimeFormat = PropBag.ReadProperty("TimeFormat", 0)
46      DisplaySeconds = PropBag.ReadProperty("DisplaySeconds", True)
47   End Sub
48
49   ''''''''''''''''''''''''''''''''''
50   ' UserControl property methods     '
51   ''''''''''''''''''''''''''''''''''
52   Public Property Get ForeColor() As OLE_COLOR
53      ForeColor = UserControl.ForeColor
54   End Property
55
56   Public Property Let ForeColor(ByVal c As OLE_COLOR)
57      UserControl.ForeColor = c
58      Call PropertyChanged("ForeColor")
59   End Property
60
61   Public Property Get TimeFormat() As clkFormatSettings
62      TimeFormat = mFormatTime
63   End Property
64
65   Public Property Let TimeFormat(ByVal value As clkFormatSettings)
66      mFormatTime = value
67      Call PropertyChanged("TimeFormat")
68   End Property
69
70   Public Property Get DisplaySeconds() As Boolean
71      DisplaySeconds = mDisplaySeconds
72   End Property
73
74   Public Property Let DisplaySeconds(b As Boolean)
75      mDisplaySeconds = b
76      Call PropertyChanged("DisplaySeconds")
77   End Property
78
```

```
79    '''''''''''''''''''''''''''''''''''
80    ' Timer event procedure             '
81    '''''''''''''''''''''''''''''''''''
82    Private Sub tmrTimer_Timer()
83       Dim t As Integer
84
85       t = Hour(Now)
86       Call Cls
87
88       If mFormatTime = [24 Hour] Then
89          Print Trim$(t);
90          Print ":" & Format$(Minute(Now), "00");
91       Else
92          Print Trim$(IIf(t < 12, t, t - 12));
93          Print ":" & Format$(Minute(Now), "00");
94       End If
95
96       If mDisplaySeconds Then
97          Print ":" & Format$(Second(Now), "00");
98       End If
99
100      If mFormatTime = [12 Hour] Then
101         Print IIf(t < 12, " AM", " PM")
102      End If
103
104      If Minute(Now) = 0 And Second(Now) = 0 Then
105         RaiseEvent OnHour
106      End If
107   End Sub
```

17.16   Create a user-drawn control that displays a "star" button. Use method **Line** to draw the button.
   ANS:

```
1    ' Exercise 17.16 Solution
2    Option Explicit
3    Dim mOffset As Integer
4    Dim mCaption As String
5    Public Event Click()
6
7    '''''''''''''''''''''''''''''''''''
8    ' UserControl Event Procedures     '
9    '''''''''''''''''''''''''''''''''''
10   Private Sub UserControl_Initialize()
11      UserControl.Width = 1800
12      UserControl.Height = 2000
13      mOffset = 50
14      mCaption = UserControl.Name
15   End Sub
16
17   Private Sub UserControl_InitProperties()
18      UserControl.BackColor = Ambient.BackColor
19   End Sub
20
21   Private Sub UserControl_ReadProperties(PropBag As PropertyBag)
22      UserControl.BackColor = PropBag.ReadProperty("BackColor", Ambient.BackColor)
23      mOffset = PropBag.ReadProperty("Offset", 50)
24      UserControl.ForeColor = PropBag.ReadProperty("ForeColor",  vbBlack)
25      mCaption = PropBag.ReadProperty("Caption", mCaption)
26   End Sub
27
28   Private Sub UserControl_WriteProperties(PropBag As PropertyBag)
29      Call PropBag.WriteProperty("Offset", mOffset)
30      Call PropBag.WriteProperty("BackColor", Ambient.BackColor)
31      Call PropBag.WriteProperty("ForeColor", ForeColor)
32      Call PropBag.WriteProperty("Caption", mCaption)
33   End Sub
```

```
34
35   Private Sub UserControl_Paint()
36       ' Note: The Paint Event is raised only if the UserControl's
37       ' AutoRedraw Property is set to False.
38
39       Call UserControl.Cls
40       Print mCaption
41
42       UserControl.Line (Width \ 2, mOffset)-(Width \ 2 + 120, _
43                                             mOffset + 360)
44       UserControl.Line (Width \ 2, mOffset)-(Width \ 2 - 120, _
45                                             mOffset + 360)
46       UserControl.Line (Width \ 2 - 120, mOffset + 360)- _
47                                (Width \ 2 - 540, mOffset + 360)
48       UserControl.Line (Width \ 2 - 540, mOffset + 360)- _
49                                (Width \ 2 - 180, mOffset + 540)
50       UserControl.Line (Width \ 2 - 180, mOffset + 540)- _
51                                (Width \ 2 - 280, mOffset + 960)
52       UserControl.Line (Width \ 2 - 280, mOffset + 960)- _
53                                (Width \ 2, mOffset + 720)
54       UserControl.Line (Width \ 2, mOffset + 720)- _
55                                (Width \ 2 + 300, mOffset + 960)
56       UserControl.Line (Width \ 2 + 300, mOffset + 960)- _
57                                (Width \ 2 + 180, mOffset + 540)
58       UserControl.Line (Width \ 2 + 180, mOffset + 540)- _
59                                (Width \ 2 + 540, mOffset + 360)
60       UserControl.Line (Width \ 2 + 540, mOffset + 360)- _
61                                (Width \ 2 + 120, mOffset + 360)
62   End Sub
63
64   Private Sub UserControl_AmbientChanged(PropertyName As String)
65
66       If PropertyName = "BackColor" Then
67           UserControl.BackColor = Ambient.BackColor
68       End If
69
70   End Sub
71
72   Private Sub UserControl_Click()
73       RaiseEvent Click
74   End Sub
75
76   ''''''''''''''''''''''''''''''''''''
77   ' UserControl Property Procedures '
78   ''''''''''''''''''''''''''''''''''''
79   Public Property Get Offset() As Integer
80       Offset = mOffset
81   End Property
82
83   Public Property Let Offset(value As Integer)
84       If value + 960 < Height Then
85           mOffset = value
86           Call UserControl_Paint
87           Call PropertyChanged("Offset")
88       End If
89   End Property
90
91   Public Property Get ForeColor() As OLE_COLOR
92       ForeColor = UserControl.ForeColor
93   End Property
94
95   Public Property Let ForeColor(color As OLE_COLOR)
96       UserControl.ForeColor = color
97       Call UserControl_Paint
98       Call PropertyChanged("ForeColor")
99   End Property
100
```

```
101   Public Property Get Caption() As String
102      Caption = mCaption
103   End Property
104
105   Public Property Let Caption(s As String)
106      mCaption = s
107      Call UserControl_Paint
108      Call PropertyChanged("Caption")
109   End Property
```

17.17   [CD] Write an "enhanced" **TextBox** control that only accepts numeric input.
            ANS:

```
1    ' Exercise 17.17 Solution
2    Option Explicit
3    Public Event Change()                               ' Expose Change event
4    Public Event KeyPress(KeyAscii As Integer)  ' Expose Keypress event
5    Public Event KeyUp(KeyCode As Integer, Shift As Integer)    ' Expose KeyUP event
6    Public Event KeyDown(KeyCode As Integer, Shift As Integer) ' Expose KeyDown event
7
8    '''''''''''''''''''''''''''''''''
9    'UserControl Event procedures '
10   '''''''''''''''''''''''''''''''''
11   Private Sub UserControl_Initialize()
12      KeyPreview = True
13   End Sub
14
15   Private Sub UserControl_KeyDown(KeyCode As Integer, Shift As Integer)
16      RaiseEvent KeyDown(KeyCode, Shift)
17   End Sub
18
19   Private Sub UserControl_KeyPress(KeyAscii As Integer)
20
21      If KeyAscii >= vbKey0 And KeyAscii <= vbKey9 Then
22         txtTextBox.Text = txtTextBox.Text & Chr$(KeyAscii)
23      End If
24
25      RaiseEvent KeyPress(KeyAscii)
26   End Sub
27
28   Private Sub UserControl_KeyUp(KeyCode As Integer, Shift As Integer)
29      RaiseEvent KeyUp(KeyCode, Shift)
30   End Sub
31
32   Private Sub UserControl_ReadProperties(PropBag As PropertyBag)
33      NumericText = PropBag.ReadProperty("NumericText", "")
34   End Sub
35
36   Private Sub UserControl_Resize()
37      txtTextBox.Width = Width
38      txtTextBox.Height = Width
39   End Sub
40
41   Private Sub UserControl_WriteProperties(PropBag As PropertyBag)
42      Call PropBag.WriteProperty("NumericText", txtTextBox.Text, "")
43   End Sub
44
```

```
45  '''''''''''''''''''''''''''''''
46  'TextBox Event procedures     '
47  '''''''''''''''''''''''''''''''
48  Private Sub txtTextBox_Change()
49      RaiseEvent Change
50  End Sub
51
52  Private Sub txtTextBox_KeyPress(KeyAscii As Integer)
53      KeyAscii = 0
54  End Sub
55
56  '''''''''''''''''''''''''''''''
57  'Property procedures          '
58  '''''''''''''''''''''''''''''''
59  Public Property Get NumericText() As String
60      NumericText = txtTextBox.Text
61  End Property
62
63  Public Property Let NumericText(ByVal stringOfDigits As String)
64      Dim length As Long, char As String, c As Long
65
66      length = Len(stringOfDigits)
67      c = 1
68
69      Do While c <= length
70          char = Mid$(stringOfDigits, c, 1)
71
72          If char < "0" Or char > "9" Then
73              stringOfDigits = ""
74              Exit Do
75          End If
76
77          c = c + 1
78      Loop
79
80      txtTextBox.Text = stringOfDigits
81      Call UserControl.PropertyChanged("NumericText")
82  End Property
```

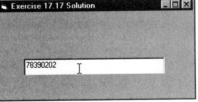

17.18   Write a control that displays images specified by the developer. The control should automatically display a different image after a specified number of seconds. Provide special effects options (e.g., inverse, etc.). Provide a minimum of one property page for the control.

17.19   Write a "ruler" user-drawn control. The control should display tick marks in units of inches, centimeters, pixels, and points. Set the ruler's **BackColor** to yellow. The ruler should have a horizontal orientation.

17.20   Enhance your solution to Exercise 17.19 to allow the developer to set either a vertical or horizontal orientation.

17.21   Enhance your solution to either Exercise 17.20 or 17.19 to allow the user to move the ruler next to an object on a form to measure it.

Chapter 18 Solutions
Database Management

18.3 **[CD]** Modify the program of Fig. 18.5 to allow the user to select any table from the **Biblio.mdb** database, then display the data in a **DataGrid** control.

ANS:

```
1   ' Exercise 18.3 Solution
2   ' Selecting tables from Biblio.mdb
3   Option Explicit
4
5   Private Sub Form_Load()
6       Call cboTables.AddItem("Authors")
7       Call cboTables.AddItem("Publishers")
8       Call cboTables.AddItem("Title Author")
9       Call cboTables.AddItem("Titles")
10      Call cboTables.AddItem("All Titles")
11      cboTables.Text = cboTables.List(0)
12      Adodc1.Caption = "Biblio.mdb: Authors"
13  End Sub
14
15  Private Sub Form_Resize()
16      cboTables.Width = ScaleWidth
17      DataGrid1.Width = ScaleWidth
18      DataGrid1.Height = ScaleHeight - cboTables.Height - Adodc1.Height
19      Adodc1.Top = cboTables.Height + DataGrid1.Height + 50
20      Adodc1.Width = ScaleWidth
21  End Sub
22
23  Private Sub cboTables_Click()
24      Adodc1.RecordSource = "[" & cboTables.Text & "]"
25      Call Adodc1.Refresh
26      Adodc1.Caption = "Biblio.mdb: " & cboTables.Text
27  End Sub
```

18.4 Using the techniques shown in this chapter, define a complete query application for the **Biblio.mdb** database. The user should be able to edit existing data and add new data to the database. Provide a series of predefined queries with an appropriate name for each query displayed in a **ComboBox**. Also allow the user to supply their own queries and add them to the **ComboBox**. Provide the following predefined queries:

  a) Select all authors from the **Authors** table.
  b) Select all publishers from the **Publishers** table.
  c) Select a specific author and list all books for that author. Include the title, year and ISBN number. Order the information alphabetically by title.
  d) Select a specific publisher and list all books published by that publisher. Include the title, year and ISBN number. Order the information alphabetically by title.
  e) Select a publisher and display its address, phone number and fax number.
  f) Provide any other queries you feel are appropriate.

For each of the preceding queries, the results should be displayed in an appropriate component. For example, the query that selects all authors from the **Authors** table should be displayed in a **DataGrid** or **Hierarchical FlexGrid** control. The queries in parts (c) and (d) might use both a **DataGrid/Hierarchical FlexGrid** and **TextBox**es for the author or publisher names. Note: If you have the Enterprise Edition of Visual Basic, investigate the **Query Designer**'s capabilities that help you graphically build queries.

    ANS:

```
1   ' Exercise 18.4 Solution
2   ' Note: Fields can be modified by editing the data's cell and selecting
3   ' a different field.
4   Option Explicit
5   Dim mSelection As Integer
6
7   Private Sub Form_Load()
8       Adodc1.Caption = Adodc1.RecordSource
9       Call cboQuery.AddItem("All authors")
10      Call cboQuery.AddItem("All publishers")
11      Call cboQuery.AddItem("A specific author")
12      Call cboQuery.AddItem("A specific publisher, all titles, year, ISBN")
13      Call cboQuery.AddItem("A specific publisher, address, phone, and fax")
14      cboQuery.Text = cboQuery.List(0)
15      DataCombo1.Enabled = False
16  End Sub
17
18  Private Sub cboQuery_Click()
19      On Error Resume Next
20
21      mSelection = cboQuery.ListIndex
22
23      Select Case mSelection
24         Case 0
25            Adodc1.RecordSource = "SELECT * FROM Authors"
26         Case 1
27            Adodc1.RecordSource = "SELECT * FROM Publishers"
28         Case 2
29            lblPrompt.Caption = "Select an author:"
30            Adodc1.RecordSource = "SELECT * FROM Authors ORDER BY Author ASC"
31            Call Adodc1.Refresh
32            DataCombo1.ListField = "Author"
33            DataCombo1.Enabled = True
34         Case 3, 4
35            lblPrompt.Caption = "Select a publisher:"
36            Adodc1.RecordSource = "SELECT * FROM Publishers ORDER BY Name ASC"
37            Call Adodc1.Refresh
38            DataCombo1.ListField = "Name"
39            DataCombo1.Enabled = True
40      End Select
41
42      Call Adodc1.Refresh
43      Adodc1.Caption = Adodc1.RecordSource
44      cboQuery.Enabled = False
45  End Sub
46
47  Private Sub DataCombo1_Click(Area As Integer)
48          DataCombo1.Enabled = False
```

```
49
50              Select Case mSelection
51                  Case 2
52                      Adodc1.RecordSource = "SELECT Titles.Title, Titles.ISBN, " & _
53                                      "Titles.[Year Published] FROM Titles " & _
54                                      "INNER JOIN ([Title Author] " & _
55                                      "INNER JOIN Authors ON [title author].Au_ID = " & _
56                                      "Authors.Au_ID) ON Titles.ISBN = " & _
57                                      "[title author].ISBN WHERE Authors.author = '" & _
58                                  DataCombo1.BoundText & "' ORDER BY Titles.Title ASC"
59                  Case 3
60                      Adodc1.RecordSource = "SELECT Titles.Title, Titles.ISBN, " & _
61                                      "Titles.[Year Published] FROM Titles " & _
62                                      "INNER JOIN Publishers " & _
63                                      " ON Publishers.PubID = " & _
64                                      "Titles.PubID WHERE Publishers.Name = '" & _
65                                  DataCombo1.BoundText & "' ORDER BY Titles.Title ASC"
66                  Case 4
67                      ' Note: Many of these fields in the database are empty
68                      Adodc1.RecordSource = "SELECT Address, Telephone, Fax" & _
69                                      " FROM Publishers WHERE Name = '" & _
70                                  DataCombo1.BoundText & "'"
71              End Select
72
73              Call Adodc1.Refresh
74      End Sub
75
76      Private Sub Adodc1_MoveComplete(ByVal adReason As ADODB.EventReasonEnum, _
77                              ByVal pError As ADODB.Error, _
78                              adStatus As ADODB.EventStatusEnum, _
79                              ByVal pRecordset As ADODB.Recordset)
80          cboQuery.Enabled = True
81      End Sub
```

18.5 Modify Exercise 18.4 to define a complete database manipulation application for the `Biblio.mdb` database. In addition to the querying capabilities, the user should be able to edit existing data and add new data to the database. Allow the user to edit the database in the following ways:

    a) Add a new author.

    b) Edit the existing information for an author.

    c) Add a new title for an author (remember that the book must have an entry in the `Title Author` table). Be sure to specify the publisher of the title.

    d) Add a new publisher.

    e) Edit the existing information for a publisher.

For each of the preceding database manipulations, design an appropriate GUI to allow the user to perform the data manipulation.

18.6 Microsoft **Access** comes with a number of predefined *database wizard templates* (music collection, video collection, wine list, book collection, etc.) that are accessible by selecting **New** from the **File** menu in Microsoft **Access** and choosing a database from **Database** tab. Create a new database using one of the templates of your choice. Perform exercises 18.4 and 18.5 using the new database and its predefined tables. Provide appropriate queries for the database you choose and allow the user to edit and add data to the database.

Chapter 19 Solutions
Networking, the Internet and the World Wide Web

19.3   [CD] Distinguish between connection-oriented network services and connectionless network services.

19.4   How does a client determine the host name of the client computer?
ANS: Using the **Winsock** control, the client can access the **LocalHostName** property to determine its name.

19.5   How does a client determine the host name of the server?
ANS: Using the **Winsock** control, the client can access the **RemoteHost** property to determine its name.

19.6   How can a client get a line of text from a server?
ANS: Using the **Internet Transfer Control**, the client could connect to a server and read the entire contents of a file using the **OpenURL** method. Using the **Winsock** control, the client can open a stream-based socket connection to a server. The server can send a line of text to the client that can be read using **Winsock** method **GetData**.

19.7   Describe how a client application can read a file from a server using the **Internet Transfer** control.
ANS: Using the **Internet Transfer Control**, the client connects to a server and reads the entire contents of a file using the **OpenURL** method. The URL of the file is supplied as the argument to **OpenURL**.

19.8   [CD] Describe how a client connects to a server.

19.9   Describe how a server sends data to a client.
ANS: Using the **Winsock** control, the client can open a stream-based socket connection to a server. The client can send data to the server using **Winsock** method **SendData**.

19.10   Describe how to prepare a server to receive a streams-based connection request from a single client.
ANS: Using the **Winsock** control, the server application must bind the server to a port on the server computer using **Winsock** property **LocalPort**. Next, the server calls **Winsock** method **Listen** to await a connection from a client.

19.11   [CD] How does a server listen for connections at a port?

19.12   Use the **Internet Transfer** control to allow a client to specify a file name to the server and have the server send the contents of the file or indicate that the file does not exist.
ANS: See Fig. 19.5 in the chapter. This exercise is actually the same as the Fig. 19.5 example.

19.13   Modify the preceding exercise to allow the client to modify the contents of the file and send the file back to the server for storage. The user can edit the file in a **TextBox**, then click a **Save Changes** button to send the file back to the server.

19.14   [CD] Modify program of Fig. 19.2 to show a list of sites in a **ComboBox** object. Allow users to add their own sites to the list and remove sites from the list.
ANS:

```
1  ' Exercise 19.14 Solution
2  ' A simple web browser using the WebBrowser Control.
3  Option Explicit
4
5  Private Sub Form_Load()
6      ' When form is loaded, go to home page
7      Call WebBrowser1.GoHome
8  End Sub
```

```
9
10   Private Sub cmdGo_Click()
11       ' if cboURL is not empty, go to URL specified in cboURL
12       On Error Resume Next
13
14       If cboURL.Text <> "" Then
15           Call WebBrowser1.Navigate(cboURL.Text)
16       End If
17
18   End Sub
19
20   Private Sub cmdBack_Click()
21       ' go to previous page
22       On Error Resume Next
23       Call WebBrowser1.GoBack
24   End Sub
25
26   Private Sub cmdForward_Click()
27       ' go to next page
28       On Error Resume Next
29       Call WebBrowser1.GoForward
30   End Sub
31
32   Private Sub cmdHome_Click()
33       ' go to home page
34       On Error Resume Next
35       Call WebBrowser1.GoHome
36   End Sub
37
38   Private Sub Form_Resize()
39       ' set dimensions of cboURL and WebBrowser1
40       On Error Resume Next
41       WebBrowser1.Width = ScaleWidth
42       WebBrowser1.Height = ScaleHeight - WebBrowser1.Top
43       cboURL.Width = ScaleWidth - cboURL.Left
44   End Sub
45
46   Private Sub WebBrowser1_DocumentComplete( _
47                   ByVal pDisp As Object, URL As Variant)
48
49       ' when download complete, display URL in cboURL
50       cboURL.Text = URL
51   End Sub
52
53   Private Sub cboURL_Click()
54       ' if cboURL is not empty, go to URL specified in cboURL
55       On Error Resume Next
56
57       If cboURL.Text <> "" Then
58           Call WebBrowser1.Navigate(cboURL.Text)
59       End If
60
61   End Sub
62
63   Private Sub cmdFavorite_Click()
64       Dim index As Integer, result As Integer
65
66       result = -1
67
68       If cboURL.ListCount > 0 Then
69           For index = 0 To cboURL.ListCount
70               If StrComp(cboURL.Text, cboURL.List(index)) = 0 Then
71                   result = index
72                   Exit For
73               End If
74           Next index
75       End If
```

```
76
77      If result = -1 Then
78          cboURL.AddItem (cboURL.Text)
79      End If
80
81   End Sub
82
83   Private Sub cmdRemove_Click()
84      Call frmRemoveItems.Show
85   End Sub
```

```
90   ' Form to remove items from sites list
91   Option Explicit
92
93   Private Sub Form_Load()
94      Dim index As Integer
95
96      For index = 0 To frmWebBrowser.cboURL.ListCount
97          Call lstSites.AddItem(frmWebBrowser.cboURL.List(index))
98      Next index
99
100  End Sub
101
102  Private Sub Form_Resize()
103     lstSites.Width = ScaleWidth
104  End Sub
105
106  Private Sub cmdRemoveItem_Click()
107     Call frmWebBrowser.cboURL.RemoveItem(lstSites.ListIndex)
108     Call lstSites.RemoveItem(lstSites.ListIndex)
109  End Sub
```

19.15 Investigate the capabilities of the **Internet Explorer** browser and use the features of the **WebBrowser** control to create your own version of **Internet Explorer**.

19.16 Develop a client/server tic-tac-toe program. The two users should alternate making moves. Your program should mediate the players moves determining whose turn it is and allowing only valid moves. The players themselves will determine when the game is over.

19.17 Develop a client/server checkers program. The two users should alternate making moves. Your program should mediate the players moves, determining whose turn it is and allowing only valid moves. The players themselves will determine when the game is over.

19.18 Develop a client/server chess-playing program modeled after the checkers program in the previous exercises.

19.19 Develop a client/server black jack card game program in which the server application deals cards to each of the client applications. The server should deal additional cards (as per the rules of the game) to each player as requested.

19.20 Develop a client/server poker card game in which the server application deals cards to each of the client applications. The server should deal additional cards (as per the rules of the game) to each player as requested.

19.21 *(Networked Morse Code)* Modify your solution to Exercise 8.26 to enable two applications to send Morse Code messages to each other through a server application. Each application should allow the user to type normal characters in **TextBox**es, translate the characters into Morse Code and send the coded message through the server to the other client. When messages are received, they should be decoded and displayed as normal characters and as Morse Code. The application should have two **TextBox**es, one for displaying the other client's messages and one for typing.

19.22 In Chapter 11, Section 11.4 discusses the use of template forms. One of the template forms is for a web browser. Rewrite the program of Exercise 19.15 to use the web browser form template.

19.23 Using the features of Fig. 19.5, the string processing capabilities of Chapter 8 and the **RichTextBox** control (see Section 11.5), write your own Hypertext Markup Language (HTML) interpreter that can parse a simple HTML file, format the text in the file and display the formatted text. Visit the World Wide Web site

```
http://www.w3.org/MarkUp/
```

for more information on HTML and the formatting tags that are found in HTML documents.

19.24   *(Dynamic Stock Portfolio Evaluator)* Create a Visual Basic application that will read a file describing an investor's stock portfolio. For each stock the investor owns, the file contains the stock ticker symbol and the number of shares of that stock the investor owns. The application then accesses some stock quotation service available over the Internet (this requires techniques from Chapter 16, Networking) and filters out only those stock transactions for the stocks in the investor's portfolio. As the application fetches new stock prices, it displays a spreadsheet on the screen and dynamically updates the spreadsheet. The spreadsheet shows each stock symbol, the latest price of that stock, the number of shares and the latest total value of shares of that stock. The spreadsheet also totals the latest value of the investor's entire portfolio. An investor could run your Visual Basic application in a small portion of his or her screen while proceeding with other work.

19.25   *(Networked Simpletron Simulator)* Modify the Simpletron Simulator exercise you created in Chapter 10 by breaking the program into a client application and a server application. Execute the SML instructions from the server application. Use the **Winsock** control to perform TCP-based communication between the client and the server. The user interface should appear on the client side. After the user enters the SML program, the program should be sent to the server application for execution. As the SML program executes on the server, the results should be sent back to the client application for display in the user interface.

19.26   *(Networked Simpletron Simulator)* Modify your solution to Exercise 19.25 to use UDP-based packet communication between the client and the server.

19.27   *(Networked Tic-Tac-Toe)* Write a client/server tic-tac-toe game in which two clients connect to a server to play. The first client to connect should be player **X** and the second client should be player **O**. The server should maintain the status of the tic-tac-toe board at all times. Each client's user interface should display the board. When a player clicks a square on the board, a message should be sent to the server and the server should validate the move. If the move is valid, the server should send messages to both clients informing them to update their boards with the appropriate moves. If the move is invalid, the server should send a message to the client indicating the invalid move and requesting that the player move again. Provide the ability to determine who wins and to play again. Use TCP-based communications between the clients and the server.

     ANS: NOTE: THREE SEPARATE INSTANCES OF VISUAL BASIC MUST BE RUNNING TO PLAY THE GAME.

```
1    ' Exercise 19.27 Solution
2    ' Tic-Tac-Toe Server
3    ' NOTE: DoEvents is heavily used to ensure proper message passing.
4    Option Explicit
5    Private mBoard(8) As Integer
6    Private mPlayersConnected As Integer
7    Private mCurrentPlayer As Integer
8    Private mPlayerX As Integer, mPlayerO As Integer
9
10   Public Enum tttResult
11       tttWin
12       tttLOSE
13       tttCONTINUE
14       tttDraw
15   End Enum
16
17   Private Sub Form_Load()
18       mPlayerX = 1
19       mPlayerO = 2
20       Call InitializeBoard
21       mCurrentPlayer = mPlayerX
22       tcpPlayer(0).LocalPort = 5000
23       Call tcpPlayer(0).Listen
24   End Sub
25
26   Private Sub Form_Resize()
27       txtOutput.Width = ScaleWidth
28       txtOutput.Height = ScaleHeight
29   End Sub
30
31   Private Sub tcpPlayer_Error(Index As Integer, ByVal Number As Integer, _
32                               Description As String, ByVal Scode As Long, _
33                               ByVal Source As String, ByVal HelpFile As String, _
34                               ByVal HelpContext As Long, CancelDisplay As Boolean)
35       Call MsgBox(Description)
36   End Sub
37
```

```
38   Private Sub tcpPlayer_SendComplete(Index As Integer)
39      Call ShowMessage("Send complete to " & Index)
40   End Sub
41
42   Private Sub tcpPlayer_SendProgress(Index As Integer, ByVal bytesSent As Long, _
43                                       ByVal bytesRemaining As Long)
44
45      Call ShowMessage("Sending to " & Index & " bytes sent: " & bytesSent & _
46                       " bytes left: " & bytesRemaining)
47   End Sub
48
49   Private Sub tcpPlayer_ConnectionRequest(Index As Integer, ByVal requestID As Long)
50
51      If mPlayersConnected < 2 Then
52         mPlayersConnected = mPlayersConnected + 1
53         Call Load(tcpPlayer(mPlayersConnected))
54         tcpPlayer(mPlayersConnected).LocalPort = 0
55         Call tcpPlayer(mPlayersConnected).Accept(requestID)
56
57         Call tcpPlayer(mPlayersConnected).SendData(mPlayersConnected)
58
59         Call ShowMessage("Player" & IIf(mPlayersConnected = mPlayerX, " X ", " O ") & _
60                          "connected")
61      End If
62
63   End Sub
64
65   Private Sub tcpPlayer_DataArrival(Index As Integer, ByVal bytesTotal As Long)
66      Dim location As Integer
67
68      Call ShowMessage("Message from player " & Index)
69
70      If mPlayersConnected <> 2 Then
71         Call tcpPlayer(Index).SendData("Waiting for another player.")
72      Else
73         Call tcpPlayer(Index).GetData(location, vbInteger)
74         Call ValidateMove(location, Index)
75      End If
76
77   End Sub
78
79   Private Sub ShowMessage(message As String)
80      txtOutput.Text = txtOutput.Text & message & vbNewLine
81      txtOutput.SelStart = Len(txtOutput.Text)
82   End Sub
83
84   Private Sub ValidateMove(location As Integer, player As Integer)
85
86      If player <> mCurrentPlayer Then
87         Call ShowMessage("Sending not your turn to " & player)
88         Call tcpPlayer(player).SendData("It is not your turn, please wait.")
89      ElseIf Not IsOccupied(location) Then
90         ' occupy position
91         mBoard(location) = mCurrentPlayer
92
93         ' send valid location to both players
94         Dim Index As Integer
95
96         Call ShowMessage("Sending move to Player X")
97         Call tcpPlayer(mPlayerX).SendData(location & " " & mCurrentPlayer)
98
99         DoEvents  ' Allow messages to arrive
100        Call ShowMessage("Sending move to Player O")
101        Call tcpPlayer(mPlayerO).SendData(location & " " & mCurrentPlayer)
102
103        Call ShowMessage("Player " & IIf(mCurrentPlayer = mPlayerX, "X", "O") & _
104                         " moved to location " & location)
```

```
105
106            Dim outCome As tttResult
107
108            outCome = GameStatus()
109
110            If outCome = tttWin Then
111                Dim temp As String
112
113                DoEvents
114                temp = IIf(mCurrentPlayer = mPlayerX, "X", "O")
115                Call tcpPlayer(mPlayerO).SendData(temp & " Wins!")
116                DoEvents
117                Call ShowMessage("Game Over. " & temp & " Wins!")
118                Call tcpPlayer(mPlayerX).SendData(temp & " Wins!")
119            ElseIf outCome = tttDraw Then
120                DoEvents
121                Call tcpPlayer(mPlayerO).SendData("Game is a Draw.")
122                DoEvents
123                Call ShowMessage("Game is a Draw")
124                Call tcpPlayer(mPlayerX).SendData("Game is a Draw.")
125            End If
126
127            mCurrentPlayer = IIf(mCurrentPlayer = mPlayerX, mPlayerO, mPlayerX)
128        Else
129            Call tcpPlayer(mCurrentPlayer).SendData("Invalid move. Try again.")
130        End If
131
132    End Sub
133
134    Private Function IsOccupied(location As Integer) As Boolean
135        ' Is position occupied
136        IsOccupied = IIf(mBoard(location) <> -1, True, False)
137    End Function
138
139    Private Sub InitializeBoard()
140        Dim x As Integer
141
142        For x = 0 To UBound(mBoard)
143            mBoard(x) = -1
144        Next
145
146    End Sub
147
148    Private Function GameStatus() As tttResult
149        Dim r As Integer, c As Integer
150
151        ' Check for a win on diagonals
152        If (mBoard(0) <> -1 And mBoard(0) = mBoard(4) And _
153            mBoard(0) = mBoard(8)) Then
154            GameStatus = tttWin
155            Exit Function
156        ElseIf (mBoard(2) <> -1 And mBoard(2) = _
157                mBoard(4) And mBoard(2) = mBoard(6)) Then
158            GameStatus = tttWin
159            Exit Function
160        End If
161
162        ' Check for win in rows
163        For r = 0 To 6 Step 3
164
165            If (mBoard(r) <> -1 And mBoard(r) = mBoard(r + 1) And _
166                mBoard(r) = mBoard(r + 2)) Then
167                GameStatus = tttWin
168                Exit Function
169            End If
170
171        Next r
```

```
172
173    ' Check for win in columns
174    For r = 0 To 2
175
176       If (mBoard(r) <> -1 And mBoard(r) = mBoard(r + 3) And _
177            mBoard(r) = mBoard(r + 6)) Then
178          GameStatus = tttWin
179          Exit Function
180       End If
181
182    Next r
183
184    ' Check for a completed game
185    For r = 0 To 8
186
187       If (mBoard(r) = -1) Then
188          GameStatus = tttCONTINUE
189          Exit Function
190       End If
191
192    Next r
193
194    GameStatus = tttDraw   ' Game is a draw
195 End Function
```

```
Tic-Tac-Toe Server
Sending to 1 bytes sent: 3 bytes left: 0
Send complete to 1
Sending move to Player O
Player O moved to location 5
Sending to 2 bytes sent: 3 bytes left: 0
Send complete to 2
Message from player 1
Sending move to Player X
Sending to 1 bytes sent: 3 bytes left: 0
Send complete to 1
Sending move to Player O
Player X moved to location 8
Sending to 2 bytes sent: 3 bytes left: 0
Send complete to 2
Sending to 2 bytes sent: 7 bytes left: 0
Send complete to 2
Game Over. X Wins!
Sending to 1 bytes sent: 7 bytes left: 0
Send complete to 1
```

```
1  ' Exercise 19.27 Solution
2  ' Tic-Tac-Toe Player
3  Option Explicit
4  Private mPlayerX As Integer, mPlayerO As Integer
5  Private mWhoAmI As Integer
6  Private mJustConnected As Boolean
7
8  Private Sub Form_Load()
9     mPlayerX = 1
10    mPlayerO = 2
11    tcpClient.RemoteHost = "127.0.0.1"
12    tcpClient.RemotePort = 5000
13    Call tcpClient.Connect
14    mJustConnected = True
15 End Sub
16
17 Private Sub lblBoard_Click(Index As Integer)
18    Call ShowMessage("Sending move " & Index)
19    Call tcpClient.SendData(Index)
20 End Sub
21
22 Private Sub tcpClient_DataArrival(ByVal bytesTotal As Long)
23
24    If mJustConnected = True Then
25       mJustConnected = False
26       Call tcpClient.GetData(mWhoAmI, vbInteger)
27       Call ShowMessage("You are player " & IIf(mWhoAmI = mPlayerX, "X", "O"))
```

```
28         Else
29            Dim data As String, location As Integer, player As Integer
30
31            Call tcpClient.GetData(data, vbString)
32
33            If IsNumeric(Left$(data, 1)) Then
34               location = CInt(Left$(data, 1))
35               player = CInt(Mid$(data, 3, 1))
36               Call DisplayMove(location, player)
37            Else
38               Call ShowMessage(data)
39            End If
40
41         End If
42   End Sub
43
44   Private Sub DisplayMove(location As Integer, player As Integer)
45      lblBoard(location).Caption = IIf(player = mPlayerX, "X", "O")
46   End Sub
47
48   Private Sub ShowMessage(message As String)
49      txtOutput.Text = txtOutput.Text & message & vbNewLine
50      txtOutput.SelStart = Len(txtOutput.Text)
51   End Sub
52
53   Private Sub tcpClient_Error(ByVal Number As Integer, Description As String, _
54                               ByVal Scode As Long, ByVal Source As String, _
55                               ByVal HelpFile As String, ByVal HelpContext As Long, _
56                               CancelDisplay As Boolean)
57
58      Call MsgBox(Description)
59   End Sub
```

19.28 *(Networked Tic-Tac-Toe)* Modify your solution to Exercise 19.27 to use UDP-based packet communication between the clients and the server.

19.29 **[CD]** *(VBScript Compound Interest Calculator)* Create an HTML document that enables the user to calculate compund interest. Provide several **TEXT** components in which the user can enter the *principal amount*, the yearly interest *rate* and the number of *years* (see the compound interest program of Figs. 5.5 through 5.7 for the calculation of interest). Provide a **BUTTON** to cause the VBScript to execute and calculate the interest. Display the result in another **TEXT** component. If any **TEXT** component is left empty, display a **MsgBox** indicating the error. Use a **Function** procedure to perform the calculation.
        ANS:

```
1    <html>
2
3    <head>
4    <title>Yearly Compound Interest Calculator</title>
5    <script LANGUAGE="VBScript">
6    <!--
7    Option Explicit
8    Dim principal, rate, years, result
9
10   Sub Calculate_OnClick()
11      result = CCur(principal) * CCur(1.0 + rate) ^ CDbl(years)
12      CompoundInterest.txtResult.Value = FormatCurrency(result, 2)
13   End Sub
14   -->
15   </script>
16   </head>
```

```
17
18   <body>
19
20   <p>Enter the principal, interest rate and number of years on deposit. Press the
21      Calculate button to determine the compounded interest. </p>
22   <hr>
23
24   <form name="CompoundInterest">
25     <p>Principal amount: <input TYPE="TEXT" NAME="txtPrincipal" SIZE="20"> </p>
26     <script FOR="txtPrincipal" EVENT="OnBlur" LANGUAGE="VBScript">
27      principal = txtPrincipal.Value
28     </script>
29
30     <p>Interest rate (e.g., .05 for 5%): <input TYPE="TEXT" NAME="txtInterest"
31                                          SIZE="20"> </p>
32     <script FOR="txtInterest" EVENT="OnBlur" LANGUAGE="VBScript">
33      rate = txtInterest.Value
34     </script>
35
36     <p>Years on deposit: <input TYPE="TEXT" NAME="txtYears" SIZE="20"> </p>
37     <script FOR="txtYears" EVENT="OnBlur" LANGUAGE="VBScript">
38      years = txtYears.Value
39     </script>
40
41     <p><input NAME="Calculate" TYPE="BUTTON" VALUE="Calculate"> </p>
42     <p>Compounded value: <input TYPE="TEXT" NAME="txtResult" SIZE="20"> </p>
43   </form>
44
45   <hr>
46   </body>
47   </html>
```

19.30   *(VBScript Compound Interest Calculator)* Modify Exercise 19.29 to use inline VBScript code.
      ANS:

```
1    <html>
2
3    <head>
4    <title>Yearly Compound Interest Calculator</title>
5    </head>
```

```
6
7   <body>
8   <p>Enter the principal, interest rate and number of years on deposit. Press
9      the Calculate button to determine the compounded interest. </p>
10  <hr>
11
12  <form name="CompoundInterest">
13     <p>Principal amount: <input TYPE="TEXT" NAME="txtPrincipal" SIZE="20"> </p>
14     <p>Interest rate (e.g., .05 for 5%): <input TYPE="TEXT"
15                                     NAME="txtInterest" SIZE="20"> </p>
16     <p>Years on deposit: <input TYPE="TEXT" NAME="txtYears" SIZE="20"> </p>
17     <p><input NAME="Calculate" TYPE="BUTTON" VALUE="Calculate"> </p>
18     <p>Compounded value: <input TYPE="TEXT" NAME="txtResult" SIZE="20"> </p>
19
20     <SCRIPT FOR="Calculate"
21            EVENT="OnClick"
22            LANGUAGE="VBScript">
23        dim result
24        result = CCur(CompoundInterest.txtPrincipal.Value) * CDbl(1.0 + _
25              CompoundInterest.txtInterest.Value) ^ _
26              CDbl(CompoundInterest.txtYears.Value)
27        CompoundInterest.txtResult.Value = FormatCurrency(result, 2)
28     </SCRIPT>
29  </form>
30
31  <hr>
32  </body>
33  </html>
```

19.31 *(VBScript Monthly Compound Interest Calculator)* Modify Exercise 19.29 to calculate the compound interest on a monthly basis. Remember that you must divide the interest rate by 12 to get the monthly rate.

　　ANS:

```
1   <html>
2
3   <head>
4   <title>Yearly Compound Interest Calculator</title>
5   <script LANGUAGE="VBScript">
6   <!--
7   Option Explicit
```

```
8   Dim principal, rate, months, result
9
10  Sub Calculate_OnClick()
11     result = CCur(principal) * CDbl(1.0 + rate) ^ CDbl(months)
12     CompoundInterest.txtResult.Value = FormatCurrency(result, 2)
13  End Sub
14  -->
15  </script>
16
17  </head>
18  <body>
19  <p>Enter the principal, interest rate and number of months. Press the Calculate
20  button to determine the compounded interest. </p>
21  <hr>
22  <form name="CompoundInterest">
23    <p>Principal amount: <input TYPE="TEXT" NAME="txtPrincipal" SIZE="20"> </p>
24    <script FOR="txtPrincipal" EVENT="OnBlur" LANGUAGE="VBScript">
25     principal = txtPrincipal.Value
26    </script>
27
28    <p>Interest rate (e.g., .05 for 5%): <input TYPE="TEXT" NAME="txtInterest"
29                                           SIZE="20"> </p>
30    <script FOR="txtInterest" EVENT="OnBlur" LANGUAGE="VBScript">
31     rate = txtInterest.Value / 12
32    </script>
33
34    <p>Months: <input TYPE="TEXT" NAME="txtMonths" SIZE="20"> </p>
35    <script FOR="txtMonths" EVENT="OnBlur" LANGUAGE="VBScript">
36     months = txtMonths.Value
37    </script>
38
39    <p><input NAME="Calculate" TYPE="BUTTON" VALUE="Calculate"> </p>
40    <p>Compounded value: <input TYPE="TEXT" NAME="txtResult" SIZE="20"> </p>
41  </form>
42
43  <hr>
44  </body>
45  </html>
```

19.32   *(VBScript Monthly Compound Interest Calculator)* Modify Exercise 19.31 to use inline VBScript code.
ANS:

```
1   <html>
2
3   <head>
4   <title>Yearly Compound Interest Calculator</title>
5   </head>
6
7   <body>
8
9   <p>Enter the principal, interest rate and number of months. Press the Calculate
10  button to determine the compounded interest. </p>
11
12  <hr>
13
14  <form name="CompoundInterest">
15     <p>Principal amount: <input TYPE="TEXT" NAME="txtPrincipal" SIZE="20"> </p>
16     <p>Interest rate (e.g., .05 for 5%): <input TYPE="TEXT" NAME="txtInterest"
17                                          SIZE="20"> </p>
18     <p>Months: <input TYPE="TEXT" NAME="txtMonths" SIZE="20"> </p>
19     <p><input NAME="Calculate" TYPE="BUTTON" VALUE="Calculate"> </p>
20     <p>Compounded value: <input TYPE="TEXT" NAME="txtResult" SIZE="20"> </p>
21
22     <SCRIPT FOR="Calculate"
23            EVENT="OnClick"
24            LANGUAGE="VBScript">
25       dim result
26
27       result = CCur(CompoundInterest.txtPrincipal.Value) * CDbl(1.0 + _
28                    CompoundInterest.txtInterest.Value / 12) ^ _
29                    CDbl(CompoundInterest.txtMonths.Value)
30       CompoundInterest.txtResult.Value = FormatCurrency(result, 2)
31     </SCRIPT>
32
33  </form>
34
35  <hr>
36  </body>
37  </html>
```

Chapter 20 Solutions
Multimedia: Images, Animation, Audio

20.2 *(Story Teller)* Record audio for a large number of nouns, verbs, articles, prepositions, etc. Then use random number generation to forms sentences and have your program speak the sentences.

20.3 *(Limericks)* Modify the limerick writing program you wrote in Exercise 8.15 to sing the limericks your program creates.

20.4 *(Background Audio)* Add background audio to one of your favorite applications by using the **Multimedia Control** to play the sound in the background while you interact with your application in the normal way.

20.5 **[CD]** *(Text Flasher)* Create a Visual Basic application that repeatedly flashes text on the screen. Do this by interspersing the text with a plain background color image. Allow the user to control the "blink speed" and the background color or pattern.

ANS:

```vb
1   ' Exercise 20.5 Solution
2   Option Explicit
3   Dim mPicture As IPictureDisp
4
5   Private Sub Form_Load()
6       Set mPicture = LoadPicture("\vb_solutions\ch20\ex20_05\yellow.gif")
7       picPict.Picture = mPicture
8   End Sub
9
10  Private Sub tmrTimer_Timer()
11      Static t As Boolean
12
13      picPict.CurrentX = 0
14      picPict.CurrentY = 0
15
16      If t Then
17         picPict.Print "TEXT"
18      Else
19         Call picPict.PaintPicture(mPicture, 0, 0)
20      End If
21
22      t = Not t
23  End Sub
24
25  Private Sub Form_Terminate()
26      Set mPicture = Nothing
27  End Sub
```

20.6   *(Image Flasher)* Create a Visual Basic application that repeatedly flashes an image on the screen. Do this by interspersing the image with a plain background color image.

ANS:

```
1   ' Exercise 20.6 Solution
2   Option Explicit
3   Dim mImage As IPictureDisp
4   Dim mBlankImage As IPictureDisp
5   Dim mSwitch As Boolean
6
7   Private Sub Form_Load()
8      Set mImage = LoadPicture("\vb_solutions\ch20\" & _
9                    "ex20_06\cool5.jpg")
10     Set mBlankImage = LoadPicture("\vb_solutions\" & _
11                    "ch20\ex20_06\white_blank.jpg")
12     BackColor = vbWhite
13     tmrTimer.Enabled = True
14  End Sub
15
16  Private Sub tmrTimer_Timer()
17     If mSwitch Then
18        Call PaintPicture(mImage, 0, 0)
19     Else
20        Call PaintPicture(mBlankImage, 0, 0)
21     End If
22
23     mSwitch = Not mSwitch
24  End Sub
```

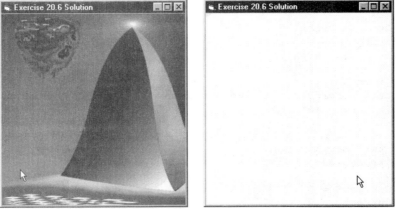

20.7   *(Towers of Hanoi)* Write an animated version of the Towers of Hanoi problem we presented in Exercise 12.6. As each disk is lifted off a peg or slid onto a peg play a "whooshing" sound. As each disk lands on the pile play a "clunking" sound. Play some appropriate background music.

20.8   *(Digital Clock)* Implement an application that displays a digital clock on the screen. You might add options to scale the clock; display day, month and year; issue an alarm; play certain audios at designated times and the like.

ANS:

```
1   ' Exercise 20.8 Solution
2   Option Explicit
3
4   Private Sub tmrTimer_Timer()
5      Call Cls
6      Print Time
7   End Sub
```

20.9   *(Analog Clock)* Create a Visual Basic application that displays an analog clock with hour, minute and second hands that move appropriately as the time changes.

20.10   *(Dynamic Customized Newsletter)* After you complete Chapter 19 you will understand how to develop Internet-based Visual Basic applications that access the World Wide Web. Develop a "newspaper of the future" in which your user uses a graphical user interface to design a customized dynamic newspaper which meets that user's unique information needs. Then have your application harvest information from the World Wide Web at the designated intervals, possibly continuously. You'll be amazed to see how many popular publications offer computerized versions at no charge on the Web.

20.11   *(Dynamic Audio and Graphical Kaleidoscope)* Develop a kaleidoscope application that displays reflected graphics to simulate the popular children's toy. Incorporate audio effects that "mirror" your application's dynamically changing graphics.

20.12   *(One-Armed Bandit)* Develop a multimedia simulation of a one-armed bandit. Have three spinning wheels. Place various fruits and symbols on each wheel. Use true random-number generation to simulate the spinning of each wheel and the stopping of each wheel on a symbol.

20.13   *(Horse Race)* Create a Visual Basic simulation of a horse race. Have multiple contenders. Use audios for a race announcer. Play the appropriate audios to indicate the correct status of each of the contenders throughout the race. Use audios to announce the final results. You might try to simulate the kind of horse race games that are often played at carnivals. The players get turns at the mouse and have to perform some skill-oriented manipulation with the mouse to advance their horses.

20.14   *(Artist)* Design a Visual Basic art application that will give an artist a great variety of capabilities to draw, use images, use animations and the like to create a dynamic multimedia art display.

20.15   *(Karaoke)* Create a Karaoke system that plays the music for a song and displays the words for your user to sing at the appropriate time.

20.16   *(Calling Attention to an Image)* If you want to emphasize an image, you might place a row of simulated light bulbs around your image. You can let the light bulbs flash in unison or you can let them fire on and off in sequence one after the other.
     ANS:

```
1    ' Exercise 20.16 Solution
2    Option Explicit
3
4    Private Sub Form_Load()
5       Dim r As Integer, c As Integer
6
7       FillStyle = vbFSSolid
8       FillColor = vbWhite
9
10      For r = 10 To ScaleWidth Step 10
11
12         For c = 10 To ScaleHeight Step 10
13            Circle (r, c), 5
14         Next c
15
16      Next r
17
18      tmrTimer.Enabled = True
19   End Sub
20
21   Private Sub Flash()
22      Dim r As Integer, c As Integer
23      Static z As Integer
24
25      FillStyle = vbFSSolid
26      FillColor = vbWhite
27
28      For r = 10 To ScaleWidth Step 10
29
30         For c = 10 To ScaleHeight Step 10
31            z = z + 1
32
33            If z Mod 2 = 0 Then
34               FillColor = vbWhite
35            Else
36               FillColor = vbYellow
37            End If
38
```

```
39              Circle (r, c), 5
40         Next c
41
42      Next r
43
44      z = IIf(z Mod 2 = 0, 0, 1)
45   End Sub
46
47   Private Sub tmrTimer_Timer()
48      Call Flash
49   End Sub
```

20.17   *(Physics Demo: Kinetics)* If you have taken physics, implement a Visual Basic application that will demo concepts like energy, inertia, momentum, velocity, acceleration, friction, coefficient of restitution, gravity and others. Create visual effects and use audios where appropriate for emphasis and realism.

20.18   *(On-Line Product Catalog)* Companies are rapidly realizing the potential for doing business on the Web. Develop an on-line multimedia catalog from which your customers may select products to be shipped. After reading Chapter 19, you are able to handle the networking aspects of this problem. If you have an actual company, you should read the latest articles on secure transmission of credit card IDs over the Internet.

20.19   *(Reaction Time/Reaction Precision Tester)* Create a Visual Basic application that moves a randomly created shape around the screen. The user moves the mouse to catch and click the shape. The shape's speed and size can be varied. Keep statistics on how much time the user typically takes to catch a shape of a given size. The user will probably have more difficulty catching faster moving smaller shapes.

   ANS:

```
1    ' Exercise 20.19 Solution
2    ' Reaction time tester
3    Option Explicit
4    Dim mCount As Integer
5
6    Private Sub Form_Load()
7       Width = Screen.Width
8       Height = Screen.Height
9       mCount = 1
10   End Sub
11
12   Private Sub picCatchIt_Click()
13      Dim response As Integer
14
15      response = MsgBox("Good catch. Do you want to try again?", vbYesNo)
16
17      If response = vbYes Then
18
19         If Timer1.Interval > 100 Then
20            Timer1.Interval = Timer1.Interval - 50
21         End If
22
```

```
23        Else
24           Call Unload(Me)         ' Unload the this form from memory
25        End If
26
27        mCount = 1
28     End Sub
29
30     Private Sub Timer1_Timer()
31        picCatchIt.Left = Rnd() * Screen.Width
32        picCatchIt.Top = Rnd() * Screen.Height
33     End Sub
34
35     Private Sub Form_Click()
36        Dim response As Integer
37
38        mCount = mCount + 1
39
40        If mCount = 20 Then
41           response = MsgBox("You have clicked 20 times. Do you want " _
42                            & "to try again?", vbYesNo)
43
44           If response = vbYes Then
45              mCount = 1
46           Else
47              Call Unload(Me)
48           End If
49
50        End If
51
52     End Sub
```

20.20   *(Image Zooming)* Create a Visual Basic application that enables you to zoom in on, or away from, an image.
         ANS:

```
1      ' Exercise 20.20 Solution
2      Option Explicit
3      Dim mImage As IPictureDisp
4
5      Private Sub Form_Load()
6         Set mImage = LoadPicture("\vb_solutions\ch20\ex20_20\cool.jpg")
7         Call PaintPicture(mImage, 0, 615, mImage.Width, mImage.Height)
8      End Sub
9
10     Private Sub cboSize_Click()
11        Dim percent As Single, s As String
12
13        Call Cls
14        s = cboSize.List(cboSize.ListIndex)
15        cboSize.Text = s
16        s = Mid$(s, 1, Len(s) - 1)    ' Remove %
17        percent = CSng(s) / 100
18
```

```
19      Call PaintPicture(mImage, 0, 615, _
20                        (mImage.Width) * percent, (mImage.Height) * percent)
21   End Sub
```

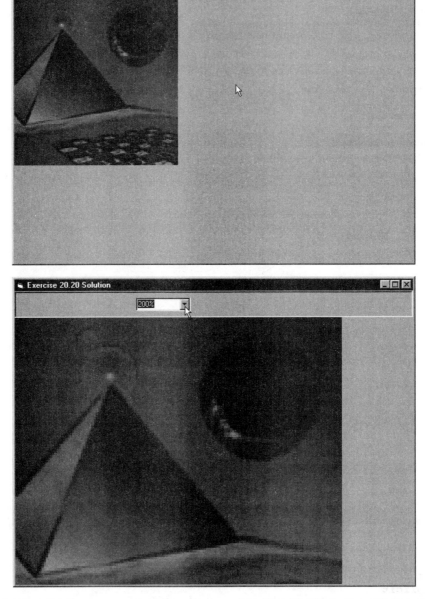

20.21   *(Calendar/Tickler File)* Create a general purpose calendar and "tickler" file. Use audio and images. For example, the application should sing "Happy Birthday" to you when you use it on your birthday. Have the application display images and play audios associated with important events. Have the application remind you in advance of important events. It would be nice, for example, to have the application give you a week's warning so you can pick up an appropriate greeting card for that special person.

20.22   *(Project: Automated Teller Machine) [Note: This project will require that you use advanced Visual Basic techniques from Chapters 14, 15, 19 and 20. This is an excellent group project.]* One of the authors had the privilege of teaching at the division of one of the largest banks in the United States that builds the hardware and software for the automated teller machines that the bank deploys worldwide. During this teaching engagement the author got a behind-the-scenes peek at the "automated teller machine of the future." Develop the framework of a Visual Basic application that implements an automated teller machine and simulates its interaction with a bank's accounts maintained by another computer. The first version of your application should simulate automated teller machines pretty much as they operate today. Then let your creative juices flow and try to design your own version of the "automated teller machine of the future." Use graphics, animation, sound and any other capabilities of Visual Basic, the World Wide Web and the Internet that you wish to employ.

20.23   *(Multimedia-Based Simpletron Simulator)* Modify the Simpletron simulator that you developed in Exercises 10.18 through 10.20 to include multimedia features. Add computer-like sounds to indicate that the Simpletron is executing instructions. Add a breaking glass sound when a fatal error occurs. Use flashing lights to indicate which cells of memory and/or which registers are currently being manipulated. Use other multimedia techniques as appropriate to make your Simpletron simulator more valuable as an educational tool to its users.

Chapter 21 Solutions
Data Structures, Collections, Dictionaries

21.6 [CD] Write a program that concatenates two linked list objects of characters. Define procedure **Concatenate**, which takes references to both list objects as arguments and concatenates the second list to the first list. The procedure should return a reference to the concatenated list.

> ANS:

```
1   ' Exercise 21.6 Solution
2   Option Explicit
3
4   Private Sub Form_Load()
5       Dim link1 As New CList
6       Dim link2 As New CList
7       Dim it As New CListIterator
8
9       Call link1.InsertAtBack("Monday")
10      Call link1.InsertAtBack("Tuesday")
11      Call link1.InsertAtBack("Wednesday")
12      Call link1.InsertAtBack("Thursday")
13      Call link1.InsertAtBack("Friday")
14
15      Call link2.InsertAtBack("Blue and Gold")
16      Call link2.InsertAtBack("Scarlet")
17      Call link2.InsertAtBack("Severe")
18      Call link2.InsertAtBack("Green wing")
19      Call link2.InsertAtBack("Hahns")
20      Call link2.InsertAtBack("Yellow-collard")
21      Call link2.InsertAtBack("Hyacinth")
22
23      Call Concatenate(link1, link2)
24
25      Set link2 = Nothing
26      Set it = link1.Iterator
27
28      While it.HasMoreItems
29          Call lstBox.AddItem(it.NextItem)
30      Wend
31   End Sub
32
33   Public Sub Concatenate(a As CList, b As CList)
34      Dim i As New CListIterator, j As New CListIterator
35      Dim node As New CListNode, node2 As New CListNode
36
37      Set i = a.Iterator
38      Set node = i.StartNode
39
40      Do Until node.NextNode Is Nothing
41          Set node = node.NextNode
42      Loop
43
```

```
44      Set j = b.Iterator
45      Set node2 = j.StartNode
46
47      node.NextNode = node2
48   End Sub
```

```
51   ' Class CList
52   Option Explicit
53   Private mFirstNode As CListNode   ' refers to first node in list
54   Private mLastNode As CListNode    ' refers to last node in list
55
56   ' determine if the list is empty
57   Public Function IsEmpty() As Boolean
58      IsEmpty = IIf(mFirstNode Is Nothing, True, False)
59   End Function
60
61   ' insert an element at the beginning of the list
62   Public Sub InsertAtFront(insertItem As Variant)
63      Dim tempNode As CListNode
64
65      If IsEmpty() Then
66         Set mFirstNode = New CListNode
67         Set mLastNode = mFirstNode
68      Else
69         Set tempNode = mFirstNode
70         Set mFirstNode = New CListNode
71         mFirstNode.NextNode = tempNode
72      End If
73
74      mFirstNode.Data = insertItem
75   End Sub
76
77   ' insert an element at the end of the list
78   Public Sub InsertAtBack(insertItem As Variant)
79      Dim tempNode As CListNode
80
81      If IsEmpty() Then
82         Set mLastNode = New CListNode
83         Set mFirstNode = mLastNode
84      Else
85         Set tempNode = mLastNode
86         Set mLastNode = New CListNode
87         tempNode.NextNode = mLastNode
88      End If
89
90      mLastNode.Data = insertItem
91   End Sub
92
93   ' remove an element from the beginning of the list
94   Public Function RemoveFromFront()
95      Dim removeItem As Variant
96
97      If IsEmpty() Then
98         Call MsgBox("List is empty")
99         RemoveFromFront = Null
100        Exit Function
101     End If
102
103     removeItem = mFirstNode.Data
104
105     If mFirstNode Is mLastNode Then
106        Set mFirstNode = Nothing
107        Set mLastNode = Nothing
108     Else
109        Set mFirstNode = mFirstNode.NextNode
110     End If
```

```
111
112        RemoveFromFront = removeItem
113    End Function
114
115    ' remove an element from the end of the list
116    Public Function RemoveFromBack()
117        Dim removeItem As Variant
118        Dim current As CListNode
119
120        If IsEmpty() Then
121            Call MsgBox("List is empty")
122            RemoveFromBack = Null
123            Exit Function
124        End If
125
126        removeItem = mLastNode.Data
127
128        If mFirstNode Is mLastNode Then
129            Set mFirstNode = Nothing
130            Set mLastNode = Nothing
131        Else
132            Set current = mFirstNode
133
134            While Not current.NextNode Is mLastNode
135                Set current = current.NextNode
136            Wend
137
138            Set mLastNode = current
139            current.NextNode = Nothing
140        End If
141
142        RemoveFromBack = removeItem
143    End Function
144
145    Public Property Get Iterator() As Variant
146        Dim iter As CListIterator
147        Set iter = New CListIterator
148        iter.StartNode = mFirstNode
149        Set Iterator = iter
150    End Property
```

```
152    ' Class CListNode
153    Option Explicit
154    Private mNodeData As Variant
155    Private mNextNode As CListNode
156
157    Public Property Get Data() As Variant
158        Data = mNodeData
159    End Property
160
161    Public Property Let Data(ByVal vNewValue As Variant)
162        mNodeData = vNewValue
163    End Property
164
165    Public Property Get NextNode() As CListNode
166        Set NextNode = mNextNode
167    End Property
168
169    Public Property Let NextNode(ByVal vNewValue As Variant)
170        Set mNextNode = vNewValue
171    End Property
```

```
172    ' Class CListIterator
173    Option Explicit
174    Private mBookmark As CListNode
175    Private mFirstNode As CListNode
```

```
176
177   Public Property Let StartNode(ByVal vNewValue As Variant)
178      Set mFirstNode = vNewValue
179      Set mBookmark = mFirstNode
180   End Property
181
182   Public Property Get StartNode() As CListNode
183      Set StartNode = mFirstNode
184   End Property
185
186   ' return next item in list
187   Public Function NextItem()
188      Dim tempData As Variant
189
190      If mBookmark Is Nothing Then
191         NextItem = Null
192      Else
193         tempData = mBookmark.Data
194         Set mBookmark = mBookmark.NextNode
195         NextItem = tempData
196      End If
197
198   End Function
199
200   Public Function HasMoreItems() As Boolean
201      HasMoreItems = IIf(Not mBookmark Is Nothing, True, False)
202   End Function
203
204   ' reset mBookmark to beginning of list
205   Public Sub ResetmBookmark()
206      mBookmark = mFirstNode
207   End Sub
```

21.7   Write a program that merges two ordered list objects of **Integer**s into a single ordered list object of **Integer**s. Define procedure **Merge**, which takes references to each of the list objects to be merged and returns a reference to the merged list object.

ANS:

```
1    ' Exercise 21.7 Solution
2    Option Explicit
3
4    Private Sub Form_Load()
5       Dim link1 As New CList, link2 As New CList
6       Dim mergedList As New CList
7       Dim it As New CListIterator
8
9       ' Insert method will insert items in order
10      Call link1.Insert(11)
11      Call link1.Insert(98)
12      Call link1.Insert(33)
13      Call link1.Insert(0)
14      Call link1.Insert(3)
15
16      Call link2.Insert(4)
17      Call link2.Insert(77)
18      Call link2.Insert(32)
19      Call link2.Insert(2)
20      Call link2.Insert(88)
21      Call link2.Insert(14)
22      Call link2.Insert(55)
```

```
23
24          ' Merge the two lists and assign the result to mergedList
25          Set mergedList = Merge(link1, link2)
26
27          ' Set references to Nothing
28          Set link1 = Nothing
29          Set link2 = Nothing
30
31          Set it = mergedList.iterator
32
33          While it.HasMoreItems
34              Call lstBox.AddItem(it.NextItem)
35          Wend
36
37      End Sub
38
39      Public Function Merge(a As CList, b As CList) As CList
40          Dim i As New CListIterator
41          Dim mergedLinkedList As New CList
42
43          Call MergeHelper(a, mergedLinkedList)  ' Copy first list
44          Call MergeHelper(b, mergedLinkedList)  ' Insert second list
45
46          Set Merge = mergedLinkedList    ' Return merged list
47      End Function
48
49      Private Sub MergeHelper(list As CList, mergedList As CList)
50          Dim iterator As New CListIterator
51
52          Set iterator = list.iterator
53
54          While iterator.HasMoreItems
55              Call mergedList.Insert(iterator.NextItem)
56          Wend
57      End Sub
```

```
59      ' Class CList
60      Option Explicit
61      Private mFirstNode As CListNode
62
63      ' Determine if the list is empty
64      Public Function IsEmpty() As Boolean
65          IsEmpty = IIf(mFirstNode Is Nothing, True, False)
66      End Function
67
68      Public Property Get Iterator() As Variant
69          Dim iter As CListIterator
70
71          Set iter = New CListIterator
72          iter.StartNode = mFirstNode
73          Set iterator = iter
74      End Property
75
76      ' Insert items in alphabetical order
77      Public Sub Insert(insertItem As Variant)
78          Dim currNode As CListNode, newNode As CListNode
79          Dim prevNode As CListNode
80
81          If IsEmpty() Then
82              Set mFirstNode = New CListNode
83              mFirstNode.Data = insertItem
84              Exit Sub
85          Else
86              Set currNode = mFirstNode
87              Set newNode = New CListNode
88              newNode.Data = insertItem
```

```
89
90        Do While (Not (currNode Is Nothing))
91
92            If (insertItem < currNode.Data) Then
93                Exit Do
94            End If
95
96            Set prevNode = currNode
97            Set currNode = currNode.NextNode
98        Loop
99
100       If (prevNode Is Nothing) Then
101           newNode.NextNode = mFirstNode
102           Set mFirstNode = newNode
103       Else
104           prevNode.NextNode = newNode
105           newNode.NextNode = currNode
106       End If
107
108    End If
109
110 End Sub
```

```
111 ' Class CListNode
112 Option Explicit
113 Private mNodeData As Variant
114 Private mNextNode As CListNode
115
116 Public Property Get Data() As Variant
117     Data = mNodeData
118 End Property
119
120 Public Property Let Data(ByVal vNewValue As Variant)
121     mNodeData = vNewValue
122 End Property
123
124 Public Property Get NextNode() As CListNode
125     Set NextNode = mNextNode
126 End Property
127
128 Public Property Let NextNode(ByVal vNewValue As Variant)
129     Set mNextNode = vNewValue
130 End Property
```

```
131 ' Class CListIterator
132 Option Explicit
133 Private mBookmark As CListNode
134 Private mFirstNode As CListNode
135
136 Public Property Let StartNode(ByVal vNewValue As Variant)
137     Set mFirstNode = vNewValue
138     Set mBookmark = mFirstNode
139 End Property
140
141 Public Property Get StartNode() As CListNode
142     Set StartNode = mFirstNode
143 End Property
144
145 ' return next item in list
146 Public Function NextItem()
147     Dim tempData As Variant
148
149     If mBookmark Is Nothing Then
150         NextItem = Null
151     Else
152         tempData = mBookmark.Data
```

```
153          Set mBookmark = mBookmark.NextNode
154          NextItem = tempData
155       End If
156
157   End Function
158
159   Public Function HasMoreItems() As Boolean
160       HasMoreItems = IIf(Not mBookmark Is Nothing, True, False)
161   End Function
162
163   ' reset mBookmark to beginning of list
164   Public Sub ResetmBookmark()
165       mBookmark = mFirstNode
166   End Sub
```

21.8 Write a program that inserts 25 random **Integer**s from 0 to 100 in order in a linked list. The program should calculate the sum of the elements and the floating-point average of the elements.

ANS:

```
1   ' Exercise 21.8 Solution
2   Option Explicit
3
4   Private Sub Form_Load()
5      Dim link1 As New CList, j As Integer
6      Dim it As New CListIterator, total As Integer
7      Dim k As Variant
8
9      Call Randomize
10
11     For j = 1 To 25
12        Call link1.Insert(Int(Rnd() * 101))
13     Next j
14
15     Set it = link1.Iterator
16
17     While it.HasMoreItems
18        k = it.NextItem
19        total = total + k
20        Call lstBox.AddItem(k)
21     Wend
22
23     Call lstBox.AddItem("Total = " & total)
24     Call lstBox.AddItem("Average = " & _
25                    Format$((total / 25), "Fixed"))
26   End Sub
```

```
27   ' Class CList
28   Option Explicit
29   Private mFirstNode As CListNode  ' refers to first node in list
30
31   ' Determine if the list is empty
32   Public Function IsEmpty() As Boolean
33       IsEmpty = IIf(mFirstNode Is Nothing, True, False)
34   End Function
35
36   Public Property Get Iterator() As Variant
37       Dim iter As CListIterator
38
```

```vb
39      Set iter = New CListIterator
40      iter.StartNode = mFirstNode
41      Set Iterator = iter
42  End Property
43
44  ' Insert items in alphabetical order
45  Public Sub Insert(insertItem As Variant)
46      Dim currNode As CListNode, newNode As CListNode
47      Dim prevNode As CListNode
48
49      If IsEmpty() Then
50          Set mFirstNode = New CListNode
51          mFirstNode.Data = insertItem
52          Exit Sub
53      Else
54          Set currNode = mFirstNode
55          Set newNode = New CListNode
56          newNode.Data = insertItem
57
58          Do While (Not (currNode Is Nothing))
59
60              If (insertItem < currNode.Data) Then
61                  Exit Do
62              End If
63
64              Set prevNode = currNode
65              Set currNode = currNode.NextNode
66          Loop
67
68          If (prevNode Is Nothing) Then
69              newNode.NextNode = mFirstNode
70              Set mFirstNode = newNode
71          Else
72              prevNode.NextNode = newNode
73              newNode.NextNode = currNode
74          End If
75
76      End If
77
78  End Sub
```

```vb
79  ' Class CListNode
80  Option Explicit
81  Private mNodeData As Variant
82  Private mNextNode As CListNode
83
84  Public Property Get Data() As Variant
85      Data = mNodeData
86  End Property
87
88  Public Property Let Data(ByVal vNewValue As Variant)
89      mNodeData = vNewValue
90  End Property
91
92  Public Property Get NextNode() As CListNode
93      Set NextNode = mNextNode
94  End Property
95
96  Public Property Let NextNode(ByVal vNewValue As Variant)
97      Set mNextNode = vNewValue
98  End Property
```

```vb
99  ' Class CListIterator
100 Option Explicit
101 Private mBookmark As CListNode
102 Private mFirstNode As CListNode
```

```
103
104    Public Property Let StartNode(ByVal vNewValue As Variant)
105        Set mFirstNode = vNewValue
106        Set mBookmark = mFirstNode
107    End Property
108
109    Public Property Get StartNode() As CListNode
110        Set StartNode = mFirstNode
111    End Property
112
113    ' Return next item in list
114    Public Function NextItem() As Variant
115        Dim tempData As Variant
116
117        If mBookmark Is Nothing Then
118           NextItem = Null
119        Else
120           tempData = mBookmark.Data
121           Set mBookmark = mBookmark.NextNode
122           NextItem = tempData
123        End If
124
125    End Function
126
127    Public Function HasMoreItems() As Boolean
128        HasMoreItems = IIf(Not mBookmark Is Nothing, True, False)
129    End Function
130
131    ' Reset mBookmark to beginning of list
132    Public Sub ResetmBookmark()
133        mBookmark = mFirstNode
134    End Sub
```

21.9   Write a program that creates a linked list object of 10 characters, then creates a second list object containing a copy of the first list, but in reverse order.

ANS:

```
1     ' Exercise 21.9 Solution
2     Option Explicit
3
4     Private Sub Form_Load()
5         Dim link1 As New CList
6         Dim link2 As New CList
7         Dim it As New CListIterator
8
9         Call link1.InsertAtBack("A")
10        Call link1.InsertAtBack("B")
11        Call link1.InsertAtBack("C")
12        Call link1.InsertAtBack("D")
13        Call link1.InsertAtBack("E")
14        Call link1.InsertAtBack("F")
15        Call link1.InsertAtBack("G")
16        Call link1.InsertAtBack("H")
17        Call link1.InsertAtBack("I")
18        Call link1.InsertAtBack("J")
19
20        Set link2 = CopyListReverse(link1)
21        Set it = link2.Iterator
22
```

```
23      While it.HasMoreItems
24          Call lstBox.AddItem(it.NextItem)
25      Wend
26   End Sub
27
28   Public Function CopyListReverse(list As CList) As CList
29      Dim i As New CListIterator
30      Dim linkList As New CList
31
32      Set i = list.Iterator
33
34      Do While i.HasMoreItems
35          Call linkList.InsertAtFront(i.NextItem)
36      Loop
37
38      Set CopyListReverse = linkList
39   End Function
```

```
42   ' Class CList
43   Option Explicit
44   Private mFirstNode As CListNode    ' refers to first node in list
45   Private mLastNode As CListNode     ' refers to last node in list
46
47   ' determine if the list is empty
48   Public Function IsEmpty() As Boolean
49      IsEmpty = IIf(mFirstNode Is Nothing, True, False)
50   End Function
51
52   ' insert an element at the beginning of the list
53   Public Sub InsertAtFront(insertItem As Variant)
54      Dim tempNode As CListNode
55
56      If IsEmpty() Then
57          Set mFirstNode = New CListNode
58          Set mLastNode = mFirstNode
59      Else
60          Set tempNode = mFirstNode
61          Set mFirstNode = New CListNode
62          mFirstNode.NextNode = tempNode
63      End If
64
65      mFirstNode.Data = insertItem
66   End Sub
67
68   ' insert an element at the end of the list
69   Public Sub InsertAtBack(insertItem As Variant)
70      Dim tempNode As CListNode
71
72      If IsEmpty() Then
73          Set mLastNode = New CListNode
74          Set mFirstNode = mLastNode
75      Else
76          Set tempNode = mLastNode
77          Set mLastNode = New CListNode
78          tempNode.NextNode = mLastNode
79      End If
80
81      mLastNode.Data = insertItem
82   End Sub
83
84   ' remove an element from the beginning of the list
85   Public Function RemoveFromFront()
86      Dim removeItem As Variant
87
88      If IsEmpty() Then
89          Call MsgBox("List is empty")
```

```
90          RemoveFromFront = Null
91          Exit Function
92      End If
93
94      removeItem = mFirstNode.Data
95
96      If mFirstNode Is mLastNode Then
97          Set mFirstNode = Nothing
98          Set mLastNode = Nothing
99      Else
100         Set mFirstNode = mFirstNode.NextNode
101     End If
102
103     RemoveFromFront = removeItem
104 End Function
105
106 ' remove an element from the end of the list
107 Public Function RemoveFromBack()
108     Dim removeItem As Variant
109     Dim current As CListNode
110
111     If IsEmpty() Then
112         Call MsgBox("List is empty")
113         RemoveFromBack = Null
114         Exit Function
115     End If
116
117     removeItem = mLastNode.Data
118
119     If mFirstNode Is mLastNode Then
120         Set mFirstNode = Nothing
121         Set mLastNode = Nothing
122     Else
123         Set current = mFirstNode
124
125         While Not current.NextNode Is mLastNode
126             Set current = current.NextNode
127         Wend
128
129         Set mLastNode = current
130         current.NextNode = Nothing
131     End If
132
133     RemoveFromBack = removeItem
134 End Function
135
136 Public Property Get Iterator() As Variant
137     Dim iter As CListIterator
138
139     Set iter = New CListIterator
140     iter.StartNode = mFirstNode
141     Set Iterator = iter
142 End Property
```

```
143 ' Class CListNode
144 Option Explicit
145 Private mNodeData As Variant
146 Private mNextNode As CListNode
147
148 Public Property Get Data() As Variant
149     Data = mNodeData
150 End Property
151
152 Public Property Let Data(ByVal vNewValue As Variant)
153     mNodeData = vNewValue
154 End Property
```

```
155
156  Public Property Get NextNode() As CListNode
157      Set NextNode = mNextNode
158  End Property
159
160  Public Property Let NextNode(ByVal vNewValue As Variant)
161      Set mNextNode = vNewValue
162  End Property
```

```
163  ' Class CListIterator
164  Option Explicit
165  Private mBookmark As CListNode
166  Private mFirstNode As CListNode
167
168  Public Property Let StartNode(ByVal vNewValue As Variant)
169      Set mFirstNode = vNewValue
170      Set mBookmark = mFirstNode
171  End Property
172
173  ' return next item in list
174  Public Function NextItem()
175      Dim tempData As Variant
176
177      If mBookmark Is Nothing Then
178         NextItem = Null
179      Else
180         tempData = mBookmark.Data
181         Set mBookmark = mBookmark.NextNode
182         NextItem = tempData
183      End If
184  End Function
185
186  Public Function HasMoreItems() As Boolean
187      HasMoreItems = IIf(Not mBookmark Is Nothing, True, False)
188  End Function
189
190  ' reset mBookmark to beginning of list
191  Public Sub ResetmBookmark()
192      mBookmark = mFirstNode
193  End Sub
```

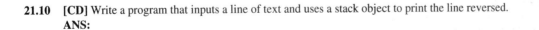

21.10   **[CD]** Write a program that inputs a line of text and uses a stack object to print the line reversed.
         ANS:

```
1   ' Exercise 21.10 Solution
2   Option Explicit
3   Private mStack As CStack
4
5   Private Sub Form_Load()
6       Set mStack = New CStack
7   End Sub
8
9   Private Sub txtInput_KeyPress(KeyAscii As Integer)
10      If KeyAscii = vbKeyReturn Then
11         Call StrTokToStack(txtInput.Text, mStack)
12         txtDisplay.Text = ReverseStackString(mStack)
13      End If
14  End Sub
```

```vb
15
16   Private Sub txtInput_Click()
17      txtInput.Text = ""
18      txtDisplay.Text = ""
19   End Sub
20
21   Private Sub Form_Terminate()
22      Set mStack = Nothing
23   End Sub
```

```vb
26   ' modStack code module
27   Option Explicit
28
29   Public Sub StrTokToStack(s As String, stack As CStack)
30      Dim tokens() As String, c As Integer
31
32      tokens = Split(s, " ")
33
34      For c = LBound(tokens) To UBound(tokens)
35         Call stack.Push(tokens(c))
36      Next c
37   End Sub
38
39   Public Function ReverseStackString(stack As CStack) As String
40      Dim s As String
41
42      While stack.IsStackEmpty = False
43         s = s & stack.Pop() & " "
44      Wend
45
46      ReverseStackString = s
47   End Function
```

```vb
49   ' Class CStack
50   Option Explicit
51   Private list As CList
52
53   Private Sub Class_Initialize()
54      Set list = New CList
55   End Sub
56
57   Public Sub Push(value As Variant)
58      Call list.InsertAtFront(value)
59   End Sub
60
61   Public Function Pop() As Variant
62      Pop = list.RemoveFromFront()
63   End Function
64
65   Public Function IsStackEmpty() As Boolean
66      IsStackEmpty = list.IsEmpty()
67   End Function
68
69   Public Property Get Iterator() As Variant
70      Set Iterator = list.Iterator
71   End Property
72
73   Private Sub Class_Terminate()
74      Set list = Nothing
75   End Sub
```

```vb
76   ' Class CList
77   Option Explicit
78   Private mFirstNode As CListNode   ' refers to first node in list
79   Private mLastNode As CListNode    ' refers to last node in list
```

```
80
81  ' determine if the list is empty
82  Public Function IsEmpty() As Boolean
83     IsEmpty = IIf(mFirstNode Is Nothing, True, False)
84  End Function
85
86  ' insert an element at the beginning of the list
87  Public Sub InsertAtFront(insertItem As Variant)
88     Dim tempNode As CListNode
89
90     If IsEmpty() Then
91        Set mFirstNode = New CListNode
92        Set mLastNode = mFirstNode
93     Else
94        Set tempNode = mFirstNode
95        Set mFirstNode = New CListNode
96        mFirstNode.NextNode = tempNode
97     End If
98
99     mFirstNode.Data = insertItem
100 End Sub
101
102 ' insert an element at the end of the list
103 Public Sub InsertAtBack(insertItem As Variant)
104    Dim tempNode As CListNode
105
106    If IsEmpty() Then
107       Set mLastNode = New CListNode
108       Set mFirstNode = mLastNode
109    Else
110       Set tempNode = mLastNode
111       Set mLastNode = New CListNode
112       tempNode.NextNode = mLastNode
113    End If
114
115    mLastNode.Data = insertItem
116 End Sub
117
118 ' remove an element from the beginning of the list
119 Public Function RemoveFromFront()
120    Dim removeItem As Variant
121
122    If IsEmpty() Then
123       Call MsgBox("List is empty")
124       RemoveFromFront = Null
125       Exit Function
126    End If
127
128    removeItem = mFirstNode.Data
129
130    If mFirstNode Is mLastNode Then
131       Set mFirstNode = Nothing
132       Set mLastNode = Nothing
133    Else
134       Set mFirstNode = mFirstNode.NextNode
135    End If
136
137    RemoveFromFront = removeItem
138 End Function
139
140 ' remove an element from the end of the list
141 Public Function RemoveFromBack()
142    Dim removeItem As Variant
143    Dim current As CListNode
144
145    If IsEmpty() Then
146       Call MsgBox("List is empty")
```

```
147         RemoveFromBack = Null
148         Exit Function
149     End If
150
151     removeItem = mLastNode.Data
152
153     If mFirstNode Is mLastNode Then
154         Set mFirstNode = Nothing
155         Set mLastNode = Nothing
156     Else
157         Set current = mFirstNode
158
159         While Not current.NextNode Is mLastNode
160             Set current = current.NextNode
161         Wend
162
163         Set mLastNode = current
164         current.NextNode = Nothing
165     End If
166
167     RemoveFromBack = removeItem
168 End Function
169
170 Public Property Get Iterator() As Variant
171     Dim iter As CListIterator
172
173     Set iter = New CListIterator
174     iter.StartNode = mFirstNode
175     Set Iterator = iter
176 End Property
```

```
177 ' Class CListNode
178 Option Explicit
179 Private mNodeData As Variant
180 Private mNextNode As CListNode
181
182 Public Property Get Data() As Variant
183     Data = mNodeData
184 End Property
185
186 Public Property Let Data(ByVal vNewValue As Variant)
187     mNodeData = vNewValue
188 End Property
189
190 Public Property Get NextNode() As CListNode
191     Set NextNode = mNextNode
192 End Property
193
194 Public Property Let NextNode(ByVal vNewValue As Variant)
195     Set mNextNode = vNewValue
196 End Property
```

```
197 ' Class CListIterator
198 Option Explicit
199 Private mBookmark As CListNode
200 Private mFirstNode As CListNode
201
202 Public Property Let StartNode(ByVal vNewValue As Variant)
203     Set mFirstNode = vNewValue
204     Set mBookmark = mFirstNode
205 End Property
206
207 ' return next item in list
208 Public Function NextItem()
209     Dim tempData As Variant
210
```

```
211    If mBookmark Is Nothing Then
212       NextItem = Null
213    Else
214       tempData = mBookmark.Data
215       Set mBookmark = mBookmark.NextNode
216       NextItem = tempData
217    End If
218
219 End Function
220
221 Public Function HasMoreItems() As Boolean
222    HasMoreItems = IIf(Not mBookmark Is Nothing, True, False)
223 End Function
224
225 ' reset mBookmark to beginning of list
226 Public Sub ResetmBookmark()
227    mBookmark = mFirstNode
228 End Sub
```

```
Exercise 21.10 Solution                                    _ □ ×
Enter a string and press Enter:  The bird's name was squawk       I

squawk was name bird's The
```

21.11 Write a program that uses a stack to determine if a string is a palindrome (i.e., the string is spelled identically backwards and forwards). The program should ignore spaces and punctuation.

ANS:

```
1  ' Exercise 21.11 Solution
2  Option Explicit
3  Dim mStack As CStack
4
5  Private Sub Form_Load()
6     Set mStack = New CStack
7  End Sub
8
9  Private Sub txtInput_KeyPress(KeyAscii As Integer)
10
11    If KeyAscii = vbKeyReturn Then
12       Dim s As String, j As Integer, c As String
13       Dim s2 As String
14
15       s = LCase$(txtInput.Text)
16
17       For j = 1 To Len(s)
18          c = Mid$(s, j, 1)
19
20          If IsLowerLetter(c) Then
21             Call mStack.Push(c)
22             s2 = s2 & c
23          End If
24       Next j
25
26       If IsPalindrome(s2) Then
27          Call MsgBox("Palindrome!")
28       Else
29          Call MsgBox("Not a palindrome.")
30       End If
31    End If
32 End Sub
33
34 Private Function IsLowerLetter(ByVal char As String) As Boolean
35
36    If Asc(char) >= 97 And Asc(char) <= 122 Then
37       IsLowerLetter = True
```

```
38        Else
39            IsLowerLetter = False
40        End If
41
42    End Function
43
44    Private Function IsPalindrome(s As String) As Boolean
45        Dim k As Integer
46
47        For k = 1 To Len(s)
48
49            If Mid$(s, k, 1) <> mStack.Pop() Then
50                IsPalindrome = False
51                Exit Function
52            End If
53
54        Next k
55
56        IsPalindrome = True
57    End Function
58
59    Private Sub Form_Terminate()
60        Set mStack = Nothing
61    End Sub
```

```
64    ' Class CStack
65    Option Explicit
66    Private mList As CList
67
68    Private Sub Class_Initialize()
69        Set mList = New CList
70    End Sub
71
72    Public Sub Push(value As Variant)
73        Call mList.InsertAtFront(value)
74    End Sub
75
76    Public Function Pop() As Variant
77        Pop = mList.RemoveFromFront()
78    End Function
79
80    Public Function IsStackEmpty() As Boolean
81        IsStackEmpty = mList.IsEmpty()
82    End Function
83
84    Public Property Get Iterator() As Variant
85        Set Iterator = mList.Iterator
86    End Property
87
88    Private Sub Class_Terminate()
89        Set mList = Nothing
90    End Sub
```

```
91     ' Class CList
92     Option Explicit
93     Private mFirstNode As CListNode    ' refers to first node in list
94     Private mLastNode As CListNode     ' refers to last node in list
95
96     ' determine if the list is empty
97     Public Function IsEmpty() As Boolean
98         IsEmpty = IIf(mFirstNode Is Nothing, True, False)
99     End Function
100
101    ' insert an element at the beginning of the list
102    Public Sub InsertAtFront(insertItem As Variant)
103        Dim tempNode As CListNode
```

```
104
105     If IsEmpty() Then
106         Set mFirstNode = New CListNode
107         Set mLastNode = mFirstNode
108     Else
109         Set tempNode = mFirstNode
110         Set mFirstNode = New CListNode
111         mFirstNode.NextNode = tempNode
112     End If
113
114     mFirstNode.Data = insertItem
115 End Sub
116
117 ' insert an element at the end of the list
118 Public Sub InsertAtBack(insertItem As Variant)
119     Dim tempNode As CListNode
120
121     If IsEmpty() Then
122         Set mLastNode = New CListNode
123         Set mFirstNode = mLastNode
124     Else
125         Set tempNode = mLastNode
126         Set mLastNode = New CListNode
127         tempNode.NextNode = mLastNode
128     End If
129
130     mLastNode.Data = insertItem
131 End Sub
132
133 ' remove an element from the beginning of the list
134 Public Function RemoveFromFront()
135     Dim removeItem As Variant
136
137     If IsEmpty() Then
138         Call MsgBox("List is empty")
139         RemoveFromFront = Null
140         Exit Function
141     End If
142
143     removeItem = mFirstNode.Data
144
145     If mFirstNode Is mLastNode Then
146         Set mFirstNode = Nothing
147         Set mLastNode = Nothing
148     Else
149         Set mFirstNode = mFirstNode.NextNode
150     End If
151
152     RemoveFromFront = removeItem
153 End Function
154
155 ' remove an element from the end of the list
156 Public Function RemoveFromBack()
157     Dim removeItem As Variant
158     Dim current As CListNode
159
160     If IsEmpty() Then
161         Call MsgBox("List is empty")
162         RemoveFromBack = Null
163         Exit Function
164     End If
165
166     removeItem = mLastNode.Data
167
168     If mFirstNode Is mLastNode Then
169         Set mFirstNode = Nothing
170         Set mLastNode = Nothing
```

```
171        Else
172           Set current = mFirstNode
173
174           While Not current.NextNode Is mLastNode
175              Set current = current.NextNode
176           Wend
177
178           Set mLastNode = current
179           current.NextNode = Nothing
180        End If
181
182        RemoveFromBack = removeItem
183     End Function
184
185     Public Property Get Iterator() As Variant
186        Dim iter As CListIterator
187
188        Set iter = New CListIterator
189        iter.StartNode = mFirstNode
190        Set Iterator = iter
191     End Property
```

```
192     ' Class CListNode
193     Option Explicit
194     Private mNodeData As Variant
195     Private mNextNode As CListNode
196
197     Public Property Get Data() As Variant
198        Data = mNodeData
199     End Property
200
201     Public Property Let Data(ByVal vNewValue As Variant)
202        mNodeData = vNewValue
203     End Property
204
205     Public Property Get NextNode() As CListNode
206        Set NextNode = mNextNode
207     End Property
208
209     Public Property Let NextNode(ByVal vNewValue As Variant)
210        Set mNextNode = vNewValue
211     End Property
```

```
212     ' Class CListIterator
213     Option Explicit
214     Private mBookmark As CListNode
215     Private mFirstNode As CListNode
216
217     Public Property Let StartNode(ByVal vNewValue As Variant)
218        Set mFirstNode = vNewValue
219        Set mBookmark = mFirstNode
220     End Property
221
222     ' return next item in list
223     Public Function NextItem()
224        Dim tempData As Variant
225
226        If mBookmark Is Nothing Then
227           NextItem = Null
228        Else
229           tempData = mBookmark.Data
230           Set mBookmark = mBookmark.NextNode
231           NextItem = tempData
232        End If
233     End Function
234
```

```
235  Public Function HasMoreItems() As Boolean
236      HasMoreItems = IIf(Not mBookmark Is Nothing, True, False)
237  End Function
238
239  ' reset mBookmark to beginning of list
240  Public Sub ResetmBookmark()
241      mBookmark = mFirstNode
242  End Sub
```

21.12   Stacks are used by compilers to help in the process of evaluating expressions and generating machine language code. In this and the next exercise, we investigate how compilers evaluate arithmetic expressions consisting only of constants, operators and parentheses.

Humans generally write expressions like **3 + 4** and **7 / 9** in which the operator (**+** or **/** here) is written between its operands—this is called *infix notation*. Computers "prefer" *postfix notation,* in which the operator is written to the right of its two operands. The preceding infix expressions would appear in postfix notation as **3 4 +** and **7 9 /**, respectively.

To evaluate a complex infix expression, a compiler would first convert the expression to postfix notation and evaluate the postfix version of the expression. Each of these algorithms requires only a single left-to-right pass of the expression. Each algorithm uses a stack object in support of its operation, and in each algorithm the stack is used for a different purpose.

In this exercise, you will write a Visual Basic version of the infix-to-postfix conversion algorithm. In the next exercise, you will write a Visual Basic version of the postfix expression evaluation algorithm.

Write class **CInfixToPostfixConverter** to convert an ordinary infix arithmetic expression (assume that a valid expression is entered) with single-digit **Integer**s such as

   (6 + 2) * 5 - 8 / 4

to a postfix expression. The postfix version of the preceding infix expression is

   6 2 + 5 * 8 4 / -

The program should read the expression into **String infix** and use the **CStack** class implemented in this chapter to help create the postfix expression in **String postfix**. The algorithm for creating a postfix expression is as follows:

   a) Push a left parenthesis **'('** on the stack.
   b) Append a right parenthesis **')'** to the end of **infix**.
   c) While the stack is not empty, read **infix** from left to right and do the following:
      If the current character in **infix** is a digit, append it to **postfix**.
      If the current character in **infix** is a left parenthesis, push it on the stack.
      If the current character in **infix** is an operator,
         Pop operators (if there are any) at the top of the stack while they have equal
            or higher precedence than the current operator and append the popped
            operators to **postfix**.
      Push the current character in **infix** on the stack.
      If the current character in **infix** is a right parenthesis,
         Pop operators from the top of the stack and append them to **postfix** until
            a left parenthesis is at the top of the stack.
         Pop (and discard) the left parenthesis from the stack.

The following arithmetic operations are allowed in an expression:
   +   addition
   –   subtraction
   *   multiplication
   /   division
   ^   exponentiation
   %   modulus

Some of the procedures you may want to provide are:
   a) Procedure **ConvertToPostfix** to convert the infix expression to postfix notation.
   b) Procedure **IsOperator**, which determines if **c** is an operator.

c) Procedure **Precedence**, which determines if the precedence of **operator1** (from the infix expression) is less than, equal to, or greater than the precedence of **operator2** (from the stack). The procedure returns **True** if **operator1** has lower precedence than **operator2**. Otherwise, **False** is returned.

d) Procedure **StackTop** (this should be added as a modification to the **CStack** class), which returns the top value of the stack without popping the stack.

ANS:

```
1    ' Exercise 21.12 Solution
2    Option Explicit
3    Dim mStack As CStack
4    Dim mInfix As CInfixToPostfixConverter
5
6    Private Sub Form_Load()
7       Set mStack = New CStack
8       Set mInfix = New CInfixToPostfixConverter
9    End Sub
10
11   Private Sub txtPush_KeyPress(KeyAscii As Integer)
12
13      If KeyAscii = vbKeyReturn Then
14         Dim s As String, j As Integer, postfix As String
15         Dim s2 As String, expression As String
16
17         s = txtPush.Text
18
19         For j = 1 To Len(s)
20            s2 = Mid$(s, j, 1)
21
22            If s2 <> " " Then
23               expression = expression & s2
24            End If
25
26         Next j
27
28         postfix = mInfix.ConvertToPostfix(expression, mStack)
29         Call MsgBox("Postfix expression is " & postfix)
30      End If
31
32   End Sub
33
34   Private Sub Form_Terminate()
35      Set mStack = Nothing
36      Set mInfix = Nothing
37   End Sub
```

```
39   ' Class CInfixToPostfixConverter
40   Option Explicit
41
42   Public Function ConvertToPostfix(infix As String, stack As CStack) As String
43      Dim postfix As String, k As Integer, c As String
44      Dim z As String
45
46      k = 1
47      Call stack.Push("(")
48      infix = infix & ")"
49      c = Mid$(infix, k, 1)
50
51      While stack.IsStackEmpty = False
52
53         If IsNumeric(c) Then
54            postfix = postfix & c
55         ElseIf c = "(" Then
56            Call stack.Push(c)
57         ElseIf IsOperator(c) Then
58            z = stack.StackTop
```

```
59
60              Do While IsOperator(z)
61
62                  If Precedence(c, z) Then
63                      postfix = postfix & stack.Pop
64                  Else
65                      Exit Do
66                  End If
67
68                  z = stack.StackTop
69              Loop
70
71              Call stack.Push(c)
72          ElseIf c = ")" Then
73              z = stack.StackTop
74
75              While z <> "("
76                  postfix = postfix & z
77                  Call stack.Pop
78                  z = stack.StackTop
79              Wend
80
81              ' Discard left parenthesis
82              Call stack.Pop
83          End If
84
85          k = k + 1
86          c = Mid$(infix, k, 1)
87      Wend
88
89      ConvertToPostfix = postfix
90  End Function
91
92  Private Function Precedence(op1 As String, _
93                              op2 As String) As Boolean
94      Dim value1 As Integer, value2 As Integer
95
96      value1 = PrecedenceHelper(op1)
97      value2 = PrecedenceHelper(op2)
98
99      If value1 < value2 Then
100         Precedence = True
101     Else
102         Precedence = False
103     End If
104 End Function
105
106 Private Function PrecedenceHelper(ByVal op As String) As Integer
107     ' Note: this procedure does not evaluate the negation operator
108
109     Select Case op
110         Case "+", "-"
111             PrecedenceHelper = 25
112         Case "*", "/"
113             PrecedenceHelper = 75
114         Case "^"
115             PrecedenceHelper = 100
116         Case "%"
117             PrecedenceHelper = 50
118     End Select
119 End Function
120
121 Private Function IsOperator(op As String) As Boolean
122     If op = "+" Or op = "-" Or op = "/" Or op = "*" Then
123         IsOperator = True
124     ElseIf op = "%" Or op = "^" Then
125         IsOperator = True
```

```
126       Else
127           IsOperator = False
128       End If
129   End Function
```

```
135   ' Class CStack
136   Option Explicit
137   Private mList As CList
138
139   Private Sub Class_Initialize()
140       Set mList = New CList
141   End Sub
142
143   Public Sub Push(value As Variant)
144       Call mList.InsertAtFront(value)
145   End Sub
146
147   Public Function Pop() As Variant
148       Pop = mList.RemoveFromFront()
149   End Function
150
151   Public Function IsStackEmpty() As Boolean
152       IsStackEmpty = mList.IsEmpty()
153   End Function
154
155   Public Property Get Iterator() As Variant
156       Set Iterator = mList.Iterator
157   End Property
158
159   Public Function StackTop() As Variant
160       Dim it As CListIterator
161
162       If mList.IsEmpty Then
163           StackTop = Null
164       Else
165           Set it = mList.Iterator
166           StackTop = it.NextItem
167       End If
168   End Function
169
170   Private Sub Class_Terminate()
171       Set mList = New CList
172   End Sub
```

```
174   ' Class CList
175   Option Explicit
176   Private mFirstNode As CListNode   ' refers to first node in list
177   Private mLastNode As CListNode    ' refers to last node in list
178
179   ' determine if the list is empty
180   Public Function IsEmpty() As Boolean
181       IsEmpty = IIf(mFirstNode Is Nothing, True, False)
182   End Function
183
184   ' insert an element at the beginning of the list
185   Public Sub InsertAtFront(insertItem As Variant)
186       Dim tempNode As CListNode
187
188       If IsEmpty() Then
189           Set mFirstNode = New CListNode
190           Set mLastNode = mFirstNode
191       Else
192           Set tempNode = mFirstNode
193           Set mFirstNode = New CListNode
194           mFirstNode.NextNode = tempNode
195       End If
```

```vbnet
196        mFirstNode.Data = insertItem
197  End Sub
198
199  ' insert an element at the end of the list
200  Public Sub InsertAtBack(insertItem As Variant)
201        Dim tempNode As CListNode
202
203        If IsEmpty() Then
204            Set mLastNode = New CListNode
205            Set mFirstNode = mLastNode
206        Else
207            Set tempNode = mLastNode
208            Set mLastNode = New CListNode
209            tempNode.NextNode = mLastNode
210        End If
211
212        mLastNode.Data = insertItem
213  End Sub
214
215  ' remove an element from the beginning of the list
216  Public Function RemoveFromFront()
217        Dim removeItem As Variant
218
219        If IsEmpty() Then
220            Call MsgBox("List is empty")
221            RemoveFromFront = Null
222            Exit Function
223        End If
224
225        removeItem = mFirstNode.Data
226
227        If mFirstNode Is mLastNode Then
228            Set mFirstNode = Nothing
229            Set mLastNode = Nothing
230        Else
231            Set mFirstNode = mFirstNode.NextNode
232        End If
233
234        RemoveFromFront = removeItem
235  End Function
236
237  ' remove an element from the end of the list
238  Public Function RemoveFromBack()
239        Dim removeItem As Variant
240        Dim current As CListNode
241
242        If IsEmpty() Then
243            Call MsgBox("List is empty")
244            RemoveFromBack = Null
245            Exit Function
246        End If
247
248        removeItem = mLastNode.Data
249
250        If mFirstNode Is mLastNode Then
251            Set mFirstNode = Nothing
252            Set mLastNode = Nothing
253        Else
254            Set current = mFirstNode
255
256            While Not current.NextNode Is mLastNode
257                Set current = current.NextNode
258            Wend
259
260            Set mLastNode = current
261            current.NextNode = Nothing
262        End If
```

```
263
264       RemoveFromBack = removeItem
265  End Function
266
267  Public Property Get Iterator() As Variant
268       Dim iter As CListIterator
269
270       Set iter = New CListIterator
271       iter.StartNode = mFirstNode
272       Set Iterator = iter
273  End Property
```

```
275  ' Class CListNode
276  Option Explicit
277  Private mNodeData As Variant
278  Private mNextNode As CListNode
279
280  Public Property Get Data() As Variant
281       Data = mNodeData
282  End Property
283
284  Public Property Let Data(ByVal vNewValue As Variant)
285       mNodeData = vNewValue
286  End Property
287
288  Public Property Get NextNode() As CListNode
289       Set NextNode = mNextNode
290  End Property
291
292  Public Property Let NextNode(ByVal vNewValue As Variant)
293       Set mNextNode = vNewValue
294  End Property
```

```
295  ' Class CListIterator
296  Option Explicit
297  Private mBookmark As CListNode
298  Private mFirstNode As CListNode
299
300  Public Property Let StartNode(ByVal vNewValue As Variant)
301       Set mFirstNode = vNewValue
302       Set mBookmark = mFirstNode
303  End Property
304
305  ' return next item in list
306  Public Function NextItem()
307       Dim tempData As Variant
308
309       If mBookmark Is Nothing Then
310          NextItem = Null
311       Else
312          tempData = mBookmark.Data
313          Set mBookmark = mBookmark.NextNode
314          NextItem = tempData
315       End If
316
317  End Function
318
319  Public Function HasMoreItems() As Boolean
320       HasMoreItems = IIf(Not mBookmark Is Nothing, True, False)
321  End Function
322
323  ' reset mBookmark to beginning of list
324  Public Sub ResetmBookmark()
325       mBookmark = mFirstNode
326  End Sub
```

21.13   Write class `CPostfixEvaluator`, which evaluates a postfix expression (assume that it is valid) such as

```
6 2 + 5 * 8 4 / -
```

The program should read a postfix expression consisting of digits and operators into a `String`. Using class `CStack` implemented earlier in this chapter, the program should scan the expression and evaluate it. The algorithm is as follows:

a)   Append a right parenthesis (`')'`) to the end of the postfix expression. When the right parenthesis character is encountered, no further processing is necessary.

b)   While the right parenthesis character has not been encountered, read the expression from left to right.
   If the current character is a digit,
      Push its `Integer` value on the stack (the value of a digit character is its value in the computer's character set minus the value of `'0'` in the computer's character set).
   Otherwise, if the current character is an *operator*,
      Pop the two top elements of the stack into variables **x** and **y**.
      Calculate **y** *operator* **x**.
      Push the result of the calculation onto the stack.

c)   When the right parenthesis is encountered in the expression, pop the top value of the stack. This is the result of the postfix expression.

Note: In b) above, if the operator is `'/'`, the top of the stack is **2** and the next element in the stack is **8**, then pop **2** into **x**, pop **8** into **y**, evaluate **8 / 2** and push the result, **4**, back on the stack. This note also applies to operator `'-'`. The arithmetic operations allowed in an expression are

   + addition
   – subtraction
   * multiplication
   / division
   ^ exponentiation
   % modulus

The stack should be maintained with the **CStack** class introduced in this chapter. You may want to provide the following procedures:

a)   Procedure **EvaluatePostfixExpression**, which evaluates the postfix expression.
b)   Procedure **Calculate**, which evaluates the expression **op1 operator op2**.
c)   Procedure **Display**, which displays the stack.

   ANS:

```
1  ' Exercise 21.13 Solution
2  Option Explicit
3  Dim mStack As CStack
4  Dim mPostfix As CPostfixEvaluator
5
6  Private Sub Form_Load()
7     Set mStack = New CStack
8     Set mPostfix = New CPostfixEvaluator
9  End Sub
10
11 Private Sub txtPush_KeyPress(KeyAscii As Integer)
12
13    If KeyAscii = vbKeyReturn Then
14       Dim s As String, j As Integer, result As Integer
15       Dim s2 As String, expression As String
16
17       s = txtPush.Text
18       Call lstOutput.Clear
19       txtPush.Text = ""
20
21       For j = 1 To Len(s)
22          s2 = Mid$(s, j, 1)
```

```
23
24             If s2 <> " " Then
25                 expression = expression & s2
26             End If
27         Next j
28
29         result = mPostfix.EvaluatePostfixExpression(expression, _
30                                                     mStack)
31         Call MsgBox("Result is " & result)
32     End If
33
34  End Sub
35
36  Public Sub Display()
37     Dim elements As New CListIterator
38
39     Call lstOutput.AddItem("The stack is:")
40     Set elements = mStack.Iterator
41
42     If elements.HasMoreItems = False Then
43         Call lstOutput.AddItem("Empty")
44         Exit Sub
45     End If
46
47     While elements.HasMoreItems
48         Call lstOutput.AddItem(elements.NextItem)
49     Wend
50
51  End Sub
52
53  Private Sub Form_Terminate()
54     Set mStack = Nothing
55     Set mPostfix = Nothing
56  End Sub
```

```
57  ' Class CPostfixEvaluator
58  Option Explicit
59
60  Public Function EvaluatePostfixExpression(e As String, _
61                              stack As CStack) As Integer
62     Dim j As Integer, c As String, popVal1 As Integer
63     Dim popVal2 As Integer
64
65     j = 1
66     e = e & ")"
67
68     c = Mid$(e, j, 1)
69
70     While c <> ")"
71         If IsNumeric(c) Then
72             Call stack.Push(CInt(c))
73             Call frmForm.lstOutput.AddItem(c)
74         Else
75             popVal2 = CInt(stack.Pop())
76             popVal1 = CInt(stack.Pop())
77             Call stack.Push(Calculate(popVal1, popVal2, c))
78         End If
79
80         Call frmForm.Display
81         j = j + 1
82         c = Mid$(e, j, 1)
83     Wend
84
85     EvaluatePostfixExpression = CInt(stack.Pop)
86     Call frmForm.Display
87  End Function
```

```vbnet
88
89   Private Function Calculate(op1 As Integer, op2 As Integer, _
90                             oper As String) As Integer
91      Select Case oper
92         Case "+"
93            Calculate = op1 + op2
94         Case "-"
95            Calculate = op1 - op2
96         Case "*"
97            Calculate = op1 * op2
98         Case "/"
99            Calculate = op1 \ op2
100        Case "^"
101           Calculate = op1 ^ op2
102        Case "%"
103           Calculate = op1 Mod op2
104     End Select
105
106  End Function
```

```vbnet
109  ' Class CStack
110  Option Explicit
111  Private list As New CList
112
113  Public Sub Push(value As Variant)
114     Call list.InsertAtFront(value)
115  End Sub
116
117  Public Function Pop() As Variant
118     Pop = list.RemoveFromFront()
119  End Function
120
121  Public Function IsStackEmpty() As Boolean
122     IsStackEmpty = list.IsEmpty()
123  End Function
124
125  Public Property Get Iterator() As Variant
126     Set Iterator = list.Iterator
127  End Property
```

```vbnet
128  ' Class CList
129  Option Explicit
130  Private mFirstNode As CListNode  ' refers to first node in list
131  Private mLastNode As CListNode   ' refers to last node in list
132
133  ' determine if the list is empty
134  Public Function IsEmpty() As Boolean
135     IsEmpty = IIf(mFirstNode Is Nothing, True, False)
136  End Function
137
138  ' insert an element at the beginning of the list
139  Public Sub InsertAtFront(insertItem As Variant)
140     Dim tempNode As CListNode
141
142     If IsEmpty() Then
143        Set mFirstNode = New CListNode
144        Set mLastNode = mFirstNode
145     Else
146        Set tempNode = mFirstNode
147        Set mFirstNode = New CListNode
148        mFirstNode.NextNode = tempNode
149     End If
150
151     mFirstNode.Data = insertItem
152  End Sub
153
```

```
154  ' insert an element at the end of the list
155  Public Sub InsertAtBack(insertItem As Variant)
156     Dim tempNode As CListNode
157
158     If IsEmpty() Then
159        Set mLastNode = New CListNode
160        Set mFirstNode = mLastNode
161     Else
162        Set tempNode = mLastNode
163        Set mLastNode = New CListNode
164        tempNode.NextNode = mLastNode
165     End If
166
167     mLastNode.Data = insertItem
168  End Sub
169
170  ' remove an element from the beginning of the list
171  Public Function RemoveFromFront()
172     Dim removeItem As Variant
173
174     If IsEmpty() Then
175        Call MsgBox("List is empty")
176        RemoveFromFront = Null
177        Exit Function
178     End If
179
180     removeItem = mFirstNode.Data
181
182     If mFirstNode Is mLastNode Then
183        Set mFirstNode = Nothing
184        Set mLastNode = Nothing
185     Else
186        Set mFirstNode = mFirstNode.NextNode
187     End If
188
189     RemoveFromFront = removeItem
190  End Function
191
192  ' remove an element from the end of the list
193  Public Function RemoveFromBack()
194     Dim removeItem As Variant
195     Dim current As CListNode
196
197     If IsEmpty() Then
198        Call MsgBox("List is empty")
199        RemoveFromBack = Null
200        Exit Function
201     End If
202
203     removeItem = mLastNode.Data
204
205     If mFirstNode Is mLastNode Then
206        Set mFirstNode = Nothing
207        Set mLastNode = Nothing
208     Else
209        Set current = mFirstNode
210
211        While Not current.NextNode Is mLastNode
212           Set current = current.NextNode
213        Wend
214
215        Set mLastNode = current
216        current.NextNode = Nothing
217     End If
218
219     RemoveFromBack = removeItem
220  End Function
```

```
221
222  Public Property Get Iterator() As Variant
223      Dim iter As CListIterator
224
225      Set iter = New CListIterator
226      iter.StartNode = mFirstNode
227      Set Iterator = iter
228  End Property
```

```
229  ' Class CListNode
230  Option Explicit
231  Private mNodeData As Variant
232  Private mNextNode As CListNode
233
234  Public Property Get Data() As Variant
235      Data = mNodeData
236  End Property
237
238  Public Property Let Data(ByVal vNewValue As Variant)
239      mNodeData = vNewValue
240  End Property
241
242  Public Property Get NextNode() As CListNode
243      Set NextNode = mNextNode
244  End Property
245
246  Public Property Let NextNode(ByVal vNewValue As Variant)
247      Set mNextNode = vNewValue
248  End Property
```

```
249  ' Class CListIterator
250  Option Explicit
251  Private mBookmark As CListNode
252  Private mFirstNode As CListNode
253
254  Public Property Let StartNode(ByVal vNewValue As Variant)
255      Set mFirstNode = vNewValue
256      Set mBookmark = mFirstNode
257  End Property
258
259  ' return next item in list
260  Public Function NextItem()
261      Dim tempData As Variant
262
263      If mBookmark Is Nothing Then
264         NextItem = Null
265      Else
266         tempData = mBookmark.Data
267         Set mBookmark = mBookmark.NextNode
268         NextItem = tempData
269      End If
270
271  End Function
272
273  Public Function HasMoreItems() As Boolean
274      HasMoreItems = IIf(Not mBookmark Is Nothing, True, False)
275  End Function
276
277  ' reset mBookmark to beginning of list
278  Public Sub ResetmBookmark()
279      mBookmark = mFirstNode
280  End Sub
```

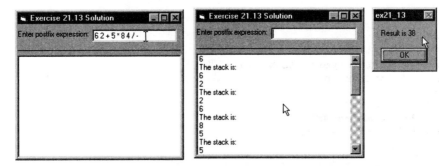

21.14   Modify the postfix evaluator program of Exercise 21.13 so that it can process **Integer** operands larger than 9.

21.15   *(Supermarket simulation)* Write a program that simulates a checkout line at a supermarket. The line should be implemented as a queue object. Customers (i.e., customer objects) arrive in random **Integer** intervals of 1 to 4 minutes. Also, each customer is serviced in random **Integer** intervals of 1 to 4 minutes. Obviously, the rates need to be balanced. If the average arrival rate is larger than the average service rate, the queue will grow infinitely. Even with "balanced" rates, randomness can still cause long lines. Run the supermarket simulation for a 12-hour day (720 minutes) using the following algorithm:

    a) Choose a random **Integer** between 1 and 4 to determine the minute at which the first customer arrives.

    b) At the first customer's arrival time

        Determine the customer's service time (random **Integer** from 1 to 4);

        Begin servicing the customer;

        Schedule the arrival time of the next customer (random **Integer** 1 to 4 added to the current time).

    c) For each minute of the day:

        If the next customer arrives,

            Say so,

            Enqueue the customer,

            Schedule the arrival time of the next customer.

        If service was completed for the last customer,

            Say so,

            Dequeue next customer to be serviced,

            Determine customer's service completion time (random **Integer** from 1 to 4 added to the current time).

Now run your simulation for 720 minutes and answer each of the following:

    a) What is the maximum number of customers in the queue at any time?

    b) What is the longest wait any one customer experiences?

    c) What happens if the arrival interval is changed from 1 to 4 minutes to 1 to 3 minutes?

21.16   [CD] Modify the program of Fig. 21.15 to allow the binary tree object to contain duplicates.
    ANS:

```
1   ' Exercise 21.16 Solution
2   Option Explicit
3   Dim mTree As CTree
4
5   Private Sub Form_Load()
6       Set mTree = New CTree
7   End Sub
8
9   Private Sub cmdInsert_Click()
10      Call mTree.InsertNode(Val(txtInput.Text))
11      txtInput.Text = ""
12      txtInput.SetFocus        ' Transfer focus to TextBox
13  End Sub
14
15  Private Sub cmdTraversals_Click()
16      Call mTree.InorderTraversal
17      lblInorderResult.Caption = mTree.Output
18      Call mTree.PreorderTraversal
19      lblPreorderResult.Caption = mTree.Output
20      Call mTree.PostorderTraversal
21      lblPostorderResult.Caption = mTree.Output
22  End Sub
```

```vb
23
24   Private Sub Form_Terminate()
25       Set mTree = Nothing
26   End Sub

27   ' Class CTree
28   Option Explicit
29   Private mRoot As CTreeNode
30   Private mOutputString As String
31
32   ' Insert a new node in the binary search tree.
33   ' If the root node is null, create the root node here.
34   ' Otherwise, call the insert procedure of class TreeNode.
35   Public Sub InsertNode(value As Variant)
36
37       If mRoot Is Nothing Then
38           Set mRoot = New CTreeNode
39           mRoot.Data = value
40       Else
41           mRoot.Insert (value)
42       End If
43
44   End Sub
45
46   ' Preorder Traversal
47   Public Sub PreorderTraversal()
48       mOutputString = ""
49       Call PreorderHelper(mRoot)
50   End Sub
51
52   ' Recursive procedure to perform preorder traversal
53   Private Sub PreorderHelper(node As CTreeNode)
54
55       If node Is Nothing Then
56           Exit Sub
57       End If
58
59       mOutputString = mOutputString & node.Data & " "
60       Call PreorderHelper(node.Left)
61       Call PreorderHelper(node.Right)
62   End Sub
63
64   ' Inorder Traversal
65   Public Sub InorderTraversal()
66       mOutputString = ""
67       Call InorderHelper(mRoot)
68   End Sub
69
70   ' Recursive procedure to perform inorder traversal
71   Private Sub InorderHelper(node As CTreeNode)
72
73       If node Is Nothing Then
74           Exit Sub
75       End If
76
77       Call InorderHelper(node.Left)
78       mOutputString = mOutputString & node.Data & " "
79       Call InorderHelper(node.Right)
80   End Sub
81
82   ' Postorder Traversal
83   Public Sub PostorderTraversal()
84       mOutputString = ""
85       Call PostorderHelper(mRoot)
86   End Sub
87
```

```
88   ' Recursive procedure to perform Postorder traversal
89   Private Sub PostorderHelper(node As CTreeNode)
90
91       If node Is Nothing Then
92          Exit Sub
93       End If
94
95       Call PostorderHelper(node.Left)
96       Call PostorderHelper(node.Right)
97       mOutputString = mOutputString & node.Data & " "
98   End Sub
99
100  Public Property Get Output() As Variant
101      Output = mOutputString
102  End Property
```

```
103  ' Class CTreeNode
104  Option Explicit
105  Private mLeft As CTreeNode
106  Private mNodeData As Variant
107  Private mRight As CTreeNode
108
109  Public Property Get Data() As Variant
110      Data = mNodeData
111  End Property
112
113  Public Property Let Data(ByVal vNewValue As Variant)
114      mNodeData = vNewValue
115  End Property
116
117  Public Property Get Left() As Variant
118      Set Left = mLeft
119  End Property
120
121  Public Property Let Left(ByVal vNewValue As Variant)
122      Set mLeft = vNewValue
123  End Property
124
125  Public Property Get Right() As Variant
126      Set Right = mRight
127  End Property
128
129  Public Property Let Right(ByVal vNewValue As Variant)
130      Set mRight = vNewValue
131  End Property
132
133  Public Sub Insert(value As Variant)
134      If value <= mNodeData Then      ' = added to allow duplicates
135          If mLeft Is Nothing Then
136              Set mLeft = New CTreeNode
137              mLeft.Data = value
138          Else
139              Call mLeft.Insert(value)
140          End If
141
142      ElseIf value > mNodeData Then
143          If mRight Is Nothing Then
144              Set mRight = New CTreeNode
145              mRight.Data = value
146          Else
147              Call mRight.Insert(value)
148          End If
149
150      End If
151
152  End Sub
```

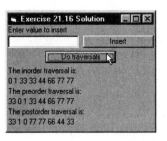

21.17 Write a program based on the program of Fig. 21.15 that inputs a line of text, tokenizes the sentence into separate words (use the **String** processing capabilities of Chapter 8), inserts the words in a binary search tree and prints the inorder, preorder and postorder traversals of the tree.

ANS:

```
1   ' Exercise 21.17 Solution
2   Option Explicit
3   Dim mTree As CTree
4
5   Private Sub Form_Load()
6      Set mTree = New CTree
7   End Sub
8
9   Private Sub txtInput_KeyPress(KeyAscii As Integer)
10     If KeyAscii = vbKeyReturn Then
11        Dim s() As String, j As Integer
12
13        s = Split(txtInput.Text)
14
15        For j = LBound(s) To UBound(s)
16           Call mTree.InsertNode(s(j))
17        Next j
18
19        Call Traversals
20     End If
21  End Sub
22
23  Private Sub Traversals()
24     Call lstIn.Clear
25     Call lstPre.Clear
26     Call lstPost.Clear
27     Call mTree.InorderTraversal
28     Call mTree.PreorderTraversal
29     Call mTree.PostorderTraversal
30  End Sub
31
32  Private Sub Form_Terminate()
33     Set mTree = Nothing
34  End Sub
```

```
37  ' Class CTree
38  Option Explicit
39  Private mRoot As CTreeNode
40
41  ' Insert a new node in the binary search tree.
42  ' If the root node is null, create the root node here.
43  ' Otherwise, call the insert procedure of class TreeNode.
44  Public Sub InsertNode(value As Variant)
45     If mRoot Is Nothing Then
46        Set mRoot = New CTreeNode
47        mRoot.Data = value
48     Else
49        Call mRoot.Insert(value)
50     End If
51  End Sub
```

```
52
53   ' Preorder Traversal
54   Public Sub PreorderTraversal()
55       Call PreorderHelper(mRoot)
56   End Sub
57
58   ' Recursive procedure to perform preorder traversal
59   Private Sub PreorderHelper(node As CTreeNode)
60       If node Is Nothing Then
61          Exit Sub
62       End If
63
64       Call frmForm.lstPre.AddItem(node.Data)
65       Call PreorderHelper(node.Left)
66       Call PreorderHelper(node.Right)
67   End Sub
68
69   ' Inorder Traversal
70   Public Sub InorderTraversal()
71       Call InorderHelper(mRoot)
72   End Sub
73
74   ' Recursive procedure to perform inorder traversal
75   Private Sub InorderHelper(node As CTreeNode)
76       If node Is Nothing Then
77          Exit Sub
78       End If
79
80       Call InorderHelper(node.Left)
81       Call frmForm.lstIn.AddItem(node.Data)
82       Call InorderHelper(node.Right)
83   End Sub
84
85   ' Postorder Traversal
86   Public Sub PostorderTraversal()
87       Call PostorderHelper(mRoot)
88   End Sub
89
90   ' Recursive procedure to perform Postorder traversal
91   Private Sub PostorderHelper(node As CTreeNode)
92       If node Is Nothing Then
93          Exit Sub
94       End If
95
96       Call PostorderHelper(node.Left)
97       Call PostorderHelper(node.Right)
98       Call frmForm.lstPost.AddItem(node.Data)
99   End Sub
```

```
105  ' Class CTreeNode
106  Option Explicit
107  Private mLeft As CTreeNode
108  Private mNodeData As Variant
109  Private mRight As CTreeNode
110
111  Public Property Get Data() As Variant
112      Data = mNodeData
113  End Property
114
115  Public Property Let Data(ByVal vNewValue As Variant)
116      mNodeData = vNewValue
117  End Property
118
119  Public Property Get Left() As Variant
120      Set Left = mLeft
121  End Property
```

```
122
123  Public Property Let Left(ByVal vNewValue As Variant)
124     Set mLeft = vNewValue
125  End Property
126
127  Public Property Get Right() As Variant
128     Set Right = mRight
129  End Property
130
131  Public Property Let Right(ByVal vNewValue As Variant)
132     Set mRight = vNewValue
133  End Property
134
135  Public Sub Insert(value As Variant)
136     If value < mNodeData Then
137        If mLeft Is Nothing Then
138           Set mLeft = New CTreeNode
139           mLeft.Data = value
140        Else
141           Call mLeft.Insert(value)
142        End If
143     ElseIf value > mNodeData Then
144        If mRight Is Nothing Then
145           Set mRight = New CTreeNode
146           mRight.Data = value
147        Else
148           Call mRight.Insert(value)
149        End If
150     End If
151  End Sub
```

21.18 In this chapter we saw that duplicate elimination is straightforward when creating a binary search tree. Describe how you would perform duplicate elimination using only a one-dimensional array. Compare the performance of array-based duplicate elimination with the performance of binary-search-tree-based duplicate elimination.

21.19 [CD] Write procedure **Depth** which receives a binary tree and determines how many levels it has.
ANS:

```
1  ' Exercise 21.19 Solution
2  Option Explicit
3  Dim mTree As CTree
4
5  Private Sub Form_Load()
6     Set mTree = New CTree
7  End Sub
8
9  Private Sub cmdInsert_Click()
10     Call mTree.InsertNode(Val(txtInput.Text))
11     txtInput.Text = ""
12     txtInput.SetFocus      ' Transfer focus to TextBox
13  End Sub
14
15  Private Sub cmdTraversals_Click()
16     Call mTree.InorderTraversal
17     lblInorderResult.Caption = mTree.Output
18     Call mTree.PreorderTraversal
19     lblPreorderResult.Caption = mTree.Output
```

```
20        Call mTree.PostorderTraversal
21        lblPostorderResult.Caption = mTree.Output
22    End Sub
23
24    Private Sub cmdDepth_Click()
25        Call MsgBox("Tree depth is " & mTree.Depth)
26    End Sub
27
28    Private Sub Form_Terminate()
29        Set mTree = Nothing
30    End Sub
```

```
31    ' Class CTree
32    Option Explicit
33    Private mRoot As CTreeNode
34    Private mOutputString As String
35    Private mDepth As Long
36
37    ' Insert a new node in the binary search tree.
38    ' If the root node is null, create the root node here.
39    ' Otherwise, call the insert procedure of class TreeNode.
40    Public Sub InsertNode(value As Variant)
41
42        If mRoot Is Nothing Then
43            Set mRoot = New CTreeNode
44            mRoot.Data = value
45        Else
46            mRoot.Insert (value)
47        End If
48
49    End Sub
50
51    ' Preorder Traversal
52    Public Sub PreorderTraversal()
53        mOutputString = ""
54        Call PreorderHelper(mRoot)
55    End Sub
56
57    ' Recursive procedure to perform preorder traversal
58    Private Sub PreorderHelper(node As CTreeNode)
59
60        If node Is Nothing Then
61            Exit Sub
62        End If
63
64        mOutputString = mOutputString & node.Data & " "
65        Call PreorderHelper(node.Left)
66        Call PreorderHelper(node.Right)
67    End Sub
68
69    ' Inorder Traversal
70    Public Sub InorderTraversal()
71        mOutputString = ""
72        Call InorderHelper(mRoot, 0)
73    End Sub
74
75    ' Recursive procedure to perform inorder traversal
76    Private Sub InorderHelper(node As CTreeNode, depthCounter As Long)
77        If node Is Nothing Then
78
79            If depthCounter > mDepth Then
80                mDepth = depthCounter
81            End If
82
83            Exit Sub
84        End If
```

```
85
86         Call InorderHelper(node.Left, depthCounter + 1)
87         mOutputString = mOutputString & node.Data & " "
88         Call InorderHelper(node.Right, depthCounter + 1)
89    End Sub
90
91    ' Postorder Traversal
92    Public Sub PostorderTraversal()
93         mOutputString = ""
94         Call PostorderHelper(mRoot)
95    End Sub
96
97    ' Recursive procedure to perform Postorder traversal
98    Private Sub PostorderHelper(node As CTreeNode)
99         If node Is Nothing Then
100            Exit Sub
101        End If
102
103        Call PostorderHelper(node.Left)
104        Call PostorderHelper(node.Right)
105        mOutputString = mOutputString & node.Data & " "
106   End Sub
107
108   Public Property Get Output() As Variant
109        Output = mOutputString
110   End Property
111
112   Public Function Depth() As Long
113        ' Depth level is calculated in InOrderHelper
114        Call InorderTraversal
115        Depth = mDepth
116   End Function
```

```
119   ' Class CTreeNode
120   Option Explicit
121   Private mLeft As CTreeNode
122   Private mNodeData As Variant
123   Private mRight As CTreeNode
124
125   Public Property Get Data() As Variant
126        Data = mNodeData
127   End Property
128
129   Public Property Let Data(ByVal vNewValue As Variant)
130        mNodeData = vNewValue
131   End Property
132
133   Public Property Get Left() As Variant
134        Set Left = mLeft
135   End Property
136
137   Public Property Let Left(ByVal vNewValue As Variant)
138        Set mLeft = vNewValue
139   End Property
140
141   Public Property Get Right() As Variant
142        Set Right = mRight
143   End Property
144
145   Public Property Let Right(ByVal vNewValue As Variant)
146        Set mRight = vNewValue
147   End Property
148
149   Public Sub Insert(value As Variant)
150        If value <= mNodeData Then
151            If mLeft Is Nothing Then
```

```
152            Set mLeft = New CTreeNode
153            mLeft.Data = value
154         Else
155            Call mLeft.Insert(value)
156         End If
157      ElseIf value > mNodeData Then
158         If mRight Is Nothing Then
159            Set mRight = New CTreeNode
160            mRight.Data = value
161         Else
162            Call mRight.Insert(value)
163         End If
164      End If
165 End Sub
```

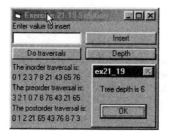

21.20   (*Recursively print a list backwards*) Write a procedure **PrintListBackwards**, which recursively outputs the items in a linked list object in reverse order. Write a test program that creates a sorted list of **Integer**s and prints the list in reverse order.

ANS:

```
1  ' Exercise 21.20 Solution
2  Option Explicit
3
4  Private Sub Form_Load()
5     Dim link1 As New CList, j As Integer
6     Dim it As New CListIterator, total As Integer
7     Dim k As Variant
8
9     Call Randomize
10
11    For j = 1 To 25
12       Call link1.Insert(Int(Rnd() * 101))
13    Next j
14
15    Set it = link1.Iterator
16
17    While it.HasMoreItems
18       k = it.NextItem
19       total = total + k
20       Call lstBox.AddItem(k)
21    Wend
22
23    Call PrintListBackwards(it.StartNode)
24 End Sub
25
26 Public Sub PrintListBackwards(node As CListNode)
27    If node Is Nothing Then
28       Exit Sub
29    Else
30       Call PrintListBackwards(node.NextNode)
31       Call lstOut.AddItem(node.Data)
32    End If
33 End Sub
```

```
36 ' Class CList
37 Option Explicit
38 Private mFirstNode As CListNode  ' refers to first node in list
39
```

```
40    ' Determine if the list is empty
41    Public Function IsEmpty() As Boolean
42        IsEmpty = IIf(mFirstNode Is Nothing, True, False)
43    End Function
44
45    Public Property Get Iterator() As Variant
46        Dim iter As CListIterator
47
48        Set iter = New CListIterator
49        iter.StartNode = mFirstNode
50        Set Iterator = iter
51    End Property
52
53    ' Insert items in alphabetical order
54    Public Sub Insert(insertItem As Variant)
55        Dim currNode As CListNode, newNode As CListNode
56        Dim prevNode As CListNode
57
58        If IsEmpty() Then
59            Set mFirstNode = New CListNode
60            mFirstNode.Data = insertItem
61            Exit Sub
62        Else
63            Set currNode = mFirstNode
64            Set newNode = New CListNode
65            newNode.Data = insertItem
66
67            Do While (Not (currNode Is Nothing))
68
69                If (insertItem < currNode.Data) Then
70                    Exit Do
71                End If
72
73                Set prevNode = currNode
74                Set currNode = currNode.NextNode
75            Loop
76
77            If (prevNode Is Nothing) Then
78                newNode.NextNode = mFirstNode
79                Set mFirstNode = newNode
80            Else
81                prevNode.NextNode = newNode
82                newNode.NextNode = currNode
83            End If
84
85        End If
86
87    End Sub
```

```
88    ' Class CListNode
89    Option Explicit
90    Private mNodeData As Variant
91    Private mNextNode As CListNode
92
93    Public Property Get Data() As Variant
94        Data = mNodeData
95    End Property
96
97    Public Property Let Data(ByVal vNewValue As Variant)
98        mNodeData = vNewValue
99    End Property
100
101   Public Property Get NextNode() As CListNode
102       Set NextNode = mNextNode
103   End Property
104
```

```
105   Public Property Let NextNode(ByVal vNewValue As Variant)
106      Set mNextNode = vNewValue
107   End Property
```

```
108   ' Class CListIterator
109   Option Explicit
110   Private mBookmark As CListNode
111   Private mFirstNode As CListNode
112
113   Public Property Let StartNode(ByVal vNewValue As Variant)
114      Set mFirstNode = vNewValue
115      Set mBookmark = mFirstNode
116   End Property
117
118   Public Property Get StartNode() As CListNode
119      Set StartNode = mFirstNode
120   End Property
121
122   ' Return next item in list
123   Public Function NextItem() As Variant
124      Dim tempData As Variant
125
126      If mBookmark Is Nothing Then
127         NextItem = Null
128      Else
129         tempData = mBookmark.Data
130         Set mBookmark = mBookmark.NextNode
131         NextItem = tempData
132      End If
133
134   End Function
135
136   Public Function HasMoreItems() As Boolean
137      HasMoreItems = IIf(Not mBookmark Is Nothing, True, False)
138   End Function
139
140   ' Reset mBookmark to beginning of list
141   Public Sub ResetmBookmark()
142      mBookmark = mFirstNode
143   End Sub
```

21.21 (*Recursively search a list*) Write a procedure **SearchList**, which recursively searches a linked list object for a specified value. Procedure **SearchList** should return the value if it is found; otherwise, **Null** should be returned. Use your procedure in a test program that creates a list of **Integer**s. The program should prompt the user for a value to locate in the list.

   ANS:

```
1    ' Exercise 21.21 Solution
2    Option Explicit
3    Dim mLink As CList
4
5    Private Sub Form_Load()
6       Dim j As Integer, it As New CListIterator
7
8       Set mLink = New CList
9
10      For j = 1 To 20
11         Call mLink.InsertAtBack(Int(Rnd() * 50))
12      Next j
```

```
13
14       Set it = mLink.Iterator
15
16       While it.HasMoreItems
17          Call lstBox.AddItem(it.NextItem)
18       Wend
19    End Sub
20
21    Public Function SearchList(node As CListNode, _
22                               ByVal key As Integer) As Variant
23
24       If (node Is Nothing) Then
25          SearchList = Null
26          Exit Function
27       ElseIf (node.Data = key) Then
28          SearchList = node.Data
29          Exit Function
30       Else
31          SearchList = SearchList(node.NextNode, key)
32       End If
33
34    End Function
35
36    Private Sub txtInput_KeyPress(KeyAscii As Integer)
37       Dim it As New CListIterator, result As Variant
38
39       Set it = mLink.Iterator
40
41       If KeyAscii = vbKeyReturn Then
42          result = SearchList(it.StartNode, txtInput.Text)
43
44          If VarType(result) = vbNull Then
45             Call MsgBox("Value was not found.")
46          Else
47             Call MsgBox("Value was found.")
48          End If
49       End If
50    End Sub
51
52    Private Sub Form_Terminate()
53       Set mLink = Nothing
54    End Sub
```

```
58    ' Class CList
59    Option Explicit
60    Private mFirstNode As CListNode   ' refers to first node in list
61    Private mLastNode As CListNode    ' refers to last node in list
62
63    ' determine if the list is empty
64    Public Function IsEmpty() As Boolean
65       IsEmpty = IIf(mFirstNode Is Nothing, True, False)
66    End Function
67
68    ' insert an element at the beginning of the list
69    Public Sub InsertAtFront(insertItem As Variant)
70       Dim tempNode As CListNode
71
72       If IsEmpty() Then
73          Set mFirstNode = New CListNode
74          Set mLastNode = mFirstNode
75       Else
76          Set tempNode = mFirstNode
77          Set mFirstNode = New CListNode
78          mFirstNode.NextNode = tempNode
79       End If
80
```

```
81        mFirstNode.Data = insertItem
82    End Sub
83
84    ' insert an element at the end of the list
85    Public Sub InsertAtBack(insertItem As Variant)
86        Dim tempNode As CListNode
87
88        If IsEmpty() Then
89            Set mLastNode = New CListNode
90            Set mFirstNode = mLastNode
91        Else
92            Set tempNode = mLastNode
93            Set mLastNode = New CListNode
94            tempNode.NextNode = mLastNode
95        End If
96
97        mLastNode.Data = insertItem
98    End Sub
99
100   ' remove an element from the beginning of the list
101   Public Function RemoveFromFront()
102       Dim removeItem As Variant
103
104       If IsEmpty() Then
105           Call MsgBox("List is empty")
106           RemoveFromFront = Null
107           Exit Function
108       End If
109
110       removeItem = mFirstNode.Data
111
112       If mFirstNode Is mLastNode Then
113           Set mFirstNode = Nothing
114           Set mLastNode = Nothing
115       Else
116           Set mFirstNode = mFirstNode.NextNode
117       End If
118
119       RemoveFromFront = removeItem
120   End Function
121
122   ' remove an element from the end of the list
123   Public Function RemoveFromBack()
124       Dim removeItem As Variant
125       Dim current As CListNode
126
127       If IsEmpty() Then
128           Call MsgBox("List is empty")
129           RemoveFromBack = Null
130           Exit Function
131       End If
132
133       removeItem = mLastNode.Data
134
135       If mFirstNode Is mLastNode Then
136           Set mFirstNode = Nothing
137           Set mLastNode = Nothing
138       Else
139           Set current = mFirstNode
140
141           While Not current.NextNode Is mLastNode
142               Set current = current.NextNode
143           Wend
144
145           Set mLastNode = current
146           current.NextNode = Nothing
147       End If
```

```
148
149      RemoveFromBack = removeItem
150  End Function
151
152  Public Property Get Iterator() As Variant
153      Dim iter As CListIterator
154
155      Set iter = New CListIterator
156      iter.StartNode = mFirstNode
157      Set Iterator = iter
158  End Property
```

```
159  ' Class CListNode
160  Option Explicit
161  Private mNodeData As Variant
162  Private mNextNode As CListNode
163
164  Public Property Get Data() As Variant
165      Data = mNodeData
166  End Property
167
168  Public Property Let Data(ByVal vNewValue As Variant)
169      mNodeData = vNewValue
170  End Property
171
172  Public Property Get NextNode() As CListNode
173      Set NextNode = mNextNode
174  End Property
175
176  Public Property Let NextNode(ByVal vNewValue As Variant)
177      Set mNextNode = vNewValue
178  End Property
```

```
179  ' Class CListIterator
180  Option Explicit
181  Private mBookmark As CListNode
182  Private mFirstNode As CListNode
183
184  Public Property Let StartNode(ByVal vNewValue As Variant)
185      Set mFirstNode = vNewValue
186      Set mBookmark = mFirstNode
187  End Property
188
189  Public Property Get StartNode() As CListNode
190      Set StartNode = mFirstNode
191  End Property
192
193  ' Return next item in list
194  Public Function NextItem()
195      Dim tempData As Variant
196
197      If mBookmark Is Nothing Then
198         NextItem = Null
199      Else
200         tempData = mBookmark.Data
201         Set mBookmark = mBookmark.NextNode
202         NextItem = tempData
203      End If
204
205  End Function
206
207  Public Function HasMoreItems() As Boolean
208      HasMoreItems = IIf(Not mBookmark Is Nothing, True, False)
209  End Function
210
```

```
211  ' Reset mBookmark to beginning of list
212  Public Sub ResetmBookmark()
213      mBookmark = mFirstNode
214  End Sub
```

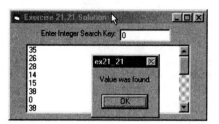

21.22 (*Binary tree delete*) In this exercise we discuss deleting items from binary search trees. The deletion algorithm is not as straightforward as the insertion algorithm. There are three cases that are encountered when deleting an item—the item is contained in a leaf node (i.e., it has no children), the item is contained in a node that has one child, or the item is contained in a node that has two children.

If the item to be deleted is contained in a leaf node, the node is deleted and the reference in the parent node is set to **Nothing**.

If the item to be deleted is contained in a node with one child, the reference in the parent node is set to reference the child node and the node containing the data item is deleted. This causes the child node to take the place of the deleted node in the tree.

The last case is the most difficult. When a node with two children is deleted, another node in the tree must take its place. However, the reference in the parent node cannot simply be assigned to reference one of the children of the node to be deleted. In most cases, the resulting binary search tree would not adhere to the following characteristic of binary search trees (with no duplicate values): *The values in any left subtree are less than the value in the parent node, and the values in any right subtree are greater than the value in the parent node.*

Which node is used as a *replacement node* to maintain this characteristic? Either the node containing the largest value in the tree less than the value in the node being deleted, or the node containing the smallest value in the tree greater than the value in the node being deleted. Let us consider the node with the smaller value. In a binary search tree, the largest value less than a parent's value is located in the left subtree of the parent node and is guaranteed to be contained in the rightmost node of the subtree. This node is located by walking down the left subtree to the right until the reference to the right child of the current node is **Nothing**. We are now referencing the replacement node, which is either a leaf node or a node with one child to its left. If the replacement node is a leaf node, the steps to perform the deletion are as follows:
   a) Store the reference to the node to be deleted in a temporary reference variable.
   b) Set the reference in the parent of the node being deleted to reference the replacement node.
   c) Set the reference in the parent of the replacement node to **Nothing**.
   d) Set the reference to the right subtree in the replacement node to reference the right subtree of the node to be deleted.

The deletion steps for a replacement node with a left child are similar to those for a replacement node with no children, but the algorithm also must move the child into the replacement node's position in the tree. If the replacement node is a node with a left child, the steps to perform the deletion are as follows:
   a) Store the reference to the node to be deleted in a temporary reference variable.
   b) Set the reference in the parent of the node being deleted to reference the replacement node.
   c) Set the reference in the parent of the replacement node reference to the left child of the replacement node.
   d) Set the reference to the right subtree in the replacement node reference to the right subtree of the node to be deleted.

Write procedure **DeleteNode**, which takes as its argument the value to be deleted. Procedure **DeleteNode** should locate in the tree the node containing the value to be deleted and use the algorithms discussed here to delete the node. If the value is not found in the tree, the procedure should print a message that indicates whether or not the value is deleted. Modify the program of Fig. 21.15 to use this procedure. After deleting an item, call the procedures **InorderTraversal**, **PreorderTraversal** and **PostorderTraversal** to confirm that the delete operation was performed correctly.

21.23 (*Binary tree search*) Write procedure **BinaryTreeSearch**, which attempts to locate a specified value in a binary search tree object. The procedure should take as an argument a search key to be located. If the node containing the search key is found, the procedure should return that node's data; otherwise, the procedure should return **Null**.
       ANS:

```
1  ' Exercise 21.23 Solution
2  Option Explicit
3  Dim mTree As CTree
4
5  Private Sub Form_Load()
6      Set mTree = New CTree
7  End Sub
```

```
 8
 9  Private Sub cmdInsert_Click()
10     Call mTree.InsertNode(Val(txtInput.Text))
11     txtInput.Text = ""
12     txtInput.SetFocus       ' Transfer focus to TextBox
13  End Sub
14
15  Private Sub cmdSearch_Click()
16     Dim v As String
17
18     v = txtInput.Text
19
20     If IsNull(mTree.BinaryTreeSearch(v)) Then
21        Call MsgBox("Value not found.")
22     Else
23        Call MsgBox("Value found!")
24     End If
25
26  End Sub
27
28  Private Sub cmdTraversals_Click()
29     Call mTree.InorderTraversal
30     lblInorderResult.Caption = mTree.Output
31     Call mTree.PreorderTraversal
32     lblPreorderResult.Caption = mTree.Output
33     Call mTree.PostorderTraversal
34     lblPostorderResult.Caption = mTree.Output
35  End Sub
36
37  Private Sub Form_Terminate()
38     Set mTree = Nothing
39  End Sub
```

```
40  ' Class CTree
41  Option Explicit
42  Private mRoot As CTreeNode
43  Private mOutputString As String
44
45  ' Insert a new node in the binary search tree.
46  ' If the root node is null, create the root node here.
47  ' Otherwise, call the insert procedure of class TreeNode.
48  Public Sub InsertNode(value As Variant)
49
50     If mRoot Is Nothing Then
51        Set mRoot = New CTreeNode
52        mRoot.Data = value
53     Else
54        Call mRoot.Insert(value)
55     End If
56
57  End Sub
58
59  ' Preorder Traversal
60  Public Sub PreorderTraversal()
61     mOutputString = ""
62     Call PreorderHelper(mRoot)
63  End Sub
64
65  ' Recursive procedure to perform preorder traversal
66  Private Sub PreorderHelper(node As CTreeNode)
67
68     If node Is Nothing Then
69        Exit Sub
70     End If
71
72     mOutputString = mOutputString & node.Data & " "
```

```
73         Call PreorderHelper(node.Left)
74         Call PreorderHelper(node.Right)
75  End Sub
76
77  ' Inorder Traversal
78  Public Sub InorderTraversal()
79      mOutputString = ""
80      Call InorderHelper(mRoot)
81  End Sub
82
83  ' Recursive procedure to perform inorder traversal
84  Private Sub InorderHelper(node As CTreeNode)
85
86      If node Is Nothing Then
87         Exit Sub
88      End If
89
90      Call InorderHelper(node.Left)
91      mOutputString = mOutputString & node.Data & " "
92      Call InorderHelper(node.Right)
93  End Sub
94
95  ' Postorder Traversal
96  Public Sub PostorderTraversal()
97      mOutputString = ""
98      Call PostorderHelper(mRoot)
99  End Sub
100
101 ' Recursive procedure to perform Postorder traversal
102 Private Sub PostorderHelper(node As CTreeNode)
103
104     If node Is Nothing Then
105        Exit Sub
106     End If
107
108     Call PostorderHelper(node.Left)
109     Call PostorderHelper(node.Right)
110     mOutputString = mOutputString & node.Data & " "
111 End Sub
112
113 Public Property Get Output() As Variant
114     Output = mOutputString
115 End Property
116
117 Public Function BinaryTreeSearch(ByVal key As Variant) As Variant
118     BinaryTreeSearch = InorderSearchTraversal(key)
119 End Function
120
121 ' Search the tree using an inorder traversal
122 Public Function InorderSearchTraversal(ByVal k As Variant) _
123                               As Variant
124     InorderSearchTraversal = InorderSearchHelper(mRoot, k)
125 End Function
126
127 Private Function InorderSearchHelper(node As CTreeNode, _
128                               ByVal k As Variant) As Variant
129     If node Is Nothing Then
130        InorderSearchHelper = Null
131        Exit Function
132     ElseIf CInt(node.Data) = CInt(k) Then
133        InorderSearchHelper = node.Data
134        Exit Function
135     End If
136
137     InorderSearchHelper = InorderSearchHelper(node.Left, k)
138     InorderSearchHelper = InorderSearchHelper(node.Right, k)
139 End Function
```

```
140  ' Class CTreeNode
141  Option Explicit
142  Private mLeft As CTreeNode
143  Private mNodeData As Variant
144  Private mRight As CTreeNode
145
146  Public Property Get Data() As Variant
147     Data = mNodeData
148  End Property
149
150  Public Property Let Data(ByVal vNewValue As Variant)
151     mNodeData = vNewValue
152  End Property
153
154  Public Property Get Left() As Variant
155     Set Left = mLeft
156  End Property
157
158  Public Property Let Left(ByVal vNewValue As Variant)
159     Set mLeft = vNewValue
160  End Property
161
162  Public Property Get Right() As Variant
163     Set Right = mRight
164  End Property
165
166  Public Property Let Right(ByVal vNewValue As Variant)
167     Set mRight = vNewValue
168  End Property
169
170  Public Sub Insert(value As Variant)
171     If value <= mNodeData Then
172        If mLeft Is Nothing Then
173           Set mLeft = New CTreeNode
174           mLeft.Data = value
175        Else
176           Call mLeft.Insert(value)
177        End If
178     ElseIf value > mNodeData Then
179        If mRight Is Nothing Then
180           Set mRight = New CTreeNode
181           mRight.Data = value
182        Else
183           Call mRight.Insert(value)
184        End If
185     End If
186  End Sub
```

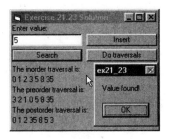

21.24 (*Level-order binary tree traversal*) The program of Fig. 21.15 illustrated three recursive procedures of traversing a binary tree—inorder, preorder and postorder traversals. This exercise presents the *level-order traversal* of a binary tree, in which the node values are printed level-by-level starting at the root node level. The nodes on each level are printed from left to right. The level-order traversal is not a recursive algorithm. It uses a queue object to control the output of the nodes. The algorithm is as follows:

    a) Insert the root node in the queue.

b) While there are nodes left in the queue,
        Get the next node in the queue;
        Print the node's value.
        If the reference to the left child of the node is not **Nothing**,
            Insert the left child node in the queue.
        If the reference to the right child of the node is not **Nothing**,
            Insert the right child node in the queue.

Write procedure **LevelOrder** to perform a level-order traversal of a **binary tree object. Modify the program of Fig 21.15** to use this procedure. (Note: You will also need to use the queue-processing **procedures of Fig. 21.11 in this program.)**
ANS:

```
1    ' Exercise 21.24 Solution
2    Option Explicit
3    Dim mTree As CTree
4
5    Private Sub Form_Load()
6        Set mTree = New CTree
7    End Sub
8
9    Private Sub cmdInsert_Click()
10       Call mTree.InsertNode(Val(txtInput.Text))
11       txtInput.Text = ""
12       Call txtInput.SetFocus
13   End Sub
14
15   Private Sub cmdTraversals_Click()
16       Call mTree.InorderTraversal
17       lblInorderResult.Caption = mTree.Output
18       Call mTree.PreorderTraversal
19       lblPreorderResult.Caption = mTree.Output
20       Call mTree.PostorderTraversal
21       lblPostorderResult.Caption = mTree.Output
22       Call mTree.LevelOrder
23       lblLevelOrderResult.Caption = mTree.Output
24   End Sub
25
26   Private Sub Form_Terminate()
27       Set mTree = Nothing
28   End Sub
```

```
29   ' Class CQueue
30   Option Explicit
31   Private mList As CList
32
33   Private Sub Class_Initialize()
34       Set mList = New CList
35   End Sub
36
37   Public Sub Enqueue(value As Variant)
38       Call mList.InsertAtBack(value)
39   End Sub
40
41   Public Function Dequeue() As Variant
42       Set Dequeue = mList.RemoveFromFront()
43   End Function
44
45   Public Function IsQueueEmpty() As Boolean
46       IsQueueEmpty = mList.IsEmpty()
47   End Function
48
49   Public Property Get Iterator() As CListIterator
50       Set Iterator = mList.Iterator
51   End Property
52
```

```
53    Private Sub Class_Terminate()
54        Set mList = Nothing
55    End Sub
```

```
56    ' Class CTree
57    Option Explicit
58    Private mRoot As CTreeNode
59    Private mOutputString As String
60
61    ' Insert a new node in the binary search tree.
62    ' If the root node is null, create the root node here.
63    ' Otherwise, call the insert procedure of class TreeNode.
64    Public Sub InsertNode(value As Variant)
65        If mRoot Is Nothing Then
66            Set mRoot = New CTreeNode
67            mRoot.Data = value
68        Else
69            Call mRoot.Insert(value)
70        End If
71    End Sub
72
73    ' Preorder Traversal
74    Public Sub PreorderTraversal()
75        mOutputString = ""
76        Call PreorderHelper(mRoot)
77    End Sub
78
79    ' Recursive procedure to perform preorder traversal
80    Private Sub PreorderHelper(node As CTreeNode)
81        If node Is Nothing Then
82            Exit Sub
83        End If
84
85        mOutputString = mOutputString & node.Data & " "
86        Call PreorderHelper(node.Left)
87        Call PreorderHelper(node.Right)
88    End Sub
89
90    ' Inorder Traversal
91    Public Sub InorderTraversal()
92        mOutputString = ""
93        Call InorderHelper(mRoot)
94    End Sub
95
96    ' Recursive procedure to perform inorder traversal
97    Private Sub InorderHelper(node As CTreeNode)
98        If node Is Nothing Then
99            Exit Sub
100       End If
101
102       Call InorderHelper(node.Left)
103       mOutputString = mOutputString & node.Data & " "
104       Call InorderHelper(node.Right)
105   End Sub
106
107   ' Postorder Traversal
108   Public Sub PostorderTraversal()
109       mOutputString = ""
110       Call PostorderHelper(mRoot)
111   End Sub
112
113   ' Recursive procedure to perform Postorder traversal
114   Private Sub PostorderHelper(node As CTreeNode)
115       If node Is Nothing Then
116           Exit Sub
117       End If
```

```
118
119       Call PostorderHelper(node.Left)
120       Call PostorderHelper(node.Right)
121       mOutputString = mOutputString & node.Data & " "
122    End Sub
123
124    Public Property Get Output() As Variant
125       Output = mOutputString
126    End Property
127
128    ' Levelorder Traversal
129    Public Sub LevelOrder()
130       Dim queue As New CQueue, node As CTreeNode
131
132       mOutputString = ""
133       Set node = mRoot
134
135       If Not (node Is Nothing) Then
136          Call queue.Enqueue(node)
137       End If
138
139       While queue.IsQueueEmpty = False
140          Set node = queue.Dequeue
141          mOutputString = mOutputString & node.Data & " "
142
143          If Not (node.Left Is Nothing) Then
144             Call queue.Enqueue(node.Left)
145          End If
146
147          If Not (node.Right Is Nothing) Then
148             Call queue.Enqueue(node.Right)
149          End If
150       Wend
151    End Sub
152
153    Private Sub Class_Terminate()
154       Set mRoot = Nothing
155    End Sub
```

```
163    ' Class CTreeNode
164    Option Explicit
165    Private mLeft As CTreeNode
166    Private mNodeData As Variant
167    Private mRight As CTreeNode
168
169    Public Property Get Data() As Variant
170       Data = mNodeData
171    End Property
172
173    Public Property Let Data(ByVal vNewValue As Variant)
174       mNodeData = vNewValue
175    End Property
176
177    Public Property Get Left() As Variant
178       Set Left = mLeft
179    End Property
180
181    Public Property Let Left(ByVal vNewValue As Variant)
182       Set mLeft = vNewValue
183    End Property
184
185    Public Property Get Right() As Variant
186       Set Right = mRight
187    End Property
188
```

```vb
189  Public Property Let Right(ByVal vNewValue As Variant)
190      Set mRight = vNewValue
191  End Property
192
193  Public Sub Insert(value As Variant)
194      If value < mNodeData Then
195          If mLeft Is Nothing Then
196              Set mLeft = New CTreeNode
197              mLeft.Data = value
198          Else
199              Call mLeft.Insert(value)
200          End If
201      ElseIf value > mNodeData Then
202          If mRight Is Nothing Then
203              Set mRight = New CTreeNode
204              mRight.Data = value
205          Else
206              Call mRight.Insert(value)
207          End If
208      End If
209  End Sub
```

```vb
216  ' Class CList
217  Option Explicit
218  Private mFirstNode As CListNode  ' refers to first node in list
219  Private mLastNode As CListNode   ' refers to last node in list
220
221  ' determine if the list is empty
222  Public Function IsEmpty() As Boolean
223      IsEmpty = IIf(mFirstNode Is Nothing, True, False)
224  End Function
225
226  ' insert an element at the beginning of the list
227  Public Sub InsertAtFront(insertItem As Variant)
228      Dim tempNode As CListNode
229
230      If IsEmpty() Then
231          Set mFirstNode = New CListNode
232          Set mLastNode = mFirstNode
233      Else
234          Set tempNode = mFirstNode
235          Set mFirstNode = New CListNode
236          mFirstNode.NextNode = tempNode
237      End If
238
239      Set mFirstNode.Data = insertItem
240  End Sub
241
242  ' insert an element at the end of the list
243  Public Sub InsertAtBack(insertItem As Variant)
244      Dim tempNode As CListNode
245
246      If IsEmpty() Then
247          Set mLastNode = New CListNode
248          Set mFirstNode = mLastNode
249      Else
250          Set tempNode = mLastNode
251          Set mLastNode = New CListNode
252          tempNode.NextNode = mLastNode
253      End If
254
255      mLastNode.Data = insertItem
256  End Sub
257
```

```
258  ' remove an element from the beginning of the list
259  Public Function RemoveFromFront() As Variant
260      Dim removeItem As Variant
261
262      If IsEmpty() Then
263          Call MsgBox("List is empty")
264          RemoveFromFront = Null
265          Exit Function
266      End If
267
268      Set removeItem = mFirstNode.Data
269
270      If mFirstNode Is mLastNode Then
271          Set mFirstNode = Nothing
272          Set mLastNode = Nothing
273      Else
274          Set mFirstNode = mFirstNode.NextNode
275      End If
276
277      Set RemoveFromFront = removeItem
278  End Function
279
280  ' remove an element from the end of the list
281  Public Function RemoveFromBack() As Variant
282      Dim removeItem As Variant
283      Dim current As CListNode
284
285      If IsEmpty() Then
286          Call MsgBox("List is empty")
287          RemoveFromBack = Null
288          Exit Function
289      End If
290
291      removeItem = mLastNode.Data
292
293      If mFirstNode Is mLastNode Then
294          Set mFirstNode = Nothing
295          Set mLastNode = Nothing
296      Else
297          Set current = mFirstNode
298
299          While Not current.NextNode Is mLastNode
300              Set current = current.NextNode
301          Wend
302
303          Set mLastNode = current
304          current.NextNode = Nothing
305      End If
306
307      RemoveFromBack = removeItem
308  End Function
309
310  Public Property Get Iterator() As Variant
311      Dim iter As CListIterator
312
313      Set iter = New CListIterator
314      iter.StartNode = mFirstNode
315      Set Iterator = iter
316  End Property
```

```
317  ' Class CListNode
318  Option Explicit
319  Private mNodeData As Variant
320  Private mNextNode As CListNode
321
```

```vb
322  Public Property Get Data() As Variant
323      Set Data = mNodeData
324  End Property
325
326  Public Property Let Data(ByVal vNewValue As Variant)
327
328      If IsObject(vNewValue) Then
329          Set mNodeData = vNewValue
330      Else
331          mNodeData = vNewValue
332      End If
333
334  End Property
335
336  Public Property Get NextNode() As CListNode
337      Set NextNode = mNextNode
338  End Property
339
340  Public Property Let NextNode(ByVal vNewValue As Variant)
341      Set mNextNode = vNewValue
342  End Property
```

```vb
343  ' Class CListIterator
344  Option Explicit
345  Private mBookmark As CListNode
346  Private mFirstNode As CListNode
347
348  Public Property Let StartNode(ByVal vNewValue As Variant)
349      Set mFirstNode = vNewValue
350      Set mBookmark = mFirstNode
351  End Property
352
353  ' return next item in list
354  Public Function NextItem() As Variant
355      Dim tempData As Variant
356
357      If mBookmark Is Nothing Then
358          NextItem = Null
359      Else
360          tempData = mBookmark.Data
361          Set mBookmark = mBookmark.NextNode
362          NextItem = tempData
363      End If
364
365  End Function
366
367  Public Function HasMoreItems() As Boolean
368      HasMoreItems = IIf(Not mBookmark Is Nothing, True, False)
369  End Function
370
371  ' reset mBookmark to beginning of list
372  Public Sub ResetmBookmark()
373      mBookmark = mFirstNode
374  End Sub
```

21.25 (*Printing trees*) Write a recursive procedure **OutputTree** to display a binary tree object on the screen. The procedure should output the tree row-by-row with the top of the tree at the left of the screen and the bottom of the tree toward the right of the screen. Each row is output vertically. For example, the binary tree illustrated in Fig. 21.19 is output as follows:

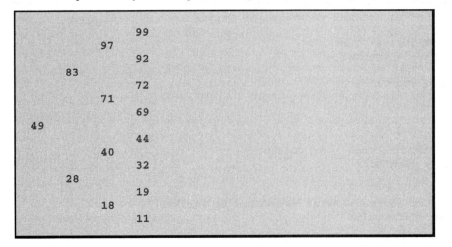

Note that the rightmost leaf node appears at the top of the output in the rightmost column, and the root node appears at the left of the output. Each column of output starts five spaces to the right of the preceding column. Procedure **OutputTree** should receive an argument **totalSpaces**, representing the number of spaces preceding the value to be output (this variable should start at zero so that the root node is output at the left of the screen). The procedure uses a modified inorder traversal to output the tree—it starts at the rightmost node in the tree and works back to the left. The algorithm is as follows:

> While the reference to the current node is not **Nothing**,
>> Recursively call **OutputTree** with the right subtree of the current node and
>>> **totalSpaces** + 5.
>> Use a **For** structure to count from 1 to **totalSpaces** and output spaces.
>> Output the value in the current node.
>> Set the reference to the current node to refer to the left subtree of the current node.
>> Increment **totalSpaces** by 5.

21.26 (*Insert/Delete Anywhere in a Linked List*) Our linked list class allowed insertions and deletions at only the front and the back of the linked list. These capabilities were convenient for us when we used composition to produce a stack class and a queue class with a minimal amount of code simply by reusing the list class. Linked lists are normally more general that those we provided. Modify the linked list class we developed in this chapter to handle insertions and deletions anywhere in the list.

21.27 (*List and Queues without Tail References*) Our implementation of a linked list (Fig. 21.3) used both a **mFirstNode** and a **mLastNode**. The **mLastNode** was useful for the **InsertAtBack** and **RemoveFromBack** procedures of the **CList** class. The **InsertAtBack** procedure corresponds to the **Enqueue** procedure of the **CQueue** class.

Rewrite the **CList** class so that it does not use a **mLastNode**. Thus, any operations on the tail of a list must begin searching the list from the front. Does this affect our implementation of the **CQueue** class (Fig. 21.11)?

21.28 (*Performance of Binary Tree Sorting and Searching*) One problem with the binary tree sort is that the order in which the data are inserted affects the shape of the tree—for the same collection of data, different orderings can yield binary trees of dramatically different shapes. The performance of the binary tree sorting and searching algorithms is sensitive to the shape of the binary tree. What shape would a binary tree have if its data were inserted in increasing order? in decreasing order? What shape should the tree have to achieve maximal searching performance?

21.29 (*Indexed Lists*) As presented in the text, linked lists must be searched sequentially. For large lists, this can result in poor performance. A common technique for improving list searching performance is to create and maintain an index to the list. An index is a set of references to key places in the list. For example, an application that searches a large list of names could improve performance by creating an index with 26 entries—one for each letter of the alphabet. A search operation for a last name beginning with 'Y' would then first search the index to determine where the 'Y' entries begin and "jump into" the list at that point and search linearly until the desired name is found. This would be much faster than searching the linked list from the beginning. Use the **CList** class of Fig. 21.3 as the basis of an **CIndexedList** class.

Write a program that demonstrates the operation of indexed lists. Be sure to include procedures InsertInIndexedList, SearchIndexedList and DeleteFromIndexedList.

Appendix

Visual Basic Multimedia Cyber Classroom: Solutions Provided on CD

This appendix contains the complete list of solutions provided on the *Visual Basic Multimedia Cyber Classroom* CD-ROM. This will help instructors avoid the exercises for which students have solutions if they purchase the Cyber Classroom product. Note that key exercises like the Knight's Tour (Chapter 7) and the Simpletron Simulator (Chapter 10) are not provided on the CD.

Chapter 1:	1.6, 1.7
Chapter 2:	2.4, 2.6a, 2.6c, 2.8
Chapter 3:	3.10, 3.11, 3.16, 3.19
Chapter 4:	4.8, 4.10, 4.16, 4.20, 4.22, 4.24, 4.25, 4.31
Chapter 5:	5.7, 5.11, 5.18, 5.20
Chapter 6:	6.6, 6.10, 6.12, 6.16, 6.26, 6.27, 6.31, 6.34, 6.40, 6.42
Chapter 7:	7.6, 7.13, 7.16, 7.24, 7.26, 7.30, 7.32
Chapter 8:	8.6, 8.7, 8.9, 8.16, 8.17, 8.21, 8.27
Chapter 9:	9.4, 9.6, 9.8, 9.12
Chapter 10:	10.3, 10.4, 10.7, 10.12
Chapter 11:	11.5, 11.12, 11.18, 11.19
Chapter 12:	12.5, 12.10, 12.15
Chapter 13:	13.3, 13.5, 13.7
Chapter 14:	14.4, 14.12
Chapter 15:	15.5, 15.12, 15.14
Chapter 16:	16.5, 16.7, 16.13, 16.15, 16.21
Chapter 17:	17.4, 17.8, 17.17
Chapter 18:	18.3
Chapter 19:	19.3, 19.8, 19.14, 19.29
Chapter 20:	20.5, 20.8
Chapter 21:	21.6, 21.10, 21.16, 21.19
Appendix D:	D.23, D.27, D.30

Appendix D Solutions
Number Systems

D.20 Some people argue that many of our calculations would be easier in the base **12** number system because **12** is divisible by so many more numbers than **10** (for base **10**). What is the lowest digit in base **12**? What might the highest symbol for the digit in base **12** be? What are the positional values of the rightmost four positions of any number in the base **12** number system?

ANS: The lowest digit is 1. The highest symbol is C. 1728, 144, 12, 1.

D.21 How is the highest symbol value in the number systems we discussed related to the positional value of the first digit to the left of the rightmost digit of any number in these number systems?

D.22 Complete the following chart of positional values for the rightmost four positions in each of the indicated number systems:

decimal	1000	100	10	1
base 6	...	...	6	...
base 13	...	169	...	...
base 3	27	...	...	...

ANS:

decimal	1000	100	10	1
base 6	216	36	6	1
base 13	2197	169	13	1
base 3	27	9	3	1

D.23 Convert binary **100101111010** to octal and to hexadecimal.
ANS: 4572, 97A.

D.24 Convert hexadecimal **3A7D** to binary.
ANS: 11101001111101.

D.25 Convert hexadecimal **765F** to octal. (Hint: First convert **765F** to binary, then convert that binary number to octal.)
ANS: 73137.

D.26 Convert binary **1011110** to decimal.
ANS: 94.

D.27 Convert octal **426** to decimal.
ANS: 278.

D.28 Convert hexadecimal **FFFF** to decimal.
ANS: 65535.

D.29 Convert decimal **299** to binary, to octal, and to hexadecimal.
ANS: 100101011, 453, 12B.

D.30 Convert the octal **4377** to hexadecimal.
ANS: 8FF.

D.31 Show the binary representation of decimal **779**. Then show the one's complement of **779**, and the two's complement of **779**.
ANS: 110000101. One's complement: 001111010. Two's complement: 001111011.

D.32 What is the result when the two's complement of a number is added to itself?

D.33 Show the two's complement of **-1** for a 32-bit **Long**.